THE RETURN OF THE
HOME STATE TO INVESTOR–STATE
DISPUTES

This book advances the idea that in order to address some of the criticisms against investor–state dispute settlement, a large majority of states have taken a 'normative' strategy, negotiating or amending investment treaties with provisions that potentially give more control and greater involvement to the contracting parties, and notably the home state. This is particularly true of agreements concluded in the past fifteen years. At the same time, there is a potential revival of the 'remnants' of diplomatic protection that have been embedded in investment treaties since the beginning of the system. But why is the home state being brought back into a domain from which it was expressly excluded several decades ago? Why would a home state be interested in intervening in these conflicts? Is this 'new' role of the home state in foreign investment disputes a 'return' to diplomatic protection of its nationals, or are we witnessing something different?

RODRIGO POLANCO is a Senior Researcher and Lecturer at the World Trade Institute, University of Bern, a Postdoctoral Researcher at the University of Lucerne, and a Visiting Professor at the Institute of International Studies at the University of Chile. He is also a former Assistant Professor of International Economic Law at the Faculty of Law, University of Chile, where he also served as Director of International Affairs.

CAMBRIDGE INTERNATIONAL TRADE AND ECONOMIC LAW

Series editors

Dr Lorand Bartels, *University of Cambridge*
Professor Thomas Cottier, *University of Berne*
Professor William Davey, *University of Illinois*

As the processes of regionalisation and globalisation have intensified, there have been accompanying increases in the regulations of international trade and economic law at the levels of international, regional and national laws. The subject matter of this series is international economic law. Its core is the regulation of international trade, investment and cognate areas such as intellectual property and competition policy. The series publishes books on related regulatory areas, in particular human rights, labour, environment and culture, as well as sustainable development. These areas are vertically linked at the international, regional and national level, and the series extends to the implementation of these rules at these different levels. The series also includes works on governance, dealing with the structure and operation of related international organisations in the field of international economic law, and the way they interact with other subjects of international and national law.

Books in the series

The Return of the Home State to Investor-State Disputes: Bringing Back Diplomatic Protection?
Rodrigo Polanco

The Public International Law of Trade in Legal Services
David Collins

Industrial Policy and the World Trade Organization: Between Legal Constraints and Flexibilities
Sherzod Shadikhodjaev

The Prudential Carve-Out for Financial Services: Rationale and Practice in the GATS and Preferential Trade Agreements
Carlo Maria Cantore

Judicial Acts and Investment Treaty Arbitration
Berk Demirkol

Distributive Justice and World Trade Law: A Political Theory of International Trade Regulation
Oisin Suttle

Freedom of Transit and Access to Gas Pipeline Networks under WTO Law
Vitalily Pogoretskyy

Reclaiming Development in the World Trading System, 2nd edition
Yong-Shik Lee

THE RETURN OF THE HOME STATE TO INVESTOR–STATE DISPUTES

Bringing Back Diplomatic Protection?

RODRIGO POLANCO

University of Bern

CAMBRIDGE
UNIVERSITY PRESS

CAMBRIDGE
UNIVERSITY PRESS

University Printing House, Cambridge CB2 8BS, United Kingdom

One Liberty Plaza, 20th Floor, New York, NY 10006, USA

477 Williamstown Road, Port Melbourne, VIC 3207, Australia

314–321, 3rd Floor, Plot 3, Splendor Forum, Jasola District Centre, New Delhi – 110025, India

79 Anson Road, #06-04/06, Singapore 079906

Cambridge University Press is part of the University of Cambridge.

It furthers the University's mission by disseminating knowledge in the pursuit of education, learning, and research at the highest international levels of excellence.

www.cambridge.org
Information on this title: www.cambridge.org/9781108473385
DOI: 10.1017/9781108628983

© Rodrigo Polanco 2019

First published 2019

Printed and bound in Great Britain by Clays Ltd, Elcograf S.p.A.

A catalogue record for this publication is available from the British Library.

ISBN 978-1-108-47338-5 Hardback

CONTENTS

TABLES

ACKNOWLEDGEMENTS

This book is an updated version of my doctoral thesis at the Graduate School of Economic Globalisation and Integration of the World Trade Institute (WTI) at the University of Bern, written during the years 2013–2015. I owe my deepest gratitude to my supervisor, Professor Thomas Cottier, and my co-supervisor, Professor Krista Nadakavukaren Schefer. Their encouragement, guidance and support made the research and writing of this work a rewarding and enriching experience. I am further indebted to my fellow doctoral researchers, my colleagues and the staff of the WTI for all the support and valuable comments received during my time as a PhD student. Special thanks to the generosity of the WTI/SECO Project for the funding of my studies, and to all the people who made my academic stay in Switzerland possible – in particular Roberto Echandi, Susan Kaplan, Shaheeza Lalani, Barry Peterson and Pierre Sauvé, as well as Dorotea López and the Institute of International Studies at the University of Chile.

I am most thankful to my parents, Carlos and Carmen, for their continuous example of love and perseverance. Most importantly, this book would not have been possible without the unconditional support and love of my dear wife Barbara and our children Tomás and Laura: this work is dedicated to them.

ABBREVIATIONS

ACHPR	African Charter on Human and Peoples' Rights
ADR	alternative dispute resolution
ALBA	Bolivarian Alliance for the Peoples of Our America
App.	appendix
Art./Arts.	article / articles
ASEAN	Association of Southeast Asian Nations
ATFA	American Task Force Argentina
ATPA	Andean Trade Preference Act
BEE	Black Economic Empowerment
BIT	bilateral investment treaty
BLEU	Belgium–Luxembourg Economic Union
CACM	Central American Common Market
CAFTA–DR	Dominican Republic–Central America–United States FTA
CANACAR	Cámara Nacional del Autotransporte de Carga
CARICOM	Caribbean Community
CCFTAC	Canada–Chile Free Trade Agreement Commission
CCIA	COMESA Common Investment Area
CCJ	Caribbean Court of Justice
CEFTA	Central European Free Trade Agreement
CEO	Corporate Europe Observatory
CEPA	closer economic partnership arrangement
CETA	Comprehensive Economic and Trade Agreement
CFIA	cooperation and facilitation investment agreement
Ch.	chapter
CIS	Commonwealth of Independent States
CMM	conflict management mechanism
COMESA	Common Market for Eastern and Southern Africa
Comm.	Commentaries
CPTPP	Comprehensive and Progressive Agreement for Trans-Pacific Partnership
CSR	corporate social responsibility
DPP	dispute prevention policy
DRC	Democratic Republic of the Congo

EC	European Commission
ECA	economic cooperation agreement
ECC	Economic Cooperation Committee
ECFA	Economic Cooperation Framework Agreement
ECJ	European Court of Justice
ECO	Economic Cooperation Organization
ECOWAS	Economic Community of West African States
ECT	Energy Charter Treaty
EEC	Eurasian Economic Community
EEU	Eurasian Economic Union
EFTA	European Free Trade Association
EPA	economic partnership agreement
ETEA	Economic and Trade Expansion Agreement
EU	European Union
FCNA	friendship, commerce and navigation agreement
FCPA	Foreign Corrupt Practices Act (United States)
FDFA	Federal Department of Foreign Affairs (Switzerland)
FDI	foreign direct investment
FET	fair and equitable treatment
FIPA	foreign investment promotion and protection agreement
fn	footnote
FPS	full protection and security
FTA	free trade agreement
FTC	Free Trade Commission
GSP	Generalized System of Preferences
IACHR	Inter-American Commission on Human Rights
IADB	Inter-American Development Bank
IAISD	International Agreement on Investment for Sustainable Development (of IISD)
IBA	International Bar Association
ICC	International Chamber of Commerce
ICCPR	International Covenant on Civil and Political Rights
ICJ	International Court of Justice
ICS	Investment Court System
ICSID	International Centre for Settlement of Investment Disputes
ICSID Convention	Convention on the Settlement of Investment Disputes between States and Nationals of Other States
ICTSD	International Centre for Trade and Sustainable Development
IEL	international economic law
IIA	international investment agreement
IISD	International Institute for Sustainable Development
ILC	International Law Commission

ILO	International Labour Organization
IMS	international minimum standard
IPA	investment protection agreement
IPFSD	Investment Policy Framework for Sustainable Development
ISA	investor–state arbitration
ISDN	Investment Dispute Settlement Navigator
ISDS	investor–state dispute settlement
JBIC	Japan Bank for International Cooperation
JC	joint committee
LDC	least-developed country
MAI	Multilateral Agreement on Investment (OECD)
MERCOSUR	Southern Common Market
MFN	most-favoured nation
MIC	multilateral investment court
MNE	multinational enterprise
NAFTA	North American Free Trade Agreement
NCM	non-conforming measure
NCP	national contact point
NDSP	non-disputing state party
NT	national treatment
OAS	Organization of American States
OECD	Organisation for Economic Co-operation and Development
OPIC	Overseas Private Investment Corporation
PAAP	Pacific Alliance Additional Protocol
PACER	Pacific Agreement on Closer Economic Relations
PCA	Permanent Court of Arbitration
PCIJ	Permanent Court of International Justice
R2P	responsibility to protect
RIA	regional investment agreement
RICO Act	Racketeer Influenced and Corrupt Organizations Act (United States)
RIT	regional investment treaty
SAA	stabilization and association agreement
SADC	Southern African Development Community
SAFTA	Singapore–Australia Free Trade Agreement
SCC	Stockholm Chamber of Commerce
SMEs	small and medium-sized enterprises
SNIS	Swiss Network for International Studies
SPA	Serbian Privatization Agency
SWF	sovereign wealth funds
TBT Agreement	Agreement on Technical Barriers to Trade
TNI	Transnational Institute

TPA	trade promotion agreement
TPP	Trans-Pacific Partnership
TRIPS Agreement	Agreement on Trade-Related Aspects of Intellectual Property Rights
TTIP	Transatlantic Trade and Investment Partnership
UAE	United Arab Emirates
UK	United Kingdom of Great Britain and Northern Ireland
UN	United Nations
UNCITRAL	United Nations Commission on International Trade Law
UNCTAD	United Nations Conference on Trade and Development
UNEP	United Nations Environment Programme
UNGC	United Nations Global Compact
UNRIAA	United Nations Reports of International Arbitral Awards
US	United States of America
USTR	United States Trade Representative
VCCR	Vienna Convention on Consular Relations
VCDR	Vienna Convention on Diplomatic Relations
VCLT	Vienna Convention on the Law of Treaties
WTO	World Trade Organization

TABLE OF CASES

Unless otherwise indicated, in addition to the sources indicated in this section, the text of awards and decisions cited in this book can be found in Investment Treaty Arbitration: www.italaw.com/

TABLE OF TREATIES

Unless otherwise indicated, in addition to the sources indicated in this section, the text of all international investment agreements cited in this book can be found in UNCTAD, International Investment Agreements Navigator: http://investmentpolicyhub.unctad .org/IIA

Bilateral Treaties

Acuerdo por Canje de Notas Interpretativo del Convenio entre la República Argentina y la República de Panamá para la Promoción y Protección Recíproca de Inversiones de 1996, 15 September 2004

Agreement between Japan and the Democratic Socialist Republic of Sri Lanka Concerning the Promotion and Protection of Investment, signed at Colombo 1 March 1982

Agreement between Japan and the Republic of the Philippines for an Economic Partnership, signed at Helsinki 9 September 2006, entered into force 11 December 2008

Agreement on Cooperation and Facilitation of Investments between the Federative Republic of Brazil and the Republic of Chile, signed at Santiago, 23 November 2015

Agreement on Cooperation and Facilitation of Investments between the Federative Republic of Brazil and the Republic of Colombia, signed at Bogota 9 October 2015 75, 76, 77

Agreement on Cooperation and Facilitation of Investments between the Federative Republic of Brazil and the United Mexican States, signed at Mexico City 26 May 2015

Agreement on Cooperation and Facilitation of Investments between the Government of the Federative Republic of Brazil and the Government of the Republic of Angola, signed at Luanda 1 April 2015

Agreement on Cooperation and Facilitation of Investments between the Government of the Federative Republic of Brazil and the Government of the Republic of Mozambique, signed at Maputo 30 March 2015

Agreement on Economic and Commercial Enlargement between the Federative Republic of Brazil and the Republic of Peru, signed at Lima, 29 April 2016

Agreement on the Encouragement and Protection of Investments between the Hashemite Kingdom of Jordan and the Government of the Syrian Arab Republic, signed 8 October 2001, entered into force 11 May 2002

Free Trade Agreement between the Government of the Republic of Korea and the Government of the Socialist Republic of Viet Nam, signed at Hanoi 5 May 2015, entered into force 20 December 2015

Free Trade Agreement between the Republic of Singapore and the Republic of Panama, signed at Singapore 1 March 2006, entered into force 24 July 2007

General Claims Commission, (Agreement 8 September 1923). (United Mexican States, United States of America), IV UNRIAA 11–14

Investment Cooperation and Facilitation Agreement between the Federative Republic of Brazil and the Republic of Malawi, signed at Brasilia 25 June 2015

Investment Promotion and Protection Agreement between Mauritius and the United Arab Emirates, signed at Dubai 20 September 2015

Investment Promotion and Protection Agreement between the Government of the Federal Republic of Nigeria and the Government of the Republic of Singapore, signed at Singapore 4 November 2016

Mainland China and Hong Kong Closer Economic Partnership Arrangement, signed at Hong Kong 28 June 2017, entered into force 28 June 2017

Reciprocal Investment Promotion and Protection Agreement between the Government of the Kingdom of Morocco and the Government of the Federal Republic of Nigeria, signed at Abuja, 3 December 2016

Segundo Acuerdo por canje de Notas Interpretativo del Convenio entre la República Argentina y la República de Panamá para la Promoción y Protección Recíproca de Inversiones de 1996, 19 October 2004

Treaty between the Federal Republic of Germany and Pakistan for the Promotion and Protection of Investments, Bonn, 25 November 1959

Treaty of Friendship, Commerce and Navigation between the United States of America and the Italian Republic. Signed at Rome, 2 February 1948

United Mexican States, United States of America, Convention of 19 November 1941, IV UNRIAA 765–769

Regional Treaties

Agreement on Investment Among the Governments of the Hong Kong Special Administrative Region of the People's Republic of China and the Member States of the Association of Southeast Asian Nations, signed at Manila, 12 November 2017

ASEAN Comprehensive Investment Agreement, signed at Cha-am 26 February 2009, entered into force 24 February 2012

Comprehensive Economic and Trade Agreement between Canada and the European Union Trans-Pacific Partnership, signed on 30 October 2016

Intra-MERCOSUR Cooperation and Facilitation Investment Protocol, signed in
  Buenos Aires 7 April 2017
Pacific Alliance Additional Protocol, signed 10 February 2014, between Chile,
  Colombia, Costa Rica and Peru
Trans-Pacific Partnership Agreement, signed on 4 February 2016, between Australia,
  Brunei, Canada, Chile, Japan, Malaysia, Mexico, New Zealand, Peru, Singapore, the
  United States, and Vietnam
Treaty establishing the Common Market for Eastern and Southern Africa, 5 November
  1993, 33 I.L.M. 1067

Multilateral Treaties

Convention on the Recognition and Enforcement of Foreign Arbitral Awards, 10 June
  1958, 21 U.S.T. 2517, T.I.A.S. No 6997, 330 U.N.T.S. 38
Convention on the Settlement of Investment Disputes between States and Nationals of
  Other States 18 March 1965, 575 U.N.T.S. 159
Energy Charter Treaty, 17 December 1994, 2080 U.N.T.S. 95; 34 I.L.M. 360 (1995)
Inter-American Convention on International Commercial Arbitration, 30 January
  1975, 1438 U.N.T.S. 245; O.A.S.TS. No 42; 14 I.L.M. 336
North American Free Trade Agreement, 17 December 1992, 32 I.L.M. 289, 605
  (1993)
Statute of the International Court of Justice, 26 June 1945, 3 Bevans 1179; 59 Stat. 1031;
  T.S. 993; 39 A.J.I.L. Supp. 215 (1945)
Unified Agreement for the Investment of Arab Capital in the Arab States, 26 November
  1980, (1988) 3 ICSID Rev. 191
United Nations Convention on Transparency in Treaty-based Investor-State
  Arbitration, 17 March 2015, 54 I.L.M. 747–57
United Nations, Charter of the United Nations, 24 October 1945, 1 U.N.T.S. XVI
Vienna Convention on Consular Relations, 24 April 1963, 21 U.S.T. 77, 596 U.N.T.S. 261
Vienna Convention on Diplomatic Relations, 18 April 1961, 23 U.S.T. 3227, 500 U.N.T.S. 95
Vienna Convention on the Law of Treaties, 1155 U.N.T.S. 331, 8 I.L.M. 679

Draft Instruments and Other Non-Binding Instruments

ILC, Draft Articles on Diplomatic Protection, with Commentaries. Report of the
  International Law Commission, 58th session (A/61/10) (2006) II *Yearbook of
  the International Law Commission* 22–100
International Law Commission, Draft Articles on Responsibility of States for
  Internationally Wrongful Acts, November 2001, Supplement No 10 (A/56/10),
  chp.IV.E.1

OECD, 'Draft Convention on the Protection of Foreign Property', *International Legal Materials*, 2 (1963), 241–67

UNCITRAL, Resolution adopted by the General Assembly 68/109, UN DOC. A/68/462 (16 December 2013)

United Nations General Assembly, 'Resolution 1803 (XVII) of 14 December 1962 – "Permanent Sovereignty Over Natural Resources", UN Doc. A/RES/17/1803' (1962)

United Nations General Assembly, 'Resolution 3281 (XXIX) of 12 December 1974 – "Charter of Economic Rights and Duties of States", UN Doc. A/RES/29/3281' (1974)

~

Introduction

> It is most expedient for the preservation of the state that the rights of
> sovereignty should never be granted out to a subject, still less to a foreigner,
> for to do so is to provide a stepping-stone whereby the grantee himself
> becomes the sovereign.
>
> Jean Bodin, *Six books of the commonwealth,* 1576 (Oxford: Blackwell,
> 1955), p. 49

A The Background

It is almost difficult to imagine now, but there was a time – not so long ago –
when foreign investment disputes were not settled using investor–state
arbitration. Such conflicts were dealt with either directly by the investor at
the host state's domestic courts or between the investor's home state and the
host state through the institution of diplomatic protection. Under special
treaties, even home state extraterritorial jurisdiction was recognized at the
host state. International arbitration between host states and foreign investors
was primarily based on contracts. Clearly, both home and host states had
a decisive role in the settlement of foreign investment disputes.

Historically, the evolution of this treatment can be briefly summarized
as follows: an initial period in which no rights for aliens were recognized
was followed by an epoch in which special rights were recognized for
foreigners – but different from those recognized for nationals. This
period was then followed by an era in which aliens were granted the
same rights – but no more – than nationals.[1] Currently, foreign investors
enjoy more rights than domestic investors, as international investment

---

[1] J. Paulsson, *Denial of Justice in International Law* (Cambridge University Press, 2005),
p. 14.

1

agreements (IIAs) include protections that are not available for nationals, notably with respect to dispute settlement.

Over the past decades, a regime of dispute settlement allowing foreign investors to initiate arbitrations against host states has been established mainly through IIAs. This investor–state dispute settlement (ISDS) system gives foreign investors the procedural alternative of pursuing international arbitration instead of going before the host state domestic courts, when they deem that their rights recognized in those treaties have been infringed upon by the host state.

The essence of ISDS is that controversies between foreign investors and host states are allegedly insulated against the political and diplomatic relations between states. In return for agreeing to independent international arbitration, the host state is assured that the investor's home state will not espouse the claim or intervene in a controversy and is theoretically relieved of the pressure of having its relations with the host state disturbed as a result of unwanted involvement in investment disputes.[2] The idea behind this system was to 'depoliticize' investment disputes.[3]

Before the system of investor–state arbitration was established, foreign investment disputes were settled either by the host state's domestic courts or through diplomatic protection, the latter being the most-used mechanism under international law. Once a state espoused a claim of a national that had invested in a foreign country, the means for resolving grievances included diplomatic and legal methods, and even the use of force. It was precisely such 'gunboat diplomacy' that triggered claims of abuse of power by the investor's home state and a reaction from affected countries – mainly from Latin America – taking the position that aliens had no greater rights than those recognized for the citizens of the host state. They held that domestic courts had a primary role in the settlement of foreign investment disputes and rejected diplomatic protection, except in cases of denial of justice or evident violation of principles of international law.[4] These ideas were dubbed the 'Calvo doctrine' and the 'Calvo clause', when contracts included provisions to renounce to diplomatic protection.[5]

[2] *Corn Products International, Inc.* v. *United Mexican States*, ICSID Case No ARB (AF)/04/1, Separate Opinion of Andreas F. Lowenfeld, 18 August 2009, para. 1.

[3] I. F. I. Shihata, 'Towards a Greater Depoliticization of Investment Disputes: The Roles of ICSID and MIGA', 1 (1986) *ICSID Review*, 1–25 at 1.

[4] S. Montt, *State Liability in Investment Treaty Arbitration: Global Constitutional and Administrative Law in the BIT Generation* (Hart Publishing, 2009), pp. 40–1.

[5] F. G. Dawson, 'The Influence of Andres Bello on Latin-American Perceptions of Non-Intervention and State Responsibility', *British Yearbook of International Law*, 57 (1987), 253–315 at 273.

However, diplomatic protection also had limitations, as it could be successfully invoked only by the home state, under strict rules on nationality of the investors and after they had exhausted local remedies available in the host state.[6] Diplomatic protection cases were almost always concerned with alleged problems in the judicial system of the host state – namely, refusal to investigate or prosecute – but generally not with failures in administrative decision-making by the host state.[7]

B The Problem

The system of diplomatic protection for the settlement of foreign investment disputes was largely abandoned after the rise of investor–state arbitration. Although consent to arbitrate investor–state disputes had already been provided for in bilateral investment treaties (BITs) signed in the late 1960s, the possibility of using this system became common only in the late 1980s – when the number of BITs containing these provisions increased dramatically.[8]

Today, around 3,300 IIAs have been concluded and around 2,600 are in force.[9] While we can trace the foundations of the system for the settlement of investment disputes in the minimum standard of treatment of aliens under customary international law, agreements focused exclusively on foreign investment have been signed since the 1959 Germany–Pakistan BIT.

Initially, these treaties were concluded between a developing and a developed country, usually at the initiative of the latter. However, with the increasing integration of the world economy as well as investment and trade liberalization, this pattern changed – especially during the 1990s, when developing countries and economies in transition started signing BITs among themselves and in large numbers. In the same decade, investment chapters began to be included within free trade agreements.[10]

The use of investor–state arbitration has augmented spectacularly in recent years. At the time of writing, investors had initiated at least 855

[6] C. F. Amerasinghe, *Diplomatic Protection* (Oxford University Press, 2008), pp. 13–20.
[7] C. McLachlan, 'Investment Treaties and General International Law', *International & Comparative Law Quarterly*, 57 (2008), 361–401 at 363.
[8] A. Newcombe and L. Paradell, *Law and Practice of Investment Treaties: Standards of Treatment* (Kluwer Law International, 2009), p. 47.
[9] UNCTAD, 'International Investment Agreements Navigator' (February 2018).
[10] R. Polanco Lazo, 'The No of Tokyo Revisited: Or How Developed Countries Learned to Start Worrying and Love the Calvo Doctrine', *ICSID Review* 30 (2015), 172–93 at 183.

known ISDS cases under IIAs, involving 134 countries. The International Centre for the Settlement of Investment Disputes (ICSID) has become the most used forum to address investor–state disputes. Other investment arbitrations take place in ad hoc panels, mainly under United Nations Commission on International Trade Law (UNCITRAL) Arbitration Rules, or in private arbitration institutions such as the Arbitration Institute of the Stockholm Chamber of Commerce (SCC).[11]

While the ability of foreign investors to choose ISDS has gained prominence, it has also progressively come under more scrutiny. There are concerns about the qualifications and independence of arbitrators, frivolous claims, 'nationality-planning' and treaty shopping, high costs, lack of transparency and coherence, expansive or inconsistent interpretations of treaty provisions, erroneous arbitral decisions, 'regulatory chill' or restrictions on the state's 'right to regulate', and a growing perception of lack of legitimacy in the system.[12] These criticisms have surfaced not only in developing countries but also in developed ones, as witnessed during the negotiations of 'mega-regionals' such as the Trans-Pacific Partnership (TPP), the Comprehensive Economic and Trade Agreement (CETA) and the Transatlantic Trade and Investment Partnership (TTIP).

C The Thesis

This book advances the idea that in order to address some of the criticisms of the ISDS system, a large majority of states have taken a 'normative' strategy, negotiating new investment treaties (or amending existing ones), with provisions that potentially give more control and greater involvement to the contracting parties, and notably the home state. This is particularly true of agreements concluded in the past fifteen years, although still these innovations are far from being found in the majority of IIAs.

Now the same states that created ISDS are 'bringing back' the home state to the realm of investment disputes, through several innovations in treaty-making that provide for a larger role for the investor's home state in these conflicts. At the same time, there is a potential revival of the 'remnants' of diplomatic protection that are embedded in investment

---

[11] UNCTAD, 'Investor–State Dispute Settlement: Review of Developments in 2017', *IIA Issues Note*, 2 (2018), 1.

[12] UNCTAD, 'Reform of Investor–State Dispute Settlement: In Search of a Roadmap', *IIA Issues Note*, 2 (2013), 2–4.

treaties since their inception – such as inter-state dispute settlement: a provision that almost all IIAs include, although it is seldom used.

Current IIAs provide for the participation of the home state in at least four different phases of an investor–state conflict: i) prior to the arbitration – through tools of dispute prevention or review of implementation of the treaty; ii) during the arbitration, via filtering of claims, joint interpretations, non-disputing state parties' submissions, regulation of the work of arbitrators, and even *renvoi* and referral mechanisms to interpret reservations or exceptions of the IIA; iii) after investor–state arbitration, facilitating the enforcement of the award or applying countermeasures to non-compliant states; and iv) instead of investor–state arbitration, through state-to-state dispute adjudication or arbitration.

But why is the home state being brought back into a domain from which it was expressly excluded several decades ago? Is this 'new' role of the home state in ISDS a 'return' to diplomatic protection of its nationals, or are we witnessing something different? Besides, having mechanisms that allow home states to participate in investment disputes does not mean that they will do so. Why would a home state be interested in doing so?

One answer to these questions would be that this normative strategy aims to bring diplomatic protection (or certain elements of it) back to the forefront in the settlement of investment disputes. The history of investment protection shows us that, before ISDS, it was the role of home states to protect their investors under international law, through diplomatic means, inter-state dispute settlement, or even with the use of force; and that role continued to be relevant even when the ISDS system was first established, as the adoption of investor–state arbitration was slow paced. Although it has taken a back seat in investor–state disputes, diplomatic protection is still relevant today as a dispute settlement mechanism in international law.

Another answer would be to consider that the increasing participation of home states – and the host states – in ISDS is a way of reasserting their control as 'masters' of the investment treaties,[13] as a reaction against a system that is providing conflicting interpretations of the obligations that were negotiated by them. This could be considered a positive development.

In theory, the involvement of home states in the prevention of investment disputes – or even in monitoring the functioning of the investment

[13] Andreas Kulick, 'Reassertion of Control: An Introduction' in A. Kulick (ed.), *Reassertion of Control Over the Investment Treaty Regime* (2017), pp. 1–29.

treaties – could favour long-term maintenance of the links between the investor and the host state, as well as decreasing the number of claims or increasing the likelihood of amicable solutions.

Similarly, it could be argued that a more active role for the home state during certain phases of investor–state arbitration could help to alleviate criticisms and improve the perception of the legitimacy of the system. Problems of lack of coherence of awards could be minimized with joint interpretations by the home and the host state of treaty provisions, or even through unilateral statements by the home state. Concerns about qualifications and independence of arbitrators could be addressed through the establishment of a roster of arbitrators selected by the states, together with the development of a joint code of conduct to guard against possible conflicts of interests. Sensitive claims could be limited using a process of filtering of claims by home and host states or their agencies acting in a coordinated way. Apprehensions about arbitrators deciding on public policies could be alleviated by setting up standing tribunals. State-to-state dispute settlement could be a mechanism to be used as a complement to or in the absence of ISDS. Enforcement of awards could be expedited with some home state participation, as a state could be better positioned than an investor to overcome the challenges that stem from a process against another state, and eventually adopt countermeasures against the non-compliant state.

This book submits the idea that the changes introduced in the treaty-making of IIAs in recent years, which give more room for home state intervention in investment disputes, allegedly with the goal of addressing some of the criticisms raised against the ISDS system, are not a 'return' to diplomatic protection, but a return of the states in order to regain control as 'masters' of the investment treaties, aiming to minimize risks in the interpretation of those agreements in potential future disputes with foreign investors. In this scenario, a home state would be willing to intervene in investment disputes only if its own public interests are affected; and these do not necessarily coincide with the interests of its investors. The normative strategy described earlier is therefore not aimed at protecting investors but at minimizing states' exposure to ISDS.

In the current literature, the large majority of these changes have been analysed as part of the phenomenon of reassertion of control or recalibration of investment treaties from the part of states in general, and not exclusively from the perspective of the home state. That framework has focused largely on host states, and include aspects that will not be analysed in this book, such as the withdrawal from investment treaties, defences based on legitimate regulatory interests, revisiting treaty standards in new treaties (such as indirect expropriation or fair and equitable treatment), and early dismissal of claims, among others.[14]

Although this work departs from that general analysis, focusing primarily on the home state, this book examines several mechanisms that require the active participation of other states (mostly host states, as the majority of investment treaties are bilateral), such as joint interpretations or the filtering of claims. Yet, the fact that the home state has a role in it justifies dedicated analysis, as it could be seen as a covered (or uncovered) mechanism of diplomatic protection.

Finally, this work also analyses mechanisms that are particular to home states, mostly relating to the prevention of investment disputes, unilateral interpretations and the enforcement of arbitral awards. The questions to analyse here are not only whether home states use such mechanisms, but also what the reasons are behind the decision to use them or not.

D Methodology

The research used in writing this book applied both historical and empirical methods, including a historical analysis of the regime of protection of foreign investors and investments before the establishment of ISDS; study of the current elements of the institution of diplomatic protection under international law; and case studies on investor–state arbitration and mechanisms involving state-to-state dispute settlement, inter-state interpretation of IIAs and even unilateral participation by the home state. The use of this methodology is consistent with a 'rules-based' approach to international law, focused on the existence of legal rules based on the sources of international investment law as they exist today (*lege lata*), especially international agreements, judicial decisions and customary international law.

---

[14] See, among others: J. E. Alvarez, 'The Return of the State', Minn. J. Int'l L., 20 (2011), 223–64; A. Kulick (ed.), *Reassertion of Control Over the Investment Treaty Regime* (2017); S. Hindelang and M. Krajewski (eds.), *Shifting Paradigms in International Investment Law: More Balanced, Less Isolated, Increasingly Diversified*, 1st edn (Oxford University Press, 2016); and S. W. Schill, '"Shared Responsibility": Stopping the Irresponsibility Carousel for the Protection of Public Interests in International Investment Law' in A. Reinisch, M. E. Footer and C. Binder (eds.), *International Law and ... Select Proceedings of the European Society of International Law* (Hart Publishing, 2016), pp. 160–9.

Special emphasis has been given to rules that stem from state consent, and its related case law, as the current ISDS regime was created by investment treaties aimed at displacing customary international law on the treatment of aliens and their property. For that reason, I have reviewed and coded all the IIAs negotiated and concluded in the past fifteen years the text of which is publicly available (1088 agreements). The study was limited to that period as, during those years, we can detect an increasing change in treaty-making in relation to the participation of home states. The number of IIAs including provisions on home state participation in that period is 568 (hereinafter the 'data set'). When changes were found to have started in previous years, an analysis of those treaties and related cases was made in order to gain a complete understanding of that specific mechanism of home state participation.

This sample of treaties was developed using several online investment treaty databases, particularly those of the United Nations Conference on Trade and Development (UNCTAD),[15] the Organization of American States (OAS) Foreign Trade Information System,[16] Transnational Dispute Management,[17] Kluwer Arbitration,[18] and Oxford's 'Investment Claims'.[19] Several agreements that were not found in those databases were collected from different governmental websites, first privately and then as part of a project funded by the Swiss Network for International Studies (SNIS).[20]

But this research is also concerned with normative arguments about how investment law should be (*lege ferenda*) as, during the examination of the home state's participation in investor–state arbitration, there is always a separate analysis of what would be the role of the home state under the treaty, what occurs in practice and what possible roles could be assumed in the future. In different sections of this work, we examine potential uses of diplomatic protection in the current system of

---

[15] UNCTAD, 'International Investment Agreements Navigator'.
[16] OAS, 'SICE the OAS Foreign Trade Information System' (February 2018).
[17] Transnational Dispute Management, 'Legal & Regulatory docs' (February 2018).
[18] Kluwer Law International, 'Kluwer Arbitration' (February 2018).
[19] Oxford University Press, 'Investment Claims' (February 2018).
[20] An Electronic Database of Investment Treaties (EDIT) was created during the implementation of the SNIS-funded project 'Diffusion of International Law: A Textual Analysis of International Investment Agreements' (2015–17). Treaty texts were collected, digitized and non-English texts translated through machine translation software, complemented with manual translation. Swiss Network for International Studies (SNIS), 'Diffusion of International Law: A Textual Analysis of International Investment Agreements' (February 2018).

settlement of investment disputes and the prospective role of home states in the prevention of such disputes.

There are, of course, limitations on this analysis. The number of IIAs that have been examined is limited by the accessibility of their texts, and thus the conclusions presented here reflect only the agreements that are publicly known. Similarly, as the focus has been to examine the state practice in IIAs treaty-making, we have reviewed texts of investment treaties that have been signed or concluded in the last fifteen years, even if they are not currently in force. Although the general tendency is that the majority of these agreements enter into force later, the conclusions presented in this work could have the bias of not representing treaties that are actually operative.

With respect to the analysis of investment disputes, this research focuses only on investor–state and state-to-state cases that are publicly available, and therefore its conclusions cannot represent the overall reality of the settlement of investor–state disputes. Likewise, due to the reserved nature of most methods of diplomatic protection, the exercise of diplomatic protections could be taking place in different forms than those described in this book, but they are not in the public domain. The conclusions made in this regard therefore also suffer from an unwanted selection bias.

E Structure

The book is divided into seven chapters, preceded by an Introduction and followed by a Conclusion. The Introduction provides the presentation of the topic, the context of the research and the main questions that guided its development. Chapter I examines the role of diplomatic protection as the main international dispute settlement mechanisms for investment disputes that were available before investor–state arbitration. This is followed by an analysis of its roots and main characteristics throughout history.

Chapter II delves into the origins of investor–state arbitration, the reasons behind its creation, and the evolution of the system, since the ICSID Convention and the consolidation of treaty-based arbitration by the end of the twentieth century, and briefly describes the backlash against ISDS that we are currently witnessing.

Chapter III explores the prospective role of the home state in the prevention of investment disputes, based on provisions included in recent IIAs, or following principles of domestic or international law.

Chapter IV examines the present role of the home state in ISDS, together with the host state, considering a wide range of mechanisms of participation, including the filtering of certain claims, joint interpretation of investment treaties, technical referrals during arbitral proceedings, and the regulation of the work of arbitrators. In each case, the relevant case law is analysed, and the characteristics of every type of intervention are considered in order to determine whether it resembles diplomatic protection.

Complementing the previous chapter, Chapter V deals with unilateral home state participation in ISDS, through non-disputing state party submissions, consultation of draft awards and enforcement of awards. Here, the relevant case law is also analysed, and the characteristics of each type of intervention are examined to define whether it corresponds to diplomatic protection.

In Chapter VI, the book deals with the 'remnants' and the future of diplomatic protection, presenting the cases in which diplomatic protection is expressly excluded from investment treaties and their consequences, and, the current mechanisms for diplomatic protection in investment disputes, concluding with an analysis of inter-state dispute settlement, its main characteristics and its interplay with investor–state arbitration. This section includes recent developments brought about by the new Brazilian approach to investment treaties and the European Union proposal for a standing investment tribunal and an appellate tribunal.

Chapter VII examines the reasons behind the actual non-intervention of home states in investment disputes, even in the presence of a legal framework that would make it possible, and draws lessons from the system for settling investment disputes before ISDS that can be useful for the current discussions in this field.

In the Conclusion, I submit that the evolution of investment treaties in recent years, including more room for the participation of home states in investment disputes, is not a return to an updated version of diplomatic protection in order to enhance the defence of its national interests. Rather, it is more a return to seeing states as masters of investment treaties, to regain control of the interpretation and application of the agreements, with the aim of avoiding expansive or unintended interpretations of IIAs against the contracting parties. In this context, the home state may have more interests in common with the host state than with its national investors.

I

The Age of Diplomatic Protection of Foreign Investors

A The Foundations of Diplomatic Protection

Diplomatic protection is an institution of customary international law where a state ('home state') spouses the claim of its national against another state and pursues it in its own name.[1]

One of the earliest doctrinal foundations of diplomatic protection comes from the writings of the Swiss Emer de Vattel, who in his book *The Law of Nations* (1758), recognized that the link between a sovereign and his citizens (and their property) continued even if they have entered or settled in a foreign territory.

> ... Whoever uses a citizen ill, indirectly offends the state, which is bound to protect this citizen; and the sovereign of the latter should avenge his wrongs, punish the aggressor, and, if possible, oblige him to make full reparation; since otherwise the citizen would not obtain the great end of the civil association, which is safety.[2]

Vattel was not in favour of the intervention of one state in another state's affairs and proclaimed the principle of 'non-intervention' as a consequence of the freedom and independence of nations, unless a ruler transgressed basic rights of his people.[3] This restricted intervention was a limit to the host state which could not claim any power over the person and property of a foreigner, but had the duty to provide

---

[1] J. E. Viñuales and D. Bentolila, 'The Use of Alternative (Non-Judicial) Means to Enforce Investment Awards against States' in L. Boisson de Chazournes, M. G. Kohen, J. E. Viñuales (eds.), *Diplomatic and Judicial Means of Dispute Settlement* (Martinus Nijhoff Publishers, 2012), pp. 248–77, p. 267.

[2] E. de Vattel, *The Law of Nations, or, Principles of the Law of Nature, Applied to the Conduct and Affairs of Nations and Sovereigns, with Three Early Essays on the Origin and Nature of Natural Law and on Luxury* (Liberty Fund, 2008), p. 298.

[3] W. G. Grewe, *The Epochs of International Law*, Revised edn (De Gruyter, 2000), p. 335.

security for them in its territory, and could be held responsible for wrongs suffered by foreigners in its territory, at the initiative of the alien's home state.[4]

By mid of the nineteenth century, states began steadily to use diplomatic means as a dispute settlement mechanism to protect its nationals and their property abroad, which led certain countries to affirm that this 'diplomatic protection' was part of customary international law.[5]

In 1913, Borchard recognizes that the diplomatic protection of citizens abroad 'is a comparatively modern phenomenon in the evolution of the state, in constitutional and in international law'.[6] Although he acknowledges as a general principle of international law that persons in a foreign country are subject to the territorial jurisdiction of the host state, this notion must be balanced with a 'complementary principle', as individuals they still owe allegiance to their own home state, which under the bond of citizenship, must watch over its citizens abroad, and intervene when their rights are violated – as measured by the 'international minimum standard' (IMS) and not by the local standard of the host state.[7] This function of 'protective surveillance' would be part of the very nature of the state, as an organization to achieve security and justice.[8] Eventually, foreign investors as aliens began to demand a treatment that met such international minimum standards, though there was no universally accepted definition of them.[9]

Soon in international practice, two elements were identified as necessary to trigger diplomatic protection. First, the injured national should exhaust all local remedies in the local courts of the host state, before his home state could invoke its right of protection.[10] Second, the link of nationality between a state and an individual is the only basis to exercise protection on her behalf.[11]

Although theoretically diplomatic protection was 'universal', in practice it was more often used by powerful and established western countries against new unsettled countries, mainly in Latin America, as European

[4] Paulsson, *Denial of Justice in International Law*, p. 14.
[5] Amerasinghe, *Diplomatic Protection*, p. 14.
[6] E. Borchard, *The Diplomatic Protection of Citizens Abroad* (New York, 1914), p. 497.
[7] Borchard, *The Diplomatic Protection of Citizens Abroad*, pp. 515, 517–18.
[8] Borchard, *The Diplomatic Protection of Citizens Abroad*, p. 520.
[9] O. E. Garcia-Bolivar, 'Sovereignty vs. Investment Protection: Back to Calvo?' (2009) 24 *ICSID Review*, 464–88.
[10] Joseph Cuthbert, *Diplomatic Protection and Nationality: The Commonwealth of Nations* (Northumberland Press, 1968), p. 4.
[11] Joseph Cuthbert, *Diplomatic Protection and Nationality*, p. 7.

colonies in Africa and Asia were not considered as separate international persons.[12] Dunn saw this merely as a result of the repeated failure of the government of these newly independent countries, which in a continued state of political disorder failed to function in an expected manner for foreign investors.[13] For some, although Latin American countries provided a judiciary for the redress of such wrongs, 'the natural inclination of the resident aliens to question the merit of the foreign justice, reinforced by many examples of maladministration of this justice, led to strong demands for international protection of their persons and property and for redress of wrongs through intervention by their home governments'.[14]

At this time, the use of diplomatic protection included both peaceful and non-peaceful means of dispute settlement and powerful countries could decide either to stand before an international tribunal or to use force unilaterally. When the latter happened, the 'diplomatic' part of the 'diplomatic protection' was 'an ironic but hardly subtle fiction'.[15] Latin American countries were especially affected by the abuse of diplomatic protection and faced armed intervention and occupation by military forces sent by the government of the investor's home state.[16]

But despite being a commonplace,[17] the hypothesis of powerful countries regularly using military force to protect its nationals and obtain payments from foreign states, has been rarely tested. In fact, the literature relies largely on anecdotes, rather than evidence of a significant relationship between state's default and foreign intervention.[18] In a detailed research focused on sovereign debt and private bondholders between 1820 and 1913, Tomz found little evidence of a systematic use of 'gunboat diplomacy' and in fact, when default and use of force coincided, it was

---

[12] Amerasinghe, *Diplomatic Protection*, pp. 14, 21.

[13] F. S. Dunn, *The Protection of Nationals: A Study in the Application of International Law* (The Johns Hopkins Press, 1932), pp. 55–56.

[14] D. R. Shea, *The Calvo Clause: A Problem of Inter-American and International Law and Diplomacy* (University of Minnesota Press, 1955), p. 10.

[15] Paulsson, *Denial of Justice in International Law*, p. 15.

[16] Shihata, 'Towards a Greater Depoliticization of Investment Disputes', 1.

[17] Dugan, C. F., D. Wallace Jr, N. D. Rubins and B. Sabahi, Investor–State Arbitration (Oxford University Press, 2008), p. 9; R. D. Bishop, J. Crawford, and W. M. Reisman, *Foreign Investment Disputes: Cases, Materials, and Commentary* (Kluwer Law International, 2005), p. 4.

[18] K. J. Mitchener and M. Weidenmier, 'How Are Sovereign Debtors Punished? Evidence from the Gold Standard Era' (2004) *Santa Clara University, Department of Economics Working Paper* at 6.

because home states had also other interests at play.[19] He concludes that 'Contrary to popular wisdom, creditor governments generally did not use – or even threaten to use – force on behalf of bondholders, and neither investors nor borrowers expected that default would lead to military intervention'.[20]

Maurer has documented the successful US intervention to defend the American property rights of Americans abroad from 1890s onwards, based not only in 'gunboat diplomacy' but using different techniques of 'sticks and carrots', ranging from the use of force (and even annexation like in the cases of the Philippines and Cuba) moving to the intimidation of use of force (usually via the threat of blockades), to access to American credit and governmental financial aid.[21]

The fact that claims for injuries to foreigners started to accumulate in the region and the fear that these would be used as excuse of territorial conquest, led to the growth of a school of thought in Latin America that vigorously opposed to diplomatic protection.[22]

1   The Calvo Doctrine and the Calvo Clause

Partially as a response to perceived abuses by foreign investors' home states, Latin American host states tried to confine investment remedies to its local courts and institutions, based on the idea that as a principle of international law, aliens have no greater rights than nationals in case of loss of life or property.[23] Under this doctrine, foreign investors were not entitled to a treatment better than that received by local investors. This doctrine has been called 'the Calvo doctrine', taking its name from the most known proponent of this idea – the Argentinean diplomat Carlos Calvo.[24]

---

[19] M. Tomz, *Reputation and International Cooperation: Sovereign Debt Across Three Centuries* (Princeton University Press, 2007), pp. 114–57.

[20] Tomz, *Reputation and International Cooperation*, p. 157.

[21] N. Maurer, *The Empire Trap: The Rise and Fall of U.S. Intervention to Protect American Property Overseas, 1893-2013* (Princeton University Press, 2013) pp. 6–7, 58–386.

[22] Dunn, *The Protection of Nationals*, p. 56.

[23] J. L. Esquirol, 'Latin America' in B. Fassbender, A. Peters (eds.), *The Oxford Handbook of the History of International Law* (Oxford University Press, 2012), pp. 553–77 p. 568.

[24] C. Calvo, *Derecho Internacional Teórico y Práctico de Europa y América* (D'Amyot, 1868), vol. i. These ideas were further elaborated in the 1896 French edition of this book ('*Le Droit International Théorique et Pratique*'). See: Manuel R. Garcia-Mora, 'The Calvo Clause in Latin American Constitutions and International Law' (1949) 33 *Marq. L. Rev.* 205 at 206.

The core of the Calvo doctrine is the principle of equality between nations and between foreigners and nationals. As explained by Montt, this equality has two dimensions, one positive and one negative. The positive side was aimed to foster investment and immigration, both much needed in post-independence Latin America in the nineteenth century, declaring that foreigners established in the region would receive the same treatment as nationals, meaning the same rights and protection before domestic courts. The negative side of this principle was the understanding that equality of treatment was the maximum treatment provided to foreigners and that governments cannot accept more responsibility towards foreigners than to their own citizens.[25] Diplomatic protection was therefore rejected except in cases of denial of justice or evident violation of principles of international law.[26]

But Calvo's ideas were not new. As it has been already pointed out by other scholars, the Venezuelan Andrés Bello advanced this principle several decades before, and Calvo had relied heavily on Bello for his own treatise on international law.[27]

Bello affirmed a limited right of diplomatic protection, clearly following Vattel's writings:[28]

> The judicial acts of a nation on the strangers who live there, if are conforming its own laws, must be respected by other nations; because by putting his foot in the territory of a foreign State, we contract, as stated above, the obligation to submit to its law, and therefore to the rules that has established for the administration of justice. But the state also contracts for its part the obligation to observe them with respect to the alien, and in the case of a manifest breach, the damage inferred to him, is an injury against the society from which he is a member. If the state instigates, approves or condones acts of injustice or violence of his subjects against foreigners, truly makes them his own, and becomes responsible for them before the other nations.

Following this view, diplomatic protection could be requested, only in the event of a denial of justice or manifest injustice.[29] Consequently, international liability could not be triggered as long as the host state

---

[25] Montt, *State Liability in Investment Treaty Arbitration*, pp. 39–40.

[26] Montt, *State Liability in Investment Treaty Arbitration*, pp. 40–41.

[27] Dawson, 'The Influence of Andres Bello on Latin-American Perceptions of Non-Intervention and State Responsibility'. Montt, *State Liability in Investment Treaty Arbitration*, pp. 31–82.

[28] A. Bello, *Principios de derecho de jentes* (Imprenta de la Opinión, 1832. Reimpresión Valentín Espinal, 1837) pp. 54–55. Translated by the author.

[29] Montt, *State Liability in Investment Treaty Arbitration*, p. 42.

provides a judicial or administrative adjudicative system that is impartial and comports with general accepted standards of due process of law, regardless of the outcome of the investor's local claim.[30]

Upholding these principles, Calvo underscored that in their dealings with Latin America, European nations had followed a different principle of intervention than in their reciprocal relations with other European states, where they had invariably maintained the view that 'the recovery of debts and the pursuit of private claims does not justify *de plano* the armed intervention of governments'.[31] As all nations were equal, the same treatment of this issue should be applied to Latin America.

But soon Latin American countries went beyond the idea of accepting diplomatic protection as a subsidiary remedy, and devised the so-called 'Calvo clause', which was inserted in contracts between foreign investors and the host state, where aliens agreed to forgo their rights to request diplomatic protection from their home state, in any dispute arising out of that contract.[32]

As with the doctrine, it seems that Carlos Calvo did not originate the Calvo clause either. According to Montt, the earliest evidence for these provisions is a decree that Peru issued in 1846 and it was also included in a contract for completion of the most important railroad line in Chile in 1861, both several years before Calvo's first edition of his treatise.[33]

The Calvo clause could take several forms, but usually had two parts, one providing that the disputes arising from the contract should be decided by the courts of the contracting host state, an another a complete or partial waiver by the foreign investor to request the protection of the contractor's home state.[34]

This is major difference with the Calvo doctrine, which did not intend automatic exclusion of diplomatic protection which could be used in cases of violation of principles of international law or denial of justice. In the Calvo clause there was a purpose to effectively restrict diplomatic protection, even if it was implemented through peaceful means. However, it was heavily debated if foreign investors could waive the right of diplomatic protection that is vested in their home state and not

---

[30] Dugan, Wallace Jr., Rubins, and Sabahi, *Investor-State Arbitration*, pp. 16, 19.
[31] A. S. Hershey, 'The Calvo and Drago Doctrines' (1907) 1 *The American Journal of International Law*, 26–45 at 27.
[32] Amerasinghe, *Diplomatic Protection*, p. 192.
[33] Montt, *State Liability in Investment Treaty Arbitration*, p. 46.
[34] Amerasinghe, *Diplomatic Protection*, p. 192.

in the investor itself.[35] The Calvo doctrine and especially the Calvo clause were contested by developed capital-exporting countries, and notably by the US.[36]

Diplomatic protection not only had customary international law as a source, and some treaties also included peaceful means of diplomatic protection. In late eighteen and early nineteenth centuries, bilateral Friendship, Commerce and Navigation Agreements (FCNAs) were signed 'to facilitate commerce, navigation, and investment between the states Parties and reciprocally to protect individuals and businesses'.[37] These agreements were concluded mostly between newly independent States and former colonial masters in order to ensure access of the latter to the expanding markets for the sale of finished goods.[38] Elements of dispute settlement involving private claims were often not part of the text of FCNAs and some early agreements even considered the possibility of war, if parties were not able to settle a dispute by negotiation.[39]

The first known treaty that included the settlement of private claims through mechanisms of peaceful diplomatic protection, was the 1794 Treaty of Amity, Commerce and Navigation between Great Britain and the United States ('Jay Treaty') signed in the aftermath of the American Independence war, which provided for three separate boards of arbitration, including one devoted to resolve British claims of property damage, expropriation and breach of contract affecting British citizens, during the conflict.[40] The system envisaged in this treaty is clearly an inter-state dispute settlement, as neither British nor American nationals were recognized direct standing, and the claims were presented by home states at their discretion. Although the treaty provided that any sum awarded would be paid directly to the claimants, the final lump-sum payment was an inter-state agreement.[41] While unsuccessful, as it did not fulfil its original purpose, the Jay Treaty opened the door for the peaceful

---

[35] Z. Douglas, *The International Law of Investment Claims* (Cambridge University Press, 2009), p. 366; Dugan, Wallace Jr., Rubins, and Sabahi, *Investor-State Arbitration*, pp. 16, 19.

[36] Shea, *The Calvo Clause*, p. 37.

[37] A. Paulus, 'Treaties of Friendship, Commerce, and Navigation' (March 2011).

[38] Dugan, Wallace Jr., Rubins, and Sabahi, *Investor-State Arbitration*, p. 37.

[39] C. Brown, *Commentaries on Selected Model Investment Treaties* (Oxford University Press, 2013), p. 6.

[40] J. H. Ralston, *International Arbitration from Athens to Locarno* (Stanford University Press, 1929), p. 191.

[41] K. Parlett, *The Individual in the International Legal System: Continuity and Change in International Law* (Cambridge University Press, 2011), pp. 50–51.

settlement of investment disputes, using inter-state arbitration or binational claims commissions.

2 Evolution of Diplomatic Protection

In early twentieth century countries like Mexico and the Soviet Union led the opposition to the protection of foreign investors through diplomatic protection, as home states strongly objected to agrarian reforms or uncompensated land seizures under the moniker not of expropriation but of 'nationalization'.[42] Other countries also continued to strongly oppose diplomatic protection and the IMS, upholding the exhaustion of local remedies in domestic courts and the national treatment (NT) standard, as the principles applicable to disputes with foreigners. Latin American countries pursued this agenda at international conferences held in the 1920s and 1930s to attempt to codify standards of treatment. Many efforts were made in this area, notably by the League of Nations, but with no avail.[43]

But the Calvo doctrine and the Calvo clause were not the only avenue that was explored to oppose forceful diplomatic protection. When it was not possible to sustain exclusive domestic jurisdiction for investment disputes, most of Latin American countries agreed on resolve such disputes using peaceful methods of diplomatic protection, mainly binational claims commissions, mixed arbitral tribunals, or ad hoc arbitrations to settle disputes involving foreigners, regarding different issues like torts, contracts and investments.[44] The solution of international conflicts arising between Latin American states, by means of arbitration was even advanced as a 'Principle of American Public Law'.[45] From 1794 to 1938, Latin American countries participated in almost 200 arbitrations, with the major number of arbitrations taking place in the century following the independence of Latin American countries from 1829 through 1910.[46]

But Latin American countries were not always keen on arbitration. Arbitration was sometimes imposed as the sole alternative to forceful

---

[42] K. Miles, *The Origins of International Investment Law: Empire, Environment and the Safeguarding of Capital* (Cambridge University Press, 2013), pp. 74–75.

[43] Montt, *State Liability in Investment Treaty Arbitration*, p. 48.

[44] Newcombe and Paradell, *Law and Practice of Investment Treaties*, pp. 13–14.

[45] Dugan, Wallace Jr., Rubins, and Sabahi, *Investor-State Arbitration*, p. 36.

[46] A. M. Stuyt, *Survey of International Arbitrations: 1794–1989* (Martinus Nijhoff Publishers, 1990).

intervention,[47] or as extension of the 'gunboat diplomacy', and home states of the foreign investors 'were seen to control the arbitral process in a way that permitted it to be used simply as a tool for extracting concessions from the host country'.[48]

Yet, these claims commissions were a clear example that diplomatic protection was not always forceful, and even provided the framework for a future understanding in substantive standards.[49] Interestingly, these commissions were never established with the Soviet Union. Despite Western powers formally protesting the confiscation of property, with few exceptions, no compensation was provided for any nationalization after the Russian Revolution of 1917.[50]

In the interwar period, the Permanent Court of International Justice (PCIJ) affirmed the doctrine of diplomatic protection, in its famous dictum of the *Mavrommatis Palestine Concessions* case:

> *It is an elementary principle of international law* that a state is entitled to protect its subjects, when injured by acts contrary to international law committed by another State, from whom they have been unable to obtain satisfaction through the ordinary channels. By taking up the case of one of its subjects and by resorting to diplomatic action or international judicial proceedings on his behalf, *a state is in reality asserting its own rights* – its right to ensure, in the person of its subjects, respect for the rules of international law.[51]

But, even though diplomatic protection was now starting to be recognized as a principle of international law, the use of forceful diplomatic protection was progressively proscribed. This process started with the partial limitation of the 1907 Hague Convention II (also known as 'Drago-Porter Convention') that restricted armed intervention as a mean of collecting public debts, except if the debtor state refused or neglected arbitration, or failed to comply with the award.[52] A more absolute restriction on the use of force for these purposes finally came about with the 1945 Charter of the United Nations (UN).[53]

---

[47] Montt, *State Liability in Investment Treaty Arbitration*, p. 38.

[48] G. Aguilar Álvarez and W. W. Park, 'The New Face of Investment Arbitration: NAFTA Chapter 11' (2003) 28 *Yale J. Int'l L.* 365 at 367.

[49] A. F. Lowenfeld, *International Economic Law* (Oxford University Press, 2003) pp. 397–403.

[50] Lowenfeld, *International Economic Law*, pp. 392–93.

[51] *Mavrommatis Palestine Concessions (Greece v. U.K.)*, 1924 P.C.I.J. (ser. B) No. 3 (August 30), p. 12.

[52] Esquirol, 'Latin America', p. 568.

[53] United Nations, Charter of the United Nations, 24 October 1945, 1 UNTS XVI, Art. 2(4).

But by mid-twentieth century, arbitration was no longer supported by Latin American countries.[54] Together with other developing countries, they tried to reaffirm an 'updated' Calvo doctrine, limiting peaceful diplomatic protection and international arbitration in the framework of the United Nations. Several declarations by the UN General Assembly addressed these issues, particularly with respect to expropriations, giving clear priority to domestic courts on the question of compensation, and leaving arbitration and other peaceful means of international dispute settlement as subsidiary, and only in the case they were freely agreed upon.[55]

However, these attempts were largely unsuccessful, and did not effectively exclude the use of diplomatic protection.[56] Today, diplomatic protection has become firmly established in customary international law, as a peaceful method of dispute settlement, even if there are still disagreements about the substantive rules governing the state responsibility for injuries to aliens.[57]

The International Law Commission (ILC) first started to consider the systematization of the principles governing diplomatic protection in 1956 as part of its codification of state responsibility. After some years, the ILC decided to leave diplomatic protection for a later study distinguishing between diplomatic protection and state responsibility for injury to aliens.[58]

In 1997 the ILC decided to prepare a draft code on diplomatic protection that was completed in 2006, based on the initial work of Mohamed Bennouna, but especially on the reports of John Dugard. In a definition that is considered declaratory of existing customary international law,[59] ILC Draft Articles on Diplomatic Protection Art. 1 defines diplomatic protection as:[60]

---

[54] L. M. Summers, 'Arbitration and Latin America' (1972) 3 *California Western International Law Journal* 1 at 7.

[55] United Nations General Assembly, 'Resolution 1803 (XVII) of 14 December 1962 – "Permanent Sovereignty Over Natural Resources", UN Doc. A/RES/17/1803' (1962), para. 4; United Nations General Assembly, 'Resolution 3281 (XXIX) of 12 December 1974 – "Charter of Economic Rights and Duties of States", UN Doc. A/RES/29/3281' (1974), para. 2 c).

[56] Amerasinghe, *Diplomatic Protection*, p. 192.

[57] Amerasinghe, *Diplomatic Protection*, p. 17.

[58] Amerasinghe, *Diplomatic Protection*, p. 61.

[59] *Case Concerning Ahmadou Sadio Diallo (Republic of Guinea v. Case Concerning Ahmadou Sadio Diallo (Republic of Guinea v. Democratic Republic of the Congo). Preliminary Objections. Judgment of 24 May 2007 (2007) para. 39.*

[60] ILC, Draft Articles on Diplomatic Protection, with Commentaries. Report of the International Law Commission, 58th session (A/61/10) (2006) II *Yearbook of the International Law Commission*, 22–100 at 24.

> [. . .] the invocation by a state, through diplomatic action or other means of peaceful settlement, of the responsibility of another State for an injury caused by an internationally wrongful act of that State to a natural or legal person that is a national of the former State with a view to the implementation of such responsibility.

As primary rules are those concerning the rights and obligations of states, and secondary rules are those necessary to enforce the primary rules, to facilitate change or lay down the rules of adjudication, the ILC Draft Articles on Diplomatic Protection are generally considered secondary rules of international law, although the secondary nature of state responsibility is not always clear, and can imply both primary and secondary rules.[61]

The commentaries to the ILC Draft Articles on Diplomatic Protection, acknowledge that investment treaties confer rights and protection on both legal and natural persons in respect of their property rights,[62] and that diplomatic protection in respect of legal persons is mainly about the protection of foreign investment.[63]

ILC Draft Articles on Diplomatic Protection Art. 17 clearly states that these articles do not apply to the alternative special regime for the protection of foreign investors provided for in bilateral and multilateral investment treaties, because such agreements abandon or relax the conditions relating to the exercise of diplomatic protection, particularly the rules relating to the nationality of claims and the exhaustion of local remedies.[64] However, these ILC Draft Articles are still subsidiary applicable to investment treaties, to the extent that they are not inconsistent with the provisions of the respective agreement.[65]

On investment disputes, diplomatic protection has increasingly become an institution of last resort, partially due to the political tensions generated after its use by developed countries after the flood of nationalizations that took place in Eastern Europe and Latin America by the middle of the twentieth century, but also with the dissatisfaction that foreign investors had with the efficacy of some of the rules governing diplomatic protection, especially the exhaustion of local remedies.[66] That

---

[61] A. Vermeer-Künzli, 'As If: The Legal Fiction in Diplomatic Protection' (2007) 18 *European Journal of International Law*, 37–68 at 50.
[62] ILC, Draft Articles on Diplomatic Protection, Comm. Art. 1 (4).
[63] ILC, Draft Articles on Diplomatic Protection, Comm. Art. 13 (1).
[64] ILC, Draft Articles on Diplomatic Protection, Comm. Art. 17 (1).
[65] ILC, Draft Articles on Diplomatic Protection, Comm. Art. 17 (3).
[66] Amerasinghe, *Diplomatic Protection*, pp. 17–19.

led to the creation of a special system of settlement of disputes for foreign investors, as we will analyse in the next chapter.

This has not diluted the availability of diplomatic protection, which still can be used, no longer as a weapon by developed against developing states, but to protect interests of investors of both countries, if it is properly rationalized.[67]

B   Diplomatic Protection in Investment Disputes

As it has been observed by the International Court of Justice (ICJ), '[...] within the limits prescribed by international law, a state may exercise diplomatic protection by whatever means and to whatever extent it thinks fit, for it is its own right that the state is asserting'.[68] The UN Charter provides an illustrative list of the methods of peaceful settlement of disputes between states under international law, including 'negotiation, enquiry, mediation, conciliation, arbitration, judicial settlement, resort to regional agencies or arrangements, or other peaceful means of their own choice'.[69]

The use of any of these mechanisms for the settlement of investment disputes, require prior diplomatic espousal, which normally consists in the intervention by the home state of the foreign investor in the form of diplomatic correspondence.[70]

Leaving aside purely diplomatic means and forceful protection, before the creation of investor–state arbitration, investment claims were asserted by four legal peaceful means of diplomatic protection: international arbitration for cases related to specifically defined claims, claims commissions or mixed arbitral tribunals for claims that derived from overall major incidents, lump-sum agreements, and international adjudication.

1   International Arbitration

Many of the disputes concerning mistreatment of foreigners that arose in the nineteenth and early twentieth centuries were resolved by ad hoc tribunals or umpires, who were charged with the case either by treaty

---

[67] Amerasinghe, *Diplomatic Protection*, pp. 19–20.
[68] *Barcelona Traction, Light and Power Company, Limited* (*Belgium* v. *Spain*), Judgment Second Phase, 5 February 1970 [1970] ICJ Rep. 32, p. 45.
[69] UN Charter Art. 33(1)
[70] Dugan, Wallace Jr., Rubins, and Sabahi, *Investor-State Arbitration*, pp. 27–28.

provision or by mutual agreement of the two governments involved to submit to neutral dispute resolution.[71] The claims were conceptualized as inter-state claims and the arbitration did not allow for direct participation of the injured individual. During the procedure the home state exercised its role of *dominus litis*, directly appointing its arbitrators and conducting the arbitration in general without intervention of its nationals that motivated the claim.[72] A right of the individual to appear or be represented in these arbitrations was exceptional and any award issued was generally paid to the respective government.[73] One of the earliest cases reported where a foreign investor was allowed to directly bring a claim against a host state using ad hoc arbitration, was the *Suez Canal Company v. Egypt* case (1864) arbitrated by a commission appointed by Napoleon III (Louis-Napoleon), the Emperor of France.[74]

But some investment disputes were also settled using institutional arbitration. The Permanent Court of Arbitration (PCA) was established by the 1899 First Hague Convention for the Pacific Settlement of International Disputes, with seat in The Hague.[75] Despite its name, the PCA is not a real court or a permanent arbitral tribunal, but rather a registry, authorized to administer ad hoc arbitral proceedings under its auspices, a feature for what it was criticized at the time.[76]

Although the PCA's early cases involved exclusively state parties and issues of public international law, several of them were relevant to the field of international investment law, as they raised issues of state responsibility involving contracts or various kinds of property claims on behalf of foreign nationals.[77] Some of these cases related to claims previously addressed by binational claims commissions, after being directly taken by home states, usually after non-compliance on the side of the host state.[78]

---

[71] Dugan, Wallace Jr., Rubins, and Sabahi, *Investor-State Arbitration*, p. 35.

[72] G. Guyomar, 'L'arbitrage concernant les rapports entre Etats et particuliers' (1959) 5 *Annuaire français de droit international*, 333–54 at 337, 340, 344.

[73] Parlett, *The Individual in the International Legal System*, p. 53.

[74] J. W. Yackee, 'The First Investor-State Arbitration: The Suez Canal Company v Egypt (1864)' (2016) 17 *The Journal of World Investment & Trade* 401–62.

[75] J. B. Scott, *Texts of the Peace Conferences at the Hague. 1899 and 1907, with English Translation and Appendix of Related Documents* (Ginn & Company, Boston and London, Published for the International School of Peace, 1908), p. 24.

[76] M. Indlekofer, *International Arbitration and the Permanent Court of Arbitration* (Kluwer Law International, 2013) p. 49.

[77] H. M. Holtzman and B. E. Shifm, *Permanent Court of Arbitration* (United Nations, 2003), vol. 1.3 p. 29.

[78] *The Pious Fund of the Californias* case (1902), was the very first case decided by the PCA. The original claim was the largest award given by the American-Mexican Claims

Other cases were related to governmental decisions, in relation to expropriation, taxes and public debt.[79]

The PCA decided few other cases related to foreign investment not previously decided by claims commissions. The *Japanese House Tax Arbitration* case dealt with the Japanese attempt of reforming the regime of 'perpetual leases' and tax exemptions that benefited aliens who were not permitted to freely own property in Japan, under several FCNA concluded between Japan and European countries. After a *compromis* with Japan, Germany, France and Great Britain, referred the dispute to an arbitral tribunal under the auspices of the PCA. An award of 22 May 1905 decided in favour of the European countries, as there was no express reservation in the treaties that limited the exemption from taxation to land. Japan strongly criticized the decision as the majority of the tribunal was integrated by nationals of the claimant's countries.[80]

2 Binational Claims Commissions and Mixed Arbitral Tribunals

After civil unrest or instability in host states, a broad spectrum of disputes often arise, also affecting foreign investors. These conflicts were several times settled by binational claims commissions with jurisdiction over a wide array of disputes,[81] including claims that could be characterized as foreign investment disputes. More than 30 different claims commissions were established between the late nineteenth century and early twentieth century.

In most of these commissions and tribunals, the home state of the injured national had control over the presentation of the claim, and generally affected nationals were entitled to direct representation for limited purposes, as they could not file a claim directly or had control

Commission of 1868. However, after Mexico refused to pay the interest on the capital of funds, the US claimed annuities before the PCA. On 14 October 1902, the PCA ruled in favour of the US ordering Mexico to both extinguish the accrued debt and continue to pay the annual allowance in perpetuity, but in currency having legal tender in Mexico. *The Pious Fund of the Californias Case (United States of America v. Mexico)*, Award, 14 October 1902, IX UNRIAA 1-14.

[79] Indlekofer, *International Arbitration and the Permanent Court of Arbitration*, pp. 94–95.

[80] Indlekofer, *International Arbitration and the Permanent Court of Arbitration*, pp. 94–95.

[81] Dugan, Wallace Jr., Rubins, and Sabahi, *Investor-State Arbitration*, p. 36.

over the presentation of the case. However, in later commissions access of individual claimants was accepted.[82]

These commissions had usually three members, one selected by each party and the third by mutual agreement of the parties, who acted as an umpire only in case of disagreement of the party-appointed commissioners. Typically, the commission had jurisdiction to decide claims including losses or damages to nationals of the contracting parties, considering natural and legal persons. Procedural instructions were generally more complete than in ad hoc arbitrations, as usually detailed rules of procedure and evidence were agreed by the states either on the treaty establishing the commission, or among the members of the commission, before reviewing the claims.

Similarly, various treaties of peace concluded at the end of World War I, established mixed arbitral tribunals in which nationals of allied and associated powers could bring claims related to property, debts and contracts against Germany, Austria, Hungary, Bulgaria and Turkey.[83] Several international claims tribunals and commissions were also established in the inter-war period (1919–1939),[84] and in the aftermath of World War II.

The mixed arbitral tribunals and claims commissions established after World War II did not have a uniform approach about the character of the claims, which included the takings of the property of nationals of the Allied Powers. On the one hand, the Italian and Japanese commissions operated exclusively on the basis of diplomatic protection, with states having complete control of the claims which were instituted by state agents. That was the case of the conciliation commissions established between Italy and the US, Great Britain, Netherlands and France, and of the 'property' commissions between Japan and the US, Great Britain and the Netherlands.[85] In contrast, the German commissions allowed individual claimants to directly initiate proceedings as parties before the Arbitral Commission on Property Rights and Interests in Germany, the Austro-German Arbitral Tribunal, and to the Mixed Commission on German External Debts.[86]

---

[82] Parlett, *The Individual in the International Legal System*, p. 55.

[83] E. Lauterpacht, *Aspects of the Administration of International Justice* (Cambridge University Press, 1991), p. 67.

[84] See: Kate Parlett, *The Individual in the International Legal System*, pp. 162–175, for a list of international claims tribunals and commissions from 1919 to 1939.

[85] Parlett, *The Individual in the International Legal System*, pp. 97–98.

[86] Parlett, *The Individual in the International Legal System*, p. 98.

3 Lump-Sum Agreements

The flood of nationalizations that took place after World War II, especially in Eastern Europe, generated several cases of diplomatic action by Western states in protection of their nationals that were dealt mainly through lump-sum agreements.[87] A common pattern of all these expropriations is that properties were usually taken without compensation ('confiscation' or 'nationalization'), or as 'a punishment for alleged wrongdoings of the owners'.[88] Although a similar phenomenon took place in Latin America, lump-sum settlements were not common place in that region, as those countries were at that time rejecting even peaceful diplomatic protection, allowing claims almost exclusively in its domestic courts.

Under a lump-sum agreement, after a politically negotiated process, the respondent state pays the claimant state a fixed amount of money or provides reparations in kind so as to settle a number of unresolved international claims, and the responsibility of distribution of the assets transferred under that agreement to individual claimants lies within the claiming state, being usually is carried out by a domestic claims authority or national claims commission.[89] Both states agreed to prohibit any further private claims arising out of the same governmental measures adopted by the host state, either under domestic or international courts.[90]

These agreements became an important method for the settlement of large or complex claims for damage and expropriation of foreign property by governments.[91] It has been reported that in the period after the end of World War II and 1995 more than 200 lump-sum agreements were concluded, covering both the settlement of property claims, but also claims concerning personal injuries due to persecution and detention.[92]

---

[87] O. T. Johnson Jr and J. Gimblett, 'From Gunboats to BITs: Evolution of Modern International Investment Law' (2012) *Yearbook on International Investment Law & Policy 2010-2011* 649–92 at 671.

[88] Z. R. Rode, 'The International Claims Commission of the United States: August 28, 1950–June 30, 1953' (1953) 47 *The American Journal of International Law* 615–37 at 616.

[89] R. Bank and F. Foltz, 'Lump Sum Agreements' (January 2009).

[90] Dugan, Wallace Jr., Rubins, and Sabahi, *Investor-State Arbitration*, p. 38.

[91] Dugan, Wallace Jr., Rubins, and Sabahi, *Investor-State Arbitration*, p. 38.

[92] B. H. Weston, D. J. Bederman, and R. B. Lillich, *International Claims: Their Settlement by Lump Sum Agreements, 1975-1995* (Martinus Nijhoff, 1999).

4 International Adjudication

Few investment disputes have been decided by international tribunals, as they were created only in the twentieth century. In the aftermath of World War I, the Permanent Court of International Justice (PCIJ) was established in the 1919 Covenant of the League of Nations. The PCIJ worked since its inaugural sitting in 1922 and was dissolved in 1946.[93]

Several judgments and opinions of the PCIJ have found their way into decisions of current investment tribunals.[94] However, only *ten* of them are directly referred to investment disputes, and from those, most of the time did not settle the dispute in favour of the foreign investor. The role of the home state is central in all of these cases, because without its espousing of a private claim and a further agreement to submit the claim before the PCIJ, no international adjudication would have been possible. The cases related to diverse forms of foreign investment, including contractual claims and expropriation of property, but also governmental decisions affecting competition, and even the review of decision of mixed arbitral tribunals.

Regarding contractual claims, the *Mavrommatis Palestine Concessions* case (1924) is certainly the milestone. The case was brought by Greece against the UK after its refusal (as the sovereign power in Palestine under a mandate by the League of Nations) to recognize the contractual rights acquired by Mavrommatis, a Greek national, through concession contracts signed with the authorities of the Ottoman Empire (the former sovereign power in Palestine). Those agreements related to the construction and operation of an electric tramway system, the supply of electric light and power and of drinking water in the cities of Jerusalem and Jaffa. The PCIJ partially upheld the preliminary objection submitted by the UK, dismissing the claim in respect of the works at Jaffa.[95] The judgment on the merits was thus rendered only with respect to the Jerusalem concession. On 26 March 1925, the PCIJ held unanimously that such concession was valid, and dismissed Greece's claim for an indemnity. Mavrommatis was entitled to have his concessions adapted to be

---

[93] International Court of Justice, *The Permanent Court of International Justice, 1922-2012* (United Nations, 2015).

[94] For a detail review of the influence of these cases in investor-state arbitration see: U. Kriebaum, 'The PCIJ and the Protection of Foreign Investments' in C. J. Tams, M. Fitzmaurice (eds.), *Legacies of the Permanent Court of International Justice* (Leiden: Nijhoff, 2013), pp. 145–73.

[95] *Mavrommatis Palestine Concessions*, p. 12.

brought into conformity with the new economic conditions in Palestine.[96]

With respect to expropriation claims, the leading case is undoubtedly the *Factory at Chorzów* case (1927). Germany sought a declaration by the PCIJ that Poland was under the duty to compensate German companies expropriated in Upper Silesia. In a famous decision, the PCIJ decided in favour on Germany and concluded that the taking by the Polish Government had been unlawful and that privately owned German property could be taken only under provisions governing expropriation, including paying compensation to prior owners,[97] declaring that 'reparation must, as far as possible, wipe out all the consequences of the illegal act and re-establish the situation which would, in all probability, have existed if that act had not been committed'.[98]

The PCIJ dictum on the *Factory at Chorzów* case, considering 'full reparation' as a standard of compensation, has been followed either directly or indirectly by several investor–state arbitration tribunals.[99]

---

[96] *Mavrommatis Jerusalem Concessions* (*Greece v. U.K.*), 1925 P.C.I.J. (ser. A) No. 5 (March 26), Judgement 26 March 1925, pp. 6–51.

[97] Lowenfeld, *International Economic Law*, pp. 396–97.

[98] *Case Concerning the Factory at Chorzów* (*Germany v. Poland*) Claim for Indemnity (Merits), 1928 P.C.I.J. (ser. A), No. 17 (13 September 1928), p. 47.

[99] A. Pellet, 'The Case Law of the ICJ in Investment Arbitration' (2013) 28 *ICSID Review – Foreign Investment Law Journal*, 223–40 at 232.

II

The Rise of and Backlash against Investor–State Arbitration

The rise of investor–state arbitration (ISA) is a process that started with the making of the Convention on the Settlement of Investment Disputes between States and Nationals of Other States (ICSID Convention),[1] an agreement that was slowly followed by consent to arbitrate investor–state disputes in bilateral investment treaties concluded in the late 1960s and 1970s.[2] Only by the end of the 1980s did the number of BITs containing investor–state dispute settlement provisions increased dramatically.[3] In the mid-1990s, investment chapters providing for ISA started to be included in certain free trade agreements (FTAs), following the example of the North American Free Trade Agreement (NAFTA).[4] Today, the vast majority of BITs and FTAs investment chapters include ISDS.[5]

However, it was not until the 1990s that this particular system of arbitration exploded, becoming one of the most fertile areas of international economic law. UNCTAD has reported that, in 2015, investors filed eighty known ISAs based on international investment agreements which constitutes the highest number of known treaty-based disputes ever filed

---

[1] Convention on the Settlement of Investment Disputes between States and Nationals of Other States 18 March 1965, 575 U.N.T.S. 159 [hereinafter 'ICSID Convention'].

[2] A BIT has been defined as 'a reciprocal agreement concluded between two sovereign States for the promotion and protection of investments by investors of the one State ("home state") in the territory of the other State ("host state")': M. Jacob, 'Investments, Bilateral Treaties', May 2011: http://opil.ouplaw.com/view/10.1093/law:epil/9780199231690/law-9780199231690-e1061 (accessed 13 January 2018).

[3] A. Newcombe and L. Paradell, *Law and Practice of Investment Treaties: Standards of Treatment* (Kluwer Law International, 2009), p. 47.

[4] North American Free Trade Agreement, 17 December 1992, 32 ILM 289, 605 (1993).

[5] D. Gaukrodger and K. Gordon, 'Investor–State Dispute Settlement: A Scoping Paper of the Investment Policy Community', *OECD Working Papers on International Investment*, No 2012/3 (2012), p. 10. The term 'international investment agreements' (IIAs) is used to refer to all investment treaties, whether FTAs or standalone BITs.

in one year – and has confirmed that foreign investors are increasingly resorting to ISA.[6]

In comparison with diplomatic protection, ISDS has several benefits for the claimant: the investor (and not the home state) has the procedural right to institute arbitration and has exclusive control of the claim, which may be initiated without the consent of the home state; and if damages are awarded they are calculated without considering inter-state concerns, and paid directly to the individual claimant.[7]

In the following sections we will briefly analyse the origins of ISA, focusing on the reasons for diplomatic protection being abandoned, and the main objectives that were taken into account in the creation of ISA. A final section explains the reasons behind the current backlash against ISA.

A   Origins and Evolution of Investor–State Arbitration

1   Before the ICSID Convention

After World War II, there were attempts to create a multilateral agreement for the protection of foreign investments that included ISDS such as the Abs–Shawcross Draft Convention (1959) and the Draft Convention on the Protection of Foreign Property (1962) developed by the Organisation for Economic Co-operation and Development (OECD). Article VII.2 of the Abs–Shawcross proposal provided that:[8]

> A national of one of the Parties claiming that he has been injured by measures in breach of this Convention may institute proceedings against the Party responsible for such measures before the Arbitral Tribunal [...], provided that the Party against which the claim is made has declared that it accepts the jurisdiction of the said Arbitral Tribunal in respect of claims by nationals of one or more Parties, including the Party concerned.

This draft still required consent by the state in a separate document, stipulating that 'parties willing to permit such claims to be brought directly against them by nationals of other parties would make a general declaration to that effect'.[9]

---

[6] UNCTAD, 'Special Update on Investor–State Dispute Settlement: Facts and Figures', *IIA Issues Note* 3 (2017), 1.

[7] K. Parlett, *The Individual in the International Legal System: Continuity and Change in International Law* (Cambridge University Press, 2011), pp. 103–7.

[8] G. Schwarzenberger, 'The Abs–Shawcross Draft Convention on Investments Abroad: A Critical Commentary', *Journal of Public Law*, 9 (1960), 147 at 162.

[9] A. R. Parra, *The History of ICSID* (Oxford University Press, 2012), p. 15.

The 1962 OECD Draft Convention also included controls on the use of ISA by nationals of a party.[10] Probably with the intention of protecting the sovereignty of the states, a state would have been allowed to preclude its nationals from instituting proceedings against another state if the claimant home state had instituted such proceedings over the same matter, or would do so within a certain time limit.[11] The tribunal could also order the claimant to give security for costs, or dismiss the claim if it appeared to be frivolous or vexatious.[12]

In the same year, the Permanent Court of Arbitration (PCA) elaborated a set of 'Rules of Arbitration and Conciliation for settlement of international disputes between two parties of which only one is a state', which seemingly inspired the subsequent adoption of the ICSID Convention.[13] However, although the PCA was established by a treaty, the rules of arbitration were not, and if countries did not comply with them that could not be characterized as a violation of an international law obligation.[14]

BITs that were starting to be signed at that time, did not include ISA. The first one – the 1959 Germany–Pakistan BIT – provided for a dispute settlement mechanism in the event of disputes as to the interpretation or application of the treaty, specifying consultation between the state parties for the purpose of finding a solution in a spirit of friendship. If no solution was possible, the dispute was to be submitted to the International Court of Justice (ICJ) if both parties so agreed, or to an ad hoc arbitration tribunal upon the request of either party.[15]

In that respect, BITs were similar to the second generation of friendship, commerce and navigation agreements that the United States (US) negotiated between 1946 and 1968 with more than forty countries, with the intention of protecting its investors and investments abroad. 'Modern' FCNAs provide that disputes arising

---

[10] Ibid., p. 17.

[11] OECD, 'Draft Convention on the Protection of Foreign Property', *International Legal Materials*, 2 (1963), 241–67, Art. 7(b)(ii).

[12] Ibid., Annex, para. 6(c).

[13] H. M. Holtzman and B. E. Shifm, *Permanent Court of Arbitration* (United Nations, 2003), vol. 1.3, p. 6.

[14] Parra, *The History of ICSID*, p. 17.

[15] Treaty between the Federal Republic of Germany and Pakistan for the Promotion and Protection of Investments, Bonn, 25 November 1959, Art. XI.

under the treaty may be submitted to the ICJ for resolution, by the state parties to the treaty.[16]

This model of dispute settlement was largely superseded after the rise of investment treaties with ISA provisions, as will be explained in the next section.

2 After the ICSID Convention

In the early 1960s, the World Bank began to work on an alternative approach to the settlement of investment disputes. The result of around four years of negotiations was the Convention establishing the International Centre for Settlement of Investment Disputes (ICSID) – a mechanism for the settlement of disputes not between states but between private parties on the one side and host states on the other.[17] The annual meeting of the World Bank's Board of Governors held in Tokyo in September 1964 approved a resolution asking the Executive Directors to formulate the final text of the Convention.[18] During that meeting, the Governor for Chile, Félix Ruiz, who was representing the Latin American countries, made a statement rejecting the proposal, known as 'the No of Tokyo'. For the first time in the Bank's history, a major resolution was met with substantial opposition to a final vote.[19]

The promotion of the ICSID Convention was central in the initial years of the Centre, which, between 1968 and 1969, published a set of model clauses to promote the insertion of provisions granting ICSID jurisdiction in contracts and BITs.[20] By the mid 1970s, the inclusion of ICSID arbitration clauses was a common feature in investment contracts, and a dozen domestic investment promotion laws were enacted with reference to the ICSID Convention.[21] That explains the fact that the first ICSID cases were all contract-based or based on domestic laws that provided consent to ICSID arbitration.

[16] J. Coyle, 'The Treaty of Friendship, Commerce, and Navigation in the Modern Era', *Columbia Journal of Transnational Law*, 51 (2013), 302 at 308, 310 and 315.

[17] A. F. Lowenfeld, *International Economic Law* (Oxford University Press, 2003), pp. 456–7.

[18] Parra, *The History of ICSID*, pp. 67–8.

[19] R. Polanco Lazo, 'The No of Tokyo Revisited: Or How Developed Countries Learned to Start Worrying and Love the Calvo Doctrine', *ICSID Review*, 30 (2015), 172 at 182.

[20] ICSID, 'Model Clauses Relating to the Convention on the Settlement of Investment Disputes Designed for Use in Bilateral Investment Agreements [September 1969]', *International Legal Materials*, 8 (1969), 1341–52.

[21] Parra, *The History of ICSID*, pp. 132–3.

The first BIT that expressly included recourse to ICSID was the 1968 Indonesia–Netherlands BIT, although, as Newcombe and Paradell point out, the drafting of the specific provision was unclear, and it could have been interpreted either as a binding offer to the investor to arbitrate or as a binding obligation on the state to agree to arbitrate if an investment dispute arose.[22] The first signed BIT clearly providing for ICSID jurisdiction with unqualified state consent seems to have been the 1969 Chad–Italy BIT.[23] Only in 1990 did an arbitral tribunal issue the first ICSID award in which jurisdiction was based on a BIT, following an arbitration clause provided in the Sri Lanka–UK BIT (1980).[24]

Belgium and the UK began including consent to ICSID in BITs in the first half of the 1970s, and France soon followed their example.[25] Notably, the US started to negotiate BITs only in the early 1980s, after abandoning its second wave of new FCNAs in 1968.[26] Other countries that originally did not include ISA in their BITs, such as Germany and Switzerland, joined the trend in the 1980s and, by the middle of that decade, BITs containing provisions with advance consent to ICSID arbitral jurisdiction were the standard.[27]

Besides ICSID and BITs, other IIAs included provisions on ISA. The 1974 Arab Investment Convention[28] created a Centre for the Settlement of Investment Disputes between host states of Arab Investments and Nationals of other Arab States (the 'Arab Centre'), an organization very similar to ICSID, but with some differences as it was circumscribed to a specific type of claimants, provided for limited annulment rules (a second award rendered was considered final) and gave jurisdiction to the same Arab Centre for disputes over the interpretation and application of the Arab Investment Convention – not to the ICJ, as in

---

[22] Newcombe and Paradell, *Law and Practice of Investment Treaties*, p. 44.
[23] Ibid., p. 45.
[24] *Asian Agricultural Products Ltd* v. *Sri Lanka*, ICSID Case No, ARB/87/3, Final award on merits and damages (1991) 6 ICSID Rev-FILJ 526.
[25] Parra, *The History of ICSID*, p. 134.
[26] Coyle, 'The Treaty of Friendship, Commerce, and Navigation in the Modern Era', 309.
[27] Parra, *The History of ICSID*, p. 134.
[28] Convention on the Settlement of Investment Disputes between Host States of Arab Investments and Nationals of Other Arab States, 10 June 1974 ('Arab Investment Convention') [1981] Rev. Arb. 348. The contracting states were Iraq, Jordan, Sudan, Syria, Kuwait, Egypt and Yemen; Libya and the United Arab Emirates (UAE) acceded later. See H. G. Gharavi, *The International Effectiveness of the Annulment of an Arbitral Award* (Kluwer Law International, 2002), p. 182.

the case of ICSID.[29] This Arab multilateral treaty was superseded by the Unified Agreement for the Investment of Arab Capital in the Arab States (1980)[30] that provides for arbitration before the Arab Investment Court, which became operational only in 2003.[31]

Another example similar to the use of ISA is the Iran–US Claims Tribunal, created after the 1981 Algiers Accords, as an international arbitral, established in The Hague, to adjudicate claims between US nationals and companies, and the government of Iran and its state-owned entities, arising out of the 1979 Islamic Revolution.[32] The Accords followed a mixed approach, distinguishing between 'small claims' (US $250,000 or less), presented at the tribunal by the home state, and 'large claims' (above US$250,000), presented by individual claimants, although in both cases the tribunal held that it was adjudicating individual rights and not those from the home state.[33] Although not all the cases before the Iran–US Claims Tribunal related to foreign investment, a number of them concern expropriation of alien property, and comparable acts.[34]

However, the most important multilateral treaty providing for ISA is the Energy Charter Treaty (ECT).[35] The fundamental objective of the ECT's provisions on investment is to ensure the creation of a 'level playing field' for the energy sector, with the purpose of reducing to a minimum the non-commercial risks associated with energy-sector investments.[36] Today, the ECT has fifty-four members, including the European Union (EU), and fifty-two states have signed or acceded to it.[37] Therefore, the ECT is the world's largest multilateral investment treaty in substantive issues.[38] Like other investment treaties, the ECT includes

---

[29] Gharavi, *The International Effectiveness of the Annulment of an Arbitral Award*, pp. 182–3.

[30] Unified Agreement for the Investment of Arab Capital in the Arab States, 26 November 1980 *ICSID Review*, 3 (1980), 191. The agreement has been ratified by all member states of the League of Arab States except Algeria and the Comoros.

[31] W. Ben Hamida, 'The First Arab Investment Court Decision', *Journal of World Investment & Trade*, 7 (2006), 699–721 at 700.

[32] Lowenfeld, *International Economic Law*, p. 461.

[33] Parlett, *The Individual in the International Legal System*, p. 99.

[34] Lowenfeld, *International Economic Law*, pp. 463–73.

[35] Energy Charter Treaty, 17 December 1994, 2080 U.N.T.S. 95; 34 I.L.M. 360 (1995).

[36] Energy Charter Secretariat, *The Energy Charter Treaty and Related Documents* (Energy Charter Secretariat, 2004), pp. 13–14.

[37] Energy Charter Secretariat, 'About the Charter'.

[38] M. D. Slater, 'The Energy Charter Treaty: A Brief Introduction to Its Scope and Initial Arbitral Awards' in Association for International Arbitration (ed.), *Alternative Dispute Resolution in the Energy Sector* (Maklu, 2009), pp. 15–54 at p. 15.

ISDS provisions, allowing the arbitration of disputes before ICSID tribunals or those constituted under the United Nations Commission on International Trade Law (UNCITRAL) or the Stockholm Chamber of Commerce (SCC) Arbitration Rules.[39] Today, 119 ISA cases are known to have been brought under the ECT, which has become the most-invoked treaty in the ISDS system.[40]

During the 1980s and the early 1990s, a major policy reversal took place in Latin America, as most countries became members of ICSID and began to sign BITs that included ISDS, in order to stimulate economic growth through foreign direct investment (FDI),[41] with the intention of presenting themselves as attractive locations for potential foreign investors.[42] The only notable exception is Brazil, which is still not an ICSID member and has not ratified almost any of the BITs that it has negotiated.[43]

B   Why Investor–State Arbitration Was Created

Several reasons led to the establishment of ISA, some of which related to the problems created by the use of diplomatic protection and others to the purported benefits of the new system. As we have seen, the traditional method for dealing with investment disputes until then – diplomatic protection – was fiercely opposed by host states, and particularly by those from the developing world. Overcoming problems arising from the use of diplomatic protection was one of the main objectives of developing a new method for the settlement of investment disputes. However, as we will see later, this development has created new resentment against the power of such international arbitral tribunals in relation to the sovereign powers of the host state.[44]

---

[39] Ibid., p. 15.
[40] UNCTAD, 'Investment Dispute Settlement Navigator': http://investmentpolicyhub
.unctad.org/ISDS (accessed 26 February 2018).
[41] K. Fach Gómez, 'Latin America and ICSID: David versus Goliath?' (2010), p. 2.
[42] A. T. Guzman, 'Why LDCs Sign Treaties That Hurt Them: Explaining the Popularity of Bilateral Investment Treaties', *Virginia Journal of International Law*, 38 (1998), 639–88 at 643–44.
[43] L. Barreiro Lemos and D. Campello, 'The Non-Ratification of Bilateral Investment Treaties in Brazil: A Story of Conflict in a Land of Cooperation', *Review of International Political Economy*, 22 (2015), 1055–86.
[44] M. E. Schneider, 'Investment Disputes – Moving Beyond Arbitration' in L. Boisson de Chazournes, M. G. Kohen and J. E. Viñuales (eds.), *Diplomatic and Judicial Means of Dispute Settlement* (Martinus Nijhoff Publishers, 2012), p. 119 at p. 125.

The main reasons for the creation of ISA can be summarized in three main aspects: to depoliticize or 'legalize' the dispute; the inherent limitations of diplomatic protection; and to overcome barriers to recovery from the host state.

1 To Depoliticize the Dispute

One of the most prominent goals that led to the creation of ISA was to 'depoliticize the dispute'. The aim was to remove the dispute from the realm of politics and diplomacy and shift it into the realm of law.[45] This was seen as being beneficial for the home state, the host state and the foreign investor.

In *Enron v. Argentina*, the tribunal explicitly mentioned as one of the merits of the ICSID Convention that 'it overcame the deficiencies of diplomatic protection where the investor was subject to whatever political or legal determination the state of nationality would make in respect of its claim'.[46]

For developed home countries, this new system had the 'healthy' effect of depoliticizing disputes, and freed governments from the pressure of affected investors who dragged them into costly diplomatic or military conflicts.[47] With respect to developing countries, depoliticizing disputes also minimized the chances that the investor's home state would be interested in exercising diplomatic protection. The hope was that developing countries would be more satisfied by dealing with a neutral arbitral tribunal rather than 'with officials from one of the world's larger economies, whose leverage over smaller states on a range of unrelated issues is likely to be considerable'.[48]

Regarding foreign investors, the creation of ISA was a turning point in international dispute settlement.[49] By its nature, diplomatic protection

---

[45] G. Kaufmann-Kohler, 'Non-Disputing State Submissions in Investment Arbitration' in L. Boisson de Chazournes, M. G. Kohen and J. E. Viñuales (eds.), *Diplomatic and Judicial Means of Dispute Settlement* (Martinus Nijhoff Publishers, 2012), pp. 307–26 at p. 308.

[46] *Enron Corp. and Ponderosa Assets, LP.v. Argentine Republic*, ICSID Case No ARB/01/3. Decision on Jurisdiction, 14 January 2004, para. 48.

[47] N. Maurer, *The Empire Trap: The Rise and Fall of US Intervention to Protect American Property Overseas, 1893–2013* (Princeton University Press, 2013), pp. 7–10.

[48] C. F. Dugan, D. Wallace Jr, N. D. Rubins and B. Sabahi, *Investor–State Arbitration* (Oxford University Press, 2008), p. 9.

[49] F. Orrego Vicuña, *International Dispute Settlement in an Evolving Global Society: Constitutionalization, Accessibility, Privatization* (Cambridge University Press, 2004), pp. 64–5.

confers on the home state a wide latitude in determining what to do about an alleged breach of international law, if anything.[50] Espousal by the investor's home state depends also on political factors, and is not available, on an equal basis, to all nationals investing abroad.[51] Thus, investors may well find that their governments refuse to espouse a meritorious claim, to avoid that being considered an unfriendly act by the host state. In ISA, the investor is 'in the driving seat', while, in diplomatic protection, the home state had complete discretion in deciding whether and how to bring a claim, and whether and when to settle.[52]

It was also presumed that granting investors direct access to specialized international arbitration would decrease the inherent limitations of diplomatic protection, giving more certainty to investors through a process of 'legalization':[53]

> The dispute settlement procedures provided for in BITs and ICSID offer greater advantages to the foreign investor than the customary international law system of diplomatic protection, as they give the investor direct access to international arbitration, avoid the political uncertainty inherent in the discretionary nature of diplomatic protection and dispense with the conditions for the exercise of diplomatic protection.

However, is not clear whether the ISDS system has achieved this objective. Some commentators have pointed out that the idea of depoliticization is, at least, superfluous and, at worst, may distract law makers or interpreters from identifying relevant issues.[54] Others have stated that all investment arbitrations should be viewed as political.[55] As we will analyse later, today, it would be either naïve or misleading to conclude that the ISDS system has been completely depoliticized.

---

[50] J. J. Coe Jr, 'Taking Stock of NAFTA Chapter 11 in Its Tenth Year: An Interim Sketch of Selected Themes, Issues, and Methods', Vand. J. Transnat'l L., 36 (2003), 1381 at 1416.

[51] Dugan et al., Investor–State Arbitration, p. 89.

[52] A. Roberts, 'Power and Persuasion in Investment Treaty Interpretation: The Dual Role of States', American Journal of International Law, 104 (2010), 179–225 at 183.

[53] ILC, 'Draft Articles on Diplomatic Protection, with Commentaries. Report of the International Law Commission, 58th session (A/61/10)', Yearbook of the International Law Commission, II (2006), Art. 17(2).

[54] M. Paparinskis, 'The Limits of Depoliticisation in Contemporary Investor–State Arbitration', Select Proceedings of the European Society of International Law, 3 (2010), 271.

[55] C. H. Brower, II, 'Obstacles and Pathways to Consideration of the Public Interest in Investment Treaty Disputes' in K. P. Sauvant (ed.), Yearbook on International Investment Law & Policy (Oxford University Press, 2009), pp. 347–78 at pp. 348–56.

2 Limitations of Diplomatic Protection

The diplomatic espousal of investment claims is not only politically costly; it is also cumbersome. Three main limitations make the use of this mechanism particularly burdensome: the rule on exhaustion of local remedies; the link with the nationality of the investor; and the available remedies due to the exercise of diplomatic protection.

(a) Exhaustion of Local Remedies

Under customary international law, diplomatic espousal is normally permissible only after previous exhaustion of all local remedies available within the judicial or administrative system of the country in which the investment is located.

This is seen as a way of respecting the sovereignty of the host state, giving it the possibility of doing justice to the injured party.[56] As the ICJ held in the *Interhandel* case:[57]

> The rule that local remedies must be exhausted before international proceedings may be instituted is a well-established rule of customary international law; the rule has been generally observed in cases in which a state has adopted the cause of its national whose rights are claimed to have been disregarded in another State in violation of international law. Before resort may be had to an international court in such a situation, it has been considered necessary that the state where the violation occurred should have an opportunity to redress it by its own means, within the framework of its own domestic legal system.

However, the scope of application of this rule can be complex. How extensive must the resort to local remedies be in order for us to consider that the host state had a proper opportunity to settle the dispute? Is the exhaustion of local remedies applicable only to remedies of a judicial nature?[58]

Regarding the scope of the exhaustion, international case law displays different opinions. In the *Finnish Ships Arbitration* case, the arbitrator stated that:[59]

---

[56] Dugan et al., *Investor–State Arbitration*, p. 30.
[57] *Interhandel case*, Preliminary Objections, p. 25.
[58] C. F. Amerasinghe, *Diplomatic Protection* (Oxford University Press, 2008), p. 144.
[59] Claim of Finnish Shipowners against Great Britain in Respect of the Use of Certain Finnish Vessels during the War. (Finland v. Great Britain). Award, 9 May 1934, 3 UNRIAA 1481, p. 1502

the raison d'être of the local remedies rule, in a case of an alleged initial breach of international law, can be solely that all the contentions of fact and propositions of law which are brought forward by the claimant Government in the international procedure as relevant to their contention that the respondent Government have committed a breach of international law by the act complained of, must have been investigated and adjudicated upon by the municipal Courts up to the last competent instance, thereby also giving the respondent Government a possibility of doing justice in their own, ordinary way.

A less strict test was articulated by the ICJ in the *ELSI* case,[60] which was preferred by the International Law Commission in its Draft Articles on Diplomatic Protection:[61]

the local remedies rule does not, indeed cannot, require that a claim be presented to the municipal courts in a form, and with arguments, suited to an international tribunal, applying different law to different parties: for an international claim to be admissible, it is sufficient if the essence of the claim has been brought before the competent tribunals and pursued as far as permitted by local law and procedures, and without success.

The same ICJ has clarified that, in cases of diplomatic protection, the burden is on the applicant to prove that local remedies have been exhausted, or to establish that exceptional circumstances relieved the allegedly injured person, whom the applicant seeks to protect, of the obligation to exhaust available local remedies.[62] If the applicant shows that exceptional circumstances justified the non-exhaustion of local remedies, it is for the respondent state to prove that effective remedies were available in its domestic legal system, and that they were not exhausted.[63]

Although the rule of exhaustion of local remedies admits some exceptions, such as cases of undue delay or lack of availability,[64] the uncertainty of its scope has meant that, in the majority of existing investment

---

[60] *ELSI case*, Judgment, p. 59.
[61] ILC, 'Draft Articles', 73.
[62] *ELSI case*, Judgment, pp. 43–6.
[63] *Diallo*, Preliminary Objections, p. 600.
[64] Under ILC Draft Articles on Diplomatic Protection, Art. 15, local remedies do not need to be exhausted when: (a) there are no reasonably available local remedies to provide effective redress, or the local remedies provide no reasonable possibility of such redress; (b) there is undue delay in the remedial process that is attributable to the state alleged to be responsible; (c) at the date of injury, there was no relevant connection between the injured person and the state alleged to be responsible; (d) the injured person is manifestly precluded from pursuing local remedies; or (e) the state alleged to be responsible has waived the requirement that local remedies be exhausted.

treaties, the investor often has immediate access to ISA, even in the absence of specific provisions.[65] Chapter 11 of NAFTA does not explicitly address whether investors are required to exhaust local remedies, and arbitral tribunals have implied that it is not needed, interpreting it such that no such customary requirement applies as a general rule, except in certain extreme cases such as denial of justice.[66]

This waiver does not derive directly from the ICSID Convention, as the host contracting state retains the power to require the exhaustion of local administrative or judicial remedies as a condition of giving its consent to arbitration under the Convention.[67] However, rarely, ICSID members have given notification that local remedies must be exhausted.[68]

(b) Nationality of the Investor

Under customary international law, a state is entitled to exercise diplomatic espousal in relation to the harm suffered by individuals and corporations, but only if the state can demonstrate a bond of nationality with the harmed person or entity.[69]

Several complex issues can arise regarding nationality. Two of the most relevant are the different rules for determining nationality of natural[70] or

---

[65] A. Van Aaken, 'The Interaction of Remedies between National Judicial Systems and ICSID : An Optimization Problem' in N. J. Calamita, D. Earnest and M. Burgstaller (eds.), The Future of ICSID and the Place of Investment Treaties in International Law (London: British Institute of International and Comparative Law, 2013), pp. 291–324 at p. 291.

[66] Coe Jr, 'Taking Stock of NAFTA Chapter 11 in Its Tenth Year', 1419–24.

[67] ICSID Convention, Art. 26.

[68] For example, in 1983 Israel gave such notification, but subsequently withdrew it in 1991. See C. Schreuer, 'Calvo's Grandchildren: The Return of Local Remedies in Investment Arbitration', Law and Practice of International Courts and Tribunals, 4 (2005), 1 at 2. Today, only Costa Rica (1993) and Guatemala (2003) have notified the Centre that they will require the exhaustion of local administrative remedies as a condition of their consent to arbitration under the ICSID Convention. See ICSID, 'Contracting States and Measures Taken by Them for the Purpose of the Convention. ICSID/8. Notifications Concerning Classes of Disputes Considered Suitable or Unsuitable for Submission to the Center': https://icsid.worldbank.org/en/Documents/icsiddocs/ICSID%208-Contracting% 20States%20and%20Measures%20Taken%20by%20Them%20for%20the%20Purpose% 20of%20the%20Convention.pdf (accessed 26 June 2017).

[69] Dugan et al., Investor–State Arbitration, p. 33.

[70] The general rule is that the nationality of natural persons is a question within the reserved domain of a state, whether by birth, descent, naturalization, succession of states, or in any other manner not inconsistent with international law. See Nationality Decrees Issued in Tunis and Morocco (French Zone) on November 8th, 1921, Advisory Opinion, 7 February 1923, (1923) PCIJ Series B 5, p. 24, and ILC Draft Articles on Diplomatic Protection, Art. 4. As a general rule, fraudulently acquired nationality is not recognized: Amerasinghe, Diplomatic Protection, p. 93.

legal persons,[71] and the eventual changes of nationality during the course of the investment ('continuous nationality rule').[72] These problems are common to both the use of diplomatic protection and ISA, to the extent that, usually, there are no specific rules about this in investment treaties, and ISDS case law has generally relied on established principles that have been developed in the context of diplomatic protection.[73]

But investment treaties including ISA can provide more precision in issues related to nationality, particularly with respect of dual nationality of natural persons, the requirement of effective links, and the rights of foreign shareholders of corporations. Although early BITs generally failed to address the determination of rules applicable in cases in which a national of a contracting party also holds the nationality of the other contracting party,[74] today, several IIAs do have rules to deal with dual nationality,[75] and Article 25(2) of the ICSID Convention excludes dual nationals, if one of the nationalities is that of the host state.

In the *Nottebohm* case, the ICJ addressed the principle of 'effective link', by which it was considered that nationality was conferred by naturalization only if there is a genuine connection between the state

[71] Nationality of corporations is rarely dealt with in domestic laws and must be derived either from the fact of incorporation or creation of a legal person, from links to a particular state (such as the main seat of business) or from the nationality of the natural persons who control the company: J. Crawford, *Brownlie's Principles of Public International Law*, 8th edn (Oxford University Press, 2012), pp. 527–8. Investment treaties use several criteria to determine whether a juridical person is a national or an investor of a particular state, the incorporation and the main seat being the most commonly used: R. Dolzer and C. Schreuer, *Principles of International Investment Law* (Oxford University Press, 2012), p. 49.

[72] Several claims commissions and post-war arbitral tribunals dealt with the question of whether nationality was a prerequisite for diplomatic protection at the time of the filing of the claim, or at any later time. Some of them required continuity of the bond of nationality until the date at which the treaty came into force (e.g. the 1924 German–US Mixed Claim Commission), while others required continuity of nationality until the date of presentation of the claim (e.g. the 1929 British–Mexican Claims Commission), and some required continuity of the nationality link until the date of the award (e.g. the 1927 French–Mexican Commission). See Parlett, *The Individual in the International Legal System*, pp. 68–70. ICSID Convention Art. 25(1) requires claimants to establish that they had the nationality of a contracting state at the date on which the parties consented to ICSID's jurisdiction and the date of registration of the request for arbitration.

[73] Dolzer and Schreuer, *Principles of International Investment Law*, p. 47.

[74] R. Dolzer and M. Stevens, *Bilateral Investment Treaties* (Martinus Nijhoff Publishers, 1995), p. 34.

[75] For example, the Canada–Lebanon BIT (1997) and the Uruguay–US BIT (2005), among others. UNCTAD, *Scope and Definition: UNCTAD Series on Issues in International Investment Agreements II* (United Nations, 2011), pp. 77–8.

and the individual concerned. An important factor to take into consideration for this link was the habitual residence of the individual concerned, and 'the centre of his interests, his family ties, his participation in public life, attachment shown by him for a given country and inculcated in his children, etc.'[76] Although it has been followed in some cases, the 'genuine link' requirement is not generally accepted or considered part of customary international law.[77] In contrast, several IIAs require a link beyond nationality to have access to the protection of the treaty and to ISDS, usually permanent residence and/or citizenship.[78]

Companies and shareholders can have a different nationality, and the diplomatic protection of foreign shareholders was not guaranteed under customary international law. In the *Barcelona Traction* case, the ICJ ruled that only the state of incorporation, rather than the state of its controlling shareholders, can invoke a claim for diplomatic protection.[79] IIAs generally recognize the protection of shareholders with a typical broad definition of 'investment', and under Article 25(2)(b) of the ICSID Convention a locally incorporated company might qualify as a foreign investor because of its foreign control. Similarly, NAFTA allows a foreign investor that owns or control a company to submit a claim of arbitration on behalf of that company.[80]

(c)   Available Remedies

The remedies available in the exercise of diplomatic protection in investment disputes could take several forms that stem from the international law on state responsibility. Some do not directly impose the obligation to act by the responsible state (e.g. termination or suspension of a treaty; or countermeasures), and others require the host state to take remedial measures for the full reparation of the injury.[81]

---

[76] *Nottebohm case*, Judgment, p. 22.

[77] ILC Draft Articles on Diplomatic Protection, Art. 4 did not adopt the *Nottebohm* rule. The ILC pointed out to the fact that 'in today's world of economic globalization and migration a strict application of the genuine link requirement would exclude millions of persons from the benefit of diplomatic protection'. See Crawford, *Brownlie's Principles of Public International Law*, 8th edn (Oxford University Press, 2012), pp. 513–17.

[78] For example, Germany–Israel BIT (1976) and Canada–Argentina BIT (1991) require permanent residency, the ECT and NAFTA require citizenship and permanent residency. See OECD, *International Investment Law: Understanding Concepts and Tracking Innovations* (OECD, 2008), pp. 13–14.

[79] *Barcelona Traction*, Judgment Second Phase, pp. 227–358.

[80] Dolzer and Schreuer, *Principles of International Investment Law*, p. 57.

[81] Amerasinghe, *Diplomatic Protection*, p. 282.

As recognized by the ILC Draft Articles on State Responsibility,[82] the reparation for the injury caused by the internationally wrongful act can take the form of restitution, compensation and satisfaction, either individually or in combination.

Because the international wrong that triggered diplomatic protection is considered to have been suffered by the home state of the foreign investor, in theory, reparation, and particularly compensation, should be to the benefit of the national state.[83] Although it is a fact that the damage to the alien constitutes the measure of reparation, the damage made to the home state is not identical with that suffered by its national.[84] The ILC Draft Articles on Diplomatic Protection include a 'recommended practice' that a state entitled to exercise diplomatic protection should 'transfer to the injured person any compensation obtained for the injury from the responsible State subject to any reasonable deductions'.[85] In its first commentary to this article, the ILC clarified that this is a desirable practice for the progressive development of the law that adds strength to diplomatic protection.[86]

In ISA, remedies are sought directly by the foreign investor and nearly always consists of monetary compensation, as restitution in kind is rarely ordered, and satisfaction[87] does not play a practical role in investment law.[88]

3 To Overcome Barriers at Host State Courts

Diplomatic protection was not the only mechanism for the settlement of investment disputes. As we have seen in the first part of this work, historically, domestic courts have had an important role in this field,

---

[82] International Law Commission, Draft Articles on Responsibility of States for Internationally Wrongful Acts, November 2001, Supplement No 10 (A/56/10), chp. IV. E.1, Art. 34.

[83] Amerasinghe, *Diplomatic Protection*, p. 319.

[84] 'The damage suffered by an individual is never therefore identical in kind with that which will be suffered by a state; it can only afford a convenient scale for the calculation of the reparation due to the state': *Case Concerning the Factory at Chorzów.* Claim for Indemnity (Merits), p. 28.

[85] ILC Draft Articles on Diplomatic Protection, Art. 19.

[86] Ibid., Art. 19, Comm. (1).

[87] ILC Draft Articles on Responsibility of States for Internationally Wrongful Acts, Art. 37 explains that satisfaction 'may consist in an acknowledgement of the breach, an expression of regret, a formal apology or another appropriate modality' that does not take a form humiliating to the responsible state.

[88] Dolzer and Schreuer, *Principles of International Investment Law*, p. 271.

but they also presented some problems that ISA was supposed to overcome: inefficiency and local bias.

The efficiency – or lack of it – of domestic courts is a concern of many foreign investors, especially in developing countries that are often perceived as lacking 'responsive, robust legal systems capable of effectively and quickly adjudicating complex claims'.[89] One unusual case in this regard is *In re Union Carbide*,[90] in which the Indian government acknowledged the inefficiency of its own courts, in resisting the defendant's efforts to transfer the cases back to India – probably through fear of the extremely high amounts that US courts are prone to awarding in personal injury cases.[91]

Some commentators mention local bias as a serious barrier to obtaining redress in host country courts, conceding that, although judges are not necessarily more sympathetic to their nationals, the contrary perception is common – in some cases with good reason.[92] Regardless of whether the 'xenophobic bias' exists in fact, there should be no controversy about the reality of the *perception* that bias exists in domestic courts against foreign investors.

But the possibility of local bias against foreigners is not an exclusive phenomenon of developing countries. The US Supreme Court had already addressed the powers of federal courts exercising jurisdiction on the ground of diversity of citizenship, in the old case of *Erie R. Co. v. Tompkins,* in which it affirmed that 'Diversity of citizenship jurisdiction was conferred in order to prevent apprehended discrimination in state courts against those not citizens of the state'.[93] Some authors have found that – consciously or not – jury decisions discriminate against foreign parties in intellectual property litigation before US courts.[94] Others have found evidence that the market reaction to the announcement of a US federal lawsuit is less negative for American corporate defendants than for foreign ones, even if the dismissal rates for US defendant firms are not reliably different from those for foreign ones.[95] In contrast, other researchers have not identify pro-domestic

---

[89] Dugan *et al., Investor–State Arbitration*, p. 15.

[90] *In Re Union Carbide Corp. Gas Plant Disaster*, 634 F. Supp. 842 (S.D.N.Y. 1986)

[91] Dugan *et al., Investor–State Arbitration*, p. 15.

[92] Ibid., p. 13.

[93] *Erie Railroad Co.* v. *Tompkins*, 304 U.S. 64 (1938)

[94] K. A. Moore, 'Xenophobia in American Courts', *Northwestern University Law Review*, 97 (2003), 1497.

[95] U. Bhattacharya, N. Galpin and B. Haslem, 'The Home Court Advantage in International Corporate Litigation', *Journal of Law and Economics*, 50 (2007), 625–60 at 652–3.

party bias providing evidence that foreigners have in fact outperformed their American counterparts when they litigate in the United States.[96] This phenomenon could be explained by the foreigners' fear of US litigation – a presumption that makes them selective in choosing strong cases to pursue to judgment.[97]

Although the empirical evidence is mixed and a theoretical basis for bias is still underdeveloped, the perception that domestic judges may favour their fellow citizens is strong[98] and, if effective, could serve as a basis for ISA, if it is available. In the award in the famous *Loewen v. US* case, regarding the conduct of a Mississippi trial court that resulted in a - $500 million damages award against a Vancouver-based funeral home company (in which repeated allusions to Loewen's Canadian nationality were made by the plaintiff),[99] the arbitral tribunal found that:[100]

> [h]aving read the transcript and having considered the submissions of the parties with respect to the conduct of the trial, we have reached the firm conclusion that the conduct of the trial by the trial judge was so flawed that it constituted a miscarriage of justice amounting to a manifest injustice as that expression is understood in international law.

Wälde has pointed out that, in some countries in which there is not a clear internal separation of powers, if the state is simultaneously a disputing party, on one hand, and sovereign regulator, on the other, governments used to controlling internal adjudication, directly or indirectly, would be prone to undue interference before domestic courts. This would impair the principle of 'equality of arms' through misconduct such as corruption, pressure on judges or arbitrators, intimidation of counsel, experts and witnesses, or in general abuses of governmental powers, particularly if the investment dispute is seen as a domestic political risk.[101]

---

[96] K. M. Clermont and T. Eisenberg, 'Xenophilia in American courts', *Harvard Law Review*, 109 (1996), 1120–43.

[97] K. M. Clermont and T. Eisenberg, 'Xenophilia or Xenophobia in US Courts? Before and After 9/11', *Journal of Empirical Legal Studies*, 4 (2007), 441–64 at 444, 464.

[98] C. A. Whytock, *Domestic Courts and Global Governance: The Politics of Private International Law* (ProQuest, 2007), pp. 89–90.

[99] *O'Keefe v. Loewen Group, Inc.*, No 91-67-423 (Miss. Circ. Ct. 1st Jud. Dist., Hinds County 1995).

[100] *The Loewen Group, Inc. and Raymond L Loewen v. United States of America*, ICSID Case No ARB(AF)/98/3, Award, 26 June 2013, para. 54.

[101] T. W. Wälde, '"Equality of Arms" in Investment Arbitration: Procedural Challenges' in K. Yannaca-Small (ed.), *Arbitration Under International Investment Agreements: A Guide to the Key Issues* (Oxford University Press, 2010), pp. 161–88 at pp. 161–79.

C   Criticisms of Investor–State Arbitration

While the ability of foreign investors to choose ISA as a mechanism for settling investment disputes has gained relevance, it has also come under progressively more scrutiny.

The criticisms of ISA have been explained in great detail elsewhere[102] but, for the purposes of this book they can be classified into two main groups: those that question the necessity of the system as such and those focused on the functioning of the arbitral procedure.

1   Against the System of Investor–State Arbitration

Critics of the regime have pointed out that it allows foreign investors to bring a dispute against the host state before a body other than the state's own courts,[103] giving to private arbitrators the ability to decide the legality of sovereign acts, and in practice contracting out the judicial function that is embedded in public law.[104]

Some have taken even bolder positions, declaring that the last decades have witnessed 'the silent rise of a powerful international investment regime that has ensnared hundreds of countries and put corporate profit before human rights and the environment',[105] pointing out that international investment arbitration does not allow consideration of other legitimate public policies affecting a state's 'right to regulate', or 'policy space'. Certain characteristics of ISDS have led to concerns about the independence and impartiality of arbitrators, like that disputing parties appoint their own arbitrator, or the way in which the arbitrators are challenged, either by colleagues arbitrators or by organs composed of

---

[102] See, among many others, Michael Waibel et al. (eds.), *The Backlash Against Investment Arbitration: Perceptions and Reality* (Wolters Kluwer Law & Business, 2010); O. Thomas Johnson and Catherine H. Gibson, 'The Objections of Developed and Developing States to Investor–State Dispute Settlement and What They Are Doing about Them' in Arthur W. Rovine (ed.), *Contemporary Issues in International Arbitration and Mediation: The Fordham Papers 2013* (2014) 253; UNCTAD, 'Reform of Investor–State Dispute Settlement'.

[103] Schneider, 'Investment Disputes – Moving Beyond Arbitration', p. 120.

[104] G. van Harten, *Investment Treaty Arbitration and Public Law* (Oxford University Press, 2008), p. 4.

[105] P. Eberhardt and C. Olivet, *Profiting from Injustice. How Law Firms, Arbitrators and Financiers Are Fuelling an Investment Arbitration Boom* (Corporate Europe Observatory (CEO) and the Transnational Institute (TNI), 2012), p. 6.

members appointed by business representatives.[106] Both types of criticisms have been rejected by other groups of scholars and practitioners.[107]

Others have stressed the imbalances of the system against developing host states, as they are subject to the most claims and at a higher level than their proportion of global investment.[108] But then others have underscored the procedural challenges that a private party has to face when litigating against a state.[109]

According to UNCTAD, there is a growing perception that the system lacks legitimacy[110] but, most importantly, that ISDS increases severance of the links between the host state and the investor, defeating the very purpose of investment promotion:[111]

> The nature of the relationship between the investor and the state involves a long-term engagement; hence a dispute resolved by international arbitration and resulting in an award of damages will generally lead to a severance of this link. Moreover, the financial amounts at stake in investor–State disputes are often very high. Time and money required conducting such investment arbitrations (large costs and increased time frame). Cases are increasingly difficult to manage, the fears about frivolous and vexatious claims, the general concerns about the legitimacy of the system of investment arbitration as it affects measures of a sovereign State, and the fact that arbitration is focused entirely on the payment of compensation and not on maintaining a working relationship between the parties.

Interestingly, this structural critique has gaining adhesion not only when disputes follow the 'classic' format of a foreign investor from a developed state in a developing host state. We are witnessing a similar debate against ISDS in the negotiations and ratification of 'mega-regional' agreements involving developed countries, such as the Trans-Pacific Partnership

---

[106] N. Bernasconi-Osterwalder and D. Rosert, *Investment Treaty Arbitration: Opportunities to Reform Arbitral Rules and Processes* (2014), p. 12.

[107] C. N. Brower and S. Blanchard, 'What's in a Meme? The Truth about Investor–State Arbitration: Why It Need Not, and Must Not, Be Repossessed by States', Colum. J. Transnat'l L., 52 (2014), 689–896; S. M. Schwebel, 'In Defense of Bilateral Investment Treaties', *Arbitration International*, 31 (2015), 181–92.

[108] K. P. Gallagher and E. Shrestha, 'Investment Treaty Arbitration and Developing Countries: A Re-Appraisal', *Global Development and Environment Institute. Working Paper No 11-01* (2011), 1–12 at 8.

[109] Wälde, 'Equality of Arms'.

[110] UNCTAD, 'Reform of Investor–State Dispute Settlement', 2–4.

[111] UNCTAD, *Investor-State Disputes: Prevention and Alternatives to Arbitration* (United Nations Publications, 2010), p. xxiii, 5, 9.

(TPP),[112] the Comprehensive Economic and Trade Agreement (CETA)[113] and the Transatlantic Trade and Investment Partnership (TTIP).[114] Some groups, including civil society, academia and certain government officials, view the proposed inclusion of ISDS in such treaties as dangerous, because it would give foreign investors access to ISA – a forum that is seen as inappropriate in legal systems with a strong tradition of rule of law and independent and impartial courts.[115]

2   Against the Functioning of Investor–State Arbitration

Next to the criticisms against the system, we can find other groups of concerns that are directed to the actual functioning of the ISA procedure.

---

[112] Trans-Pacific Partnership Agreement, signed on 4 February 2016, between Australia, Brunei, Canada, Chile, Japan, Malaysia, Mexico, New Zealand, Peru, Singapore, the US and Vietnam. After the withdrawal of the US on 30 January 2017, the remaining TPP-11 countries decided to continue with the agreement, with the exception of a small number of technical articles and the suspension of application of certain provisions. Renamed Comprehensive and Progressive Agreement for Trans-Pacific Partnership (CPTPP), negotiations concluded on 23 January 2018, and the new agreement was signed on 8 March 2018 in Santiago de Chile. New Zealand Ministry of Foreign Affairs and Trade, 'Comprehensive and Progressive Agreement for Trans-Pacific Partnership' (February 2018). The CPTPP incorporates, by reference, the provisions of the TPP, so I have kept all the citations to that treaty in this book. In the case of TPP, the main objections against investor–state arbitration came from Australia and at a certain extent from the United States. See Leon E. Trakman, 'Investor–State Dispute Settlement under the Trans-Pacific Partnership Agreement' in Tania Voon (ed.), *Trade Liberalisation and International Co-operation: A Legal Analysis of the Trans-Pacific Partnership Agreement* (Edward Elgar Publishing, 2013), pp. 179–206.

[113] Comprehensive Economic and Trade Agreement between Canada and the European Union Trans-Pacific Partnership, signed on 30 October 2016. In this case, the debate has been taking place in both negotiating parties, Canada and the EU, and even its signature was at risk, after the opposition of the Walloon government in Belgium. See J. Adriaensen, 'The Future of EU Trade Negotiations: What Has Been Learned from CETA and TTIP?', November 2017: http://blogs.lse.ac.uk/europpblog/ (accessed 28 February 2018). CETA has been in partial provisional application since 21 September 2017.

[114] In the case of the TTIP, the European Commission held an online public consultation process, receiving a total of 149,399 contributions. European Commission, 'Online Public Consultation on Investment Protection and Investor-to-State Dispute Settlement (ISDS) in the Transatlantic Trade and Investment Partnership Agreement (TTIP)' (2014). A group of 121 academic experts spoke against the inclusion of ISA in the TTIP. See P. Muchlinski et al., 'Statement of Concern about Planned Provisions on Investment Protection and Investor-State Dispute Settlement (ISDS) in the Transatlantic Trade and Investment Partnership (TTIP)', July 2014: www.kent.ac.uk/law/isds_treaty _consultation.html (accessed 4 August 2017).

[115] Polanco Lazo, 'The No of Tokyo Revisited', 2.

UNCTAD has summarized different problems in this regard: i) transparency, as both disputing parties can keep proceedings fully confidential even in cases in which the dispute involves public interest matters; ii) 'nationality planning', as investors may gain access to ISDS using corporate structuring, without effective business in the 'home' state; iii) consistency of arbitral decisions, as arbitral tribunals have had divergent legal interpretations of identical or similar treaty provisions; iv) limited powers to correct erroneous decisions, as there is generally no appeal mechanism and ICSID annulment committees have very limited review powers; and v) arbitrators' independence and impartiality, as some disputing parties perceive them as biased or profiting from the system through repeated appointments.[116]

Reacting against this 'procedural' set of criticisms, innovative forms of rule-making have been taking place in recent years, both in IIAs and in arbitration rules. In order to discourage frivolous claims by investors, some IIAs have included a particular procedure for addressing preliminary objections by respondents.[117] After being amended in 2006, the ICSID Arbitration Rules now allow arbitral tribunals to dismiss proceedings summarily if they find that the underlying claims are 'manifestly without legal merit'.[118]

To minimize the possibilities of treaty and forum shopping, or overall 'nationality planning', several recent IIAs include a clause on 'denial of benefits', with the aim of excluding the protection provided by those treaties to investors or enterprises with no substantial business activity in the in the territory of the party under whose law it is constituted or organized.[119]

Several steps have been taken in order to increase transparency in the ISDS, aiming to improve the knowledge of the dispute, the access to the proceedings by non-disputing parties, and the publicity of awards and other arbitral documents. Efforts towards a more transparent investment arbitration system are reflected in most recent FTAs and BITs, particularly

---

[116] UNCTAD, 'Improving Investment Dispute Settlement: UNCTAD's Policy Tools', *IIA Issues Note*, 4 (2017), at 6.

[117] M. Potestà and M. Sobat, 'Frivolous Claims in International Adjudication: A Study of ICSID Rule 41 (5) and of Procedures of Other Courts and Tribunals to Dismiss Claims Summarily', *Journal of International Dispute Settlement*, 3 (2012), 131–62 at 22.

[118] A. Antonietti, 'The 2006 Amendments to the ICSID Rules and Regulations and the Additional Facility Rules', *ICSID Review – Foreign Investment Law Journal*, 21 (2006), 427–48 at 438–47.

[119] For a detailed explanation on these clauses, see L. A. Mistelis and C. M. Baltag, 'Denial of Benefits and Article 17 of the Energy Charter Treaty', Penn St. L. Rev., 113 (2008), 1301.

those signed by the United States and Canada.[120] In 2006, ICSID amended its Rules of Arbitration, including provisions on the publication of awards and opening of hearings to the public, allowing the possibility of *amicus curiae* submissions, among others.[121] Further steps towards transparency were achieved on 1 April 2014, with the entry into force of the UNCITRAL Rules on Transparency in treaty-based investor–state arbitration,[122] and on 10 December 2014, with the adoption of the UN Convention on Transparency in Treaty-based Investor-State arbitration (also known as the 'Mauritius Convention'), which has been in force since 18 October 2017.[123]

However, what is more interesting for the purpose of this work is that some of these criticisms against the functioning of ISA have been addressed in the negotiation and renegotiation of new IIAs, increasingly conferring an important role on the home state of the foreign investor. This is particularly true in relation to problems of interpretations of treaty provisions, filtering of claims, regulation of the work of arbitrators, and enforcement of awards, as we will analyse in detail in the later chapters of this book.

There is no single approach to addressing the criticisms against the international investment regime. However, the treaty practice that has been observed in recent years can lead us to the conclusion that the majority of countries do not seem to be against IIAs or ISA per se, but against the consequences of having certain standards broadly defined or the way in which those standards are interpreted in practice by private arbitrators. Evidence of this is the continuously growing number of investment treaties and the steady state practice of negotiating and concluding IIAs with ISA or other methods of investor-state dispute settlement even in the legitimacy crisis of recent years.

Although some countries, such as Bolivia, Ecuador, Venezuela and South Africa, have totally or partially 'disengaged' from the system, in the face of criticisms against ISA, the large majority have taken an 'intra-system' and 'normative' strategy, actively participating in the negotiation

---

[120] OECD, *Transparency and Third Party Participation in Investor–State Dispute Settlement Procedures* (2005), p. 5.

[121] Antonietti, 'The 2006 Amendments to the ICSID Rules and Regulations and the Additional Facility Rules', 432–7.

[122] UNCITRAL, Resolution adopted by the General Assembly 68/109, U.N. DOC. A/68/462 (16 December 2013).

[123] United Nations Convention on Transparency in Treaty-based Investor-State Arbitration, 17 March 2015, 54 ILM 747–57.

and renegotiation of new investment treaties to correct the system's numerous problems.[124]

If we analyse this new generation of treaties, we can see that they give more control and stronger involvement to the contracting parties, and notably we find a more active participation of the home state in investment disputes, in several roles such as the prevention or management of such disputes, the filtering of certain claims, in built-in treaty mechanisms for interpreting or clarifying provisions, in the regulation of the work and conduct of arbitrators, and in the enforcement of arbitral awards. These developments are not addressing the 'systemic' criticisms against the ISDS and the legitimacy of the system as such, but mostly those against the functioning of the arbitral procedure.

Several reasons explain the inclusion of stronger inter-governmental elements in IIAs. The first IIA that included detailed provisions in this regard was NAFTA, and Alschner believes that when it was negotiated, Canada and the United States felt potentially exposed to investment claims, and used tighter state control as a solution to moderating their risk in the face of bidirectional investment flows.[125] Van Aaken points out that contracting parties might retain authoritative interpretation for themselves or delegate it to other persons or institutions (such as joint commissions), if arbitrators are not trusted by states, either because they feel expertise is missing or because they are behaving in an unwanted manner.[126] According to Roberts, these institutional provisions have advantages over 'ad hoc' interpretations or clarifications, as they form part of the general regulatory framework of the agreement, which therefore 'substantially reduces concerns about detrimental reliance by investors'.[127] For Kulick, states have never lost their ability to make treaty interpretations, sharing this role with investor–state tribunals, only for the specific disputes between investors and home states.[128]

[124] R. Polanco Lazo, 'Is There a Life for Latin American Countries after Denouncing the ICSID Convention?', *Transnational Dispute Management*, 11 (2014).

[125] W. Alschner, 'The Return of the Home State and the Rise of "Embedded" Investor–State Arbitration' in S. Lalani and R. Polanco (eds.), *The Role of the State in Investor-State Arbitration* (Brill /Martinus Nijhoff, 2014), pp. 303–5.

[126] A. Van Aaken, 'Delegating Interpretative Authority in Investment Treaties: The Case of Joint Commissions', *Transnational Dispute Management*, 11 (2014) at 10.

[127] Roberts, 'Power and Persuasion', 208.

[128] Kulick, 'State–State Investment Arbitration as a Means of Reassertion of Control. From Antagonism to Dialogue' in A. Kulick (ed.), *Reassertion of Control Over the Investment Treaty Regime* (2017), pp. 128–52 at p. 146.

This phenomenon is simultaneously something 'new' and something 'old'. It is novel, in the sense that, with the rise of ISA, the home state had little to do with it, being virtually cast aside from the settlement of investment disputes. However, as we have seen in the first part of this work, this is also something 'old', as it implies the revisiting of a historical trend that saw home states involved in investment disputes, particularly through the use of peaceful means of diplomatic protection. Although most of these 'new' mechanisms are used jointly by the home state and the home state – a feature that has been described as the 'reassertion' of state control over the investment treaty regime[129] – a number of these mechanisms can also be triggered directly and solely by the home state. But is this new role of the home state in ISDS a 'return' to diplomatic protection, or we are witnessing a different type of home state participation?

In the chapters that follow, a detailed typology of the different kinds of participation of the home state is provided. This encompasses the whole range of investor–state disputes, from prevention and management of conflicts to participation at different stages of ISA, until the enforcement and implementation of arbitral awards. In each case we will examine whether this intervention constitutes diplomatic protection, based on the survey of IIAs negotiated, concluded and signed in the last fifteen years.

---

[129] Kulick (ed.), *Reassertion of Control Over the Investment Treaty Regime* (2017).

III

Home States and the Prevention of Investment Disputes

In this chapter we will examine a prospective role of the home state in the prevention of investment conflicts. In principle, it is not evident why home states would be involved in investment dispute prevention at all. But as Schreuer has pointed out, investor–state arbitration under international investment agreements serves not only the investor's personal interests but also the public interests of the contracting states and the broader interest of the international community in the avoidance of international conflicts.[1] However, what would these home states' 'public interests' be? Which grounds would justify their intervention in the prevention of investment disputes? Can this be considered diplomatic protection?

A   Home State Interests in Preventing Investment Disputes

As briefly analysed in the preceding chapter, in recent years there has been a critical reflection on the impact of ISA as a mechanism for settling foreign investment disputes. One of the proposed paths to reforming that system has been the use of methods of alternative dispute resolution (ADR) as well as dispute prevention policies (DPPs) and conflict management mechanisms (CMMs), which enable investors and governments to manage foreign investment conflicts before they escalate into disputes under international investment agreements.[2]

---

[1] C. Schreuer, 'Investment Protection and International Relations' in A. Reinisch and U. Kriebaum (eds.), *The Law of International Relations: Liber Amicorum Hanspeter Neuhold* (Eleven International Publishing, 2007), pp. 345–58 at p. 357.

[2] Echandi has defined DPPs as 'any course of action adopted and pursued by one or more governments specifically aimed at preventing investor-State conflicts arising under IIAs from escalating into full-blown disputes under those agreements', and CMMs as 'concrete procedural mechanisms, established either by law or contract, to enable investors and host states to early manage investment-related conflicts and prevent dispute escalation'.: R. Echandi, 'Complementing Investor–State Dispute Resolution: A Conceptual

53

However, the tools of prevention or management of foreign investment disputes traditionally consider the participation only of the host state and the concerned investor, and there is no clarity about what role (if any) the home state could have in the prevention of investment disputes.

Generally speaking, state efforts on conflict-prevention involve early diplomatic action aimed at preventing new disputes and the escalation of existing tensions, as well as limiting the spread of ongoing conflicts. In the context of armed conflicts, this has been dubbed 'preventive diplomacy'.[3]

The prevention of investment disputes between foreign investors and the host state could be relevant for home states if it is directly related to legitimate public policies that are either shared with other states or particular to the home state.

Different shared interests between home and host states can be foreseen in this regard, such as those related to national security, economic and regulatory interests, and common concerns. Examples of national security issues include conflicts that arise between national investors and host states with which the home state has pending or latent military problems, such as territorial claims or peace negotiations. Economic interests that would foster home state interest in preventing investment disputes can include dependency on exports or imports of goods or services from the host state, pending or projected negotiations of preferential trade agreements, regional integration, or the like. But, also, a home state may have shared regulatory concerns in the policies advanced by the host state, and therefore be willing to support regulations enacted by other states even if they affect its own investors abroad. For example, if the home state is planning to apply similar regulations as those applied by the host state – e.g. on plain packaging of cigarettes – it could be interested in preventing disputes in such areas in case it envisages potential conflicts with foreign or national investors. These shared on public interests could also be part of common concerns between home states and host states. If the home state has failed, or has been unable, to act in the pursuit of shared public goods – e.g. climate change mitigation – it might have an incentive to prevent investment disputes between its nationals and a host state that has been able to act in the pursuit of the same goals.

Framework for Investor–State Conflict Management': Prospects in International Investment Law and Policy (Cambridge University Press, 2013), pp. 295–6.

[3] M. Jenča, 'The Concept of Preventive Diplomacy and Its Application by the United Nations in Central Asia', *Security and Human Rights*, 24 (2013), 183–94 at 184.

However, home states could also act in their own interests in the prevention of investment disputes. Several reasons could lead countries to do this, including their concern to promote specific policies, reputational gains or political goals. Certain home states could have an interest in promoting specific policies that they consider desirable that national investors follow while investing abroad, such as corporate responsibility practices in areas like human and labour rights or environmental protection. This would induce home states to work in the prevention of investment disputes that are related to these issues. Home states could also foresee reputational gains in the prevention of investment disputes between their national investors and host states, endorsing certain types of 'responsible' investment from their nationals, which would reduce potential conflicts with the host state, under the assumption that conflicts are less likely to happen between host states and 'responsible' investors. In the absence of mechanisms of investor–state dispute settlement, home states would be interested in preventing investment disputes that could increase the possibilities of a request of diplomatic espousal by national investors – especially if they have no interest in 'politicizing' such disputes for other competing domestic political priorities.

Nowadays, preventive diplomacy is conducted by multiple international actors, using a wide range of tools. This has been possible thanks to the establishment of a normative framework that encourages international efforts to prevent violent conflict.[4] Unfortunately, there is no such framework for the prevention of investment disputes.

What, then, would be the legal basis of home state participation in the prevention of investor–state conflicts? As currently conceived, diplomatic protection takes place after the violation of primary rules concerning the treatment of aliens.[5] For that reason, 'classic' diplomatic protection would not be a useful basis on which to justify the role of home states in the prevention of disputes of their investors abroad, due to its distinctive remedial character: the invocation of the responsibility of another state for an injury already caused by an internationally wrongful act.[6]

IIAs do not generally provide for a role for the home state in the prevention of investment conflicts. Thus, the basis for such participation

---

[4] Ibid., 185.
[5] C. F. Amerasinghe, *Diplomatic Protection* (Oxford University Press, 2008), p. 37.
[6] See the definition of diplomatic protection in Art. 1 of the International Law Commission Draft Articles on Diplomatic Protection: ILC, 'Draft Articles on Diplomatic Protection, with commentaries', 24.

should be found somewhere else. In the next sections we will examine the different tools that might be used by the home state for this purpose.

B   Tools for Prevention of Investment Disputes Involving Home States

1   Prevention of Disputes in IIAs

In theory, IIAs could provide for a series of home state rights and obligations, but, so far, these provisions have not generally been included in these treaties, with the notable exception of some recent agreements (mainly concluded by Brazil) and of certain model bilateral investment treaties that envisage different roles for the home state. According to Bottini, these roles could include assisting developing and least-developed countries (LDCs) in facilitating foreign investment, providing information to the host state regarding a home investor or investment, and ensuring that home states' legal systems allow for claims relating to investor liability for damages in the host state.[7]

(a)   Investment Facilitation and Investor Liability in Model IIAs

Two model treaties developed in recent years contain provisions on home state rights and obligations, and some of them can be considered relevant for the prevention of investment disputes, particularly those related to investment facilitation and investor liability. These are the 2005 International Institute for Sustainable Development (IISD) Model International Agreement on Investment for Sustainable Development (IAISD)[8] and the 2012 Southern African Development Community (SADC) Model BIT,[9] which was also developed with technical support provided by the IISD.

Investment facilitation activities are those carried out by both home and host states that make it easier for foreign investors to establish or expand

---

[7] G. Bottini, *Extending Responsibilities in International Investment Law*. E15 Initiative (International Centre for Trade and Sustainable Development (ICTSD) and World Economic Forum, 2015), p. 4.

[8] International Institute for Sustainable Development, H. L. Mann, K. von Moltke, L. E. Peterson and A. Cosbey, 'IISD Model International Agreement on Investment for Sustainable Development' (2005).

[9] Southern African Development Community (SADC), *SADC Model Bilateral Investment Treaty Template with Commentary* (2012).

their investments, as well as to conduct their day-to-day business.[10] One can argue that certain provisions on investment facilitation could help to prevent investment disputes, as they are directed towards improving the conditions in which the investment is established in the host state.

The IISD Model IAISD includes some provisions on investment facilitation that could improve the 'quality' of the foreign investment, such as home state assistance to host states in environmental and social impact assessments, provision of information on home state standards that might apply to the investment proposed by its investor (e.g. the home state environmental impact assessment process), and overall cooperative efforts to promote sustainable investments.[11]

Investment liability provisions are those directed to guarantee investors' responsibility for corruption, damage or injuries in the host state, produced in connection with their investments. For the purpose of dispute prevention, these provisions should work as a deterrent for investors to be involved in such conducts or activities, and therefore they could reduce the possibilities of a dispute with the home state. Some of these clauses provide for a direct role for the home state, particularly for dispute resolution and corruption issues.

For example, both the IISD Model IAISD and the SADC Model BIT stipulate that investors shall be liable in their home state for acts or decisions made in relation to the investment when they lead to significant damage, personal injuries or loss of life in the host state. Investors' liability can be pursued by the host state, a private person or an organization, using civil actions before the home state courts. Home states shall ensure that their legal rules and systems allow for, or do not prevent or restrict, the bringing of these civil actions against the investor,[12] using *forum non conveniens* or similar rules.[13]

These provisions are not intended to create a presumption of guilt of the investor, but rather to provide remedies through home state's courts for harm caused by its national companies (or those headquartered in its territory) acting in prejudice of the host state or its communities.

---

[10] UNCTAD, *Investment Facilitation: A Review of Policy Practices. Follow-up to UNCTAD's Global Action Menu for Investment Facilitation* (2017), p. 3.

[11] IISD Model IAISD, Arts. 29 and 30.

[12] Ibid., Arts. 17, 18 c), f), 31; SADC Model BIT, Arts. 17, 19.4.

[13] International Institute for Sustainable Development, Mann, von Moltke, Peterson and Cosbey, 'IISD Model International Agreement on Investment for Sustainable Development', 16.

The legal process of the home state, together with the standard and burden of proof, etc., would continue to apply to the proceedings.[14]

One important difference between both model treaties is that the IISD Model explicitly mentions that host state laws shall be applicable to liability proceedings against the investor in the home state, while in the SADC model liability is restricted to decisions taken by the parent company within the home state.

Regarding corruption, both model IIAs provide for common obligations against corruption for the host and the home state. Under these provisions, the home state shall prosecute their investors involved in bribing or similar activities, to any public official of the host state, either directly or indirectly.[15] In the IISD model, host states additionally have the right to seek information in its home state about a potential investor, its corporate governance history and its practices.[16]

The implementation of these provisions is aimed not only at criminal punishment, but also at the abrogation of the investor's treaty rights, either because the definition of investment requires it to be made in accordance with domestic law (being a corrupted investment, it is no longer a covered investment),[17] or because those rights are explicitly rescinded in the treaty.[18]

Reactions to these model IIAs, particularly in the Western, capital-exporting states have not been positive, and an observer may well be concerned whether they tilt towards the state to such an extent that it makes investment protection odious.[19] In fact, treaties that follow these templates even partially by including home state commitments relating to the prevention of investment disputes are scarce, and will be addressed in the following sections. Not even the SADC or its members have followed its own model in the conclusion of recent IIAs.

---

[14] Southern African Development Community (SADC), *SADC Model Bilateral Investment Treaty Template with Commentary*, p. 38.

[15] IISD Model IAISD, Art. 32; SADC Model BIT, Art. 10.

[16] IISD Model IAISD, Art. 28.

[17] Southern African Development Community (SADC), *SADC Model Bilateral Investment Treaty Template with Commentary*, p. 32.

[18] IISD Model IAISD, Art. 18 c). The same consequence is foreseen if the investor persistently fails to comply with its obligations in a manner that circumvents international environmental, labour, human rights or corporate governance obligations to which the host state and/or home state are parties.

[19] M. Sornarajah, *Resistance and Change in the International Law on Foreign Investment* (Cambridge University Press, 2015), p. 359.

However, some key elements of these model treaties have been echoed in more recent policy guidelines. The United Nations Conference on Trade and Development (UNCTAD)'s Global Action Menu for Investment Facilitation considers one of its action lines to complement investment facilitation through enhancing international cooperation for investment promotion and development. Among the possible mechanisms for achieving this goal are including in IIAs provisions that encourage home countries to provide facilitation services or outward investment support (such as political risk insurance) linked with high standards of corporate governance and responsible business conduct by outward investors.[20]

(b)   The New Brazilian Model

As mentioned, few IIAs include provisions on the prevention of investment disputes, and even fewer provide for a role for home states in it. Rare exceptions include the cooperation and facilitation investment agreements (CFIAs) concluded by Brazil with Mozambique, Angola, Mexico, Malawi, Colombia, Chile, Ethiopia and Suriname, a model that was also included in the investment chapter of the Economic and Trade Expansion Agreement (ETEA) concluded between Brazil and Peru in 2016, and in the 2017 Intra-MERCOSUR Investment Facilitation Protocol.

CFIAs are notable because they do not include ISA. Brazil made a conscious decision not to include ISDS provisions in these agreements, opting instead for creating mechanisms of risk mitigation and dispute prevention, which actively involve both home and host states.[21]

From the point of view of dispute prevention, the CFIAs adopt two different and interrelated levels for the settlement of any 'issue of interest of an investor'. First, the creation of focal points or 'ombudspersons';[22]

---

[20] UNCTAD, *Investment Facilitation: A Review of Policy Practices. Follow-up to UNCTAD's Global Action Menu for Investment Facilitation*, p. 17.

[21] F. Morosini and M. Ratton Sánchez-Badin, 'The New Brazilian Agreements on Cooperation and Facilitation of Investments (ACFIs): Navigating between Resistance and Conformity with the Global Investment Regime' (2015), 25.

[22] Agreement on Cooperation and Facilitation of Investments between the Government of the Federative Republic of Brazil and the Government of the Republic of Mozambique, signed at Maputo 30 March 2015, Art. 5; Agreement on Cooperation and Facilitation of Investments between the Government of the Federative Republic of Brazil and the Government of the Republic of Angola, signed at Luanda 1 April 2015, Art. 5; Agreement on Cooperation and Facilitation of Investments between the Federative Republic of Brazil and the United Mexican States, signed at Mexico City 26 May 2015, Art. 15; Investment Cooperation and Facilitation Agreement between the Federative Republic of Brazil and the Republic of Malawi, signed at Brasilia 25 June 2015, Art. 4;

and, second, the establishment of a joint committee (JC) appointed by the contracting parties.[23] The home state is involved in both levels of dispute prevention, together with the host state. If those mechanisms fail, the treaties provide for resort to inter-state mechanisms that may or not involve arbitration.[24]

The first level of dispute prevention involves the ombudspersons, who are in charge of preventing, managing and settling disputes between foreign investors and the host state. Among other duties, the ombudspersons have several tasks that fall within the scope of dispute prevention, such as interacting with the relevant government authorities to assess and recommend referrals for suggestions and complaints received from the government and investors of the other party; provide timely and useful information on regulation applicable to general investment or on specific projects; and mitigating conflicts and facilitating their resolutions in coordination with relevant government authorities and in partnership with pertinent private bodies.[25] All the ombudspersons designated in CFIAs are governmental entities of the home and the host state.

If the ombudspersons do not manage to resolve the conflict, dispute prevention escalates to a second level: the joint committee. The JC is established with the primary general task of supervision of the implementation and execution of the CFIAs, and in that context it ought to facilitate the exchange of information between the contracting parties,

Agreement on Cooperation and Facilitation of Investments between the Federative Republic of Brazil and the Republic of Colombia, signed at Bogota 9 October 2015, Art. 17; Agreement on Cooperation and Facilitation of Investments between the Federative Republic of Brazil and the Republic of Chile, signed at Santiago, 23 November 2015, Art. 19; Agreement on Economic and Commercial Enlargement between the Federative Republic of Brazil and the Republic of Peru, signed at Lima, 29 April 2016, Art. 2.16; Intra-MERCOSUR Cooperation and Facilitation Investment Protocol, signed at Buenos Aires 7 April 2017, Art. 18; Agreement on Cooperation and Facilitation of Investments between the Federative Republic of Brazil and the Federal Democratic Republic of Ethiopia, signed at Addis Ababa, 11 April 2018, Art.18; and Agreement on Cooperation and Facilitation of Investments between the Federative Republic of Brazil and the Republic of Suriname, signed at Brasilia, 02 May 2018, Art.19.

[23] Brazil-Mozambique CFIA (2015), Art. 4; Brazil-Angola CFIA (2015), Art. 4; Brazil-Mexico CFIA (2015), Art. 14; Brazil-Malawi CFIA (2015), Art. 3; Brazil-Colombia CFIA (2015) Art. 18; Brazil-Peru ETEA (2016), Art. 2.15; Intra-MERCOSUR Investment Facilitation Protocol (2017), Art. 17; Brazil-Ethiopia CFIA (2018), Art. 17; Brazil-Suriname CFIA (2018), Art. 18.

[24] P. Martini, 'Brazil's New Investment Treaties: Outside Looking . . . Out?' (June 2015).

[25] Morosini and Ratton Sánchez-Badin, 'The New Brazilian Agreements on Cooperation and Facilitation of Investments (ACFIs)', 26.

strengthen mutual investment and create mechanisms for interaction between the private sector and governments.[26]

The JC has also the task of developing the thematic cooperation and investment facilitation agendas between the contracting parties, which consider a number of topics that can improve the establishment and management of the investment in the host state (e.g. payments and transfers, visas and technical and environmental regulations), and therefore theoretically minimizing the chances of disputes arising about these issues.[27]

If a conflict arises, the JC – composed of representatives of both the home and the host state – shall try to resolve any issue or dispute concerning the parties' investment in an amicable manner. A party may submit a concern to the JC, specifying the name of the interested investor and the encountered challenges and difficulties. The concerned investor could also participate in these bilateral meetings, as well as representatives of governmental or non-governmental entities involved in the measure or situation under consultation.[28] The JC functions as a type of mediator, issuing a summarized report[29] – a task that, in certain treaties, has a previously defined short timeframe (generally sixty days, extendable by mutual agreement by sixty additional days).[30]

If the dispute is not settled within the JC, the parties (including the home state) may resort to inter-state arbitration mechanisms, if it is

---

[26] N. Monebhurrun, 'Novelty in International Investment Law: The Brazilian Agreement on Cooperation and Facilitation of Investments as a Different International Investment Agreement Model', *Journal of International Dispute Settlement* (2016), 79–100 at 85.

[27] Brazil–Mozambique CFIA (2015), Art. 8 and Annex I; Brazil–Angola CFIA (2015), Art. 8 and Annex I; Brazil–Mexico CFIA (2015), Art. 20 and Annex I; Brazil–Malawi CFIA (2015), Art. 7 and Annex I; Brazil–Colombia CFIA (2015), Art. 24 and Annex I; Intra-MERCOSUR Investment Facilitation Protocol (2017), Art. 25 and Annex I; Brazil–Ethiopia CFIA (2015), Art. 25 and Annex I. Brazil–Chile CFIA, Art. 26; Brazil–Peru ETEA (2016), Art. 2.22; and Brazil–Suriname CFIA (2018), Art. 26, do not define a specific cooperation and facilitation agenda.

[28] The CFIAs include a rare feature, as they allow the participation of the private sector and of civil society in the meetings of the JC, by formal invitation or by requesting invitation 'to participate in the formulation of norms or policies regarding the implementation of foreign investments': Monebhurrun, 'Novelty in International Investment Law', 85.

[29] Morosini and Ratton Sánchez-Badin, 'The New Brazilian Agreements on Cooperation and Facilitation of Investments (ACFIs)', 26.

[30] Brazil–Mexico CFIA (2015), Art. 18.3; Brazil–Malawi CFIA (2015), Art. 13.3; Brazil–Colombia CFIA (2015), Art. 22.3; Intra-MERCOSUR Investment Facilitation Protocol (2017), Art. 23; Brazil-Ethiopia CFIA (2018), Art. 23; Brazil–Suriname CFIA (2018), Art. 24. Under Brazil–Chile CFIA (2015), Art. 24.3 the timeframe is ninety days, and under Brazil–Peru ETEA (2016), Art. 2.20.3 it is 120 days.

deemed convenient for them, and only after a written request. In any case, the previous exhaustion of negotiations and consultations at the JC level is mandatory to initiate inter-state arbitral proceedings between states.[31] As we have seen, the roles of both the JC and the ombudspersons are, primarily, to promote regular exchange of information and prevent disputes and, if a dispute arises, to implement the settlement mechanism, based on consultations, negotiations and mediation. Although state-to-state arbitration is mentioned in CFIAs, Brazilian public officials have noted that it shall not be the foremost mechanism for settling disputes, favouring consultations, negotiations and mediation, through the JC and the ombudspersons.[32] In fact, both the ombudspersons and the JCs are considered as operating in addition to existing diplomatic channels between the contracting parties.

(c) Other Treaties

Besides the new Brazilian CFIAs, a few other IIAs include specific provisions on prevention of investment disputes that involve the home state. One of them is the South Korea–Vietnam FTA[33] that establishes contact points – at both state and local government levels – for improving the investment environment, which have, among other tasks, 'to receive the complaints from investors of the other Party with regard to its administrative action of governments and to provide assistance in resolving difficulties of investors of the other Party'. Although this preventive activity does not involve the home state directly, the Committee on Investment established on the treaty – where the home state participates – has the role of discussing and reviewing the implementation and operation of these provisions (which are explicitly excluded from both investor–state and state-to-state dispute settlement).[34]

Another treaty that includes more detailed provisions on dispute prevention involving the home state is the Morocco–Nigeria BIT.[35]

---

[31] Martini, 'Brazil's New Investment Treaties'.

[32] F. Morosini and M. Ratton Sánchez-Badin, 'The Brazilian Agreement on Cooperation and Facilitation of Investments (ACFI): A New Formula for International Investment Agreements?' (August 2015).

[33] Free Trade Agreement between the Government of the Republic of Korea and the Government of the Socialist Republic of Viet Nam, signed at Hanoi, 5 May 2015, entered into force 20 December 2015, Art. 12.19.

[34] South Korea–Vietnam FTA, Arts. 12.17, 12.19.

[35] Reciprocal Investment Promotion and Protection Agreement between the Government of the Kingdom of Morocco and the Government of the Federal Republic of Nigeria, signed at Abuja, 3 December 2016, Arts. 2, 4 and 26.

Apart from being mentioned as one of the core objectives of the agreement, dispute prevention receives lengthy treatment in the treaty. Before initiating any arbitration procedure, a dispute between the host state and an investor of the home state is to be previously assessed by the joint committee, composed of representatives of both contracting parties, which shall seek to resolve any issues or disputes concerning investment in an amicable manner. The home state may submit to the JC a specific question of interest to its investors, in writing, and specifying the name of the interested investor and the encountered challenges and difficulties. The JC shall have ninety days, extendable by mutual agreement by sixty additional days, to submit relevant information about the case. Special meetings could be considered, if needed to facilitate the search for a solution. Representatives of the investor shall participate in such meetings whenever possible, as well as non-party entities involved in the measure or situation under consultation.

The procedure ends, at the request of 'any party', with the adoption by the JC of a report summarizing the dialogue and bilateral consultation that took place, identifying the investors, the description of the measure under consultation and the position of the parties concerning the measure. Except for this report, the meetings of the JC, and all the related documentation and steps taken at this preventive stage, shall remain confidential. If the dispute cannot be resolved within six months from the date of the written request for consultations and negotiations, the investor may resort to international arbitration mechanisms, but only after exhausting local remedies, or to the domestic courts of the host state.

For Gazzini, Article 26 of the Morocco–Nigeria BIT is 'intriguing' and 'ambiguous', as it deals with investor–state disputes and, without further explanation, refers to disputes and solutions 'between the Parties'. Moreover, this provision does not indicate what the position of investors is beyond their possible participation in the 'bilateral meeting' of the JC. Also, it does not define the meaning, nature or legal significance of 'assessment' of the dispute, or the meaning of 'consultations and negotiations'.[36]

The Morocco–Nigeria BIT also includes provisions on investment facilitation and investment liability, closely following the IISD Model

---

[36] T. Gazzini, 'Nigeria and Morocco Move Towards a "New Generation" of Bilateral Investment Treaties', May 2017: www.ejiltalk.org/nigeria-and-morocco-move-towards-a-new-generation-of-bilateral-investment-treaties/ (accessed 17 January 2018).

IAISD on both issues. On investment facilitation, both parties shall agree on standards for conducting a social impact assessment of the potential investment, as well as on corporate governance adopted at the meeting of the JC. On anti-corruption, both the host and the home state shall prosecute and convict penalized persons who have breached their applicable domestic laws on corruption. Finally, the treaty includes a number of promotion and facilitation activities in which the home state should assist the host state, some of which could have a positive impact on reducing the possibility of a dispute between the investor of the home state and the host state (e.g. support for cooperative efforts to promote sustainable investments).

On investment liability, the treaty declares that investors shall be subject to civil actions for liability in the judicial process of their home state for acts or decisions made in relation to the investment, where such acts or decisions lead to significant damage, personal injuries or loss of life in the host state. In the same line, the treaty provides that a host state has the right to seek information from a potential investor in its home state about its corporate governance history and its practices as an investor.[37]

Another Nigerian treaty – this time with Singapore – also has a minor facilitation provision involving the home state, allowing the latter to request specific information on home state laws, regulations, administrative rulings of general application, and international agreements pertaining to or affecting investment, to which the host state shall promptly respond.[38]

Finally, two recent IIAs concluded by Hong Kong, with Mainland China and the Association of Southeast Asian Nations (ASEAN), also include provisions on investment facilitation which might be useful in the prevention of investment disputes, as both parties should cooperate to facilitate investments through several activities, including improving investment environment and simplifying procedures for investment applications and approvals.[39]

---

[37] Morocco–Nigeria BIT, Arts. 14, 17, 19, 20, 21 and 25.

[38] Investment Promotion and Protection Agreement between the Government of the Federal Republic of Nigeria and the Government of the Republic of Singapore, signed at Singapore 4 November 2016, Art. 27.

[39] Mainland China and Hong Kong Closer Economic Partnership Arrangement, signed at Hong Kong 28 June 2017, entered into force 28 June 2017, Art. 15; and Agreement on Investment Among the Governments of the Hong Kong Special Administrative Region of the People's Republic of China and the Member States of the Association of Southeast Asian Nations, signed at Manila, 12 November 2017, Art. 16.

Table 3.1. *IIAs with provisions on review of implementation*

	Direct Review by Contracting Parties	Review by a Treaty Body
Number of IIAs	222	109
% of total data set	39	19

2 Prevention by Review of IIAs' Implementation

Several IIAs include provisions that allow contracting parties to express their views on the implementation, application or operation of the agreement – usually through diplomatic channels. As discussed in other chapters of this book, these clauses may also provide that the parties could discuss any matter relating to the interpretation of the agreement, or even become a type of inter-state dispute settlement mechanism. The following section will then focus exclusively on the use of these provisions for the purposes of dispute prevention of foreign investment conflicts involving the home state.

Seemingly, the first IIA that included explicit provisions on the review of its implementation was the 1982 Japan–Sri Lanka BIT, which provides that: 'Each Contracting party shall accord sympathetic consideration to, and shall afford adequate opportunity for consultation regarding, such representations as the other Contracting party may make with respect to any matter affecting the operation of the present Agreement'.[40]

More than half of the IIAs concluded in the last fifteen years (328 agreements, representing around 58 per cent of the total data set examined in this book), include provisions that allow the parties – home and host states – to review the implementation of the agreement, either directly by the contracting parties or through the creation of dedicated treaty bodies.

Clauses on the review of IIAs' implementation aim to preserve the relationship between the parties, guiding the overall implementation of the treaty although no consequences are assigned to the lack of agreement in such reviews.

Home states could help in the training of host states' public servants, in order to identify and manage these conflicts at an early stage. UNCTAD

---

[40] Agreement between Japan and the Democratic Socialist Republic of Sri Lanka Concerning the Promotion and Protection of Investment, signed at Colombo 1 March 1982, Art. 13.1.

has recognized that including provisions to facilitate the implementation of the IIA could help to maximize its sustainable development impact – for example, if activities on technical assistance, or capacity building on investment promotion and facilitation, are considered.[41] In this regard, home states could assist host states in assessing the environmental, social and human rights impact of potential large-scale investments. This Would be particularly important for LDCs due to their limited capacity and resources for performing such analysis. The assumption here is that having a clearer assessment of the sustainable development impacts of foreign investment in the host state, decreases the likelihood of having a dispute between that state and a foreign investor.

Provisions on review of the implementation of an IIA could allow a bigger role for the home state in the prevention of investment disputes, through the clarification of the overall operation of the treaty, even in the absence of a current dispute. Consultation might facilitate the understanding of certain provisions and avoid the escalation of a dispute to arbitration between a home state's investor and the host state that might endanger the contracting parties' relationship.[42]

There are several examples of the preventive use of these provisions. Under the Mauritius–UAE BIT, the contracting parties shall hold consultations on the settlement of investment disputes.[43] The Japan–Philippines economic partnership agreement (EPA) explicitly provides for general consultations 'for the avoidance and settlement of disputes', establishing that the contracting parties shall make every effort to avoid possible disputes through consultations.[44] In the Panama–Singapore FTA, even a working group may be established to review claims by a party that a measure of the other party has affected the effective implementation of the undertakings in the agreement.[45] Along the same lines, the Jordan–Syria BIT creates an 'Agreement Implementation Follow-up Committee', with one of its tasks being 'to perform conciliating role for disputes related to the investment

---

[41] UNCTAD, *Investment Policy Framework for Sustainable Development (IPFSD)* (2015), p. 85.

[42] J. W. Salacuse, *The Law of Investment Treaties* (Oxford University Press, 2010), p. 361.

[43] Investment Promotion and Protection Agreement between Mauritius and the United Arab Emirates, signed at Dubai, 20 September 2015, Art. 14.

[44] Agreement between Japan and the Republic of the Philippines for an Economic Partnership, signed at Helsinki, 9 September 2006, entered into force 11 December 2008, Art. 150.

[45] Free Trade Agreement between the Republic of Singapore and the Republic of Panama, signed at Singapore 1 March 2006, entered into force 24 July 2007, Art. 17.2(c).

activity and to solve them amicably'.[46] The ASEAN Investment Agreement considers it a function of the ASEAN Investment Area Council to facilitate the 'avoidance and settlement of disputes arising from the agreement'.[47]

We also find a type of 'preventive interpretation' of IIAs, aimed at clarifying the intention of the contracting parties, before there is even an actual conflict or concrete query about its implementation. An example is the joint interpretative instrument of CETA, signed by Canada and the EU in October 2016. This document provides, in the sense of Article 31 of the Vienna Convention on the Law of Treaties (VCLT),[48] a 'clear and unambiguous statement' of what both contracting parties had agreed in a number of CETA provisions that have been the object of public debate and concerns, like the 'right to regulate' in the public interest, investment protection and dispute resolution, as well as sustainable development, labour rights, environmental protection, government procurement and small and medium-sized enterprises (SMEs). The document even includes a concordance table referenced to the CETA text, for the purpose of assisting in the interpretation of the agreement, by relating the statement of the intention of the parties in that instrument to the relevant provisions of CETA.[49] Undoubtedly, preventive interpretation is not only directed towards effectively avoiding conflicts between investors and host states, but is also important as a political signal to the constituencies of both home and host states, as well as those of third parties. However, the effectiveness of this preventive interpretation is yet to be seen.

(a) Direct Review by the Contracting Parties

From the sample of available treaties concluded in the last fifteen years, 222 IIAs (39 per cent) include a clause providing for the review of the implementation of the agreement directly by the parties as a part of

---

[46] Agreement on the Encouragement and Protection of Investments between the Hashemite Kingdom of Jordan and the Government of the Syrian Arab Republic, signed 8 October 2001, entered into force 11 May 2002, Art. 8.

[47] ASEAN Comprehensive Investment Agreement, signed at Cha-am 26 February 2009, entered into force 24 February 2012, Art. 42.3(e). Similar provisions are included in other IIAs, e.g.: Australia–Chile FTA (2008), Art. 20.1.3(d); Malaysia–Pakistan CEPA (2007), Art. 8; China–Pakistan FTA (2006), Art. 76(c).

[48] Vienna Convention on the Law of Treaties, 1155 U.N.T.S. 331, 8 I.L.M. 679, entered into force 27 January 1980.

[49] Canada, EU, 'Joint Interpretative Declaration on the Comprehensive Economic and Trade Agreement (CETA) between Canada and the European Union and Its Member States' (October 2016).

a consultation or cooperation mechanism. The large majority (194) are included in BITs that follow the 'classic' formulation of holding consultations for the general purpose of reviewing the implementation of the agreement that shall be held at a time agreed on through appropriate channels.[50] Usually there is no designation of a specific governmental authority in charge of these consultations, although it is provided for in a few BITs.[51]

No specific procedural rules and no fixed timeframe is provided for these consultations, although implicitly the consultation should take place promptly.[52] Certain BITs include a precise timeframe for such consultations. The Senegal–US BIT was apparently the first one to include a periodical review of the status of the treaty and its application, providing for consultations between representatives of the two contracting parties, at a time and place to be determined by mutual accord, every two years beginning from the date in which the treaty entered into force.[53]

While is not always explicit in the text, these consultations should take place at the request of either contracting party.[54] Most agreements go further, in demanding that consultations should be requested 'in writing' with respect to any matter that it considers might affect the operation of the agreement.[55]

In some cases, direct review by the contracting parties of the treaty is provided for in free trade or regional investment treaties (RITs). In the data set twenty-six FTAs and three RITs provide for this type of review, usually under cooperation commitments in addition to existing institutional consultation mechanism in treaty bodies, such as 'joint' or 'implementing' committees, as will be examined in the next section.[56]

---

[50] E.g. Egypt–Finland BIT (2004), Art. 16; Belarus–Denmark BIT (2004), Art. 11; Croatia–Oman BIT (2004), Art. 14.

[51] See Belarus–Venezuela BIT (2007), Art. 11, which designates 'coordinating organs' for each contracting party.

[52] E.g.: Bosnia and Herzegovina–Lithuania BIT (2007), Art. 10 provides that consultations should begin 'without undue delay', upon request by either contracting party.

[53] Senegal–US BIT (1983), Art. VI.3.

[54] E.g.: Portugal–UAE BIT (2011), Art. 13; India–Slovenia BIT (2011), Art. 16; Macedonia–Montenegro BIT (2010), Art. 10.

[55] E.g.: Canada–Mongolia BIT (2016), Art. 38; Canada–Hong Kong BIT (2016), Art. 36; Canada–Guinea BIT (2015), Art. 39.

[56] E.g.: Australia–China FTA (2015), Art. 16.5; EEU–Viet Nam FTA (2015), Art. 8.6; CARICOM–Costa Rica FTA (2004), Art. XIII.01. CARICOM is the Caribbean Community, and includes the following countries: Antigua and Barbuda, Barbados, Belize, Costa Rica, Dominica, Grenada, Guyana, Jamaica, St Kitts and Nevis, St Lucia,

Review of the IIA between the contracting parties can also be directed to specific subject matters of the treaty, in sensitive issues such as the control of an investment, transparency of investment contracts, implementation of intellectual property, denial of benefits, temporary safeguards and investment subsidies.

In a number of Australian BITs, a consultation process between contracting parties should take place with respect to any question concerning the control of a company or an investment.[57] An analogous provision is included in at least one Canadian BIT.[58]

Several Japanese BITs include a provision allowing the contracting parties to request information to the other contracting party, relating to contracts that the latter enters into with regard to investment. According to this clause, a home state could directly require information about the implementation of a contract between one of its investors and the host state.[59] Some of these treaties also specify the obligation of home and host states to consult with each other on intellectual property rights promptly and, depending on the results of the consultations, the host state shall, in accordance with its applicable law and regulations, take appropriate measures to remove the factors that are recognized as having adverse effects on the investments of investors of the home state.[60]

Several BITs concluded by the United States,[61] Japan[62] and other countries[63] provide for a consultation mechanism in the event that one

St Vincent and the Grenadines, Suriname, and Trinidad and Tobago. Some notable exceptions are the Korea–Singapore FTA (2005), in which the review of the treaty is in charge of the ministers in charge of trade negotiations of the parties or their designated officials (Art. 22.1). This also happens in a couple of RITs: the ASEAN – Korea Investment Agreement (2009), Art. 25, and the ASEAN Comprehensive Investment Agreement (2009), Art. 43. In contrast, the Agreement on Promotion and Protection of Investments among the member states of the ECO (2005) does not have a treaty body for its implementation.

[57] K. Gordon and J. Pohl, *Investment Treaties over Time - Treaty Practice and Interpretation in a Changing World* (2015), p. 31.

[58] Canada–Hungary BIT (1991), Art. 1(4).

[59] E.g. Cambodia–Japan BIT (2008), Art. 8.2; Japan–Laos BIT (2008), Art. 9.2; Japan–Uzbekistan BIT (2008), Art. 7.2.

[60] E.g. Japan–Vietnam BIT (2003), Art. 18.3; Cambodia–Japan BIT (2008), Art. 21.3; Japan–Laos BIT (2008), Art. 21.3.

[61] E.g. Senegal–US BIT (1983), Art. I.b); Haiti–US BIT (1985), Art. I.b); Bangladesh–US BIT (1986), Art. I.b).

[62] E.g. Japan–Kenya BIT (2016), Art. 23.2; Japan–Mozambique BIT (2013), Art. 25.2; Japan–Laos BIT (2008), Art. 26.2.

[63] New Zealand–South Korea FTA (2015), Art. 10.14; Mauritius–Saudi Arabia BIT (2015), Art. 15.2; Singapore–Turkey FTA (2015), Art. 12.22.2; Mexico–UAE BIT (2016), Art. 30;

contracting party triggers the 'denial of benefits' clause, and thus whenever that contracting party concludes that the benefits of the treaty should not be extended to a company of the other party, if nationals of any third country control such company, 'it shall promptly consult with the other Party to seek a mutually satisfactory resolution of the matter'.[64] Some Japanese BITs also require that the host state engages in prior joint consultation with the home state before triggering temporary safeguard measures,[65] or reviewing the treatment of subsidies related to investments or investors.[66]

(b)   Institutional Review of the Agreement

From the group of IIAs concluded in the last fifteen years, 109 (19 per cent) include a more elaborated mechanism for the review of the implementation of the agreement, via a treaty body created in the same IIA, either specially for investment purposes or for the general administration of the treaty.

The idea of creating a treaty body to review the implementation of an investment agreement is not a new one. The Netherlands–Singapore BIT has already established a 'joint committee' composed of representatives of the contracting parties, which would meet at the request of either party for the purpose of discussing any matter pertaining to the implementation of the agreement.[67] However, this feature is rarely found in later BITs – only in some concluded by Japan,[68] the Netherlands,[69] Korea[70] and China,[71] among other countries.[72]

A more complex consultation mechanism between the contracting parties was created in the NAFTA. Articles 2001 and 2002 established a free trade commission (FTC), comprising ministerial-level

---

Jordan–Saudi Arabia BIT (2017), Art. 22(2). A similar but less binding provision (only 'to the extent practicable') is also found in the South Korea–Turkey Investment Agreement (2015), Art. 1.15.2; and South Korea–Vietnam FTA (2015), Art. 9.11.2.

[64] Gordon and Pohl, *Investment Treaties over Time*, pp. 31–2.

[65] Nigeria–Singapore BIT (2015), Art. 5.4; and Morocco–Nigeria BIT (2016), Art. 12.4

[66] SAFTA (amended 2016), Ch. 8, Art. 17.

[67] Netherlands–Singapore BIT (1972), Art. XIII.

[68] China–Japan BIT (1988), Art. 14; Japan–Mongolia BIT (2001), Art. 16; Japan–Korea BIT (2002), Art. 20; Japan–Vietnam BIT (2003).

[69] Netherlands–Singapore BIT (1972), Art. XIII; Netherlands–Sri Lanka BIT (1984), Art. 11; Netherlands–Pakistan BIT (1988), Art. 12.

[70] China–Korea BIT (1992), Art. 14; Japan–Korea BIT (2002), Art. 20; Korea–UAE BIT (2002), Arts. 7–8.

[71] China–Japan BIT (1988), Art. 14; China–Korea BIT (1992), Art. 14.

[72] See also: Greece–Israel BIT (1993), Art. 5; Jordan–Syria BIT (2001), Art. 8; and Morocco–Nigeria BIT (2016), Art. 4.

representatives from the three member countries and endowed with its own Secretariat.[73] The FTC has the task of supervising the implementation and further elaboration of the agreement, and resolving disputes arising from its interpretation. It also oversees the work of the NAFTA committees, working groups and other subsidiary bodies.[74]

Following NAFTA's experience, its member states included this feature in the negotiation of later agreements with other countries and between themselves – notably in the TPP.[75] After NAFTA, the FTAs concluded by the United States with Singapore and Chile in 2003 included a similar commission.[76] In the last fifteen years, the United States has continued the inclusion of a FTC in its FTAs with Australia, the Dominican Republic and Central America (CAFTA–DR), Morocco, Oman, Colombia, Panama, Peru and Korea.[77] The United States also included this commission in its BITs with Kyrgyzstan, Moldova, Ecuador, Jamaica, Ukraine, Estonia, Trinidad and Tobago, Latvia, Honduras, Croatia, Bolivia, Mozambique and El Salvador.[78]

Subsequently to NAFTA, Canada established a similar commission in its FTAs concluded with Chile and Costa Rica.[79] In the last fifteen years, Canada has also continued to include this feature in its FTAs with Colombia, Peru, Panama, Honduras and South Korea,[80] as well as in its BITs with Jordan and Benin.[81] Closely following NAFTA, Mexico replicated the creation of a FTC for the review of the agreement, in its FTAs signed with Colombia and Venezuela,[82] Bolivia,[83] Nicaragua,[84] Chile[85]

---

[73] Salacuse, *The Law of Investment Treaties*, p. 361.

[74] NAFTA, Art. 2001.

[75] TPP, Art. 27.1.

[76] Singapore–US FTA (2003), Art. 20.1, Chile–US FTA (2003), Art. 21.1.

[77] E.g.: Australia–US FTA (2004), Art. 21.1; CAFTA–DR (2004), Art. 19.1; US–Morocco (2004), Art. 19.2.

[78] E.g. Bolivia–US BIT (1998), Art. V; Croatia–US BIT (1996), Art. IX; Kyrgyzstan–US BIT (1993).

[79] Canadian–Chile FTA (1996), Arts. N-01, N-02; Canada–Costa Rica FTA (2001), Arts. XIII.1–3.

[80] E.g. Canada–Colombia FTA (2008), Arts. 2001, 2002; Canada–Peru FTA (2008), Arts. 2001, 2002; Canada–Panama FTA (2010), Arts. 21.01, 21.02.

[81] Canada–Jordan BIT (2009), Art. 51; Canada–Benin BIT (2013), Arts. 47–49.

[82] Colombia–Mexico–Venezuela FTA (1995), Arts. 20-01, 20-02. Venezuela withdrew from this FTA in 2006.

[83] Bolivia–Mexico FTA (1995), Arts. 18-01 and 18-02. Bolivia denounced this treaty in 2009, and it was replaced by another FTA without an investment chapter: OAS, 'Trade Policy Developments: Bolivia – Mexico' (June 2010).

[84] Mexico–Nicaragua FTA (1997), Arts. 19-01, 19-02.

[85] Chile–Mexico FTA (1998), Arts. 17-01, 17-02.

and Uruguay.[86] In the last fifteen years, Mexico has also included this treaty body in its FTAs with Japan, Peru, Central America[87] and Panama, and in the Pacific Alliance Protocol.[88]

However, the influence of NAFTA in this regard goes beyond its contracting parties. From 2004 onwards, at least 75 FTAs have included an investment chapter or an investment side agreement, providing for the establishment of a treaty body comprising officials of each party at a ministerial level – an FTC or a JC – to review the implementation of the agreement, among other duties. Furthermore, some FTAs also include additional agreement coordinators.[89]

Interestingly, an increasing number of BITs include this type of commission or committee. From only ten BITs that had such bodies before 2004, in the last ten years we find at least thirty-four BITs[90] – notably those concluded by Japan[91] and Brazil[92] – and six RITs[93] establishing a treaty body for the general review of the agreement. In some cases, the agreement makes a referral to a body previously created by an existing treaty.[94] In one particular case, in 2004 an FTA and a BIT were concluded in parallel between Jordan and Singapore, providing for the same feature.[95]

The functioning of such treaty bodies is very similar in all these treaties. Typically, the commissions or committees convene

---

[86] Mexico–Uruguay FTA (2003), Arts. 17-01, 17-02.

[87] Central America includes Costa Rica, El Salvador, Guatemala, Honduras and Nicaragua.

[88] E.g. Japan–Mexico EPA (2004), Art. 165; Mexico–Peru FTA (2011), Arts. 17.1–17.4; PAAP (2014), Arts. 16.1, 16.2. Pacific Alliance Additional Protocol, signed 10 February 2014, between Chile, Colombia, Costa Rica and Peru.

[89] E.g. Argentina–Chile FTA (2017), Art. 17.2; Brazil–Peru ETEA (2016), Art. 2.15; Singapore–Turkey FTA (2015), Art. 8.1. The PACER Plus Agreement (2017), Arts. 22 and 23, provides that the review of commitments is also undertaken through points of contacts provided by the parties.

[90] E.g. Chile–Hong Kong Investment Agreement (2016), Art. 34; Morocco–Nigeria BIT (2016). Art. 4; Japan–Iran BIT (2016), Art. 20.

[91] E.g. Japan–Uruguay BIT (2015), Art. 26; Japan–Ukraine BIT (2015), Art. 24; Japan–Myanmar BIT (2013), Art. 24.

[92] See the eight Brazilian CFIAs referred to in the preceding section.

[93] E.g. China–Japan–Korea Trilateral Investment Agreement (2012), Art. 24; ASEAN–China Investment Agreement (2009), Art. 22; ASEAN Korea Investment Agreement (2009), Arts. 24, 26 and 27.

[94] E.g.: Japan–Saudi Arabia BIT (2013), Art. 19, establishes an Investment Working Group within the framework of the joint committee established by Article 6 of the Agreement on Economic and Technical Cooperation between Japan and Saudi Arabia (1975).

[95] Jordan–Singapore BIT (2004), Art. 23, Jordan–Singapore FTA (2004), Art. 8.1.2(e).

regularly, at least once a year[96] or upon the request of a contracting party,[97] and usually in person – although some treaties provide that such meetings can take place using videoconferencing or by any other technological means.[98] Generally, a commission can adopt its own rules of procedure,[99] although some explicitly provide rules of procedure,[100] or for decisions to be taken by consensus or mutual agreement.[101] Besides supervising the implementation of the agreement, other tasks include issuing interpretations of the provisions of the treaty, considering, deciding or proposing amendments and establishing committees or working groups, or supervising its work.[102]

However, a few FTAs include a treaty body exclusively devoted to investment issues, although this is a tendency present in FTAs recently negotiated by the EU[103] and China.[104] When established, a committee or sub-committee on investment has the functions of exchanging information on investment matters, reviewing and monitoring the implementation and operation of the agreement,[105] in coordination and reporting to the JC. Characteristically, these committees are composed of

---

[96] Israel–Myanmar BIT (2014), Art. 15; Benin–Canada BIT (2013), Art. 49; Japan–Switzerland ECA (2009), Art. 148; Colombia–EFTA FTA (2008), Art. 11.1.4 provide for meetings every two years.

[97] E.g. Japan–Mozambique BIT (2013), Art. 23.6; Japan–Saudi Arabia BIT (2013), Art. 19. In the Colombia–Japan BIT (2010), Art. 20, the Committee shall meet within 12 months after the entry into force of the agreement and then as agreed by the parties. Similarly, in the Peru–Singapore FTA (2008), Art. 16.1.5, the Commission shall convene within two years of the entry into force of the agreement, and subsequently as and when the parties agree it to be necessary.

[98] Burkina Faso–Canada BIT (2015), Art. 40; Mexico–Peru FTA (2011), Art. 17.1.3; Colombia–EFTA FTA (2008), Art. 11.1.5.

[99] E.g. Australia–Korea FTA (2014), Art. 21.3(d); Canada–Korea FTA (2014), Art. 20.1.3 (f); Japan–Myanmar BIT (2013), Art. 24.4.

[100] China–New Zealand FTA (2008), Art. 181.

[101] E.g.: Canada–Korea FTA (2014), Art. 20.1.6; Mexico–Panama FTA (2014), Art. 17.1.5; Japan–Myanmar BIT (2013), Art. 24.2.

[102] E.g. Canada–Korea FTA (2014), Art. 20.1.5; Japan–Myanmar BIT (2013), Art. 24.5; Japan–Mozambique BIT (2013), Art. 23.5.

[103] A Committee on Services and Investment is established in CETA Art. 8.44; a Committee on Trade in Services, Investment and Government Procurement under EU–Vietnam FTA, Art. 34.1; and a Committee on Investments in EU-Singapore IPA (April 2018), Art. 4.1.

[104] A Committee on Investment is established in China–Korea FTA (2015), Art. 12.17; Australia–China (2015) Art. 9.7; Chile-Hong Kong Investment Agreement (2016), Art. 35; China–Hong Kong CEPA Investment Agreement (2017), Art. 17.

[105] India–Malaysia ECA (2011), Art. 15.2; New Zealand–Malaysia FTA (2009), Art. 10.18.

representatives of the parties, and in some cases may invite other relevant entities or experts in the issues to be discussed.[106] Meetings are usually scheduled at times and venues agreed by the parties,[107] although sometimes at least a yearly meeting is provided for.[108]

3 Prevention of Investment Disputes Based on Principles of International Law

As we have seen in the preceding section, a legal basis for the participation of the home state in the prevention of investment disputes is found in a limited number of IIAs with explicit provisions on dispute prevention or via mechanisms of review of its implementation. However, a more active involvement of the home state in this preventive role can be drawn from some existing and emerging principles of international law.

Leading international organizations, such as the UN, the OECD and the International Labour Organization (ILO), as well as some scholars, have already articulated principles that provide a clear basis for home states' involvement in dispute prevention activities.

(a) International Principles and Standards on Corporate Social Responsibility

Corporate social responsibility (CSR) is a management concept that promotes certain types of conduct and principles in business operations on core issues such as environment, human rights, labour rights, and anti-corruption, as well as on other issues such as fair operating practices, consumer rights, community involvement, society development and organizational governance. CSR instruments provide corporations with tools and mechanisms for incorporating those principles within their business activities, at global, regional and sector-specific levels, taking different forms, such as reporting initiatives, comprehensive guidelines, governance and management standards.[109]

---

[106] Canada–Korea FTA (2014), Art. 20.3(b); PAAP (2014), Art. 10.33.5; Japan–Myanmar BIT (2013), Art. 24.3; Japan–Mozambique BIT (2013), Art. 23.3; Brunei–Japan EPA (2007), Art. 72.4.

[107] Australia–Japan Economic Partnership (2014), Art. 14.18.

[108] ASEAN–Australia–New Zealand FTA (2009), Art. 17.2. Burkina Faso–Canada BIT (2015), Art. 40.3, provides for a meeting at least every five years.

[109] United Nations Environment Programme (UNEP), 'Corporate Social Responsibility and Regional Trade and Investment Agreements' (2011), 15–17.

CSR is a dynamic and constantly evolving concept, with ongoing conflicts about its content and significance. Different groups have different understandings of the meaning, definition and scope of CSR, with some favouring its voluntary nature, and others the impact that enterprises have in the society.[110]

While firms could be motivated to adopt CRS instruments for several reasons – because of their own mission and vision, to improve their reputation, or to gain an advantage over competitors – home states could also be interested in promoting these principles abroad, as often the image of corporations abroad also affects the image of their country of origin.[111]

Home states could have an interest in advancing CSR as a way of promoting 'responsible investment' – a type of investment that may reduce the possibility of conflicts between its national investor and the host state, because of its approach that explicitly acknowledges the relevance to the investor of environmental, social and governance issues, recognizing that 'the generation of long-term sustainable returns is dependent on stable, well-functioning and well governed social, environmental and economic systems'.[112]

Although CSR is mostly understood as voluntary self-regulation by corporations – consider, for example, the ISO 2600 on Social Responsibility[113] – nowadays it is also recognized in several domestic systems, such as the UK's 2003 Corporate Responsibility Bill, and France's 2001 Nouvelles Regulations Economiques.[114] However, depending on the host country in which the investment takes place, an obligation to comply with a corporate code of conduct or a national law may not be enough to ensure that acceptable standards are upheld.[115] For that

---

[110] D. Kinderman, 'Global and EU-Level Corporate Social Responsibility: Dynamism, Growth, and Conflict' in H. Backhaus-Maul, M. Kunze and S. Nährlich (eds.), *Gesellschaftliche Verantwortung von Unternehmen in Deutschland* (Springer Fachmedien Wiesbaden, 2018), pp. 101–13 at p. 111.

[111] C. Lopez, Manto Gotsi and C. Andriopoulos, 'Conceptualising the Influence of Corporate Image on Country Image', *European Journal of Marketing*, 45 (2011), 1601–41 at 1601.

[112] United Nations, 'Introducing Responsible Investment' (January 2015).

[113] International Organization for Standardization, 'ISO 26000 – Social Responsibility' (2010).

[114] I. Bantekas, 'Corporate Social Responsibility in International Law', B.U. Int'l L.J., 22 (2004), 309 at 325–27.

[115] L. Cotula, *Foreign Investment, Law and Sustainable Development: A Handbook on Agriculture and Extractive Industries* (2016), p. 31.

reason, the development of CSR international principles and standards is particularly important to ensure its implementation.

A large number of articles and books have been written about CSR international principles and standards. Here, we will focus only on those principles and standards that involve the home state and that can serve as a basis for the prevention of investment disputes. Therefore an important CSR initiative, such as the 1999 United Nations Global Compact (UNGC), will not be analysed, as it focuses on companies that voluntarily align their operations with ten universal principles in the area of human rights, labour standards, the environment and anti-corruption.[116]

The first attempt at developing international CSR frameworks arose in the 1970s, with the adoption of the OECD Guidelines for multinational enterprises (MNEs),[117] which provide voluntary principles and standards for responsible business conduct in areas such as human rights, employment, environment, combating bribery, consumer interests and taxation. Adhering governments cooperate with each other to strengthen the international legal and policy framework in which business is conducted, with the common aim of encouraging the positive contributions that MNEs can make to economic, environmental and social progress and minimizing the difficulties to which their various operations may give rise,[118] thereby decreasing the chances of having an investment dispute.

Another important international instrument is the OECD Anti-Bribery Convention. On this sensitive issue both home and host states should collaborate in assisting enterprises confronted with solicitation of bribes and with extortion, as is recognized by the Convention.[119] However, it is important to recall that anti-corruption treaties create obligations for states and do not directly create obligations for companies to take measures to combat corruption. Therefore, actual enforcement

---

[116] Kinderman, 'Global and EU-Level Corporate Social Responsibility', 104–5.
[117] The Guidelines were first adopted in 1976, as part of the OECD Declaration on International Investment and Multinational Enterprises, and have been reviewed five times since then, with the most recent update having taken place in 2011. Today, the adhering governments are all thirty-five OECD countries and thirteen non-OECD countries – namely Argentina, Brazil, Colombia, Costa Rica, Egypt, Jordan, Kazakhstan, Latvia, Lithuania, Morocco, Peru, Romania and Tunisia: OECD, 'Guidelines for MNEs' (2018).
[118] OECD, OECD Guidelines for Multinational Enterprises, 2011 edn (OECD Publishing, 2011), pp. 14–15.
[119] OECD, Convention on Combating Bribery of Foreign Public Officials in International Business Transactions (OECD Publishing, 2011), Art. 8.

largely depends on domestic law that could include the treaty's extraterritorial application, empowering authorities to investigate and prosecute corruption that occurred overseas (e.g. the UK's Bribery Act of 2010, or the US Foreign Corrupt Practices Act (FCPA) of 1977).[120] If either inter-state collaboration or home state extraterritorial jurisdiction is effective, it could operate to deter investment disputes.[121]

But probably the most relevant CSR international principles and standards for fostering the role of home states in the prevention of investment disputes are the 'Ruggie Principles', which, for that reason, will be examined separately in the next section.

(b)   Principles on Business and Human Rights

In 2011, the UN Human Rights Council endorsed the Guiding Principles on Business and Human Rights: Implementing the United Nations 'Protect, Respect and Remedy' elaborated by John Ruggie, Special Representative of the Secretary-General, on human rights and transnational corporations and other business enterprises.[122] As states are not generally required, under international law, to regulate extraterritorial activities of businesses domiciled in their jurisdiction, several 'Ruggie principles' deal with actions that can be undertaken by home states in this regard. The assumption here is that the effective implementation of these principles would tend to prevent investment disputes, as the respect of human rights by foreign investors should reduce the chances of conflict with the host state.

Principle 2 declares that 'States should set out clearly the expectation that all business enterprises domiciled in their territory and/or jurisdiction respect human rights throughout their operations'. The commentary to this principle delves into the underlying reasons that home states could have for implementing such a policy, including ensuring predictability for business enterprises and preserving the state's own reputation.[123]

---

[120] Cotula, *Foreign Investment, Law and Sustainable Development*, p. 120.
[121] Claims of bribery in ISDS cases are not unusual. See, among others: *Metal-Tech Ltd v. Republic of Uzbekistan*, ICSID Case No ARB/10/3; *Inceysa Vallisoletana S.L. v. Republic of El Salvador*, ICSID Case No ARB/03/26; *Plama Consortium Ltd v. Republic of Bulgaria*, ICSID Case No ARB/03/24; and *Siemens AG v. Argentine Republic*, ICSID Case No ARB/02/8.
[122] J. Ruggie, 'Report of the Special Representative of the Secretary-General on the issue of human rights and transnational corporations and other business enterprises', *Neth. Q. Hum. Rts*, 29 (2011), 224.
[123] United Nations Human Rights Council, *Guiding Principles on Business and Human Rights: Implementing the United Nations 'Protect, Respect and Remedy' Framework, endorsed by the United Nations Human Rights Council on 16 June 2011* (2011), pp. 3–4.

Principle 4 proclaims that states should take additional steps to protect against human rights abuses by business enterprises that are controlled or owned by the state (state-owned enterprises). One mechanism envisaged for this purpose is to require human rights due diligence for the concession and renewal of outward investment incentives (such as export credit agencies, political risk insurance, or guarantee agencies) that provide substantial support of those businesses. The SADC Model BIT offers an example on how to implement this principle, as home states may provide investment financing and investment guarantee facilities for their investors from the territory of the other state party if they promote compliance with the obligations of investors set forth in the agreement, which include the duty to respect human rights in the state in which they are located.[124] This provision would allow home states to require their investors to comply with human rights obligations as a condition of state financing or insuring of the investment.[125]

The Ruggie Principles declare that home states have an even higher responsibility for regulating their outward investment in conflict-affected areas, having to act before situations on the ground deteriorate, as the host state may be unable or unwilling to protect human rights adequately due to a lack of effective control or government failures.[126] This is particularly important governance for extractive industries in zones of weak governance, in which an important governance gap persists with respect to the human-rights impact conduct of foreign extractive corporations.[127]

According to Principle 7, home states should help to ensure that business enterprises operating in those countries – which comprise investors – are not involved with human rights abuses, through different measures that could include:

1. ensuring the effectiveness of home state policies, legislation, regulations and enforcement measures to address the risk of business involvement in gross human rights abuses;
2. engaging at the earliest stage possible to help identify, prevent and mitigate the human rights-related risks of business enterprises activities and relationships;

---

[124] SADC Model BIT, Arts. 15.1 and 23.3.
[125] Southern African Development Community (SADC), *SADC Model Bilateral Investment Treaty Template with Commentary*, p. 44.
[126] United Nations Human Rights Council, *Guiding Principles on Business and Human Rights*, p. 9.
[127] P. Simons and A. Macklin, *The Governance Gap: Extractive Industries, Human Rights, and the Home State Advantage* (Routledge, 2015), pp. 16–17.

3. providing adequate assistance in assessing and addressing the heightened risk of abuse, especially on sexual violence and gender-based and sexual violence; and

4. denying access to home state' support and services to business enterprises that are involved with gross human rights abuses and refuses to cooperate in addressing them.

In order to achieve greater coherence in the implementation of the abovementioned policies, the commentary of Principle 7 recommends that home states should develop 'early-warning indicators' to alert government actors and investors to such problems; assign consequences to enterprises that fail to cooperate, including the denial, withdrawal, of existing or future public support or services; and overall to foster closer cooperation among national and foreign entities, including development assistance agencies, ministries of trade and foreign affairs, embassies and export finance institutions.[128]

Under Principle 26, the involvement of the home state is also foreseen in order to ensure the effectiveness of domestic judicial mechanisms when addressing business-related human rights abuses. This could include granting jurisdiction to home state courts where human rights claimants face legal, practical and other relevant barriers that could lead to a denial of justice in home state courts, regardless of the merits of the claim.[129] However, Principle 26 makes no explicit recommendation that home states remove jurisdictional and other barriers for victims of extraterritorial human rights abuses by national business actors or domiciled within their jurisdiction[130] – a feature that is included in both the IISD and SADC model IIAs.

(c) ILO and UNCTAD Frameworks

The ILO and UNCTAD have also advanced principles that provide a basis for the further participation of the home state in the prevention of investment disputes.

The ILO approved the 'Tripartite Declaration of Principles concerning Multinational Enterprises and Social Policy' (MNE Declaration) at its 204th Session in November 1977, and they have been amended since

---

[128] United Nations Human Rights Council, *Guiding Principles on Business and Human Rights*, p. 9.

[129] Ibid., p. 29.

[130] Simons and Macklin, *The governance gap*, p. 96.

then, with the latest version being approved in March 2017.[131] The MNE Declaration sets out roles and responsibilities for both home and host states, multinational enterprises, and workers' and employers' organizations to solve decent work challenges and identify opportunities for inclusive growth. Its principles cover areas of employment, training, conditions of work and life and industrial relations.[132]

According to the MNE Declaration, governments of home states should promote good social practice among their multinational enterprises operating abroad, 'having regard to the social and labour law, regulations and practices in host countries as well as to relevant international standards'. Governments of both host and home states should be prepared to have consultations with each other, whenever the need arises, on the initiative of either.[133]

From the point of view of the prevention of investment disputes, again here the assumption is that if the home state proactively consults with its investors abroad and with the host states in order to implement the MNE Declaration, the less likely it is that investment disputes will arise.

In 2012, UNCTAD launched an Investment Policy Framework for Sustainable Development (IPFSD),[134] which was updated in 2015.[135] This framework includes core 'Principles for Investment Policymaking', which aim to guide the development of national and international investment policies.

Principle 10, on 'International Cooperation', advocates home states' support of outward investment that is conducive to sustainable development, conditioning the grant of loans and investment guarantees against political risks, on an assessment of social and environmental impacts of the investment. If home states can help host states to avoid a 'race to the bottom' on sustainable development provisions for attracting foreign investment, and fostering sustainable investment on the side of their investors, the chances of their having investment disputes with the host state should be lower.

---

[131] International Labour Organization (ILO), 'Tripartite Declaration of Principles concerning Multinational Enterprises and Social Policy (MNE Declaration, 5th ed.)' (2017).

[132] International Labour Organization (ILO), 'Translating the 2030 Agenda for Sustainable Development into Action: Integrating Trade, Investment and Decent Work Policies. Background Note' (Nairobi, Kenya, 2016), p. 5.

[133] International Labour Organization (ILO), 'Tripartite Declaration of Principles concerning Multinational Enterprises and Social Policy (MNE Declaration, 5th ed.)', para. 12.

[134] UNCTAD, *Investment Policy Framework for Sustainable Development* (2012).

[135] Ibid.

With the aim of translating these core principles into concrete options for policymakers, UNCTAD has developed a companion framework for IIAs with policy options to operationalize sustainable development objectives in IIAs. In this detailed design of treaty provisions, UNCTAD suggests several choices to policymakers for incorporating sustainable development considerations in the text of the IIAs and promoting responsible investment, and some of them explicitly refer to home states and have the clear potential to prevent investment disputes.

A first option is to consider that home states can monitor or regulate the foreign activities of their companies in issues related to human rights, the environment or corruption. A second option is that home states encourage investors to comply with CSR principles and standards, such as the UNGC or the OECD Guidelines for MNEs, through a 'best endeavour' clause. A third option goes further, conditioning the provision of investment guarantees and other outward investment incentives to the investment and investors' compliance with CSR principles and standards. A fourth option can involve the work of a special committee set up under the IIA and tasked to discuss CSR-related issues.[136]

(d)   Emerging Principles of International Law

With respect to emerging principles of international law, certain scholars have advanced the idea that states have a 'common' or 'shared' responsibility to protect public interests.

Based on the principles of responsibility to protect (R2P)[137] and common concern of mankind, Nadakavukaren Schefer and Cottier have advocated a 'principle of common concern', as a basis for cooperation and joint responsibilities in the production of global public goods that could be used to justify the intervention of home states in the prevention of investment disputes. In this context, any problem that concerns the entire international community and that cannot be solved by an affected state should be considered one in which all states have responsibility for protecting, assisting or responding.[138] Examples of such collective action problems are found in global commons problems

---

[136] Ibid., pp. 109, 110 and 112.

[137] N. T. Hooge, *Responsibility to Protect (R2P) as Duty to Protect?: Reassessing the Traditional Doctrine of Diplomatic Protection in Light of Modern Developments in International Law* (University of Toronto, 2010).

[138] K. Nadakavukaren Schefer and T. Cottier, 'Responsibility to Protect (R2P) and the Emerging Principle of Common Concern' (2012) *NCCR Working Paper No 2012/29* at 18–19.

such as climate change,[139] public corruption, massive financial instability, extremely high levels of unemployment, and general concerns that cannot be resolved by one state alone. Moreover, common concern could also develop into a foundation for state responsibility if corresponding obligations are not met.[140]

Schill has advanced the idea of 'shared responsibility', suggesting that all actors – home and host states, but also tribunals, international organizations and the international community – bear joint responsibility for achieving common goals or public policies, through the protection of public interests, such as 'the environment, human rights, labour standards, public health and morals, or international peace and security'.[141] In this framework, different actors have different forms of action. Home states can work together with host states to recalibrate IIAs, clarifying that investment treaties 'cannot unduly restrict governments' policy space to protect public interests' or 'can agree on joint interpretations of existing investment treaties to that effect, in particular where investment tribunals do not sufficiently take account of public interests in their decision-making practice'.[142] This principle could also be used to justify unilateral actions of the home state directed at preventing disputes involving its investors and another state.

4   Implementing Rules and Principles for the Prevention of Investment Disputes

Currently, most IIAs promote foreign investment only through the granting of investment protection and do not contain commitments by home states to promote responsible investment from the perspective of their nationals who benefit from that agreement.[143] Sauvant has pointed out that IIAs' purpose could be expanded to include promoting sustainable development and FDI flows that support this objective. IIAs should

---

[139] T. Cottier, P. Aerni, B. Karapinar, S. Matteotti, J. de Sépibus and A. Shingal, 'The Principle of Common Concern and Climate Change', *Archiv des Völkerrechts*, 52 (2014), 293–324.

[140] Nadakavukaren Schefer and Cottier, 'Responsibility to Protect (R2P) and the Emerging Principle of Common Concern', 18–19.

[141] S. W. Schill, '"Shared Responsibility" Stopping the Irresponsibility Carousel for the Protection of Public Interests in International Law' in A. Reinisch, M. E. Footer and C. Binder (eds.), *International Law and ... Select Proceedings of the European Society of International Law* (Hart Publishing, 2016), pp. 160–9 at p. 12.

[142] Ibid., p. 14.

[143] UNCTAD, *Investment Policy Framework for Sustainable Development*, p. 39.

be adapted while recognizing that host and home states preserve certain policy space and that investors commit themselves to responsible business conduct.[144]

Using CSR instruments, home states could foster outward foreign investment with proper respect towards human rights, environmental and labour standards to prevent a 'race to the bottom' based on competition for foreign investment, and may collaborate in the development of preventive and management policies of investment conflicts (DPPs and CMMs) at the host state.[145] It is expected that firms build and maintain systems that prevent abuses, disputes or adverse impacts on CSR core issues from occurring.[146] Foreign corporations could step in to substitute for missing or inadequate government regulation, or a governance gap in the host state.[147]

The range of policies that home states could enact to foster the abovementioned rules of principles, found in either IIAs, international or even domestic law – and thus the prevention of investment disputes – is quite broad.

First, the inclusion of CSR language in IIAs has the potential to reinforce its benefits, particularly in the areas of coherence, legitimacy and implementation,[148] but also in dispute prevention. UNCTAD has suggested that IIAs need to incorporate provisions where the home state places conditions on the granting of outward investment promotion incentives or guarantees, on an investor's socially and environmentally sustainable behaviour or compliance with CSR standards.[149] Some IIAs concluded in the past fifteen years include provisions on CSR, although these references are still relatively limited. From this group, IIAs concluded

---

[144] K. P. Sauvant, *The Evolving International Investment Law and Policy Regime: Ways Forward. E15 Task Force on Investment Policy – Policy Options Paper. E15 Initiative* (International Centre for Trade and Sustainable Development (ICTSD) and World Economic Forum, 2016) p. 21.

[145] Echandi, 'Complementing Investor–State Dispute Resolution', 295–6.

[146] See D. Kovick and C. Rees, 'International Support for Effective Dispute Resolution Between Companies and Their Stakeholders: Assessing Needs, Interests, and Models. Working Paper No 63' (June 2011); and R. B. Paton, 'Corporate Social Responsibility: From Conflict Resolution to Conflict Anticipation', *Reflections*, 7 (2012)

[147] J. S. Knudsen, *Bringing the State Back In? US and UK Government Regulation of Corporate Social Responsibility (CSR) in International Business* (2014) p. 10.

[148] R. Peels, E. Echeverria, J. Aissi and A. Schneider, 'Corporate Social Responsibility in International Trade and Investment Agreements', ILO Research Paper, International Labour Office, 13(2016), at 18.

[149] UNCTAD, *Investment Policy Framework for Sustainable Development*, pp. 36–7.

mainly by Canada,[150] Brazil[151] and Colombia,[152] also include commitments of the contracting parties to encourage enterprises operating within its territory or jurisdiction voluntarily to incorporate internationally recognized CSR standards. These obligations are only 'best efforts' and therefore it would be difficult to initiate a claim again the home state if in practice its national companies do not abide by CSR principles.[153]

Secondly, home countries could condition the granting of outward investment incentives on an assessment of human rights, labour and environmental impacts. Some countries have started to do just that. For example, the Dutch government has made adherence to the OECD Guidelines for MNEs mandatory for every company receiving official development aid funding.[154] In the United States, the Overseas Private Investment Corporation (OPIC) conditions the granting of investment guarantees on an assessment of social and environmental impacts,[155] and, for example, requires that a project meets the workers' rights standards of the ILO.[156] Similarly the Japan Bank for International Cooperation (JBIC) conducts a review of environmental and social conditions when deciding on funding and conducts monitoring and follow-up after the decision has been made.[157]

Thirdly, home states could be the point of contact for the management of investment conflicts – before they escalate to disputes. According to the OECD Guidelines for MNEs, when issues arise with respect to these enterprises, they will generally be dealt with first at a national level by the

---

[150] E.g.: Canada–Côte d'Ivoire BIT (2014), Art. 15; Canada–Mali BIT (2014), Art. 15; Canada–Senegal BIT (2014), Art. 16.

[151] Brazil-Ethiopia CFIA (2018), Art. 14; Brazil-Suriname CFIA (2018), Art. 15. Intra-MERCOSUR Investment Facilitation Protocol (2017), Art. 14; Brazil–Peru ETEA (2016), Art. 2.13; Brazil–Angola CFIA (2015), Art. 10 and Annex II; Brazil–Mozambique CFIA (2015), Art. 10 and Annex II; Brazil–Malawi CFIA (2015), Art. 9; Brazil–Mexico CFIA (2015), Art. 13; Brazil–Colombia CFIA (2015), Art. 13; Brazil–Chile CFIA (2015), Art. 15.

[152] Colombia–France BIT (2014), Art. 11; PAAP (2014), Art. 10.30.2; Colombia–Panama FTA (2013), Art. 14.15; Colombia–Costa Rica FTA (2013), Art. 12.9.

[153] These provisions are also found in the TPP, Art. 9.17. Similarly, the Singapore–US FTA (2008), Art. 18.9, refers to 'principles of corporate stewardship' and the SADC Investment Protocol (2006), Art. 10, refers to 'corporate responsibility', but in the sense that foreign investors shall abide by the laws, regulations, administrative guidelines and policies of the host state.

[154] OECD and WTO, *Aid for Trade at a Glance 2015* (OECD Publishing, 2015), p. 232.

[155] OPIC, 'Environmental and Social Policy Statement' (January 2017).

[156] OPIC, 'Finance Eligibility Checklist' (2017).

[157] Japan Bank for International Cooperation (JBIC), 'Japan Bank for International Cooperation Annual Report 2016'.

national contact point (NCP) of the country in which the issues have arisen, and, where appropriate, pursued at the bilateral level. The NCP of the host state should consult with the NCP of the home state in its efforts to assist the parties in resolving the issues. If an enterprise's activity or organization takes place in several adhering countries, the NCPs involved should consult with a view to agreeing on which NCP will take the lead in assisting the parties.[158] The same guidelines provide that in the event that issues arise in a non-adhering country, the NCP of the home state will take steps to develop an understanding of the issues involved, including contacting the management of the enterprise in the home state, and embassies and government officials in the non-adhering country.[159]

Fourthly, home states could play a role in providing important information that may deter enterprises' conduct against the abovementioned principles of international law. The home state could be particularly useful with respect to accounting offences, as they will generally occur in the company's home state (when the bribery offence itself may have been committed in another country). Host states could be provided access to home state judiciaries in cases of bribery.[160]

Fifthly, home states could also assist in the implementation of domestic DPPs or CMMs in the host state through capacity building to governmental agencies, on the content and potential impact of IIAs. In this context, the use of review and consultation tools in IIAs could help to manage investment-related conflicts before they escalate into full disputes. In the same vein, state-to-state mechanisms of interpretation of IIAs – which will be analysed in detail in the next chapter – could work as DPPs in practice, considering that clearer obligations of a home state in theory would diminish future potential investment conflicts.

Finally, it is important to note that the duty to respect core CSR principles, such as human rights, should not be borne solely by the states. As the arbitral tribunal in *Urbaser* v. *Argentina* has declared, 'international law accepts corporate social responsibility as a standard of crucial importance for companies operating in the field of international commerce. This standard includes commitments to comply with human

---

[158] OECD, 'Implementation Procedures of the OECD Guidelines for Multinational Enterprises', *OECD Guidelines for Multinational Enterprises*, 2011 edn (OECD Publishing, 2011), pp. 65–89 at p. 82.
[159] Ibid., p. 86.
[160] Sauvant, *The Evolving International Investment Law*, p. 28.

rights in the framework of those entities' operations conducted in countries other than the country of their seat or incorporation'.[161]

We should also consider that having a larger involvement for the investor's home state would not necessarily make prevention of disputes more efficient or less expensive, and they could also risk making it a longer, more expensive or more difficult process, if the home state intervention is excessive and not adapted to the needs of both its national investors and the home state. All these tools of dispute prevention should be handled with care, as they could lead to the perception of constituting an informal way to exercise diplomatic protection in disguise, or as undue intervention or meddling in the sovereign affairs of another state, and even problems of conflict of interest could be foreseen.

5   The Nature of Home State Prevention of Investment Conflicts

What is the nature of the participation of the home state in the prevention of investment disputes, whether based on explicit or implicit IIA provisions on dispute prevention or principles of international law? Is this diplomatic protection or something else?

The answer to that question seems to be clear with regard to the preventive mechanisms based on the joint activity of both the home and the host state, such as the review of the implementation of the treaty. In these cases, the participation of the home state would not amount to diplomatic protection, as it is not possible to implement these mechanisms only by a joint decision.

However, even in cases in which the mechanisms of dispute prevention can be triggered only by one state, home state participation in them would not necessarily fit the 'classic' notion of diplomatic protection, which is remedial by nature. Therefore, these activities would normally not be directed at determining the responsibility of another state for an injury caused by an internationally wrongful act with a view to the implementation of such responsibility, which are both requisites of diplomatic protection, according to the ILC Draft Articles on Diplomatic Protection.[162]

In the *Pac Rim* v. *El Salvador* case, the claimant argued that the procedures of consultations envisaged by Article 20.4 CAFTA–DR with

---

[161] *Urbaser SA and Consorcio de Aguas Bilbao Bizkaia, Bilbao Biskaia Ur Partzuergoa v. Argentine Republic*, ICSID Case No ARB/07/26. Final Award, 8 December 2016, para. 1195.

[162] International Law Commission, Draft Articles on Diplomatic Protection, Art. 1.

respect to an actual or proposed measure or matter that might affect the operation of the agreement, amounted to diplomatic protection, and they should be therefore precluded under Article 27(1) of the ICSID Convention. The tribunal in that case concluded that this type of intervention 'fall short of diplomatic protection', adding that Article 16 of the ILC Draft Articles on Diplomatic Protection distinguishes between diplomatic protection from other states' actions and procedures to resort under international law in order to secure redress for injury suffered by a national as a result of an internationally wrongful act.[163]

Therefore, home state participation in the prevention of investment disputes would usually be closer to the notion of 'consular assistance', which is largely preventive and aimed mainly at avoiding a situation in which a national is subjected to an internationally wrongful act.[164]

However, in some cases, a home state could perform actions of a preventive nature, after a conflict has arisen regarding an alleged injury suffered by a national investor as a result of a breach of international law by a foreign host state, but before it escalates into a fully fledged dispute. Two IIAs examined in this chapter provide examples of this situation.

In the recent Brazilian CFIAs, a state party to the agreement can submit a specific question that is of interest to the investor's interest to the JC established in the same treaty. It would therefore mean that in the event of a conflict, the home state would need to start consultation procedures before the JC, in the investor's name. As in diplomatic protection, the investors would have to refer to the home state to trigger this mechanism, as they could not act alone, and the home state has no obligation to start this procedure. Monebhurrun has criticized this, in pointing out that it would increase the administrative burden for the JC, which will be surely involved in a time-consuming 'triangular relationship' where a bilateral one would suffice, adding that 'a say could have been given directly to private companies – at least at this stage which does not imply litigation – with an eventual State intervention in case of failure in the negotiations'.[165]

As previously discussed, under Article 26 of the Nigeria–Morocco BIT, the home state could have a role in the prevention of an investment

---

[163] *Pac Rim Cayman LLC* v. *Republic of El Salvador*, ICSID Case No ARB/09/12, Decision on the Respondent's Jurisdictional Objections, 1 June 2012, paras. 488 and 489.

[164] International Law Commission, 'Draft Articles on Diplomatic Protection', Art. 1, Comm. 9.

[165] Monebhurrun, 'Novelty in International Investment Law', 89.

dispute – or, to be more precise, avoiding a conflict escalating to full arbitration. In my view, it is a characteristic of diplomatic protection that the home state is not obliged to submit the issue raised by its investor to the JC, and that is not clear whether, in such circumstances, the investor can even start an ISA – with the already existing complication that, previously, the investor would also need to exhaust local remedies at the host state.

For Gazzini, this provision blurs the roles and positions of states and investors, undermining one essential element of ISDS: insulation from political considerations. He adds that 'the very fact that the procedure under Art. 26 is activated by the national State is questionable and may raise several problems ... abandoning direct negotiations between the investor and the host State as pre-condition for international arbitration seems rather counterproductive'.[166]

---

[166] Gazzini, 'Nigeria and Morocco Move towards a "New Generation" of Bilateral Investment Treaties'.

IV

Home State Role in ISDS Together with the Host State

In this chapter we will examine the different mechanisms in which the home state can participate in investor–state arbitration, together with the host state to the dispute. There are at least four mechanisms whereby this participation can take place: the filtering of claims before the start of the arbitral procedure; the joint interpretation of provisions of international investment agreements; technical referral procedures of interpretation to domestic authorities of each state; and the regulation of the work of arbitrators beyond the terms already established in the respective IIA.

A   Filtering of Claims

Several IIAs concluded in the last fifteen years include a 'filter mechanism' of investment claims, allowing the use of investor–state dispute settlement to challenge certain measures of the host state only if the competent authorities of both the home and the host states agree on the qualification of the nature of such measures, its consequences, and that they are not covered by any exception or reservation in the treaty.

Until now, the treaty practice on filtering of claims has been largely limited to taxation measures. One important exception is found in the Australia–China FTA, in which the filtering mechanism is extended beyond taxation measures, suspending the initiation of the arbitral procedure, but without having the effect of completely excluding the claim in the event that both contracting parties reach an agreement.

In treaty-making practice, the filtering mechanism has increasingly been considered and, during the last fifteen years, has been found in at least seventy-seven new IIAs, mostly in investment chapters of FTAs (forty-three FTAs from the data set), although it is also found in bilateral investment treaties or regional investment treaties (thirty

Table 4.1 *IIAs with provisions on filtering of claims*

	Filtering of Tax Claims	Filtering of Public Welfare Claims
Number of IIAs	77	1
% of Total Data Set	14	0.2

BITs and four RITs). A filtering mechanism for tax measures is provided for in the 2005 IISD Model BIT.[1]

1 Types of Filtering Mechanisms

(a) Taxation Measures

Although there is a wide range of different ways in which states deal with taxation in IIAs, many countries share the position that tax matters should generally be excluded from investment treaties and are better dealt with by specific bilateral tax treaties.[2] Thus, as a general rule, taxation measures are not under the scope of application of IIAs and, if they are, such agreements usually include carve-out provisions or the exclusion of certain treaty aspects from application to tax matters. For example, under NAFTA, taxation measures are excluded from the application of Article 1105 (minimum standard of treatment), but Article 2103 does permit claims against such measures, with some exceptions, based on Article 1102 (national treatment).

However, some IIAs signed in the last fifteen years allow the application of their provisions on expropriation and compensation to taxation measures. Under these 'clawback' provisions, if there is a dispute on whether a taxation measure constitutes an expropriation, the investor has to refer the case to the competent tax authorities of the contracting states of the IIA, prior to submitting a claim to arbitration. These authorities can then make a binding determination that the measure does or does not amount to an expropriation. Only if they fail to agree

---

[1] IISD Model BIT, Art. 50(D).
[2] C. Tietje and K. Kampermann, 'Taxation and Investment: Constitutional Law Limitations on Tax Legislation in Context' in S. W. Schill (ed.), *International Investment Law and Comparative Public Law* (Oxford University Press, 2010), pp. 569–97 at pp. 571–2.

after a short period of time ('negative deadlock'),[3] can the matter be referred to an arbitral tribunal. Thus, the home and the host states are dealing with a legal question that involves the assessment of facts, of the relevant treaty and of the international case law.[4]

In treaty-making, there are two basic forms of this filtering mechanism. In one, the power to determine the expropriatory character is, in effect, assigned to the two tax authorities of the home and the host states acting jointly with binding effect (the 'NAFTA' model). In the other, a joint tax consultation mechanism is considered before an investment claim becomes admissible, only with recommendatory effect (the 'Energy Charter Treaty (ECT)' model).

The filter mechanism for taxation measures was first introduced in 1992, in Article 2103(6) of NAFTA. Under that provision, the investor shall refer the issue of whether the measure is not an expropriation for determination by the appropriate competent tax authorities, at the time that it gives notice of intent to submit a claim to arbitration. If the competent taxation authorities do not agree to consider the issue or, having agreed to consider it, fail to agree that the measure is not an expropriation, within a period of six months of such referral; the investor is entitled to submit its claim to arbitration.

A filtering mechanism for taxation measures was also included in Article 21(5) of the ECT ('carve-out'), but with some important differences to the NAFTA model. First, it must be used not only to determine whether a tax constitutes an alleged expropriation, but also to resolve whether the tax is discriminatory. Secondly, such a determination must be made by the competent tax authorities of the contracting parties within a period of six months of the referral, but their decision is not binding on an ISDS arbitral tribunal, which 'may take into account any conclusions arrived at by the Competent Tax Authorities regarding whether the tax is an expropriation'.[5]

The majority of filter mechanisms for taxation measures typically follow the model of Article 2103(6) of NAFTA. Not surprisingly, the main vectors of diffusion of this tool in IIAs are NAFTA parties.

---

[3] W. W. Park, 'Arbitration and the Fisc: NAFTA's "Tax Veto"', *Chicago Journal of International Law*, 2 (2001), 231–41 at 236.

[4] A. Kolo, 'Tax "Veto" as a Special Jurisdictional and Substantive Issue in Investor–State Arbitration: Need for Reassessment?', *Suffolk Transnational Law Review*, 32 (2009), 475 at 481.

[5] ECT, Art. 21(5)(b)(iii).

In the decade following NAFTA, Canada continued the inclusion of the filtering mechanism for taxation measures in its FTA with Chile[6] and in almost all its BITs,[7] using NAFTA as a starting point, but introducing some important variations. For example, in almost all recent Canadian BITs the competent taxation authorities of each contracting party can determine not only whether the measure in question constitutes an expropriation, but also whether a tax measure of a contracting party is in breach of an 'investment agreement' – an agreement between the central government authorities of a contracting party and the investor concerning an investment (also dubbed a 'legal stability agreement', 'investment authorization', etc.).[8] A similar wording is included in the Canada–Costa Rica BIT, but here the taxation authorities have broader faculties, as they can jointly determine that a claim 'is without foundation and consequently, there are no grounds for submitting such claim to arbitration'.[9]

Canada has included this filtering mechanism in all BITs that it has concluded in the last fifteen years, and in its FTAs with Colombia, Peru, Panama, Honduras and Korea, as well as in the TPP. In almost all these BITs, the filtering mechanism on taxation measures is applicable to both expropriation and investment agreements.[10] In contrast, the Canadian FTAs largely follow the NAFTA model and only provide for the filtering mechanism for taxation measures that are tantamount to expropriation.[11]

With regard to the United States, tax matters were generally excluded from the coverage of the BITs concluded after NAFTA, and the filtering

---

[6] Canada–Chile FTA (1996), Art. O-03.6.

[7] The filtering of claims is included in almost all Canadian BITs concluded after NAFTA. One of the few exceptions is the Canada–Singapore BIT (1997), Art. VIII, in which taxation measures are explicitly included as measures that could have an effect equivalent to expropriation, but no filtering mechanism is provided for in this case. Canadian BITs with Czech Republic (2009) and Slovakia (2010) have no filter mechanism and no explicit mention that tax measures could be tantamount to expropriation.

[8] E.g. Canada–Ukraine BIT (1994), Art. XII; Canada–Latvia (1995), Art. XII; Canada–Trinidad and Tobago BIT (1995), Art. XII.

[9] Canada–Costa Rica BIT (1998), Art. XI(2).

[10] E.g. Canada–Peru BIT (2006), Arts. 16.3, 22.3, 23.3 and. 26.4; Canada–Romania BIT (2009) Art. XII; Canada–Latvia BIT (2009), Art. XII. Of the Canadian IIAs concluded in the last fifteen years, only the Canada–China BIT (2012), Art. 14; and Canada–Mongolia BIT (2016), Art. 21 provide for the filtering mechanism only in relation to expropriation.

[11] Canada–Colombia FTA (2008), Arts. 821.4, 2208.7; Canada–Peru FTA (2008), Arts. 819.2, 820.2, 823.4, 2203.8, 2203.9(d), 2203.10–11; Canada–Panama FTA (2010), Arts. 9.22.5, 23.04.8–9; CETA, Art. 28.7.7; TPP, Art. 29.4.8. Of all these treaties, only CETA has a broader scope for the filtering mechanism, as will be explained later.

mechanism was only included again in the FTAs signed with Singapore and Chile in 2003.[12] In the last fifteen years, the United States has also considered this device for investment claims related to taxation measures in its FTAs with Korea, Panama, Colombia, Peru and Oman,[13] in the TPP, and also in its BITs with Rwanda and Uruguay.[14]

A similar provision is provided for in the Australia–US FTA, although in this treaty there is no ISDS. A contracting party may claim in writing that a taxation measure of the other party is an expropriation. In that case, that other party's designated authority may request, in writing, consultations between the designated tax authorities, which have the sole responsibility for determining whether the taxation measure is an expropriation under the FTA and would give rise to an inconsistency with any tax convention between the parties. Unless the designated authorities agree on this matter within sixty days after receipt of the request for consultations (a period that might be extended by mutual agreement of the designated authorities), the party alleging an expropriation may pursue the issue the state-to-state dispute settlement procedures established in the same treaty.[15]

After NAFTA, the filter mechanism on taxation measures was included by Mexico in several FTAs – especially in those signed with Latin American countries such as Nicaragua, Chile, Uruguay, Central America, Peru and Panama, in the Pacific Alliance Protocol (PAAP), and in the TPP.[16] The only country outside Latin America with which Mexico has included such a mechanism in its FTA is Japan.[17]

Overall, the majority of treaties that include a filtering mechanism for taxation measures follow the NAFTA model, with some minor differences. As in NAFTA, the large majority provide for a six-month period for competent tax authorities to determine whether the challenged

---

[12] Singapore–US (2003), Art. 21.3.6; Chile–US FTA (2003), Art. 23.3.6.
[13] Korea–US FTA (2007), Art. 23.3.6; Panama–US FTA (2007), Art. 21.6, Annex 21.3; Colombia–US FTA (2006), Art. 22.3.6; Peru–US FTA (2006), Art. 22.3.6; Oman–US FTA (2006), Art. 21.3.6.
[14] Rwanda–US BIT (2008), Art. 21.3; Uruguay–US BIT (2005), Art. 21.3.
[15] Australia–US FTA (2004), Art. 22.3.6. A similar provision is found in the China–Hong Kong CEPA Investment Agreement (2017), Art. 24 (a treaty that also does not provide for ISDS), but there is no time limit for the tax authorities to make a joint determination.
[16] Mexico–Nicaragua FTA (1997), Arts. 13–20; Chile–Mexico FTA (1998), Art. 19–05.4; Mexico–Uruguay FTA (2003), Art. 19–05.4; Central America–Mexico FTA (2011), Arts. 11.24.2, 11.25.1; Mexico–Peru FTA (2011), Art. 18.4.4; Mexico–Panama FTA (2014), Art. 19.5.4, Annex 19.5; PAAP (2014), Art. 18.4.7–8.
[17] Mexico–Japan FTA (2004), Arts. 170.4 and 21.3.6.

measure is an expropriation, the time generally being counted from the point that the investor gives notice of intent to submit a claim to arbitration,[18] although certain IIAs count it from the date on which the written request for consultation is submitted to the disputing contracting party.[19] An important number of treaties provide for roughly the same timeframe but expressed as a period of 180 days.[20] Some IIAs provide for a different period of five months.[21] In a few others, the designated authorities seized of a tax issue may agree to modify the time period allowed for their consideration of the issue.[22] A small number of treaties do not specify a duration for this process, merely indicating that 'the Parties, including representatives of their tax administrations, shall hold consultations'.[23]

Although the scope of the filtering clause typically covers only expropriation claims, some IIAs – notably those concluded by Canada – go beyond that, towards determination of whether a measure has an effect equivalent to expropriation. Certain treaties establish a similar procedure for prior determination of whether a challenged measure is a taxation one in the first place.[24] Furthermore, some treaties includes provisions in the event that there is a conflict with a tax convention, determining whether it prevails over the IIA.[25] More importantly, some Canadian IIAs extend the filtering mechanism with respect to taxation measures in broader terms, to breaches of 'all the relevant provisions' of the agreement,[26] or generally to provisions on non-discriminatory treatment (national treatment, most-favoured nation, senior management and boards of directors) or

---

[18] E.g.: Chile–Hong Kong Investment Agreement (2016), Art. 14.5; China–Korea FTA (2015), Art. 21.3.5–6; Honduras–Peru FTA (2015), Art. 18.3.7.

[19] China–Japan–Korea Trilateral Investment Treaty (2012), Art. 21.5.

[20] E.g.: Japan–Uruguay BIT (2015), Art. 25; Australia–Korea FTA (2014), Art. 22.3.5; Colombia–Korea FTA (2013), Art. 21.3.6. It is also expressed in these terms in the Canada–Korea FTA (2014), Art. 22.3.7; Rwanda–US BIT (2008), Art. 21.3; Korea–US FTA (2007), Art. 23.3.6; Oman–US FTA (2006), Art. 21.3.6; Uruguay–US BIT (2005), Art. 21.3; Japan – Mexico EPA (2004), Art. 170.4 (b), and in US Model BIT (2004) (2012), Art. 21.2.

[21] Indonesia–Japan EPA (2007), Art. 73.4.

[22] Canada–Mongolia BIT (2016), Art. 21.6; Canada–Honduras FTA (2013), Art. 22.4.11; Canada–Peru FTA (2008), Art. 2203.11.

[23] China–New Zealand FTA (2008), Art. 204.4.

[24] K. Gordon and J. Pohl, *Investment Treaties over Time – Treaty Practice and Interpretation in a Changing World* (2015), p. 30.

[25] E.g.: Canada–Peru FTA (2008), Art. 2203.9(d); Canada–Colombia FTA (2008), Art. 2204.8(d), Canada–Panama FTA (2010), Art. 23.04.10; Canada–Honduras FTA (2013), Art. 22.4.9; Chile–Hong Kong Investment Agreement (2016), Art. 14.4.

[26] Canada–Mongolia BIT (2017), Art. 21.4.

investment protection (fair and equitable treatment, full protection and security, transfers, subrogation and compensation for losses and expropriation).[27]

Taxation authorities for the purposes of the filtering mechanism are usually designated in the IIA, although some agreements leave that task to the disputing party and the non-disputing party (through a process of consultations)[28] or provide that each party shall notify the other party the identity of such taxation authorities, by diplomatic note.[29] Certain treaties provide specific guidelines for these authorities, in order to determine whether the taxation measure constitutes an expropriation, establishing that the mere imposition of taxes does not generally constitute expropriation, especially when they are consistent with policies, principles and internationally recognized tax practices (such as to prevent the avoidance or evasion of taxes), and when they are applied on a non-discriminatory basis, non-targeting investors of a particular nationality.[30]

In the Common Market for Eastern and Southern Africa (COMESA)[31] Investment Agreement there is a slightly different filtering procedure, as an investor that seeks to challenge a taxation measure through ISDS must first refer to the Secretary-General of COMESA whether that taxation measure involves an expropriation, at the time that it gives its notice of intention to arbitrate. The Secretary–General, in turn, shall ask the competent authorities of the host state and home state whether they do not agree to consider the issue or, having agreed to consider it, fail to agree that the measure is not an expropriation within a period of six months of such referral, in which case the investor may submit its claim to arbitration.[32]

---

[27] CETA, Art. 28.7.7.
[28] ASEAN–Australia–New Zealand FTA (2009), Art. 25.6.
[29] Canada–Côte d'Ivoire BIT (2014), Art. 14.
[30] Colombia–Costa Rica FTA (2013), Art. 21.3.6 (a); Colombia–Korea FTA (2013), Art. 21.3.6; Guatemala–Peru FTA (2011), Art. 18.3.7; Panama–Peru FTA (2011), Art. 21.3.7; Costa Rica–Peru FTA (2011), Art. 18.3.7; Korea–Peru FTA (2010), Art. 24.4.7; New Zealand–Malaysia FTA (2009), Art. 10.24.4–5; Panama–Singapore FTA (2006), Art. 18.3.6.
[31] COMESA is the Common Market for Eastern and Southern Africa, which include Burundi, Comoros, Democratic Republic of Congo, Djibouti, Egypt, Eritrea, Ethiopia, Kenya, Libya, Madagascar, Malawi, Mauritius, Rwanda, Seychelles, Sudan, Swaziland, Uganda, Zambia and Zimbabwe. Treaty establishing the Common Market for Eastern and Southern Africa, 5 November 1993, 33 I.L.M. 1067.
[32] COMESA Investment Treaty, Art. 23.2.

In the large majority of these agreements, the decision by the competent tax authorities is binding on an ISDS arbitral tribunal. However, a few of them – closer to the ECT model – only give to that determination a persuasive authority, establishing that the tribunal shall accord 'serious consideration'[33] to the decision of the tax authorities of the disputing party and of the non-disputing party (home state), or there is no mention whether that determination is binding or not.[34] The ECT model is completely replicated only in the Economic Community of West African States (ECOWAS) Energy Protocol.[35]

(b)   Public Welfare Measures

Filtering mechanisms also exist outside taxation. Under the Australia-China FTA, the respondent state may, within thirty days of the date on which it receives a request for consultations, declare that it considers that a measure alleged to be in breach of an obligation that allows the use of ISDS is a 'public welfare measure', meaning a non-discriminatory measure for the legitimate public welfare objectives of public health, safety, the environment, public morals or public interest, and therefore it shall not be the subject of an ISDS claim.[36] Notably, this agreement does not include a filtering mechanism for taxation measures.

To activate this mechanism, the respondent host state shall deliver to the claimant and to the non-disputing party (the home state) a notice specifying the basis for its position (a 'public welfare notice'), which shall trigger a ninety-day period of consultation between the home and the host states, suspending the ISA during this period. The respondent state shall promptly inform the claimant, and make available to the public, the outcome of any consultations. The outcome of these consultations seems to be merely persuasive, as the arbitral tribunal shall not draw any adverse inference from the absence of a decision between the host state and the home state. Similarly, the arbitral tribunal shall not draw any adverse inference from the non-issuance of a public welfare notice by the respondent state.[37]

Yet, it seems highly unlikely that a joint agreement between the home and the host states regarding the public welfare nature of a measure challenged by an investor could be so easily disregarded by an arbitral

---

[33] ASEAN–Korea Investment Agreement (2009), Art. 18.8-11; ASEAN Comprehensive Investment Agreement (2009), Art. 36.8.
[34] COMESA Investment Treaty, Art. 23.2.
[35] ECOWAS Energy Protocol, Art. 21.
[36] Australia–China FTA (2015), Art. 9.11.4-5.
[37] Australia–China FTA (2015), Art. 9.11.6-8.

tribunal, as it would look closely similar to a joint interpretation by the contracting parties.

2 Use of Filtering Mechanisms in ISDS

Filtering procedures have not been widely used in practice, but the existing cases can illustrate the issues that may arise due to the use (or lack thereof) of the filtering mechanism.

In three NAFTA cases, this mechanism was triggered with respect to a Mexican tax ('IEPS tax' – a 20 per cent tax applicable to soft drinks, hydrating and rehydrating drinks and syrups or concentrates for preparing soft drinks, sweetened with high-fructose corn syrup), in which the United States (the home state of all claimants) consistently did not agree that the IEPS tax was *not* an expropriation. In all three cases – *Cargill*,[38] *CPI*[39] and *ADM*,[40] the expropriation claims were finally rejected by the arbitral tribunals.

Also under NAFTA, the tax authorities of the home state (the United States) and the host state (Mexico) agreed to strike out one of the three alleged expropriation measures challenged by the claimant in *Feldman v. Mexico*,[41] but could not agree on the other two measures, and thus the arbitration went ahead on those claims. However, in the award, the arbitral tribunal gave some deference to that previous determination, holding that the comparison with the excluded measure was 'inescapable' and that, at minimum, it suggests that 'tax law and policy changes are intended to be given relatively broad leeway under NAFTA, even if their effect is to make it impractical for certain business activities to continue'.[42]

---

[38] *Cargill, Inc.* v. *United Mexican States*, ICSID Case No ARB(AF)/05/2, Award, 18 September 2009, paras. 16, 17, 378, 551.

[39] *Corn Products International, Inc.* v. *United Mexican States*, ICSID Case No ARB (AF)/04/1, Decision on Responsibility, 15 January 2008, paras. 81–94.

[40] *Archer Daniels Midland Co and Tate & Lyle Ingredients Americas, Inc.* v. *United Mexican States*, ICSID Case No ARB (AF)/04/5, Award, 21 November 2007, paras. 237–52.

[41] Mexico's action in enacting legislation that restricted the availability of rebates of excise taxes to those who purchase cigarettes in the 'first sale' within Mexico was not considered an expropriation under Article 1110 of NAFTA (Letter of 17 February 1999 from Assistant US Treasury Secretary Donald C. Lubick to Mexican Under Secretary of Revenue Tomas Ruiz). Marvin Roy Feldman Karpa v. United Mexican States, ICSID Case No ARB(AF)/99/1, Award, 16 December 2002 (2002) para. 116.

[42] *Feldman v. Mexico*, Award, para. 116.

In *Gottlieb Investors* v. *Canada*, arbitration was fully prevented. Gottlieb intended to submit a claim alleging that a change in the tax treatment of Canadian income trusts in the energy sector, announced in 2006, led to an unlawful expropriation of its investment in Canada. However, the tax authorities of the home state (the United States) and the host state (Canada) agreed that the challenged measures were not an expropriation under Article 1110 of NAFTA. The claimant was barred from bringing a claim merely by an exchange of letters between the heads of the respective tax agencies, agreeing that the Canadian taxation measures cited in the claimant's notice of intent were not an expropriation under NAFTA, without any explanation of the reasoning for both states considering that the challenged measure was non-expropriatory.[43]

In *Resolute Forest Products Inc.* v. *Canada*, the claim was brought without prior use of the filtering mechanism, even though it partially involved certain taxation measures. Canada submitted that Article 2103(6) NAFTA clearly limits the jurisdiction of the arbitral tribunal to consider taxation measures, excluding them from dispute resolution unless the clearly prescribed procedural requirements are met: that the claimant has sought a determination from the NAFTA parties that the measure is an expropriation. By non-disputing state party (NDSP) submissions, both the United States and Mexico agreed with Canada's interpretation.[44] The claimant affirmed that the type of tax contemplated in the prerequisite of Article 2103(6) consists of 'affirmative tax measures burdening an investor to the point of expropriation. Tax breaks favouring a competitor without affirmatively burdening an investor, particularly when asserted as the basis for a constructive expropriation claim in conjunction with other measures conferring competitive advantages, are not "taxation measures" requiring referral'.[45] The award of the tribunal is still pending at the time of writing.

Under the ECT, the non-use of the referral procedure to the competent tax authority by the claimant was one of the reasons that a claim against

---

[43] *Gottlieb Investors Group* v. *Government of Canada.* Determination under NAFTA Article 2103-6 on expropriation claim. Letter to Gottlieb Investors Group indicating determination, 29 April 2008, TDM, www.transnational-dispute-management.com/legal-and-regulatory -detail.asp?key=5448.

[44] *Resolute Forest Products Inc.* v. *Government of Canada*, PCA Case No 2016-13. Respondent's Comments on Article 1128 Submissions from USA and Mexico, 12 July 2017, para. 29

[45] *Resolute Forest Products Inc.* v. *Government of Canada*, PCA Case No 2016-13. Claimant's Comments on Article 1128 Submissions from USA and Mexico, 12 July 2017, para. 30.

Bulgarian taxation measures was rejected in *Plama* v. *Bulgaria*.[46] In the three arbitrations in the *Yukos* dispute, the tribunal took a different view, downplaying the relevance of the filtering mechanism, under the extraordinary circumstances of the case. Firstly declared that any measures falling under the taxation carve-out of Article 21(1) of the ECT are also covered by the scope of the expropriation clawback in Article 21(5) of the ECT,[47] and that the referral mechanism therefore cannot be avoided on the basis of a narrow interpretation of the term 'tax' in Article 21(5)(b)(i) of the ECT. The arbitral tribunal then found that any referral to the competent taxation authorities in these cases would clearly have been futile, dispensing the prescribed procedure because it would not produce the result that it seeks to achieve.[48]

> the Tribunal finds that, in any event, the carve-out of Article 21(1) can apply only to bona fide taxation actions, i.e., actions that are motivated by the purpose of raising general revenue for the state. By contrast, actions that are taken only under the guise of taxation, but in reality aim to achieve an entirely unrelated purpose (such as the destruction of a company or the elimination of a political opponent) cannot qualify for exemption from the protection standards of the ECT under the taxation carve-out in Article 21(1).[49]

Following that reasoning, the tribunal concluded that it had jurisdiction to rule on the claimants' claims under Article 13 of the ECT due to the fact that the filtering mechanism does not apply to Russia's measures

---

[46] *Plama Consortium Ltd* v. *Republic of Bulgaria*, Award, 27 August 2008, paras. 266–7. In this case, the claimant complained that a discounted debt unfairly gave rise to a paper profit that it was liable to pay under Bulgarian company income tax law.

[47] This could be considered rather obvious, but the respondent submitted that, the use of the expression 'taxation measures' in the carve-out of the ECT, Art. 21(1), and merely of 'taxes' in the clawback of the ECT, Art. 21(5), would result in a wide carve-out and a narrow clawback, reinstating protection from expropriation only in relation to charges and payments, but not collection and enforcement measures or interests and fines. Siding with the claimants, the Tribunal disagreed with such an interpretation holding that it would lead to a gap in the ECT where investors would stand completely unprotected from expropriatory taxation, something that would defeat the object and purpose of the ECT itself. *Yukos Universal Ltd (Isle of Man)* v. *Russian Federation*, PCA Case No AA 227, Final Award, 18 July 2014, paras. 1410–16; *Veteran Petroleum Ltd (Cyprus)* v. *Russian Federation*, UNCITRAL, PCA Case No AA 228, Final Award, 18 July 2014, paras. 1410–16; and *Hulley Enterprises Ltd (Cyprus)* v. *Russian Federation*, PCA Case No AA 226, Final Award, 18 July 2014, paras. 1410–16.

[48] *Yukos* v. *Russia*, Final Award, paras. 1410–16; *Veteran Petroleum* v. *Russia*, Final Award; and *Hulley Enterprises* v. *Russia*, Final Award, paras. 1417–28.

[49] The same interpretation has been advanced by the claimant in *Resolute Forest Products* v. *Canada*.

because they were not a bona fide exercise of its tax powers. To rule otherwise would mean that the mere labelling of a measure as 'taxation' would be sufficient to bring such a measure within the scope of Article 21(1) of the ECT, and produce a loophole in the protective scope of the treaty. In addition, the tribunals held that submitting these issues to the preliminary examination of the same authorities of a state that participated in measures against an investor would add little value for an arbitral tribunal.[50]

Outside NAFTA and the ECT, a binding tax filtering clause was relevant in *EnCana* v. *Ecuador*. In that case, based on Article XII(4) of the Canada–Ecuador BIT, the claimant notified its claim to the tax authorities of the home state (Canada) and the host state (Ecuador). However, both states failed to make a joint determination within six months, so that the claim could proceed to arbitration, in order to determine whether the measures taken by Ecuador constituted expropriation or had an equivalent effect. That claim was finally rejected by the majority of the arbitral tribunal.[51]

Treaty practice in the abovementioned cases shows that, until now, these filtering mechanisms have operated solely through an exchange of letters between the competent tax authorities, which communicate a formal decision to the claimant without an explanation of the grounds of the decision. That does not mean that home and host states have always agreed on the expropriatory character of the taxation measure that is challenged, but such a decision is taken without giving the affected investors the chance to present their case before them or to contend the arguments of the tax authorities of the host state.

3   The Nature of Filtering Mechanisms in ISDS

Undoubtedly, the filtering mechanism introduces an element of politics into the settlement of investment disputes, subordinating the adjudicatory power of investment treaty tribunals to the power of the governments when they act jointly.[52] But is this diplomatic protection? It does

---

[50] *Yukos* v. *Russia*, Final Award, paras. 1430–45; *Veteran Petroleum* v. *Russia*, Final Award, paras. 1430–45; and *Hulley Enterprises* v. *Russia*, Final Award, paras. 1430–45.

[51] *EnCana Corp.* v. *Republic of Ecuador*, LCIA Case No UN3481, UNCITRAL (formerly EnCana Corp. v. Government of the Republic of Ecuador), Award, 3 February 2006, para. 109.

[52] T. Wälde and A. Kolo, 'Investor–State Disputes: The Interface Between Treaty-Based International Investment Protection and Fiscal Sovereignty', *Intertax*, 35 (2007), 424–49 at 446.

not seem to fulfil the traditional requirements of that institution:[53] first, because the filtering is not invoked by the home state but by the claimant, in order to comply with the treaty requirements established for the submission of claims and, secondly, the determination of whether the taxation measure amounts to expropriation, constitutes discrimination, is in violation of the IIA, a tax convention or an investment agreement, or is a public welfare measure, is taken by both the home and the host states together, not as a unilateral right of the home state. Plus, with respect to taxation measures, if both states determine that the claim must be excluded from ISDS through this filtering mechanism, rather than protecting its national investor, the home state would be siding with the host state, blocking a tax claim to be settled under ISA. Yet, as the three IEPS tax cases show, the home state can also side with its investor.

Although filtering mechanisms cannot be used by the host state to delay ISAs unduly, as they should normally be exercised under strict time limitations, they may effectively prevent a legal issue from being determined by an arbitral tribunal.[54] For that reason, some commentators have dubbed this procedure, when applied to taxation measures, a 'tax veto'[55] – a label that does not seem accurate. Traditionally, a 'veto' is a unilateral act to block an action of another body[56] – something that in this case might be done only by unanimity (the agreement of all appropriate competent tax authorities). Plus, the decision of the competent authorities is not always binding. In that sense, rather than vetoing, states are acting as 'gatekeepers'.[57]

In *CPI* v. *Mexico*, the arbitral tribunal held that Article 2103(6) of NAFTA gave the home state a limited power regarding a claim for expropriation based upon a taxation measure, 'but this is exceptional and, in any event, does not give the investor's State of nationality control

---

[53] International Law Commission, 'Draft Articles on Diplomatic Protection, with Commentaries. Report of the International Law Commission, 58th session (A/61/10)', *Yearbook of the International Law Commission*, II (2006), 22–100, Art. 1.

[54] Wälde and Kolo, 'Investor–State Disputes', 447.

[55] See Tietje and Kampermann, 'Taxation and Investment: Constitutional Law Limitations on Tax Legislation in Context', 572; Park, 'Arbitration and the Fisc: NAFTA's "Tax Veto"'; and Kolo, 'Tax "Veto" as a Special Jurisdictional and Substantive Issue in Investor–State Arbitration: Need for Reassessment?'.

[56] See, for example, the several types of veto described in B. A. Garner, *Black's Law Dictionary, Standard Ninth Edition*, 9th edn (West, 2009), pp. 1700–1.

[57] T. Posner, 'The Role of Non-Disputing States in Investment Dispute Settlement, 22nd Investment Treaty Forum (ITF), British Institute of International and Comparative Law (BIICL), 8 May 2014' (2014).

over the proceedings; rather its effect is that the State of nationality and the respondent State, if agreed, can together effectively preclude such a claim by determining that the measure in question was not an expropriation'.[58]

But why do taxation measures benefit from this special treatment in investment law? Alschner believes that there are technical and political reasons for including such provisions.[59] They are technical, as tax matters require considerable expertise that is more likely to be held by the competent authorities of the contracting states than by tribunals. The OECD believes that this reflects the perception that special knowledge must be available to assess issues related to tax matters that are unlikely to be available to arbitration panels.[60] They are also political, since taxation power is one of the most sensitive areas of national sovereignty that provides a major source of revenue and, as such, is more out of the need for policy flexibility.[61] Even though states seem to recognize that expropriatory taxation can be a particularly deceptive way to take property in ways that are apparently lawful, tax authorities do not want to give up their powers even in this egregious case.[62]

For some authors, there is no justifiable reason for tax matters being treated differently in the investment regime. Kolo believes that the filtering mechanism raises a serious question over its compatibility with the due process of law, as the decision on whether a taxation measure is equivalent to deprivation of property rights 'should be made by a neutral and independent tribunal, rather than the administrative agency whose actions formed the basis of the dispute'.[63] Park questions why the 'triage' of tax claims must be made administratively, if arbitrators are trusted to decide on issues with significant national interests – such as expropriation of natural resources – and claiming that is not evident 'why there should be a presumption against an arbitral tribunal examining expropriations that implicate tax measures'.[64] Another feature of this

---

[58] CPI v. Mexico, Decision on Responsibility, para. 173, fn 70.

[59] W. Alschner, 'The Return of the Home State and the Rise of "Embedded" Investor–State Arbitration' in S. Lalani and R. Polanco (eds.), The Role of the State in Investor–State Arbitration (Brill/Martinus Nijhoff, 2014), p. 322.

[60] Gordon and Pohl, Investment Treaties over Time, p. 31.

[61] See Tietje and Kampermann, 'Taxation and Investment: Constitutional Law Limitations on Tax Legislation in Context', pp. 569–70.

[62] Wälde and Kolo, 'Investor–State Disputes', 446.

[63] Kolo, 'Tax "Veto" as a Special Jurisdictional and Substantive Issue in Investor–State Arbitration: Need for Reassessment?', 479.

[64] Park, 'Arbitration and the Fisc: NAFTA's "Tax Veto"', 241.

mechanism that could be in contradiction with due process is that there is no obligation on tax authorities to provide affected investors with the opportunity to present their cases before them or to contest the arguments of the host state tax authorities.[65]

Although filtering procedures have been used in only a few ISDS cases, as was analysed in the preceding section, both Kolo and Park have criticized the potential for state abuse of this mechanism. Alschner thinks that these fears are overstated, as the procedure would be highly legalized and moderated in both procedural and substantive terms, with a clear allocation of factual and interpretive authority and strict timelines.[66] However, in order to assess whether this is true, we need to examine the case law with respect to filtering procedures carefully. As we have seen in the preceding section, in some cases in which this mechanism has been used, the authorities of both the home and host states have agreed to strike out investors' claims related to tax measures, by mere exchange of formal letters, without further clarification of the basis for their decisions.

B   Joint State Interpretation of IIAs

Interpretation of treaties is not the exclusive task of states,[67] let alone the home state. It is also the duty of tribunals to interpret the meaning of terms used in a treaty, particularly when that is the question in an investment dispute.[68] But even if states have delegated the task of ruling on investor claims to arbitral tribunals, contracting parties of IIAs – meaning both home and host states – are the 'masters' of their treaties,[69] retaining a degree of interpretive authority and control over them, and they can elucidate their authentic intentions in clarifying the language or meaning of an agreement, through an authoritative interpretation.[70]

---

[65] Kolo, 'Tax "Veto" as a Special Jurisdictional and Substantive Issue in Investor–State Arbitration: Need for Reassessment?'.

[66] Alschner, 'The Return of the Home State', pp. 323–4.

[67] J. R. Weeramantry, *Treaty Interpretation in Investment Arbitration* (Oxford University Press, 2012), p. 31.

[68] *Camuzzi International SA v. Argentine Republic*, ICSID Case No ARB/03/2, Decision on Objection to Jurisdiction, 11 May 2005, para. 135.

[69] S. Hindelang and C.-P. Sassenrath, *The Investment Chapters of the EU's International Trade and Investment Agreements in a Comparative Perspective* (Publications Office, 2015), p. 17.

[70] UNCTAD, 'Interpretation of IIAs: What States Can Do', *IIA Issue Note* (2011) at 3.

In 1923, the PCIJ declared, in the *Jaworzina* Advisory Opinion, 'that the right of giving an authoritative interpretation of a legal rule belongs solely to the person or body who has power to modify or suppress it'.[71] In the *Kasikili/Sedudu Island* case, the ICJ held that an agreement by the parties as to the interpretation of a provision reached after the conclusion of the treaty represents an authentic interpretation.[72] The right of the contracting parties to issue an authentic interpretation of their treaty is addressed in Article 31 of the Vienna Convention on the Law of Treaties (VCLT), if unanimous agreement among them is obtained:[73]

1. A treaty shall be interpreted in good faith in accordance with the ordinary meaning to be given to the terms of the treaty in their context and in the light of its object and purpose.

2. The context for the purpose of the interpretation of a treaty shall comprise, in addition to the text, including its preamble and annexes:

   (a) Any agreement relating to the treaty which was made between all the parties in connexion with the conclusion of the treaty;

   (b) Any instrument which was made by one or more parties in connexion with the conclusion of the treaty and accepted by the other parties as an instrument related to the treaty.

3. There shall be taken into account, together with the context:

   (a) Any subsequent agreement between the parties regarding the interpretation of the treaty or the application of its provisions;

   (b) Any subsequent practice in the application of the treaty which establishes the agreement of the parties regarding its interpretation;

   (c) Any relevant rules of international law applicable in the relations between the parties.

4. A special meaning shall be given to a term if it is established that the parties so intended.

Fauchald points out that Article 31 of the VCLT distinguishes between two forms of agreement between the parties to a treaty: (i) an agreement made in connection with the conclusion of the treaty, which is part of its 'context'; and (ii) a subsequent agreement regarding the interpretation of the treaty, which comes in addition to the 'context'.[74] Joint

---

[71] *Question of Jaworzina*, Advisory Opinion, 1923 P.C.I.J. (ser. B) No 8 (December 6), p. 37.
[72] *Kasikili/Sedudu Island (Botswana v. Namibia)*, 1999 I.C.J. 1045 (December 13), p. 1075.
[73] Weeramantry, *Treaty Interpretation in Investment Arbitration*, p. 32.
[74] O. K. Fauchald, 'The Legal Reasoning of ICSID Tribunals – An Empirical Analysis', *European Journal of International Law*, 19 (2008), 301–64 at 328.

interpretations by the contracting parties of an IIA are a type of the latter agreement.

Nolte has underlined an important difference between Article 31(3)(a) and Article 31(3)(b) of the VCLT. While the former refers to a subsequent agreement between the parties (whether written or not), the latter refers to subsequent practice between the parties, which encompasses all other forms of later conduct by one or more parties that can contribute to the manifestation of an agreement.[75] When this agreement can be proven, we consider such subsequent joint statements by states as equivalent to formal joint interpretations.

But express provisions on the treaty can modify the VCLT interpretive principles, either by broadening the interpretive powers of contracting parties (e.g. by making joint interpretation binding) or by restricting them (e.g. by not permitting interpretations in pending disputes).[76]

What is the difference, then, between interpretations (which clarify the meaning of the text of the treaty) and amendments (which change that meaning)? Most commentators accept that interpretations and amendments are situated on the same spectrum and that the difference between them is usually one of degree,[77] but some important differences can be established: amendments are more likely to have a prospective effect – as they reflect a change in the treaty – than interpretations, which could have prospective and retrospective effect because they reveal the intention of the parties on an existing text of a treaty.[78] Interpretations that clearly depart from the text would be binding only if they were made by those with the power to amend the treaty.[79] However, as a matter of practice, it will often be difficult to make a distinction between what is a true interpretation and what is an amendment.[80]

Although the bulk of IIAs that have a provision on joint interpretations include a separate one on amendments, usually there is no express distinction on their binding character, except in some cases in which

---

[75] George Nolte, 'First Report on Subsequent Agreements and Subsequent Practice in Relation to Treaty Interpretation', UN Doc. A/CN.4/660 (19 March 2013) *International Law Commission Sixty-fifth session* at 31.

[76] A. Roberts, 'Power and Persuasion in Investment Treaty Interpretation: The Dual Role of States', *American Journal of International Law*, 104 (2010), 179–225 at 208.

[77] Ibid., 201.

[78] Alschner, 'The Return of the Home State', 321.

[79] Roberts, 'Power and Persuasion', 201.

[80] G. Kaufmann-Kohler, 'Interpretive Powers of the Free Trade Commission and the Rule of Law' Fifteen Years of NAFTA (JurisNet, LLC, 2011), pp. 175–94 at p. 191.

joint interpretation is made directly by the parties, as will be detailed in the following section.

Overall, the large majority of IIAs include clauses referring the interpretation of treaty provisions, either directly by the contracting parties via consultation or cooperation, or indirectly through a treaty body with senior representatives of each state, usually a joint commission or committee, which typically also has the task of monitoring the implementation of the treaty.[81] NAFTA was the first IIA that introduced the mechanism of 'institutionalized' authoritative interpretations by the parties of an IIA – a scheme that, since then, has been reproduced in several FTAs. Similar provisions can be found in BITs, and in most of them the contracting parties retain the task of issuing interpretations, rather than delegating it to their representatives.[82]

If we analyse the IIAs concluded in the last fifteen years, 196 (around 35 per cent) provide for a mechanism of joint interpretation of the treaty, either directly by the contracting states or through a dedicated treaty body. But both types of interpretation are not exclusive, and several IIAs include a direct interpretation of the contracting parties and at the same time a joint interpretation by a treaty body.[83]

Joint interpretations that take place largely 'in abstract' are not related to a specific dispute. However, some IIAs include provisions that provide for the possibility of authoritative interpretations in pending arbitral procedure ('intra-arbitral' interpretation), typically regarding general issues of interpretation, or specific provisions on financial measures, reservations, non-conforming measures (NCMs) or exceptions to the treaty. The mechanism provided for these interpretations is a referral (or

---

[81] M. Ewing-Chow and J. J. Losari, 'Which Is to Be the Master?: Extra-Arbitral Interpretative Procedures for IIAs', *Transnational Dispute Management*, 11 (2014), 1–20 at 8.

[82] Alschner, 'The Return of the Home State', 317.

[83] Korea–New Zealand FTA (2015), Art. 10.25.1-2; Korea–Vietnam FTA (2015), Art. 9.24.1; China–New Zealand FTA (2008), Art. 155; China–Peru FTA (2009), Art. 170; Japan–Switzerland ECA (2009), Art. 137; Colombia–Peru BIT (2007), Art. 34.1; Panama–United States FTA (2007), Art. 20.1; Colombia–United States FTA (2006), Art. 21.1; Canada–Peru BIT (2006), Art. 47.1, 48; Japan–Philippines EPA (2006), Arts. 13, 106; Chile–Peru FTA (2006), Art. 16.1; Nicaragua–Taiwan FTA (2006), Art. 22.01; Peru–United States FTA (2006), Art. 21.1; Panama–Singapore FTA (2006), Art. 15.1; Oman–United States FTA (2006), Art. 20.1; Guatemala–Taiwan FTA (2005), Art. 18.01; Korea–Singapore FTA (2005), Art. 20.1; New Zealand–Thailand EPA (2005), Art. 17.2; CAFTA–DR (2004), Art. 20.1; Morocco–United States FTA (2004), Art. 20.1; CARICOM–Costa Rica FTA (2004), Art. XIII.01.

Table 4.2 *IIAs with joint interpretation provisions*

	Abstract Interpretation		Intra-Arbitral Interpretation
	Direct Interpretation by Contracting Parties	Interpretation Through Treaty Body	Referral or *Renvoi*
Number of IIAs	135	54	78
% of Total Data Set	24	10	14

renvoi[84] from the tribunal to the contracting parties or a treaty body, with a strict timeframe within which to issue the interpretation. During that time, the procedure is suspended and, in the absence of an agreed interpretation after the period has elapsed, the tribunal shall decide the issue.

There is an important difference between direct and indirect interpretation of an IIA by the contracting parties. In almost all the treaties in which the joint interpretation of the agreement is made by a treaty body or directly by the contracting parties, the interpretation has a binding character for tribunals established under the treaty, as part of the governing law of the IIA. For example, all Mexican BITs signed since the 1998 BIT with the Netherlands[85] declare that an interpretation jointly formulated and agreed by the contracting parties of a provision of the agreement shall be binding on any tribunal established under the dispute settlement mechanism included in the same treaty. This is repeated in the Mexican BITs with Portugal, Korea, Greece, Cuba and the Czech Republic.[86]

Only a few treaties do not explicitly recognize a binding character for these interpretations,[87] and instead provide that they 'must be taken into account' and not be seen as amendments to or modifications of the

---

[84] United Nations Conference on Trade and Development (UNCTAD), 'Interpretation of IIAs: What States Can Do', *IIA Issue Note* (2011), 3 at 12; and Alschner, 'The Return of the Home State', 293–333.

[85] Mexico–Netherlands BIT (1998), Appendix, Art. 8.

[86] Mexico–Portugal BIT (1999), Art. 15.2; Korea–Mexico BIT (2000), Art. 14.2; Greece–Mexico BIT (2000), Art. 16.2; Cuba–Mexico BIT (2001), App., Art. 7.2; Czech Republic–Mexico BIT (2002), Art. 16(2).

[87] E.g. Colombia–Korea FTA (2013), Art. 19.1.3; China–Peru FTA (2009), Art. 170; Japan–Switzerland ECA (2008), Art. 148.2(d).

agreement.[88] Conversely, when a joint interpretation is made as part of the consultation mechanism, there is usually no unambiguous mention of its non-binding character, and some agreements are explicit in according only 'sympathetic consideration' to the request of consultations.[89]

As a general rule, no strict timeline is provided for an 'abstract' joint interpretation of an IIA, meaning that when such interpretations are not requested in a specific ISDS case there is no specific period for issuing the interpretation, although certain IIAs provides that that should take place 'without undue delay',[90] or that parties should agree 'promptly'[91] or 'immediately'[92] to such mechanism. Other agreements state that the time and place for such consultations shall be agreed by the parties through diplomatic channels.[93] In CETA, the joint committee may decide that an interpretation shall have binding effect from a specific date.[94]

Here, there is a significant difference with 'intra-arbitral' interpretations, which generally have strict timelines. Although 'abstract' interpretations are mainly 'extra-arbitral',[95] the lack of a time limit for these proceedings can pose some problems if arbitration is pending. As experience with NAFTA shows, an interpretation issued during the procedure of an ongoing case will not necessarily be considered by the tribunal. In *Pope & Talbot v. Canada* there was a lengthily discussion of whether NAFTA's Free Trade Commission interpretation should be applied even if it affected prior findings made by the tribunal in the same case. Even if the tribunal considered the interpretation to be binding, in the award on damages, the arbitrators were able to accommodate the interpretation of the FTC without overturning its previous decisions, as they deemed that it led to the same conclusion that there was a breach by Canada of its obligations under Article 1105 of NAFTA.[96]

---

[88] Colombia–Israel FTA (2013), Art. 13.3.d.

[89] E.g. UAE–Portugal BIT (2011), Art. 10; Saint Vincent and the Grenadines–Taiwan BIT (2009), Art. XIII; Canada–Romania BIT (2009), Art. XIV.

[90] E.g. Bosnia and Herzegovina–San Marino BIT (2011), Art. 12; Albania–Bosnia and Herzegovina BIT (2008), Art. 9; Bosnia and Herzegovina–Lithuania BIT (2007), Art. 10

[91] E.g.: India–Lithuania BIT (2011), Art. 15; Canada–Slovakia BIT (2011), Art. XI; Macedonia–Montenegro BIT (2010), Art. 10.

[92] Armenia–Lithuania BIT (2006), Art. 11.

[93] E.g.: Kazakhstan–Macedonia BIT (2012), Art. 15; Portugal–Serbia BIT (2010), Art. 12; Angola–Russia BIT (2009), Art. 12.

[94] CETA, Art. 8.31.3.

[95] Ewing-Chow and Losari, 'Which Is to Be the Master?', 8–9.

[96] *Pope & Talbot Inc. v. Government of Canada*, UNCITRAL. Award in Respect of Damages, 31 May 2002, para. 52.

Probably, having this context into consideration, in the initial text of the EU–Singapore FTA (2014), a provision was included, establishing that the Committee on Trade in Services, Investment and Government Procurement 'should exercise due restraint in recommending interpretations of any provision already submitted to a tribunal in a dispute between a party and a claimant of the other Party where a final award has yet to be made'.[97]

1 Abstract Interpretation

(a) Direct Interpretation by the Parties

Since early times, IIAs have included provisions that allow contracting parties to express their views on the implementation or operation of the treaty, through diplomatic channels. Usually these clauses also provide that the parties could discuss any matter relating to the interpretation of the agreement. If implemented, these provisions could allow the home state to participate together with the host state if a problem of interpretation of the treaty arises in ISDS.

A direct interpretation is provided in 135 IIAs that have been signed in the last fifteen years, mostly through a mechanism whereby the parties agree to consult promptly, on the request of either, to resolve any disputes or to discuss any matter relating to the interpretation of the treaty. Provisions of joint interpretation by the parties are present predominantly in BITs, although some FTAs[98] and RITs[99] also include this feature. Notably, some FTAs concluded by NAFTA countries also provide for this type of interpretation, in addition to the institutionalized interpretation by a treaty body (as in NAFTA).[100]

Seemingly, the first investment treaty that included this feature was the 1983 Senegal–US BIT:[101]

> The Parties agree to consult promptly, on the request of either, to resolve any disputes in connection with the Treaty, or to discuss any matter relating to the interpretation or application of the Treaty, including any

---

[97] EU–Singapore FTA (October 2014), Art. 9.22.3.1. This provision is not in found in Art. 3.13 of the EU-Singapore Investment Protection Agreement (April 2018).

[98] E.g. Korea–New Zealand FTA (2015), Art. 10.25.1-2; Korea–Vietnam FTA (2015), Art. 9.24.1; Japan Switzerland ECA (2009), Art. 137; EEC (2008), Art. 11.

[99] CACM Agreement on Investment and Trade Services (2002), Art. 3.33.2. CACM member states are Costa Rica, El Salvador, Guatemala, Honduras and Nicaragua.

[100] E.g. Panama–US FTA (2007), Art. 20.1; Colombia–US FTA (2006), Art. 21.1; Peru–US FTA (2006), Art. 21.1.

[101] Senegal–US BIT (1983), Art. VI.

matter or procedures, adjudicatory decisions, or policies of one Party that pertain to or affect investments of nationals or companies of the other Party.

Several BITs concluded afterwards by the United States provide for this type of interpretation via consultation or cooperation between the contracting parties. This mechanism is included in the United States' BITs with Haiti, the Democratic Republic of Congo, Morocco, Turkey, Bangladesh, Grenada, Tunisia, Sri Lanka, the Czech Republic, Slovakia, Argentina, Kazakhstan, Romania, Armenia and Bulgaria.[102]

The United States continues to include these provisions in its recent BITs, with a more specific focus on treaty interpretation. Both the 2004 US Model BIT and the current version (of 2012), establish that a joint decision of the parties declaring their interpretation of a provision of the treaty shall be binding on a tribunal and any decision or award issued by a tribunal must be consistent with that joint decision.[103] The same provision is found in the United States' BITs with Uruguay and Rwanda.[104]

In the IIAs concluded in the last fifteen years, in which a direct joint interpretation by the contracting parties is provided for, in the majority of the cases it is included indirectly, as a part of a consultation or cooperation mechanism, and therefore is not necessarily binding on the parties or a tribunal.[105] Only in certain treaties is joint interpretation explicitly included with a binding character,[106] usually as part of the governing law of the agreement and therefore binding on the ISDS tribunals.[107] However, these two types of interpretation are not exclusive, as several IIAs include both kinds of provisions.[108]

Although provisions on joint interpretation by the contracting parties are commonly applicable to the treaty in general, some IIAs provide for interpretation on specific issues. For example, under the India–Mexico BIT, both states agree to consult each other on having a joint

---

[102] E.g. Haiti–US BIT (1983), Art. VI; Democratic Republic of Congo–US BIT (1984), Art. VI; Morocco–US BIT (1985), Art. V.

[103] US Model BIT (2004) (2012), Art. 30.3.

[104] Uruguay–US BIT (2005), Art. 30.3; Rwanda–US BIT (2008), Art. 30.3.

[105] E.g. Colombia–Singapore BIT (2013), Art. 22; Russia–Uzbekistan BIT (2013), Art. 10; Haiti–Spain BIT (2012), Art. 13.

[106] Canada–Czech Republic BIT (2009), Art. X(6).

[107] E.g. Korea–Turkey Investment Agreement (2015), Art. 1.17.16; Korea–New Zealand FTA (2015), Art. 10.25.1-2; Burkina Faso–Canada BIT (2015), Arts. 34.1, 40(b).

[108] E.g. Canada–Côte d'Ivoire BIT (2014), Arts. 32, 38.2(b); Canada–Mali BIT (2014), Arts. 32, 38.2(b); Canada–Senegal BIT (2014), Arts. 33, 39.2(b).

interpretation on the article on expropriation (Article 7) at any time after the entry into force of the agreement.[109] There is usually no timeframe in which to reach a joint interpretation of the treaty by the parties, but some recent agreements provide for a period of sixty days.[110] In any case, the absence of agreement does not have a specific assigned effect.

(b) Interpretation by a Treaty Body

An interpretation of an IIA by a treaty body created in the same agreement is provided for in fifty-four IIAs signed in the last fifteen years. Several of these provisions derive from Article 1131(2) of NAFTA, which establishes that an interpretation by the FTC of a provision of the treaty shall be binding on a tribunal established under Chapter 11 of NAFTA, being considered as part of the governing law of the dispute.

NAFTA's FTC has the aim of 'clarifying' and 'reaffirming' the meaning of its provisions,[111] and in fact preventing expansive interpretations by arbitral tribunals, departing from what contracting parties originally agreed. According to Coe, the drafters of NAFTA anticipated unacceptable departures from their intended meaning of the treaty, and for that reason retained for themselves the prerogative of interpreting the text conclusively.[112]

The drafting of NAFTA granting interpretative powers to the FTC was replicated by its member states in the negotiation of later FTAs with investment chapters in the subsequent decade. Mexico included this feature in its FTAs with Colombia and Venezuela, Bolivia, Nicaragua, Chile and Uruguay.[113] While the United States included it in its FTAs with Singapore and Chile,[114] Canada did so in its FTAs with Chile and Costa Rica.[115]

---

[109] India–Mexico BIT (2007), Art. 29(2).
[110] Korea–New Zealand FTA (2015), Art. 10.25.1-2; Canada–Guinea BIT (2015), Arts. 331.1, 39(b); Canada–Mongolia BIT (2016), Arts. 32.1, 38.2.2
[111] North American Free Trade Agreement (NAFTA) – Free Trade Commission, 'Notes of Interpretation of Certain Chapter 11 Provisions' (July 2001).
[112] J. J. Coe Jr, 'Taking Stock of NAFTA Chapter 11 in Its Tenth Year: An Interim Sketch of Selected Themes, Issues, and Methods', Vabd. J. Transnat'l L., 36 (2003), 1426.
[113] Colombia–Mexico–Venezuela FTA (1995), Art. 20.2; Bolivia–Mexico FTA (1995), Art. 15-32.2; Mexico–Nicaragua FTA (1997), Art. 16-33; Chile–Mexico FTA (1998), Arts. 9–32; Mexico–Uruguay FTA (2003), Arts. 13–31.
[114] Singapore–US FTA (2003) Art. 20.1; Chile–US FTA (2003), Art. 21.1.
[115] Canada–Chile FTA (1996), Arts. N-01 and N-02; Canada–Costa Rica FTA (2001), Arts. XIII.1, XIII.2 and XIII.3.

In the last fifteen years, Mexico has also included FTCs with inter-pretative powers in its FTAs with Japan, Peru, Central America and Panama, and in the Pacific Alliance Protocol.[116] While the United States included this feature in its FTAs with Australia, the Dominican Republic and Central America (CAFTA–DR), Morocco, Oman, Colombia, Panama, Peru and Korea.[117] Canada did so in its FTAs with Colombia, Peru, Panama, Honduras and Korea, as well as in its BITs with Jordan and Benin.[118] It was also included in the TPP.[119]

Some of the countries that concluded IIAs with NAFTA members replicated this feature in their own treaties. That was the case for Chile, Colombia, El Salvador and Honduras.[120] This mechanism is also included in investment chapters of FTAs recently negotiated by the EU with Canada, Vietnam and Singapore,[121] and at least in one BIT con-cluded by the European Free Trade Association (EFTA).[122] However, the interpretation of the agreement by a treaty body is still a salient char-acteristic of NAFTA members' treaties. In fact, some BITs concluded by NAFTA countries even follow that model of 'institutionalized' author-itative interpretations by a treaty body.[123]

Treaty bodies issuing interpretations of IIAs – either joint commis-sions or committees – usually take decisions by mutual agreement or consensus. There is generally no timeframe within which to reach a joint interpretation of the treaty by the parties, although some recent agree-ments provide for a period of ninety days.[124] In any case, the absence of agreement does not have an assigned effect.

---

[116] E.g: Japan–Mexico (2004), Art. 84.2; Mexico–Peru FTA (2011), Arts. 11.29.2. Central America–Mexico FTA (2011), Arts. 11.26.2, 19.1.3.

[117] E.g: Peru–US FTA (2006), Arts. 10.22.3, 20.1; Panama–US FTA (2006), Arts. 10.22.3, 19.1.3.c; Colombia–US FTA (2006), Arts. 10.22.3, 20.1.3.c.

[118] E.g: Canada–Colombia FTA (2008), Art. 832.1; Canada–Peru FTA (2008), Arts. 837.3, 2001; Canada–Panama FTA (2010), Art. 9.32.1.

[119] TPP, Art. 9.24.3.

[120] E.g: Colombia–Northern Triangle FTA (2007), Arts. 12.25, 17.1.3(e); El Salvador–Honduras–Taiwan FTA (2007), Arts. 10.33.3, 14.01.2(d); Chile–China Supplementary Agreement on Investment (2012), Art. 27.

[121] CETA, Arts. 8.31.3, 8.44.3(a) and 26.1.5(e); EU–Vietnam FTA, Ch. 8, Art. 16(4); EU–Singapore IPA (April 2018), Art. 3.13.

[122] EFTA–Korea BIT (2005), Art. 21.

[123] E.g: Kyrgyzstan–US BIT (1993), Art. V; Canada–Venezuela BIT (1996), Art. XII.7; Mexico–Korea BIT (2000), Art. 14.2.

[124] Australia–China FTA (2015), Arts. 9.7.3(b), 9.18.2; Chile–Hong Kong Investment Agreement (2016), Art. 29.2; Argentina–Chile FTA (2017), Art. 8.36.2.

2   Intra-Arbitral Interpretation

As mentioned, some IIAS provide for a mechanism of referral (or *renvoi*) to the contracting parties of the treaty, or to a treaty body, regarding general or specific issues of interpretation of the treaty.

In this mechanism, the interpretation of such sensitive provisions returns to the contracting parties, which retain the facility for direct or indirect authoritative treaty interpretation – a task that was originally delegated to the arbitral tribunals constituted under the IIA. *Renvoi* is usually triggered when the interpretation of certain questions explicitly defined in the treaty is invoked as a defence by the respondent state in a specific arbitration.[125]

We find at least three different types of *renvoi* mechanisms in the IIAs concluded in the past fifteen years: firstly, for the general interpretation of any IIA provisions; secondly, for the interpretation of reservations, exceptions, or NCMs; and, thirdly, for the interpretation of provisions on financial measures.

(a)   General *Renvoi*

From the sample of investment treaties concluded in the last fifteen years, only eight IIAs include general *renvoi* for intra-arbitral interpretation of any provision of the IIA, by the contracting parties or a treaty body.[126]

A binding intra-arbitral interpretation could be done by a joint commission or other treaty body established in the IIA with representatives of the contracting parties. In the last fifteen years, this type of interpretation has been included in the investment chapters of the Mexican FTAs with Japan and Peru and in the Mexican BITs with Chile and Uruguay.[127] Similarly, in the Canada–Chile FTA and in the TPP, the FTC has been granted general interpretative powers.[128] In all these agreements, the commission shall submit in writing any decision declaring its interpretation to the tribunal within a strict timeframe (within sixty days from the request), and if it fails to do so, the tribunal shall decide the issue.

Some IIAs require the arbitral tribunal to request a joint interpretation of a treaty provision that is in dispute 'by the parties', even if there is

---

[125] T. H. Yen, *The Interpretation of Investment Treaties* (Martinus Nijhoff Publishers, 2014), p. 254.

[126] Japan–Mexico FTA (2004), Art. 84; China–New Zealand FTA (2008), Art. 155; New Zealand–Malaysia FTA (2009), Art. 10.26.

[127] Mexico–Japan FTA (2004), Art. 84; Chile–Mexico FTA (1998), Art. 9-32.2; Mexico–Uruguay FTA (2003), Art. 13-31.2.

[128] Canada–Chile FTA (1996), Arts. N-01 and N-02; TPP, Art. 9.24.3.

a treaty body that could perform that task, such as a joint committee.[129] This provision is included in the Malaysian FTAs with India and New Zealand, and in the China–New Zealand FTA.[130] In all these treaties if the contracting parties fail to submit an interpretation in writing within a specific time – usually sixty days from the date of the request – the tribunal shall decide the issue.[131] We find similar provisions in IIAs concluded in the decade that preceded our analysis, such as the Mexican IIAs with Netherlands and Portugal.[132]

Usually, general *renvoi* is triggered a request of the respondent state, but in some treaties this power is also given to the tribunal on its own account,[133] or even at the request of the investor.[134]

(b)   Interpretation of Reservations, Exceptions or NCMs

Several recent IIAs include a specific *renvoi* procedure for the interpretation of reservations, exceptions or NCMs of the treaty, usually contained in annexes of the same agreement. This interpretation is generally in the power of a treaty body (mostly in FTAs) or the contracting parties (in some BITs).

Article 1132 of NAFTA provides that where a disputing party asserts as a defence that the measure alleged to be a breach is within the scope of a reservation or exception set out in NAFTA Annexes, the tribunal shall request the interpretation of the FTC on the issue. Within sixty days of delivery of the request, the commission shall submit to the tribunal its written interpretation, which shall be binding. If the FTC fails to submit an interpretation within sixty days, the tribunal shall decide the issue.

The experience of NAFTA has been taken into consideration by its member states in other IIAS. After NAFTA, the United States granted

---

[129] M. Feldman, 'Joint Interpretation under a Divided TPP Investment Chapter' in W. Shan and J. Su (eds.), *China and International Investment Law: Twenty Years of ICSID Membership* (Martinus Nijhoff Publishers, 2014), pp. 408–28 p. 416.

[130] India–Malaysia ECA (2011), Art. 10.14.21-22; New Zealand–Malaysia FTA (2009), Art. 10.26; China–New Zealand FTA (2008), Art. 155.

[131] E.g. New Zealand–Taiwan ECA (2013), Ch. 12, Art. 24. Ch. 22, Art. 2.2.(f); ASEAN–Australia–New Zealand FTA (2009), Art. 27.2-3; ASEAN Comprehensive Investment Agreement (2009), Art. 40.2-3.

[132] Mexico–Netherlands BIT (1998), App., Art. 8; Mexico–Portugal BIT (1999), Art. 15.2.

[133] E.g. India–Malaysia ECA (2011), Art. 10.14.21-22; New Zealand–Malaysia FTA (2009), Art. 10.26; ASEAN–Australia–New Zealand FTA (2009), Art. 27.2-3.

[134] India–Malaysia ECA (2011), Art. 10.14.21-22; New Zealand–Malaysia FTA (2009), Art. 10.26.

interpretative powers to the FTCs for the interpretation of reservations and exceptions included in the annexes of the FTAs with Singapore and Chile.[135] In the last fifteen years, the United States has continued to include this feature in its FTAs such as CAFTA-DR and those with Morocco, Oman, Colombia, Panama, Peru and Korea.[136] Canada replicated this model in its FTAs concluded with Chile[137] and has included it in its FTAs with Colombia, Peru, Panama, Honduras and Korea.[138] A similar provision was included in the 2004 Canada model foreign investment promotion and protection agreement (FIPA), leaving the interpretation to a commission comprising cabinet-level representatives of the parties or their designees, and it is found in its BITs with Peru and Jordan.[139] Mexico included this feature in its FTAs with Colombia and Venezuela, Bolivia, Nicaragua, Chile, Uruguay, Japan, Peru, Central America and Panama, and the Pacific Alliance Protocol.[140]

However, the influence of NAFTA in this regard goes beyond its contracting parties and, in the following decade, other countries have also included a procedure of interpretation of exceptions, reservations or NCMs via a treaty body, such as the Central American Common Market (CACM), which includes this provision,[141] and some other IIAs concluded by Latin American countries, which are mainly FTAs.[142]

Of the IIAs signed in the last fifteen years, fifty-two include provisions on intra-arbitral joint interpretation of reservations and exceptions. The majority are included in the investment chapters of FTAs (thirty-five treaties) providing for the interpretation by a joint commission or committee on investment. In all these treaties, if the respondent state asserts, as a defence, that a challenged measure is within the scope of reservations, exceptions or NCMs, the tribunal has a duty to request the

---

[135] Singapore-US FTA (2003) Art. 15.22, Chile-US FTA (2003), Art. 10.22.
[136] E.g. CAFTA-DR (2004), Art. 10.23; Morocco-US FTA (2004), Art. 10.22; Oman-US FTA (2006), 10.22.
[137] Canada-Chile FTA (1996), Art. G-33.
[138] E.g. Canada-Colombia FTA (2008), Art. 832.2; Canada-Peru FTA (2008), Art. 838; Canada-Panama FTA (2010), Art. 9.32.2.
[139] Canada Model FIPA (2004), Art. 41; Canada-Peru BIT (2006), Art. 41; Canada-Jordan BIT (2009), Art. 41.
[140] E.g. Colombia-Mexico-Venezuela FTA (1995), Annex 17-16, Rule 11; Bolivia-Mexico FTA (1994), Art. 15-33; Mexico-Nicaragua FTA (1997), Art. 16-34.
[141] CACM Agreement on Investment and Trade Services (2002), Art. 3.34.
[142] In Colombia-Peru BIT (2007), Art. 28, a bilateral treaty commission has the duty of issuing these interpretations.

interpretation of the respective provision or annex by the respective treaty body.[143] Only if the treaty body fails to submit an interpretation within a short period (which in almost all treaties is sixty days from the date of the request), the tribunal shall decide the issue.[144] However, this does not mean that the parties are obliged to convene to discuss the issue. The Panama–Singapore FTA clarifies that a request by a tribunal to make a joint interpretation of a provision shall not be construed as requiring the convening of a session of the treaty body of the agreement ('Administrative Commission').[145]

In FTAs with more than two contracting parties, some agreements provide that the interpretation adopted by the treaty body, will be binding only with respect to the parties that had adopted the decision.[146]

Some BITs also include a similar provision but, in the absence of a joint commission or committee, the authoritative interpretation is made directly by the contracting parties. This feature has been included largely in the Canadian BITs with Kuwait, China, Côte d'Ivoire, Serbia, Nigeria, Cameroon, Guinea, Burkina Faso, Hong Kong and Mongolia.[147] It is also included in the United States' BITs with Rwanda and Uruguay, as well as in the US Model BITs of 2004 and 2012, and in the 2010 Chile–Uruguay BIT.[148] In all these treaties, when a respondent state asserts, as a defence, that a measure alleged to be a breach is within the scope of an annex of the treaty, the tribunal shall request the interpretation of the contracting parties on the issue. The contracting parties shall submit to the tribunal, in writing, any joint decision declaring their interpretation within sixty days of delivery of the request that shall be binding on a tribunal. If the parties fail to issue such a decision within that period, the tribunal shall decide the issue.

---

[143] E.g. Korea–Vietnam FTA (2015), Art. 9.24.2; Honduras–Peru FTA (2015), Art. 12.24; Colombia–Panama FTA (2013), Art. 14.31.2.

[144] Under the Australia–China FTA (2015), Arts. 9.19.2 and 9.19.3, and in the TPP, Art. 9.25, the Committee on Investment has a timeframe of ninety days within which to issue a binding interpretation of annexes or NCMs.

[145] Panama–Singapore FTA (2006), Art. 17.3.

[146] Mexico–Central America FTA (2011), Art. 19.1.9.

[147] E.g. Canada–Kuwait BIT (2011), Art. 32.2; Canada–China BIT (2012), Arts. 8, 30.2 and Annex B8; Canada–Côte d'Ivoire BIT (2014), Art. 32.2.

[148] Rwanda–US BIT (2008), Art. 31; Uruguay–US BIT (2005), Art. 31; US Model BIT 2004 and 2012, Art. 31; Chile–Uruguay BIT (2010), Art. 24.

(c) Financial Measures

In the last fifteen years, we find eighteen IIAs with a special *renvoi* mechanism on financial measures, with a referral to the contracting parties for interpretation, mainly concluded by Canada and Peru.

Canada has included one in its BITs with Côte d'Ivoire, Mali, Senegal, Serbia, Nigeria, Cameroon, Tanzania, Benin, Kuwait, Jordan, Romania, Latvia and Peru.[149] These agreements apply the referral procedure where an investor submits a claim to arbitration and the respondent state invokes certain exceptions with respect to financial measures: (i) limitations of transfers by a financial institution relating to maintenance of the safety, soundness, integrity or financial responsibility of financial institutions; (ii) reasonable measures for prudential reasons;[150] and (iii) measures of general application taken by a public entity in pursuit of monetary and related credit or exchange rate policies.

At the request of the respondent state, the tribunal shall require a report in writing from the contracting parties on the issue of whether, and to what extent, the invoked defences are valid in the claim of the investor. The tribunal may not proceed pending receipt of this report. If the parties cannot agree on the report, they can submit the issue to an arbitral panel established in accordance with the ISDS procedures of the agreement. Only if, after seventy days from the referral, no request for the establishment of a state-to-state panel has been received, the arbitral tribunal may decide the matter.

In these IIAs, the expertise qualifications are shifted to the arbitrators, establishing that where an investor or respondent party claims that a dispute involving measures relating to financial institutions or exceptions in this regard are invoked, the arbitrators shall have experience in financial services law or practice. Unfortunately, these treaties do not clarify what happens if the members of the tribunal were appointed prior to one of the issues in the proceedings arising.

The same type of *renvoi* that is included in the abovementioned Canadian BITs is provided for in the Colombia–Peru BIT.[151] However,

---

[149] E.g. Canada–Côte d'Ivoire BIT (2014), Art. 22; Canada–Mali BIT (2014), Art. 22; Canada–Senegal BIT (2014), Art. 23.

[150] These measures typically include those (i) directed to protect investors, depositors, financial market participants, policyholders, policyclaimants, or persons to whom a fiduciary duty is owed by a financial institution; (ii) to maintain the safety, soundness, integrity or financial responsibility of financial institutions; and (iii) to ensure the integrity and stability of a party's financial system.

[151] Colombia–Peru BIT (2007), Art. 23.

other Peruvian IIAs have adopted a slightly different approach. In the Peruvian FTAs with Costa Rica, Guatemala, Panama and Honduras, if the respondent state invokes, as a defence, certain 'prudential measures' – those directed at safeguarding the balance of payments, and preventing or delaying a transfer or payment under certain domestic laws – the tribunal shall request interpretation by the contracting parties of the validity of such defence. If, after ninety days from the request, there is no joint agreement, the tribunal can decide the issue on its own.[152]

However, *renvoi* is not the only mechanism that is provided for to deal with sensitive financial measures. In several IIAs, a referral to technical authorities of the contracting parties is provided for as an alternative, as will be explained later. A few treaties provide for both mechanisms. This is the case in the Peru–Panama FTA, which contemplates *renvoi* to the contracting parties for the analysis of defences based on 'prudential measures' to safeguard the balance of payments,[153] and to a committee of financial services (integrated by authorities responsible of financial services of the contracting parties), to examine the validity of defences based on other prudential measures, such as those adopted to maintain the safety, soundness, integrity or financial responsibility of individual financial institutions or cross-border financial service providers, or other exceptions in the treaty referring to financial measures.[154]

Some detail on the procedure of how the parties or the committees of financial services work would be interesting to examine, in order to determine whether they have similar or different methods of interpretation, but both *renvoi* procedures and technical referrals have not yet been widely used in ISA, to be able to make such a comparison.[155]

3   The Effective Use of Joint Interpretations

While the number of IIAs including provisions on joint interpretations has increased substantially in the last fifteen years, greatly improving the control of states over the treaties that they have concluded, until now, home and host states have often refrained from using this mechanism. According to UNCTAD states have 'largely neglected their role in

---

[152]   E.g. Guatemala–Peru FTA (2011), Art. 12.19; Panama–Peru FTA (2011), Art. 12.19; Costa Rica–Peru FTA (2011), Art. 12.19.

[153]   Panama–Peru FTA (2011), Art. 12.19

[154]   Ibid., Arts. 14.11, 14.18.

[155]   Alschner, 'The Return of the Home State', 321.

interpreting IIAs. Instead, they left the task of giving meaning to treaty provisions solely to arbitral tribunals'.[156]

In fact, the more active treaties in this regard are from the 1990s (NAFTA, the Canada–Chile FTA and the Argentina–Panama BIT) and joint interpretation procedures under these treaties only took place in the 2000s. Sometimes a joint interpretation has not been requested, even in cases in which it would have been needed. For example, in *Mobil* v. *Canada*, the respondent state unsuccessfully contended that the challenged measure fell within the scope of its NAFTA reservations. However, Canada did not refer the question to the FTC for a binding interpretation pursuant to Article 1132.[157]

One of the reasons given in explanation for joint interpretations being harder to find is that contracting parties might lack sufficient commonality of interest to reach such agreements, when, in most cases, one state has only defended cases, and the other has only had its nationals bringing claims. NAFTA is unusual in this regard, because all the parties have been respondents, and nationals of all contracting states have brought claims – even between developed countries.[158]

Another explanation relates to the fact that, even if states use that power, nothing guarantees that arbitral tribunals will always follow such interpretations. Some NAFTA tribunals have challenged the letter and the spirit of the FTC's interpretations and thereby undermined its real effectiveness,[159] as will be analysed in the next section.

However, the possibility that home and host states agree on interpretations of an IIA is always latent. The question that this book tries to answer is whether the effective use of this mechanism would imply the return of a classic or an updated form of diplomatic protection, or whether the home state would mainly support governmental interests in the interpretation of the provision that has triggered the *renvoi* by the host state, and not the defence or assistance of its claimant investor.

---

[156] UNCTAD, 'Interpretation of IIAs: What States Can Do', 3.
[157] *Mobil Investments Canada Inc. and Murphy Oil Corp.* v. *Canada*, ICSID Case No ARB(AF)/07/4, Canada's Counter-Memorial 1 December 2009, paras. 214–40. Alschner, 'The Return of the Home State', 323.
[158] Roberts, 'Power and Persuasion', 224.
[159] For example, tribunals in the cases Pope & Talbot, Mondev, ADF, and Merrill & Ring interpreted customary international law broadly by emphasizing its evolutionary character, going at least implicitly, beyond the FTC interpretation on NAFTA Art. 1105. P. Dumberry, *The Fair and Equitable Treatment Standard: A Guide to NAFTA Case Law on Article 1105* (Kluwer Law International, 2013), pp. 313–14.

(a)   NAFTA Free Trade Commission Interpretations

In 2001, the NAFTA FTC, using Article 1131(2), issued a note of interpretation that dealt with two topics that had been controversial in early ISDS cases under that treaty: Firstly, to interpret Article 1120(2) of NAFTA with respect to access to documents, declaring that nothing in the treaty precluded the parties from providing public access to documents submitted to, or issued by, an ISDS tribunal constituted under Chapter 11 of NAFTA, with the exception of confidential business information, privileged information and information that a party must withhold pursuant to the relevant arbitral rules. Secondly, to clarify and reaffirm the meaning of Article 1105(1) – limiting the scope of the fair and equitable treatment (FET) and full protection and security (FPS) standards as not requiring treatment in addition to or beyond that required by the customary international law minimum standard of treatment of aliens, and that a breach of another provision of the NAFTA, or of a separate international agreement, does not establish that there has been a breach of Article 1105(1).[160]

The second part of this note proved to be controversial, as an interpretation was issued by the FTC in reaction to three controversial rulings rendered by NAFTA arbitral tribunals in 2000–1: *Metalclad* v. *Mexico*,[161] *S. D. Myers* v. *Canada*,[162] and *Pope & Talbot* v. *Canada*.[163] As Dumberry mentions, the first two paragraphs of the note were aimed at overruling the award on merits in *Pope & Talbot*, holding that the FET standard should be considered only in addition to the international minimum standard of treatment. They also intended to address the expanding interpretation of the tribunal in *Metalclad* that the FET standard included an obligation of transparency. The third paragraph of the note corrected the reasoning of the *S. D. Myers* partial award that a breach of one provision of NAFTA's Chapter 11 could create a breach of another provision.[164]

The FTC interpretation generated divergent and spirited views among tribunals and commentators.[165] The FTC note was criticized as an

---

[160] North American Free Trade Agreement (NAFTA) – Free Trade Commission, 'Notes of Interpretation of Certain Chapter 11 Provisions'.

[161] *Metalclad Corp.* v. *United Mexican States*, ICSID Case No ARB(AF)/97/1, Award, 30 August 2000.

[162] *S. D. Myers, Inc.* v. *Government of Canada*, UNCITRAL, Partial Award, 13 November 2000.

[163] *Pope & Talbot Inc.* v. *Government of Canada*, UNCITRAL. Award on the Merits of Phase 2, 10 April 2001.

[164] Dumberry, *The Fair and Equitable Treatment Standard*, p. 310.

[165] Coe Jr, 'Taking Stock of NAFTA Chapter 11 in Its Tenth Year', 1429.

opportunistic method put in place by the parties in order to avoid liability in ongoing arbitration cases, acting as both party and rule-maker in these proceedings.[166] In fact, the FTC adopted the minority's view in *S. D. Myers* v. *Canada* partial award, in which the dissenting arbitrator, Bryan Schwartz, was not fully convinced that transparency was part of the IMS,[167] and the partially dissenting opinion of Edward Chiasson held that breach of another provision of the NAFTA is not a basis for finding a breach of Article 1105.[168] The same proposition – that the FET standard should be reduced to the customary international law minimum standard – was later adopted in the new 2004 US Model BIT.[169]

Nevertheless, this joint interpretation has mostly been considered to be an 'authoritative statement' of the governing law of the treaty by subsequent tribunals. In *Methanex* v. *United States*,[170] the tribunal held that the note is a subsequent agreement falling under Article 31(3)(a) of the VCLT, given the definitive meaning of Article 1105.[171] The tribunals in *Loewen* v. *United States*,[172] *Glamis* v. *United States*,[173] *UPS* v. *Canada*,[174] *Cargill* v. *Mexico*,[175] *Chemtura* v. *Canada*,[176] *Grand River* v. *United States*,[177] and *Thunderbird* v. *Mexico*,[178] recognized the binding nature of such interpretations, and the tribunal in *ADF* v. *United States*[179] showed an even greater degree of deference, stating that no more authentic and authoritative source of instruction is possible.[180] A lighter

---

[166] Dumberry, *The Fair and Equitable Treatment Standard*, p. 311.

[167] *S. D. Myers, Inc.* v. *Government of Canada*, UNCITRAL, Separate Opinion by Dr Bryan Schwartz, 13 November 2000, para. 255.

[168] *Pope & Talbot* v. *Canada*, Award on the Merits of Phase 2, para. 267.

[169] US Model BIT (2004), Art. 5(1).

[170] *Methanex Corp.* v. *United States of America*, UNCITRAL, Final Award of the Tribunal on Jurisdiction and Merits, 3 August 2005, pt. II, ch. H, para. 23.

[171] Dumberry, *The Fair and Equitable Treatment Standard*, p. 311.

[172] *Loewen Group* v. *US*, Award, paras. 126–8.

[173] *Glamis Gold, Ltd* v. *United States of America*, UNCITRAL, Award, 8 June 2009, para. 599.

[174] *United Parcel Service of America Inc.* v. *Government of Canada*, UNCITRAL, Award on Jurisdiction, 22 November 2002, para. 96.

[175] *Cargill, Inc.* v. *Mexico*, Award, para. 268.

[176] *Chemtura Corp.* v. *Government of Canada*, UNCITRAL (formerly *Crompton Corp.* v. *Government of Canada*), Award, 2 August 2010, para. 120.

[177] *Grand River Enterprises Six Nations, Ltd et al.* v. *United States of America*, UNCITRAL, Award, 12 January 2011, para. 175.

[178] *International Thunderbird Gaming Corp.* v. *United Mexican States*, UNCITRAL, Award, 26 January 2006, paras. 192–3.

[179] *ADF Group Inc.* v. *United States of America*, ICSID Case No ARB (AF)/00/1, Award, 9 January 2003, para. O.177.

[180] Alschner, 'The Return of the Home State', 318.

approach was taken in *Mondev* v. *United States*, as the award considered that the FTC note contained relevant 'clarifications'.[181]

Some tribunals have undermined the effectiveness of the FTC note, following two different sets of arguments. Firstly, some have held that the level of protection offered to foreign investors under Article 1105 of NAFTA is superior to the minimum standard of treatment under customary international law, which is considered an 'evolving and flexible concept',[182] and that the FTC's Notes of Interpretation cannot be taken to mean that a NAFTA tribunal must entirely disregard the terms 'fair and equitable' and 'full protection and security' when considering whether the customary international law standard of treatment set out in the provision has been met.[183]

Secondly, certain tribunals[184] have taken the position that the FET standard has become some kind of customary international law rule in and of itself.[185] Nevertheless, in recent years, the controversy about the FTC's Note of Interpretation has diminished, and most NAFTA tribunals have now accepted it, partly because NAFTA expressly empowered the FTC to issue binding interpretations.

In fact, some argue that the narrow joint interpretation of the FET standard has benefited the NAFTA contracting parties, as, in the majority of the recent claims brought under Chapter 11, tribunals have found in favour of investors on their FET claims 22 per cent of the time, in contrast with non-NAFTA cases in which the investor alleged a breach of the FET obligation, and in which tribunals have found that the host state violated that standard in 62 per cent of cases.[186]

---

[181] *Mondev International Ltd* v. *United States of America*, ICSID Case No ARB(AF)/99/2, Award, 11 October 2002, paras. 121–2.

[182] *Merrill & Ring Forestry L.P.* v. *Government of Canada*, UNCITRAL, ICSID Administered Case, Award 31 March 2010, paras. 192–4, the tribunal adverts that the binding character of the FTC interpretation does not mean that necessarily reflects the current state of customary and international law.

[183] *Mesa Power Group, LLC* v. *Government of Canada*, UNCITRAL, PCA Case No 2012-17, Award, 24 March 2016, para. 357.

[184] *Pope & Talbot Inc.* v. *Canada*, Award on the Merits of Phase 2, para. 118. The tribunal interpreted Art. 1105 to require that 'covered investors and investments receive the benefits of the fairness elements under ordinary standards applied in the NAFTA countries, without any threshold limitation that the conduct complained of be "egregious", "outrageous" or "shocking", or otherwise "extraordinary"'.

[185] Dumberry, *The Fair and Equitable Treatment Standard*, pp. 312–13.

[186] L. Johnson and M. Razbaeva, 'State Control Over Treaty Interpretation' (2014) p. 5. These percentages where calculated using UNCTAD's statistics of investment treaty cases decided by October 2010.

A second group of interpretations of NAFTA's FTC, made by a series of statements on 7 October 2003, was less conflictive. The first statement on date was issued on 'Notices of Intent to Submit a Claim to Arbitration',[187] aimed at providing a standard format for these notifications. However, the text only recommends its use to investors, as a legal obligation in this respect could be created only by an amendment to NAFTA.[188] The second FTC statement was on non-disputing party participation, allowing *amicus curiae* submissions both on law and on facts.[189] Mexico had initially opposed the admission of *amicus curiae* submissions in the *Methanex*[190] and *UPS* cases,[191] on the ground that their participation was not expressly included in NAFTA texts and that this institution was not accepted under Mexican domestic law. The FTC note brought Mexico into a consensus of the three NAFTA parties on this topic – a change that was applauded.[192]

A sort of third statement was made only unilaterally by Canada[193] and the United States on 7 October 2003,[194] affirming that they would consent, and request the consent of disputing investors and tribunals, to hearings being open to the public in every investor–state dispute, except to guarantee the protection of confidential information. Mexico joined this position in July 2004, during a formal meeting of the FTC,[195] creating some kind of protracted consensus on this issue. The practice of the large majority of NAFTA's Chapter 11 tribunals has generally accepted that non-disputing parties are allowed to attend the hearings, even when they have been *in camera*.[196] One exception arose in the case *Detroit*

---

[187] NAFTA Free Trade Commission, 'Statement of the Free Trade Commission on Notices of Intent to Submit a Claim to Arbitration' (2003).

[188] H. Mann, 'The Free Trade Commission Statements of October 7, 2003, on NAFTA's Chapter 11: Never-Never Land or Real Progress?' (2003) p. 2.

[189] NAFTA Free Trade Commission, 'Statement of the Free Trade Commission on Non-Disputing Party Participation' (2004).

[190] *Methanex Corp. v. United States of America*, UNCITRAL, Decision of the Tribunal on Petitions from Third Persons to Intervene as '*amici curiae*', 15 January 2001, para. 9.

[191] *United Parcel Service of America Inc. v. Government of Canada*, UNCITRAL, First Mexican 1128 Submission, 11 June 2001.

[192] Mann, 'The Free Trade Commission Statements of October 7, 2003, on NAFTA's Chapter 11: Never-Never Land or Real Progress?', p. 3.

[193] Canada, 'Statement of Canada on Open Hearings in NAFTA Chapter Eleven Arbitrations' (2003).

[194] United States, 'Statement on Open Hearings in NAFTA Chapter Eleven Arbitrations'.

[195] NAFTA Free Trade Commission, '2004 NAFTA Commission Meeting – Joint Statement, San Antonio 16 July 2004' (July 2004).

[196] *Eli Lilly and Co v. Government of Canada*. Government of Canada Submission on Procedural Issues, 2 May 2014, p. 46.

International Bridge Co v. *Canada*, in which the arbitral tribunal – under UNCITRAL Arbitration Rules – held that, because the confidentiality order did not specifically refer to the presence of non-disputing parties at the hearings, and those hearings are *in camera*, non-disputing parties could not be present.[197]

What is more interesting about this second group of interpretations is that they are not binding per se, as their application depends on external factors (such as the position of investors and tribunals and the applicable rules of arbitration). Thus, they could not be equated to a treaty amendment, but to a subsequent agreement or practice by the contracting parties.

(b)   CCFTAC Notes of Interpretation

Outside NAFTA, there has been little public activity by IIA treaty bodies that is specifically related to treaty interpretation. One of the few exceptions is the Canada–Chile Free Trade Agreement Commission (CCFTAC), which, until now, has issued three notes of interpretation, under the Canada–Chile FTA, which, in this respect, follow the NAFTA model.[198]

The CCFTAC's first note of interpretation (2002) deals with access to documents and the minimum standard of treatment in accordance with international law, in very similar terms to those in the NAFTA FTC's first Note of Interpretation, declaring that nothing in the treaty imposes a general duty of confidentiality on the disputing parties to an ISDS arbitration – with the exceptions of confidential, privileged and other information that the party must withhold pursuant to the relevant arbitral rules. The note reiterates that the customary international law minimum standard of treatment is the minimum to be afforded to the investments of investors of another party, that the concepts of FET and FPS do not require treatment in addition to or beyond that minimum, and that a breach of another provision of the treaty, or of a separate international agreement, does not establish that there has been a breach of the minimum standard of treatment.[199]

The second Note of Interpretation (2004) refers to non-disputing party participation, declaring that no provision of the Canada–Chile FTA

---

[197] *Detroit International Bridge Co* v. *Government of Canada* (UNCITRAL), Procedural Order N° 6, 18 March 2014, and Procedural Order N° 7, 25 Mar 2014.

[198] Canada–Chile FTA (1996), Art. N-01.2(c).

[199] Canada – Chile Free Trade Commission, 'Notes of Interpretation of Certain Chapter G Provisions' (October 2002).

limits a tribunal's discretion to accept written submissions from a person
or entity that is not a disputing party, establishing a procedure for
applications and submissions in that character, and affirming that both
states will consent, and request the consent of disputing investors and
tribunals, to having open hearings in investor–state cases that ensure the
protection of confidential information.[200]

The third CCFTAC Note of Interpretation deals with indirect expropriation (2010), declaring that the concept of a 'measure tantamount to
nationalization or expropriation'[201] can also be labelled 'indirect expropriation', which results from a measure or series of measures of a party
that has an effect equivalent to direct expropriation without formal
transfer of title or outright seizure. The note further elaborates that
such determination requires a case-by-case, fact-based inquiry that considers several factors, such as the economic impact of the measure, the
extent to which it interferes with distinct and reasonable expectations,
and the character of the measure or series of measures. In addition, it
affirms that 'non-discriminatory measures of a party that are designed
and applied to protect legitimate public welfare objectives, such as health,
safety and the environment', do not constitute indirect expropriations,
except in rare circumstances, such as when they are so severe in the light
of their purposes that they cannot be viewed as having been adopted and
applied in good faith.[202] In issuing this interpretation, the commission
follows, almost verbatim, the 2004 Canada Model FIPA.[203]

The CCFTAC Notes of Interpretation are relevant not only because
they are one of the few examples outside NAFTA of IIA interpretation by
contracting parties, but also because they have been made in a bilateral
context, addressing issues on which NAFTA FTC has not publicly
agreed – such as indirect expropriation – and, more remarkably, that
the interpretation mechanism has been triggered by the interest of the
contracting parties, and not in reaction to a specific arbitration, as, until
now, the Canada–Chile FTA has never been used as the basis for an ISDS
case.

---

[200] Canada – Chile Free Trade Commission, 'Declaration of the Free Trade Commission on
Non-Disputing Party Participation' (November 2004).
[201] Canada–Chile FTA (1996), Art. G-10.
[202] Canada–Chile Free Trade Commission, 'Decision of the Canada–Chile Free Trade
Commission. Interpretation of Article G-10' (April 2010).
[203] Canada, Model Foreign Investment Protection Agreement (FIPA) (2004), Annex
B.13(1).

(c) Joint Interpretative Statements by States

Although the subsequent practice of states could eventually create a subsequent agreement, as recognized in Article 31(3)(b) of the VCLT, outside the institutionalized mechanisms of joint interpretation examined previously, it is rather uncommon that treaty parties reach explicit interpretive agreements, and few tribunals have relied on them, particularly in relation to BITs.[204]

A rare exception is the Argentina–Panama BIT (1996), in which both contracting parties had two series of exchanges of diplomatic notes in 2004, with the purpose of making an 'interpretative agreement', which in some cases was claimed to reflect the treaty-making practice of Argentina.

The first exchange took place in September 2004, in which, through declarations by both parties, Argentina and Panama agreed on the interpretation of several issues:[205]

(i) that the most-favoured nation (MFN) clause in the BIT did not extend to provision on dispute resolution;

(ii) that the choice of forum clause was deemed to have been exercised by the submission to the jurisdiction of the courts of the contracting party in whose territory the investment was made;

(iii) that the provisions agreed in the BIT were not to be considered as having been violated by acts or omissions of a contracting party if such acts or omissions were of general scope and non-discriminatory;

(iv) that the provisions of the BIT regarding expropriation, had been agreed, in the sense that one or a series of non-discriminatory legislative or regulatory acts adopted by a contracting party for the purpose of protecting general welfare objectives, such as public policy, public health, public safety, social, economic, monetary, exchange rate and tax policy, did not constitute direct or indirect expropriation or nationalization or a similar measure and therefore would not be subject to compensation;

---

[204] C. Schreuer and M. Weiniger, 'A Doctrine of Precedent?' in P. Muchlinski, F. Ortino and C. Schreuer (eds.), *The Oxford Handbook of International Investment Law* (Oxford University Press, 2008), pp. 1188–206 at p. 1199.

[205] Acuerdo por Canje de Notas Interpretativo del Convenio entre la República Argentina y la República de Panamá para la Promoción y Protección Recíproca de Inversiones de 1996, 15 September 2004. Translation made by the author.

(v) that the contracting parties understood the provisions on FET, in the sense that they established the minimum standard of treatment of aliens recognized by customary international law; and

(vi) that financial institutions might be subject to coercive measures, such as seizure and execution, in connection with proceedings before a court of the other contracting party, only with respect to obligations by such financial entities on their own.

Argentina and Panama made a second interpretation of their BIT in October 2004, in which both parties declared, with regard to Article 5 of that treaty – on transfer of investment and returns – that 'the temporary adoption of control measures to exchange on a non-discriminatory basis by a Contracting party, does not modify the intention expressed . . ., in the sense of ensuring the transfer of listed investments and returns'.[206]

Interestingly, both joint interpretations were issued right after the decision on jurisdiction in *Siemens v. Argentina* in August 2004, a case in which the tribunal upheld the application of the MFN clause of the Argentina–Germany BIT, to import dispute settlement provisions from the Argentina–Chile BIT.[207] This could be relevant for Argentina, as the Argentina–Panama BIT is very similar to the Argentina–Germany BIT.

Citing the first Argentina-Panama joint interpretation, the tribunal in *National Grid v. Argentina* – a case initiated under the Argentina–UK BIT – held that it had not received 'any evidence that the Argentine Republic adopted similar interpretations of the MFN clause incorporated in the more than 50 bilateral investment treaties concluded with other state parties. While it is possible to conclude from the UK investment treaty practice contemporaneous with the conclusion of the Treaty that the UK understood the MFN clause to extend to dispute resolution, no definite conclusion can be reached regarding the Argentine Republic's position at that time'.[208]

A less substantive joint interpretation – although more important as far as numbers were concerned – took place in 2003, between the United

---

[206] Segundo Acuerdo por canje de Notas Interpretativo del Convenio entre la República Argentina y la República de Panamá para la Promoción y Protección Recíproca de Inversiones de 1996, 19 October 2004. Translation made by the author.

[207] *Siemens AG v. Argentine Republic*, ICSID Case No ARB/02/8, Decision on Jurisdiction, 3 August 2004, paras. 108–10.

[208] *National Grid plc v. Argentine Republic*, UNCITRAL. Decision on Jurisdiction, 20 June 2006 para. 85.

States, and eight European countries with which it had previously signed investment treaties, and they were at that time acceding or candidate countries to the EU. The exchange of diplomatic notes in relation to its BITs signed in the 1990s with Bulgaria, the Czech Republic, Estonia, Latvia, Lithuania, Poland, Romania and Slovakia, was aimed at clarifying specific aspects of these BITs, on the interpretation of both the essential security exception and the restriction on performance requirements, and in order to be consistent with EU law in a way in which these treaties could be maintained in force after the accession process.[209]

This mechanism of interpretation had been agreed after a series of discussions and meetings from mid 2002, by the United States, the acceding and candidate countries, and the European Commission, which had identified, EU measures in certain sectors that raised questions of compatibility in relation to obligations of the acceding and candidate countries in the BITs concluded with the United States.[210]

Another joint interpretative statement using the consultation mechanism of the Czech Republic–Netherlands BIT took place in *CME* v. *Czech Republic*, arriving at a common position between the Dutch and Czech governments in relation to the interpretation of three issues: (i) the correct interpretation of Article 8.6 of the BIT, which specifies the law to be applied by a tribunal in resolving an investment dispute; (ii) the manner in which the BIT should be applied to claims of predecessors of an investment bringing claims in an investment dispute; and (iii) the manner in which the BIT should be applied to investment disputes that had previously been raised by an indirect holder of the same investment of different nationality under a comparable BIT. Representatives of the Netherlands and the Czech Republic held a series of meetings to discuss the issues raised and decided at their last meeting (held in The Hague on 4–5 April 2002), that they had reached 'common positions' on all three issues, which were recorded and signed in agreed minutes dated 1 July 2002.[211] The tribunal used this joint act to support its findings in the final award.[212] This agreement has been criticized as 'post facto

---

[209] Johnson and Razbaeva, 'State Control Over Treaty Interpretation', 6.

[210] US Department of State, 'Understanding Concerning Certain US Bilateral Investment Treaties, signed by the US, the European Commission, and acceding and candidate countries for accession to the European Union' (September 2003).

[211] *CME Czech Republic BV* v. *Czech Republic*, UNCITRAL, Final Award, 14 March 2003, paras. 87–93.

[212] A. Newcombe and L. Paradell, *Law and Practice of Investment Treaties: Standards of Treatment* (Kluwer Law International, 2009), p. 117.

interpretation in favour of the host state', considering that the common position of both contracting parties was adopted after the partial award was issued, and in which the respondent was found liable to the claimant in respect of several violations of the BIT.[213] Kaufmann-Kohler has implied that this interpretation was an example of diplomatic protection, as the prohibition on using diplomatic protection in the UNCITRAL Rules is not applicable, nor was diplomatic protection addressed in the BIT.[214]

Under general international law, joint interpretations could be also made by the contracting parties without an explicit provision in an IIA authorizing them to do so, and they could have authoritative value regardless of their legal form.[215] However, the interpretative value of these interpretations might be questioned if they were not contained in a subsequent agreement or a common understanding by the parties. Exchange of diplomatic notes[216] and common respondent pleadings;[217] have not been considered joint interpretations. Therefore, the coincidence of unilateral statements by contracting parties does not constitute a joint interpretation unless the statements relate to each other and there is evidence that the parties intended them to constitute an agreement.[218]

[213] M. Hunter and A. Barbuk, 'Procedural Aspects of Non-Disputing Party Interventions in Chapter 11 Arbitrations', Asper Review of International Business and Trade Law, 3 (2003), 151 at 157.
[214] Kaufmann-Kohler, 'Non-Disputing State Submissions in Investment Arbitration', 315.
[215] UNCTAD, 'Interpretation of IIAs: What States Can Do', 11.
[216] In Gruslin v. Malaysia, exchanges of 'note verbale' between Malaysia and Belgium, were downplayed by the latter. However, the tribunal considered those notes as a formal communication between states, which, although they did not have the effect of a direct amendment of the treaty, were regarded 'as an enduring and authoritative engagement expressing to the Belgo–Luxemburg Union the manner in which the Respondent regards and applies the terms of the IGA [investment treaty] with regard to investments made in its territory by nationals of the Belgo–Luxemburg Union'. Philippe Gruslin v. Malaysia, ICSID Case No ARB/99/3, Award, 27 November 2000, para. 23.4
[217] The tribunal in Gas Natural v. Argentina dismissed the possibility that the position of Argentina in the case, and the position of Spain (the home state of the investor) as a defendant in another case, could reflect subsequent practice between the parties according to VCLT Art. 31(3)(b). Gas Natural SDG, SA v. Argentine Republic, ICSID Case No ARB/03/10, Decision of the Tribunal on Preliminary Questions on Jurisdiction, 17 June 2005, para. 47, fn 12. For Roberts, legitimate concerns might arise about the validity of these interpretations as respondent states 'might be adopting expedient interpretations to avoid liability in particular cases rather than considered interpretations that they would wish to have general application': Roberts, 'Power and Persuasion', 218.
[218] Fauchald, 'The Legal Reasoning of ICSID Tribunals', 328.

In fact, in the absence of formal proceedings, proving the existence of a joint interpretation can be a difficult and fact-intensive process.[219] In *Aguas del Tunari* v. *Bolivia*,[220] the tribunal rejected the existence of a subsequent practice establishing an agreement between Bolivia and the Netherlands (the home state of the investor), based on the apparent coincidence of certain statements made by Dutch diplomats before their Parliament, with the Bolivian position.[221] In *Sempra* v. *Argentina*, the arbitral tribunal rejected the view that arguments put forward by counsel defending a state, obligated that state, as an expression of a unilateral act,[222] on the basis that counsel have a duty to present the arguments that they deem appropriate to defend their clients' positions, 'and the tribunal cannot presume that intention if it is not expressly stated'.[223]

The existence of joint interpretive statements by states could be the subject of a dispute. In *Sanum* v. *Laos* – a case brought by casino and gaming investors incorporated in Macao – the arbitral tribunal held that the 1993 China–Laos BIT was applicable to Macao, after the handover of the former Portuguese territory to China in 1999.[224] Laos challenged this jurisdictional ruling in the seat of arbitration (Singapore), pursuant to Singapore's International Arbitration Act, based on an exchange of letters between Laos and China (dated 7 and 9 January 2014) that purportedly confirmed that the BIT contracting parties did not intend the treaty to apply to Macao.[225] In a judgment dated 20 January 2015, the High Court of the Republic of Singapore deemed those letters sufficiently persuasive to consider them a subsequent agreement confirming the intention of China and Laos not to extend the BIT to Macao.[226] Although, in this case, the actions of the home state were relevant to the decision of Singapore's High Court, the investment dispute was

---

[219] UNCTAD, 'Interpretation of IIAs: What States Can Do', 11.

[220] *Aguas del Tunari, SA* v. *Republic of Bolivia*, ICSID Case No ARB/02/3, Decision on Respondent's Objections to Jurisdiction, 21 October 2005, para. 262.

[221] Newcombe and Paradell, *Law and Practice of Investment Treaties*, pp. 117–18.

[222] Ibid., p. 118.

[223] *Sempra Energy International* v. *Argentine Republic*, ICSID Case No ARB/02/16, Decisions on Objections to Jurisdiction, 11 May 2005, para. 146.

[224] *Sanum Investments Ltd* v. *Lao People's Democratic Republic*, UNCITRAL, PCA Case No 2013-13, Award on Jurisdiction, 13 December 2013.

[225] L. E. Peterson, 'Singapore Court Rejects Arbitrators' Extension of Chinese Investment Treaty to Macao', January 2015: www.iareporter.com/articles/20150121_1 (accessed 26 January 2018).

[226] *Government of the Lao People's Democratic Republic* v. *Sanum Investment Ltd*, SGHC 15 (High Court of Singapore, Judgment of 20 January 2015).

settled in parallel, by an agreement between the parties dated 15 June 2014.[227]

4   The Nature of Joint State Interpretations in ISDS

We do not find, in joint interpretations, some important elements of the classic definition of 'diplomatic protection'. Firstly, in the majority of cases, joint interpretations take place as an 'abstract' interpretation of the agreement, and generally outside an arbitration process. Thus, the intervention of the host state in this regard could aim to prevent a future dispute over an 'incorrect' interpretation of the agreement, or to clarify 'erroneous' interpretations by previous arbitral tribunals. In these situations, the remedial character of diplomatic protection is therefore absent.[228] Secondly, another element of the diplomatic protection is missing, as neither a respondent state nor a home state can issue a subsequent binding interpretation alone; an agreement of the contracting parties is required for this purpose. There is no direct right of the state of nationality of the investor in this regard.[229]

At least one ISDS case negates the character of diplomatic protection to joint state interpretations. In *Pac Rim* v. *El Salvador* the tribunal discussed whether the consultation mechanism with interpretative features provided for in Article 20.4 of CAFTA–DR[230] constituted a mechanism for diplomatic protection. The claimant suggested that it was, and that therefore such a mechanism was excluded from the arbitral procedure, following Article 27(1)of the ICSID Convention. Contesting the position of the claimant, Costa Rica intervened in an NDSP submission, declaring that such consultations 'are aimed at elucidating Treaty interpretation and application issues between two States Party to it', and not to determine the responsibility of one of the contracting states with regard to a national of another contracting state. Adding that if 'a state Party wish to exercise diplomatic protection of one of its nationals, the consultations under Article 20.4 would not be the appropriate mechanism to do so'.

---

[227] *Sanum Investments Ltd* v. *Lao People's Democratic Republic*, UNCITRAL, PCA Case No 2013-13. Settlement Agreement, 15 June 2014.
[228] C. F. Amerasinghe, *Diplomatic Protection* (Oxford University Press, 2008), p. 37.
[229] International Law Commission, Draft Articles on Diplomatic Protection, Art. 3.
[230] Under CAFTA–DR Art. 20.4, any party 'may request in writing consultations with any other Party with respect to any actual or proposed measure or any other matter that it considers might affect the operation of this Agreement'.

The tribunal accepted the reasoning of Costa Rica's submission, based on Articles 1 and 16 of the ILC Draft Articles on Diplomatic Protection, declaring that such articles distinguish between diplomatic protection and resort to other actions and procedures that can be taken by a state to secure redress for injury suffered as a result of an internationally wrongful act that does not constitute diplomatic protection. In the tribunal's view, the consultation mechanism with interpretative features of CAFTA–DR 'fall short of diplomatic protection under international law'.[231] On the other hand, since Article 27(1) of the ICSID Convention only suspends the right of diplomatic protection, other rights of the states are not affected,[232] including those provided for in IIAs to make consultations, reviews or interpretations of a treaty.

What is, then the true nature of joint state interpretations? Although their effective utilization has been limited, the possible impact of their use has been the subject of a controversial debate among scholars, on both substantive and procedural issues.

On the first group, some fear that states could use joint interpretations to water down protection standards, creating a bias in favour of host states,[233] or to influence proceedings to which they are respondents[234] – a position that Ewing-Chow and Losari have characterized as 'self-serving', implying that states will always act to the detriment of investors.[235] Schreuer and Weiniger believe that joint interpretations – although efficient – have a serious disadvantage, as states will attempt to issue official interpretations to influence pending proceedings to which they are parties.[236]

Other type of substantial criticisms consider that joint interpretations could be amendments in disguise, rather than interpretations.[237] This concern has been voiced particularly in relation to NAFTA's FTC interpretations. Brower believes that the 'Free Trade Commission's purported 'interpretation' of Article 1105 actually constitutes a 'modification', it represents an ultra vires, attempted amendment that has no binding

---

[231] Pac Rim Cayman v. El Salvador, Decision on the Respondent's Jurisdictional Objections, paras. 4.88, 4.89.
[232] M. Paparinskis, 'Investment Arbitration and the Law of Countermeasures', British Yearbook of International Law (2008), 265–352 at 313.
[233] Alschner, 'The Return of the Home State', 318.
[234] R. Dolzer and C, Schreuer, Principles of International Investment Law (Oxford University Press, 2012), p. 35.
[235] Ewing-Chow and Losari, 'Which Is to Be the Master?', 14.
[236] Schreuer and Weiniger, 'A Doctrine of Precedent?', 1201.
[237] Ewing-Chow and Losari, 'Which Is to Be the Master?', 16.

force'.[238] Alvarez and Park have warned that 'the Commission's de facto amendment of NAFTA would imperil the stability and predictability of the investor protection regime'.[239] For Weiler, the NAFTA ministers attempted to amend NAFTA by using interpretative authority to include a view that is 'simply not supported in the text of the provision and reflects neither the current state of IEL nor the broad objectives of NAFTA'.[240]

However, other commentators have a more positive take on joint interpretations by contracting partners. For Van Aaken, the competence retained by states to issue binding interpretations, taking back the delegation to tribunals, has the advantage of flexibility without giving away too much control.[241] Alschner points out that true joint interpretation is likely to strive for moderation, as 'every contracting State has a de facto veto power to prevent any interpretation that goes against its interests'.[242] For Roberts, the subsequent agreements and practice of the treaty parties remain highly relevant, and reaching joint interpretations with other treaty parties is a way for states to take an active role in interpreting their IIAs, generating state practice that tribunals could take into account when interpreting them, in an ongoing 'dialogue' between states and tribunals.[243] Ewing-Chow and Losari believe that it is quite unlikely that host states will always act to the detriment of investors 'because they want to attract them rather than repulse them', and that home states, non-disputing parties, are more likely to act as a safeguard against any potential abuse, considering their own interests as both capital-exporting and capital-importing countries.[244] Methymaki and Tzanakopoulos quickly dismiss the due process concerns, pointing out that states – and not the

---

[238] C. H. Brower, II, 'Investor–State Disputes Under NAFTA: The Empire Strikes Back', *Columbia Journal of Transnational Law*, 40 (2002), 43–88 at 71. See also: C. H. Brower, II, 'Why the FTC Notes of Interpretation Constitute a Partial Amendment of NAFTA Article 1105', *Virginia Journal of International Law*, 46 (2005), 347.

[239] G. Aguilar Álvarez and W. W. Park, 'The New Face of Investment Arbitration: NAFTA Chapter 11', Yale J. Int'l L., 28 (2003), 365 at 398.

[240] T. Weiler, 'NAFTA Investment Law in 2001: As the Legal Order Starts to Settle, the Bureaucrats Strike Back', *The International Lawyer*, 36 (2002), 345–53 at 347.

[241] A. Van Aaken, 'Control Mechanisms in International Investment Law' in Z. Douglas, J. Pauwelyn and J. E. Viñuales (eds.), *The Foundations of International Investment Law: Bringing Theory into Practice* (Oxford University Press, 2014), pp. 409–35 at pp. 428–9.

[242] Alschner, 'The Return of the Home State', 319.

[243] Roberts, 'Power and Persuasion', 185, 194.

[244] Ewing-Chow and Losari, 'Which Is to Be the Master?', 14–15.

tribunal or the investor – are the true masters of the treaty and therefore know exactly where the goalposts of the agreement are.[245]

On the procedural side, joint interpretations have raised some concerns about due process of law, as the 'dual character' of the states – as parties of the investment treaty and as respondent host states – could violate fundamental procedural rights. For Kaufmann-Kohler, although *in abstracto*, interpretative powers are beneficial as they increase predictability, the exercise of such powers may undermine the rule of law, if they are used retroactively to change the governing law in pending proceedings, or are issued without any prior public consultation – including of the claimants – and may violate the principle of equal treatment of parties.[246] In the same vein, Dolzer and Schreuer consider undesirable and incompatible with the principles of fair procedure a mechanism whereby 'a party to a dispute is able to influence the outcome of judicial proceedings, by issuing an official interpretation to the detriment of the other party'.[247] Schreuer elaborates that if a binding interpretation is relevant to pending proceedings, it gives rise to serious concerns about the fairness of the procedure and infringes the independence of the international tribunal.[248]

Desierto has pointed out that binding joint interpretations, and particularly those issued while a case is pending, are not mere 'subsequent agreements' under Article 31(3)(a) of the VLCT, as the arbitral tribunal has to defer to them completely, 'regardless of the actual terms of the joint decision in relation to the treaty text, the relevant applicable law to the treaty, or States' own prior historical practices that evidence their understanding of the treaty standards subject of the joint decision'.[249]

Fauchald objects to the use of joint interpretations because they may reduce the transparency of IIAs, in the sense that 'investors cannot trust that the treaty constitutes the final regulatory framework'.[250] But one can

---

[245] E. Methymaki and A. Tzanakopoulos, 'Masters of Puppets? Reassertion of Control through Joint Investment Treaty Interpretation' in A. Kulick (ed.), *Reassertion of Control Over the Investment Treaty Regime* (2017), pp. 155–81 at p. 180.

[246] Kaufmann-Kohler, 'Interpretive Powers of the Free Trade Commission and the Rule of Law', 187–9.

[247] Dolzer and Schreuer, *Principles of International Investment Law*, p. 35.

[248] Schreuer, 'Investment Protection and International Relations', 353.

[249] D. A. Desierto, 'Joint Decisions by State Parties: Fair Control of Tribunal Interpretations?' (June 2012).

[250] Fauchald, 'The Legal Reasoning of ICSID Tribunals', 332.

say that when powers of interpretation are expressly provided for in a treaty, they must be considered part of the regulatory framework. The issue of an 'abstract' joint interpretation by the contracting parties of an IIA, while ISA is pending under the same treaty, also presents us with the question of to whom the obligations of an investment treaty are owed. If the obligations set forth in an investment treaty are a direct right for investors, they crystallize when the individual qualifies as an investor under the IIA. From that moment on, the host state owes international treaty obligations to an individual, who can invoke them before an international arbitral tribunal, or waive them, without the consent of the home state.[251] It could then be argued that any interpretation between both state parties to the IIA would not necessarily be opposable by the claimant, especially if it has a restrictive reading of the investor's rights.

If the substantive obligations of the IIA are owed on an inter-state basis,[252] the right to arbitrate using ISDS only enforces rights that are, in origin, the rights of the home state and the claimant acts only as a proxy of the state of its nationality. Douglas has discussed two models that could explain this. The first is a 'derivative rights theory',[253] in which investment treaties 'institutionalise and reinforce' the system of diplomatic protection, and therefore no direct rights are conferred on foreign

---

[251] K. Parlett, *The Individual in the International Legal System: Continuity and Change in International Law* (Cambridge University Press, 2011), p. 133.

[252] In the *Methanex* case, in a non-disputing party submission, Canada declared that 'When interpreting the NAFTA, tribunals should recall that the NAFTA is a treaty among three Parties, namely the sovereign states of the United Mexican States, the United States and Canada. *The obligations undertaken by the three Parties, including those under NAFTA Chapter Eleven obligations, are owed by the Parties to one another and are subject to the dispute settlement procedures in NAFTA Chapter Twenty. They are not owed directly to individual investors. Nor do investors derive any rights from obligations owed to the Party of which they are nationals.* Rather, the disputing investor must prove that the Party claimed against has breached an obligation owed to another Party (. . .) and that loss or damage has thereby been incurred': *Methanex Corp. v. United States of America*, UNCITRAL, Second Submission of Canada Pursuant to NAFTA Article 1128, 30 April 2001, para. 2. Similar statements where made by Canada in *Feldman: Marvin Roy Feldman Karpa v. United Mexican States*, ICSID Case No ARB(AF)/99/1, Canada's NAFTA Second Article 1128 Submission, 28 June 2001, para. 8; and by Mexico in *Loewen Group, Inc. and Raymond L. Loewen v. United States of America*, ICSID Case No ARB(AF)/98/3, Mexico Third 1128 Submission 2 February 2002, para. 9.

[253] Z. Douglas, *The International Law of Investment Claims* (Cambridge University Press, 2009), pp. 10–38.

investors by the IIA,[254] but remains a mere agent of its home state.[255] The second is what Parlett calls the 'procedural-direct theory' that deviates from the previous one recognizing that, on the filing of the notice of arbitration, the claimant enters into a direct relationship with the respondent host state. Only prior to that crystallization are the substantive obligations of the BIT owed on an inter-state basis.[256] This model not only rules out the possibility of a waiver by the claimant prior to the notice of arbitration (as the right is owed by the home state), but also leaves open the possibility that the respondent state claims circumstances precluding wrongfulness with respect to the home state (and not the investor),[257] or that both host and host state issue a joint interpretation of an IIA that changes the understanding of such a treaty dramatically.

Juratowitch has submitted that when a right has been conferred on an investor by an IIA, that right 'inheres' in that investor. States have now provided widespread consent to individual investors bringing actions directly against host states, precisely to avoid the difficulties inherent in diplomatic protection. If investors are bringing actions against host states by way of subrogation to the rights of their home state, that would not explain why several IIAs provide for subrogation to those rights when a state or its agency makes a payment to any of its investors under a guarantee or a contract of insurance into which it has entered in respect of an investment. If states were the primary holders of rights conferred in investment treaties, then there would be no need for them to provide for subrogation of those rights to themselves.[258]

Roberts advocates an intermediate position, submitting that those IIAs create 'interdependent' procedural and substantive rights for *both* investors and home states. Any rights granted to investors are subject to express and implied limits imposed by the IIAs and the general international law. Due to this commonality, claims to vindicate these rights can be brought by either by the home state or the investor, but not generally

---

[254] *Loewen Group* v. *US*, Award, para. 233.

[255] Paparinskis prefers to use the terminology 'delegated rights', as derivative rights may be misleading because such term can also be used to describe the lawmaking process from which the rights are derived: M. Paparinskis, 'Investment Treaty Arbitration and the (New) Law of State Responsibility', *European Journal of International Law*, 24 (2013), 617–47 at 625.

[256] Parlett, *The Individual in the International Legal System*, p. 110.

[257] Ibid., pp. 110–11.

[258] B. Juratowitch, 'The Relationship between Diplomatic Protection and Investment Treaties', *ICSID Review*, 23 (2008), 10–35 at 24–7.

by both.[259] This position is based on the conclusions of the *Avena* case, in which, in interpreting the 1963 Vienna Convention on Consular Relations (VCCR), the ICJ clarified that violations of the rights of an individual may entail violation of the rights of the home state, and that violations of the rights of the latter may entail violation of the rights of the individual. In light of these special circumstances of 'interdependence', the home state may submit, at the same time claims in its own name, for alleged violations directly suffered, and on behalf of its nationals, for the violation of individual rights, not placing on the nationals the burden of first exhausting local remedies.[260]

But regardless the nature of these rights – something that, as Paparinskis rightly points out, is a ultimately a matter of treaty interpretation[261] – it is incorrect to assume that contracting parties cannot adopt *de jure* or de facto amendments to an investment treaty. Once given, investor rights can be altered via various means, including interpretation, amendment, withdrawal and termination. As long as investors have the knowledge that, within the IIA general regulatory framework, their treaty protections may change, they cannot legitimately expect that their treaty rights will be absolute and irrevocable.[262]

The problem does not seem to be with the power to make joint interpretations, but in the way in which this power is used. Time seems to be of the essence. Roberts believes that a strong argument can be made to impose timing constraints in order to balance the interests of the contracting parties and investors' legitimate expectations. The earlier interpretation is made, the more likely it is to be consistent with the investor's reliance.[263] Thus, even if a respondent state cannot issue a subsequent agreement on interpretation alone – requiring the acquiescence of the other contracting parties – an 'abstract' interpretation made during a pending procedure is less likely to be considered by the tribunal, as it could be a reaction to the specificities of the case at hand, and might not reflect the common interests of the contracting states while negotiating the treaty. Ideally, states should take steps to clarify the meaning of

---

[259] A. Roberts, 'State-to-State Investment Treaty Arbitration: A Hybrid Theory of Interdependent Rights and Shared Interpretive Authority', Harv. Int'l L.J., 55 (2014), 1 at 29, 35.
[260] *Avena and Other Mexican Nationals* (Mexico v. US), 2004 I.C.J. 12 (March 31), para. 40.
[261] Paparinskis, 'Investment Treaty Arbitration', 326.
[262] Roberts, 'Power and Persuasion', 210–11.
[263] Ibid., 212–14.

their investment treaties on a prompt and steady basis, especially before disputes arise.[264]

In this regard, Ishikawa has suggested that a good time for discussing such joint interpretations might be the consultation period provided for in the large majority of IIAs between the submission of the notice of dispute to the host state and the beginning of arbitration proceedings. This could be implemented voluntarily, as both the contracting parties to an IIA and the investor would be interested in having clarity on the interpretation of investment agreements. Certain elements might be included in the inter-state consultation mechanisms to make them more compulsory, such as the obligation on the contracting parties to have consultations on the interpretation of the treaty during that period of time, or imposing an obligation on the disputing investor to notify its home state after submitting the notice of dispute.[265]

C   Technical Referral to Domestic Authorities

Investment treaties increasingly include referral mechanisms to domestic agencies of both the home and host states to issue authoritative interpretations after an arbitral procedure has already started ('intra-arbitral' interpretation). These provisions are frequently found regarding two sensitive issues: determination of whether a taxation measure is tantamount to expropriation and of whether a financial measure can qualify as a prudential carve-out or a monetary policy exception. In both cases, the analysis encompasses questions of fact and law.

Here, we make a distinction with the *renvoi* procedures analysed in the previous section, as, in this case, the contracting parties or the treaty bodies are not expected to issue an authoritative interpretation directly. This task is assigned to 'technical' domestic agencies or 'experts' of each contracting party.

In the IIAs concluded in the last fifteen years, the majority of intra-arbitral technical referrals are found in relation to financial measures. We find technical referrals in fifty-two IIAs (around 9 per cent of the sample), forty-seven of which refer to the interpretation of technical questions on financial services and only nineteen to those on taxation measures. Overall, this mechanism is found mostly in the investment

---

[264] Johnson and Razbaeva, 'State Control Over Treaty Interpretation', 11.

[265] T. Ishikawa, 'Keeping Interpretation in Investment Treaty Arbitration "on Track": The Role of States Parties', *Transnational Dispute Management*, 11 (2014), at 27–30.

Table 4.3 *IIAs with technical referral provisions*

	Referral on Taxation Measures	Referral on Financial Measures
Number of IIAs	19	47
% of Total Data Set	3	8

chapters of FTAs, but there is an increasing number of BITs in which the interpretation of these sensitive issues is taken away from investment tribunals and given to the respective agencies of the home and the host states.[266]

The technical referral is triggered when the interpretation of certain 'competent authorities' is required – generally by request of the respondent state. Strict timelines are a common feature of all of these referral provisions, before the question reverts to the arbitral tribunal, ranging from sixty days (the most common period) to 180 days. In all cases, the interpretation of the parties or of the treaty body is binding on an ISDS tribunal.

1 Taxation Measures

We have already mentioned that in order to determine whether taxation measures constitute expropriations, several IIAs provide that an investor has to refer a case to the competent tax authorities of the contracting parties *before* submitting a claim to arbitration. This filtering procedure operates when it is clear *ex ante* that the challenged measure is a taxation measure.

But other IIAs – notably most of those concluded by Canada[267] – also deal with this situation when, in connection with a claim already in arbitration between an investor and a host state, an issue arises to determine whether a measure is a taxation one. In such cases, the respondent state *may* refer the issue to the designated competent

---

[266] In the sample there are twenty-five FTAs and twenty-two BITs that include a technical referral for interpretation of exceptions or carve-outs on financial services. With respect to taxation measures, the distribution is more favourable for bilateral treaties, with thirteen BITs and six FTAs.

[267] E.g. Canada–Mongolia BIT (2016), Arts. 1, 21.5; Canada–Hong Kong BIT (2016), Art. 14.6; Canada–Guinea BIT (2015), Art. 14.7.

authorities of the contracting parties. However, a decision of the taxation authorities shall bind a tribunal formed under the treaty. A tribunal seized of a claim in which this issue arises *may* not continue with the arbitral procedure, pending receipt of the decision of the designated authorities. Only if they fail to agree within a strict period of time (generally six months)[268] can the matter be decided by the arbitral tribunal.

As we can see, the technical referral in taxation measures operates in a softer way than the filtering of taxation claims, as it is neither mandatory for the respondent state to refer the issue to the competent tax authorities,[269] nor obligatory for the tribunal to suspend the arbitral procedure, although this is to be recommended, as, in the majority of cases, a decision of the taxation authorities shall bind a tribunal constituted under the treaty.[270]

A similar technical referral regarding taxation measures is included in CETA, with some substantial and procedural differences from the mechanism described before. On substance, the respondent state *may* refer a matter for consultation and joint determination by the contracting parties during an ISDS procedure: (i) if a challenged measure is a taxation measure, (ii) if it is found to be a taxation measure whether it breaches obligations on non-discriminatory treatment, or investment protection, and (iii) if there is an inconsistency between the obligations in CETA that are alleged to have been breached and those of a tax convention. Each party shall ensure that its delegation for the consultations to be conducted shall include persons with relevant expertise on the issues, including representatives from the relevant tax authorities of each party.[271]

---

[268] Under ASEAN–Australia–New Zealand FTA, Ch. 15, Art. 3.4; New Zealand–Thailand FTA, Art. 15.7.4; and Australia–Thailand FTA, Art. 1607.2, there is no specific period for the consultation process. In the Canadian BITs with Cameroon and Mongolia, taxation authorities may agree to modify the time period allowed for their consideration of the issue. In all the other Canadian BITs and in the Chile–Hong Kong Investment Agreement (2016), Art. 14.6, the timeframe is six months.

[269] In almost all these IIAs the taxation authorities are not identified in the text of the treaty, and they must be notified to each contracting party by diplomatic note. The only exceptions are the Canada–Mongolia BIT and the Chile–Hong Kong Investment Agreement.

[270] One of the few exceptions in this regard is the ASEAN–Australia–New Zealand FTA, in which a joint decision of the 'relevant parties' – home and host states including representatives of their tax administrations – shall be accorded 'serious consideration' by an arbitral tribunal.

[271] CETA, Art. 28.7.7(a),(e).

Procedurally, there is a significant difference on the timeframe. This referral cannot be made later than the date that the tribunal fixes for the respondent to submit its counter-memorial. Where the respondent makes such a referral, the arbitral proceedings are suspended for 180 days. If the contracting parties do not agree to consider the issue, or fail to make a joint determination, the investor may proceed with its claim. If the contracting parties agree, a joint determination by the parties shall be binding on the tribunal.[272]

2 Financial Services

Regarding financial services, the technical referrals in IIAs are generally directed to a treaty body – a financial services committee – in order to review the validity of a defence invoked by the respondent state. A special feature of this mechanism is that it may follow many different patterns in the agreements in which it is considered.

The first technical referral mechanism on financial services was created in Article 1415 of NAFTA, which allows the referral of certain issues in a pending ISDS case to the NAFTA Financial Service Committee (consisting of representatives from the contracting states' financial authorities) in order to determine whether a measure invoked in defence by a respondent falls under Article 1410 of NAFTA,[273] which provides for, among other exceptions: (i) the adoption of 'reasonable measures' for 'prudential reasons';[274] (ii) non-discriminatory measures of general application in pursuit of monetary, credit or exchange rate policies; and (iii) the limitation of transfers through measures relating to maintenance of the safety, soundness, integrity or financial responsibility of financial institutions or cross-border financial service providers.

This mechanism is triggered at the request of the respondent state. The tribunal is obliged to refer the matter, in writing, to the committee for a decision, and the arbitration may not continue pending receipt of

---

[272] Ibid., Art. 28.7.7.(b).

[273] Alschner, 'The Return of the Home State', 321.

[274] According to NAFTA Art. 1410, prudential measures include: (a) the protection of investors, depositors, financial market participants, policyholders, policy claimants, or persons to whom a fiduciary duty is owed by a financial institution or cross-border financial service provider; (b) the maintenance of the safety, soundness, integrity or financial responsibility of financial institutions or cross-border financial service providers; and (c) ensuring the integrity and stability of a party's financial system. The limitation of transfers considered in the same provision is only a valid exception if the measure was applied in non-discriminatory, good faith and equitable fashion.

such a decision. If the committee agrees on the validity of the defence to the investor's claim, this shall be binding on the tribunal.[275] Where the committee has not decided the issue within sixty days of receipt of the referral, the respondent state or the home state of the disputing investor may request the establishment of an arbitral panel, triggering the state-to -state arbitration mechanism under Article 2008 of NAFTA. Where no request for the establishment of such a panel has been made within ten days of the expiration of the sixty-day period, the tribunal may proceed to decide the matter (seventy days, in total, after the referral was made).

Not surprisingly, the main vectors of diffusion of this mechanism in IIAs are NAFTA parties. In the decade following NAFTA, Canada continued to include a technical referral on financial measures in several BITs,[276] although some important variations were introduced. Firstly, the consultations shall be between the financial services authorities of the contracting parties – and not by a special treaty body as in NAFTA. Secondly, the technical referral does not explicitly include non-discriminatory measures of general application in pursuit of monetary, credit or exchange rate policies, being applicable only to 'reasonable measures' for 'prudential reasons', or measures to limit or prevent trans-fers by financial institutions. Thirdly, the suspension of the arbitral proceedings is generally seventy days,[277] from the tribunal's referral to the competent authorities, without an express mention that the lack of agreement could trigger the state-to-state dispute settlement mechanisms of the BITs.

In the last fifteen years, Canada has also included these technical referral provisions in a number of BITs that go back and follow closely Article 1415 of NAFTA, with some differences, such as that the limitation on transfers does not refer to cross-border financial service providers, and, most importantly, that the decision on validity of the defence is taken directly by the contracting parties – the home and the host states – and not by domestic financial services authorities.[278]

An exception to this is the Canada–China BIT, which, again, follows another pattern, looking closely to the NAFTA model, but with some

---

[275] NAFTA, Art. 1415.

[276] E.g.: Canada–Ukraine BIT (1994), Art. XI; Canada–Trinidad and Tobago BIT (1995), Art. XI; Canada–Philippines BIT (1995), Annex, Section 5.

[277] In the Canada–South Africa BIT (1995), Art. XI, the suspension of the arbitral proceed-ings is for sixty days; in the Canada–Barbados BIT (1996), Art. XI, it is ninety days.

[278] E.g.: Canada–Mongolia BIT (2016), Art. 22.3-5; Canada–Hong Kong BIT (2016), Art. 22.3-5; Canada–Burkina Faso BIT (2015), Art. 24.3-5.

minor variations. For example, the mechanism is applicable only to 'reasonable measures' for 'prudential reasons'. More importantly, if, after sixty days from the referral, the financial services authorities of the contracting parties are unable to reach a joint decision, the issue shall be referred by either of them, within thirty days, to a state-to-state arbitral tribunal established pursuant to the treaty, and all the members of which shall have expertise or experience in financial services law or practice, which may include the regulation of financial institutions.[279]

The referral mechanism in financial issues is also included in several FTAs concluded by Canada in the last fifteen years, with Korea, Colombia, Peru, Panama and Honduras.[280] These agreements also delegate the authority to issue a binding decision to a financial services committee at the request of the respondent state, applying the referral procedure for general measures in pursuit of monetary and related credit or exchange rate policies – as in NAFTA – and also including the adoption or enforcement of measures necessary to secure compliance with the domestic laws or regulations of a contracting party, comprising those relating to the prevention of deceptive and fraudulent practices or to deal with the effects of a default on financial services contracts, inasmuch as those measures do not constitute a means of arbitrary or unjustifiable discrimination, or a disguised restriction on investment in financial institutions or cross-border trade in financial services. Procedurally, this mechanism suspends the arbitral proceedings for a total of seventy days from the referral. If the committee has not decided on the issue within sixty days, either the respondent state or the home state may trigger state-to-state arbitration.

A similar provision has been included in CETA, but with some important differences, as referral is provided for only for prudential measures, and not for general measures for monetary, credit or exchange rate policies, or in the case of limitation of transfers. Procedurally, the referral cannot be made later than the date that the tribunal fixes for the respondent to submit its counter-memorial, and the financial services committee has an extended timeframe of three months within which to agree on a decision, with the arbitral proceedings being suspended during that time. If the committee decides that the carve-outs or exceptions are a valid defence to the claim in their entirety, the investor shall be deemed

---

[279] Canada–China BIT (2012), Arts. 20.2, 33.3.
[280] E.g. Canada–Korea FTA (2014), Arts. 10.10, 10.19; Canada–Honduras FTA (2013), Arts. 13.10, 13.18; Canada–Panama FTA (2010), Arts. 12.11, 12.18.

to have withdrawn its claim and proceedings shall be discontinued. If such a joint determination is only in relation to parts of the claim, the decision will be binding on the tribunal only in relation to those parts, and the investor may proceed with any remaining parts of the claim. It is explicitly stated that no adverse inference can be drawn from the fact that the committee did not agree on a joint determination, and there is no referral to ISDS mechanisms in the event of disagreement.[281]

After NAFTA, the United States did not include this mechanism in many IIAs. Only the FTAs with Singapore, Chile and Morocco, and CAFTA-DR,[282] consider it, with the drafting being very similar to Article 1415 of NAFTA, but adding to the group of measures subject to referral those adopted to prevent deceptive and fraudulent practices or to deal with the effects of default in financial services contracts. This text was later followed in the Panama–US FTA.[283]

Building on this slightly modified NAFTA framework, the US Model BITs of 2004 and 2012[284] provided for technical referral on financial measures – with some further important changes in relation to the NAFTA Model:

(i) The respondent state has 120 days within which to submit the issue for referral to the competent financial authorities, from the date on which the claim is submitted to arbitration. The failure of the respondent to make such a request is without prejudice to the right of the respondent state to invoke defences at any appropriate phase of the arbitration.

(ii) If, before the respondent submits the request for a joint determination, the presiding arbitrator has been appointed, such arbitrator shall be replaced at the request of either disputing party, and the tribunal shall be reconstituted, appointing someone with expertise or experience in financial services law or practice.

---

[281] CETA, Arts. 13.16 and 13.21, Annex 13-B.

[282] E.g. Singapore–US FTA (2003), Arts. 10.10, 10.19; Chile–US FTA (2003), Arts. 12.10, 12.18; CAFTA–DR (2004), Arts. 12.10, 12.19.

[283] Panama–US FTA (2007), Arts. 12.10, 12.19. In these models the term 'prudential reasons' also includes the maintenance of the safety and financial and operational integrity of payment and clearing systems; and measures of general application taken in pursuit of monetary and related credit policies or exchange rate policies do not include measures that expressly nullify or amend contractual provisions that specify the currency of denomination or the rate of exchange of currencies.

[284] US Model BIT (2004) (2012), Art. 20.3.

(iii) If, within 120 days of the date by which the competent financial authorities have received the respondent's written request for a joint determination, they have not made a determination, the tribunal shall decide the issue or issues left unresolved by the competent financial authorities. The tribunal shall draw no inference from the fact that the competent financial authorities have not made a determination.

(iv) The home state, acting as non-disputing party, may make oral and written submissions to the tribunal regarding the issue of whether and to what extent the invoked defences are valid to the claim. More importantly, *unless it makes such a submission, the home state shall be presumed, for purposes of the arbitration, to take a position not inconsistent with that of the respondent host state* (emphasis added).

(v) The arbitral proceeding suspended during the referral may resume ten days after the competent financial authorities' joint determination has been received, or ten days after the expiration of the 120-day period provided to the competent financial authorities.

(vi) Finally, the tribunal shall address and decide the issues left unresolved by the competent financial authorities prior to deciding the merits of the claim, if is requested by the respondent state within thirty days after the expiration of the 120-day period for a joint determination.

The abovementioned text was included in the US BITs with Uruguay and Rwanda,[285] and in its FTAs with Colombia, Peru, Oman and Korea. In its FTAs with Oman and Korea there is a minor variation giving to the financial authorities only sixty days to reach a joint agreement after the referral.[286] Another difference is found in the FTAs with Colombia and Peru, in which, strangely, it is considered to be the participation of other 'non-disputing party' besides the home state of the investor (when there is none), in the referral procedure before the responsible financial authorities, if they have substantial interest in the joint determination.[287]

After NAFTA, the referral mechanism on financial measures was also included by Mexico in its FTAs with Colombia, Venezuela, Bolivia and Nicaragua.[288] All these agreements closely resemble Article 1415 of

---

[285] Uruguay–US BIT (2005), Art. 20.3; Rwanda–US BIT (2008), Art. 20.3.
[286] Oman–US FTA (2006), Arts. 12.10, 12.19; Korea–US FTA (2007), Arts. 13.10, 13.19.
[287] Colombia–US FTA (2006), Arts. 12.10, 12.19; Peru–US FTA (2006), Arts. 12.10, 12.19.
[288] Colombia-Mexico-Venezuela FTA (1994), Art. 12-09, 12-20; Bolivia–Colombia FTA (1994), Arts. 12-09, 12-20 (which provided for referral to a 'Working Group' on financial services); Mexico–Nicaragua FTA (1997), Art. 13-20.

NAFTA, with the minor variation that, in the FTA with Colombia and Venezuela, and in the FTA with Nicaragua, the suspension of the arbitral proceeding is for only sixty days, and there is no express mention that the lack of agreement by the financial services committee could serve as basis for initiating the state-to-state dispute settlement mechanisms of the FTAs. In the last fifteen years, Mexico has replicated Article 1415 of NAFTA in its FTA with Peru,[289] and included a similar provision in its FTA with Panama, and in the Pacific Alliance Protocol.[290] The main difference with the NAFTA model in the two latter FTAs is the inclusion of another group of measures in the scope of the referral: those adopted to prevent deceptive and fraudulent practices or to deal with the effects of default in financial services contracts. No Mexican BIT provides for this referral mechanism. The Pacific Alliance Protocol also provides for a procedure to allow the participation of members of the Alliance in the referral, besides the host and the home state, if they have substantial interest in the subject matter of the referral.[291]

Outside the NAFTA contracting parties, other FTAs that include this mechanism initially tended to follow the NAFTA model, which was replicated in the Panama–Taiwan FTA[292] and briefly adjusted in the FTAs between Nicaragua and Taiwan; Australia and Chile; Korea and Peru; Panama and Peru; and Colombia and Costa Rica, which added to the measures that are subject to referral those adopted to prevent deceptive and fraudulent practices or to deal with the effects of default in financial services contracts.[293] Plus, if the committee has not decided the issue within sixty days following receipt of the referral, either party may, within ten days thereafter, request the establishment of a panel under the state-to-state dispute settlement mechanism of the same treaty. If no request for the establishment of a panel has been made within ten days after the sixty-day period of referral, the tribunal may proceed to

---

[289] Mexico–Peru FTA (2011), Arts. 12.9 and 12.20.

[290] PAAP (2014), Arts. 11.11, 11.21; Mexico–Panama FTA (2014), Arts. 11.12, 11.20.

[291] Under PAAP (2014), Art. 11.21, fn 5, if, within fifteen days of the date of receipt of a request for a decision, any of the other contracting parties submits a written request to the respondent state and the home state of the investor, stating its substantial interest in the subject matter of the referral, the authorities responsible for financial services of such third party may participate in the discussions on the matter, if agreed to by the authorities responsible for financial services of the respondent and the home state of the complainant party (translated by the author).

[292] Panama–Taiwan FTA (2003), Arts. 12.09, 12.19.

[293] E.g.: Nicaragua–Taiwan FTA (2006), Art. 12.19; Australia–Chile FTA (2008), Arts. 12.11, 12.18; Korea–Peru FTA (2010), Art. 12.19.

decide the matter. In addition, the Korea–Singapore FTA[294] also provides for a referral to the financial services committee when the respondent state invokes safeguards on financial measures.[295]

However, more recent FTAs have adopted the variations of the NAFTA model contained in the US Model BITs of 2004 and 2012, with an extended timeframe for the referral process, and the possibility that the home state could act as non-disputing party before the competent financial authorities of the contracting parties. This is so in the case of the Australia–Korea FTA.[296]

Very few BITs have included this referral procedure outside the NAFTA member states. In the Colombia–Spain BIT,[297] within thirty days after the submission of a claim to arbitration, the respondent state may request consultation with the financial authorities of the contracting parties to determine whether the origin of the dispute is a financial-sector prudential measure.[298] These consultations will be held for 120 days and, if the financial authorities of both contracting parties consider that the origin of the dispute is a fair, non-discriminatory and good faith, prudential measure, the responsibility of the contracting party to the dispute shall be excluded. In the EFTA–Korea BIT, the respondent state may make a referral to the Sub-Committee on Financial Services on the treaty, which, in a period of ninety days, shall decide whether, and to what extent, defences to the claim to the claim of the investor on prudential measures, temporary safeguard measures, monetary and exchange rate policies invoked by the respondent are valid. Where the treaty sub-committee finds that none of the defences is valid or has not reached a decision within ninety days of receipt of the referral, the investor may proceed to submit the claim to international arbitration.[299]

Finally, one of the most recent BIT including a technical referral procedure is the Chile–Hong Kong Investment Agreement, which, in

---

[294] Korea–Singapore FTA (2005), Arts. 10.12, 12.6, 12.13.
[295] According to the treaty, these are those adopted or maintained in the event of serious balance of payments or external financial difficulties or threat thereof or where, in exceptional circumstances, payments and capital movements between the parties cause or threaten to cause serious difficulties for the operation of monetary policy or exchange rate policy in either party.
[296] Australia–Korea FTA (2014), Arts. 8.10, 8.19.
[297] Colombia–Spain BIT (2005), Art. 10.7.
[298] The term 'prudential measures' in the financial sector in this BIT means those that are taken to maintain the safety, soundness, integrity or financial responsibility of financial institutions (translated by the author).
[299] EFTA–Korea BIT (2005), Arts. 6, 7, 10, 17.

substance, follows closely the Chile–US FTA, with some important procedural differences:[300]

(i) The respondent state shall submit in writing to the authorities of the home state that are responsible for financial services a request for a joint determination on the issue of whether the exceptions are a valid defence, no later than the date that the tribunal fixes for the respondent to submit its defence, or its response to the amendment to the claim.

(ii) Secondly, the authorities of the respondent state and of the non-disputing party shall attempt, in good faith, to make a determination that shall be binding and transmitted promptly to the disputing parties and the ISDS tribunal. *Yet there is no explicit suspension of the proceedings.*

(iii) If the authorities have not made a determination within 120 days, either contracting party may request the establishment of an arbitral panel to decide the issue, triggering the state-to-state dispute settlement mechanism of the treaty. The final report of the arbitral panel shall be binding on the contracting parties and the ISDS tribunal.

(iv) If no request for the establishment of an arbitral panel has been made within ten days of expiration of the 120-day period, the ISDS tribunal established may proceed on the claim, but drawing no inference from the fact that the authorities have not made a determination.

(v) As in the US Model BITs of 2004 and 2012, the home state may make oral and written submissions to the tribunal regarding the issue of whether the exceptions are a valid defence to the claim. Unless it makes such a submission, the non-disputing party shall be presumed to take a position that is not inconsistent with that of the respondent host state.

3   The Nature of Technical Referrals in ISDS

This system of delegation of public interpretation to technical agencies or experts has received less attention from practitioners and scholars. Some have stressed problems in specific treaties – as in the case of CETA, highlighting that a prudential carve-out for financial services has been

---

[300] Chile–Hong Kong Investment Agreement (2016), Art. 22.3-5.

included, but that it is procedurally and substantively weaker than the one in NAFTA, as has previously been explained.[301]

Others have pointed out that the 'technical authorities' are not neutral judges of the dispute. For Kolo, in relation to tax measures, they are interested-parties to the case, 'being the very department whose conduct is either in question (in respect of the host state) or might be in future (with regard to the home state). Hence it is probably in the self-interest of both authorities to agree that the disputed measure is not an expropriation'.[302] This problem could be present – especially if agencies are political or dependent of each government, and they find consensus against the investor – a truly 'diplomatic protection' in disguise. For Van Aaken, delegation to independent, non-political bodies could mitigate opportunist use or behaviour of expert agencies, but does not guarantee that those bodies will not be subject to political or regulatory capture.[303]

If states want experts to have an optimal decision on such issues, there are other mechanisms that can provide expertise to the tribunal. Expertise can be imported into tribunals in at least two other ways: either by having the tribunal appointing external experts in the respective subject matter; or by appointing experts as arbitrators[304] – something that several IIAs in the data set already provide for in relation to financial services.

However, there are political and knowledge reasons to consider this kind of delegation. Where subject matter or factual expertise is needed, usually states delegate not to courts but to specialized agencies (either independent or not). Politically, the fact that independent agencies jointly decide on the violation of an IIA can solve information asymmetry problems, and there is a bigger chance that their decision will filter out opportunistic behaviour of the host state, since, in the event of dissent of the agencies, the case will be left to the arbitral tribunal. What happens here is that contracting state parties are withdrawing the delegated duty to solve certain questions (taxation measures and the prudential

---

[301] S. Sinclair, 'Financial Services' in S. Sinclair, S. Trew and H. Mertins-Kirkwood (eds.), *Making Sense of the CETA* (Canadian Centre for Policy Alternatives, 2014), pp. 18–23 at pp. 19–23.

[302] Kolo, 'Tax "Veto" as a Special Jurisdictional and Substantive Issue in Investor–State Arbitration: Need for Reassessment?', 481.

[303] Van Aaken, 'Control Mechanisms in International Investment Law', 430–1.

[304] Van Aaken, 'Delegating Interpretative Authority in Investment Treaties', 18.

regulation of financial markets) from ISDS tribunals *ex ante* and delegating it instead to specialized agencies of the contracting states.[305]

If the contracting parties truly believe that the other's agency is completely independent and not home biased, interpretative delegation to them makes sense. In *Fireman's Fund* v. *Mexico*, the tribunal acknowledged with respect the design of the NAFTA that 'it is evident that the drafters carved out the financial sector from significant portions of the general provisions, because none of the state Parties was prepared to engage in the kind of harmonization and deregulation that would have been necessary to treat banks, insurance companies, and securities firms ... in the same way ... All of these differences, it is clear, are designed to leave room for national decision-making rather than harmonization, and to limit the opportunity of investors from another state Party to resort to international dispute settlement to challenge regulatory measures taken by the respective national authorities'.[306]

But is this technical referral an expression of diplomatic protection? Again, we find here that one key element of that institution is not present, as the determination of the validity of the exceptions invoked by the respondent state is a decision that is taken jointly by the competent authorities – if they achieve a consensus – and not unilaterally by the home state. This is true, even if the position of each domestic agency is presented unilaterally. This was exactly the procedure followed in *Gottlieb Investors* v. *Canada*, in which the US and Canadian tax authorities agreed that the challenged measures were not an expropriation under Article 1110 of NAFTA merely through an exchange of letters.[307]

As in the other types of home state intervention analysed previously, rather than offering diplomatic protection, this phenomenon seems to be a way of reasserting control of states, instead recalibrating the interpretive authority of an investment treaty to the contracting parties to investor–state tribunals.[308]

---

[305] Ibid., 15–19.

[306] *Fireman's Fund Insurance Co* v. *United Mexican States*, ICSID Case No ARB(AF)/02/1, Decision on the Preliminary Question, 17 July 2003, para. 83.

[307] *Gottlieb Investors Group* v. *Canada*. Although this case refers to what we have classified as 'filtering of claims', the procedure of intra-arbitral referral basically follows the same pattern.

[308] A. Roberts, 'Recalibrating Interpretive Authority' (2014) *Columbia FDI Perspectives*. *Vale Columbia Center on Sustainable International Investment*.

D   Regulating the Work of Tribunals

Some investment treaties provide for more active participation by the home state in the ISDS proceedings outside the interpretation of the agreement, through different means of regulating the work of tribunals in charge of settling the dispute, such as the mechanisms for appointment of arbitrators – or even the creation of standing investment tribunals, the adoption of codes of conduct for arbitrators (or judges of special standing tribunals), and of supplemental rules of procedure.

Although some of these mechanisms are extremely important – the creation of international investment tribunals could be a groundbreaking change in the existing investment regime – there are still very few IIAs that contain this type of provision, as Table 4.4 depicts regarding our data set of the past fifteen years.

In the following sections we will examine how these different mechanisms have been conceived in recent IIAs. It is important to stress that we will focus on the home state's participation in regulating the work of investment tribunals (arbitral or standing) *after* the conclusion of the treaty.

1   Selection of Arbitrators

Some IIAs provide for an active role for states – including the home state – in the nomination of arbitrators in ISA, through the establishment of a roster of arbitrators to appoint possible presidents of the arbitral tribunal. This mechanism is very similar to the ICSID system, in which the Centre maintains a roster of qualified persons ('Panel of Arbitrators') in order to appoint arbitrators where the parties have not reached an agreement to appoint the presiding arbitrator, or they fail to appoint their own arbitrator.[309]

This feature has already been provided for in at least nine IIAs. The majority of them have in common that in all of them the appointing authority is the Secretary-General of ICSID, regardless of the rules of arbitration applicable in a particular case. Also, as a general rule, if the

---

[309] ICSID Convention, Arts. 3, 12–15 and 37–8. Each contracting state may designate to this panel four persons who may but need not be its nationals, and shall be persons of high moral character and recognized competence in the fields of law, commerce, industry or finance, who may be relied upon to exercise independent judgment. Panel members serve for renewable periods of six years. The full list of members of the Panels of Conciliators and Arbitrators is available at the ICSID web page: International Centre for Settlement of Investment Disputes (ICSID), 'Members of the Panels of Conciliators and Arbitrators' (February 2018).

Table 4.4 *IIAs with provisions regulating the work of tribunals*

	Selection of Arbitrators	Standing Investment Courts	Adoption of Code of Conduct	Supplemental Rules of Procedure
Number of IIAs	3	2	7	18
% of Total Data Set	0.5	0.4	1	3

tribunal has not been constituted within ninety days from the date on which the claim was submitted to arbitration, the appointing authority shall, at the request of a disputing party, appoint the arbitrator or arbitrators not yet appointed from such a roster, provided that the arbitrator shall not be a national of the respondent state or a national of the home state of the disputing investor.

The first agreement in which we find this roster is NAFTA, where the parties are to establish and maintain, a roster of *forty-five* presiding arbitrators who should be experienced in international law and investment matters and meet the qualifications mentioned in the ICSID Convention, the ICSID Additional Facility Rules and the UNCITRAL Arbitration Rules. The roster members are to be appointed by consensus and without regard to nationality. In the event that no such presiding arbitrator is available to serve, the ICSID Secretary-General is to appoint a presiding arbitrator, who is not a national of any of the parties, from the ICSID Panel of Arbitrators.[310] A similar provision is provided for in other IIAs, with the difference that the roster of arbitrators has either *thirty*[311] or *six*[312] members. In another variation of this model the roster is facilitative, as the contracting parties *may* agree on establishing and maintaining a roster of *twenty* presiding arbitrators.[313]

In certain IIAs, the roster is established by a treaty body. In the Australia–China FTA, the committee on investment shall establish a list of at least *twenty* individuals who are willing and able to serve as arbitrators. Each contracting party shall select at least five individuals to

---

[310] NAFTA, Art. 1124.
[311] Canada–Chile FTA (1996), Art. G-25.
[312] Panama–Taiwan FTA (2003), Art. 10.25.
[313] Japan–Mexico EPA (2004), Art. 82; Chile–Korea FTA (2003), Art. 10.28.

serve as arbitrators. The parties shall also jointly select at least ten individuals who are not nationals of either party to act as chairpersons of the tribunals.[314] In the CACM, each party shall nominate up to *five* arbitrators with the same qualifications as are detailed in the ICSID Convention and experience in international law and in matters relating to investments. The members of the list will be appointed consensually by the parties, regardless of nationality, for a period of two years, which is renewable. The appointing authority will use that list, in case a disputing party does not appoint an arbitrator or an agreement is not reached in the appointment of the president of the court.[315] In COMESA, establishing and maintaining a roster of qualified arbitrators is mandatory for the COMESA Secretariat. Yet, its use is facilitative for the disputing parties, who may select arbitrators from that list or not.[316]

In the initial text of the EU–Singapore FTA (2014), the trade committee shall establish a list of at least *fifteen* individuals who are willing and able to serve as arbitrators, no later than one year after the entry into force of the agreement, upon the recommendation of the committee on trade in services, investment and government procurement. For that purpose, each contracting party shall propose five individuals to serve as arbitrators who may not act as chairpersons or sole arbitrators; and a list of individuals, who are not nationals of either party, who may act as chairpersons or sole arbitrators.[317]

Yet, the text of this treaty, changed in April 2018, for two important reasons: first, due to the new EU proposal of establishing standing investment tribunals (which will be analysed in the next section); and secondly, after the opinion delivered by the European Court of Justice (ECJ) on 16 May 2017 to clarify the EU's competence to sign and ratify the FTA with Singapore. The Court identified two important matters of shared competence that can be exercised by the EU or by its member states: portfolio investment and ISDS.[318] Following that opinion, a debate between the Council and the European Parliament on the best architecture for EU trade agreements and investment protection agreements (IPAs) took place. Now the text of the FTA

---

[314] Australia–China FTA (2015), Arts. 9.7.3, 9.15.2-6.
[315] CACM Agreement on Investment and Trade Services (2002), Arts. 3.26–27.
[316] COMESA Investment Agreement (2007), Art. 30.
[317] EU–Singapore FTA (October 2014), Arts. 9.18.3, 9.30.2.
[318] European Court of Justice, Opinion of the Court 2/15 (Full Court), 16 May 2017, *(EU–Singapore Free Trade Agreement) of 16. 5. 2017. Opinion Pursuant To Article 218(11) TFEU*, ECLI:EU:C:2017:376.

with Singapore (and with Vietnam) does not include an investment chapter, but a parallel IPA.[319]

Although the selection of arbitrators has been promoted as an important improvement in the context of the ISA system,[320] it can pose exactly the problem that states are trying to overcome, if lists are put together in a non-public process and selecting mainly 'pro-state' arbitrators, thus creating a bias against foreign investors. Others make the criticism that the roster only works as a backup and that it neither has the power of an exclusive list of arbitrators nor fulfils strict conditions of independence and impartiality.[321]

This discussion takes place in the context of a broader debate in international arbitration, as to whether party autonomy to nominate arbitrators should be abandoned in favour of another system. Some have advanced the idea that an arbitral institution should appoint all arbitrators, under the assumption that, if arbitrators are nominated by a neutral third party, they will be free of bias in relation to the disputing parties. Other scholars have taken the view that such a system would take an important advantage from the disputing parties, handing over the appointing decision to a bureaucratic body with political procedures.[322] But not all share these concerns. Some believe that tenured panellists appointed by states with the awareness that they will be deciding disputes are also less likely to raise concerns about bias towards investors or states 'and perhaps collectively may be more likely to have a diverse disciplinary and personal background'.[323]

2 The New EU Approach: Standing Investment Courts

The interest in a multilateral court for the settlement of investment disputes has arisen in the wake of rules embedded in a growing number

---

[319] European Commission – Trade, 'Singapore' (September 2017).

[320] European Commission, 'Fact sheet on investment provisions in the EU–Singapore Free Trade Agreement' (2014) p. 3.

[321] N. Bernasconi-Osterwalder and H. Mann, 'A Response to the European Commission's December 2013 Document "Investment Provisions in the EU–Canada Free Trade Agreement (CETA)"' (2014) p. 22.

[322] J. A. Huerta Goldman, A. Romanetti and F. X. Stirnimann, 'Cross-Cutting Observations on Compositions of Tribunals' in J. A. Huerta Goldman, A. Romanetti and F. X. Stirnimann (eds.), WTO Litigation, Investment Arbitration, and Commercial Arbitration (Wolters Kluwer Law & Business, Kluwer Law International, 2013), pp. 129–34 at pp. 131–2.

[323] T. Voon, 'Consolidating International Investment Law: The Mega-Regionals as a Pathway towards Multilateral Rules', World Trade Review, 17 (2018), 33–63 at 8.

of FTAs, starting with the EU's proposal, on 16 September 2015, to establish a standing Investment Tribunal and an Appellate Tribunal (the 'Investment Courts System' (ICS)) as part of the negotiations of the Transatlantic Trade and Investment Partnership (TTIP) with the United States.[324] This revised system seems to be 'modelled after' the World Trade Organization (WTO) dispute settlement system, with lower and appellate decision-making bodies, and claims to be subject to accountable, transparent and democratic principles.[325]

Several other proposals have been put forward to remedy the drawbacks of the ISDS through the creation of a permanent investment court. This mechanism was envisaged in a 2015 German Model BIT with ISDS for 'industrial countries', and in a French proposal put forward in the same year for creating a hybrid institution that was called a 'court' but resembled an arbitral tribunal.[326] In 2015, UNCTAD also considered an international investment court as one of the reform options for the ISDS system.[327]

In December 2016, the European Commission and Canada announced that they were working together to establish a multilateral investment court (MIC). The ultimate aim of such efforts is to establish a single permanent body to decide investment disputes, thus moving away from the prevailing ad hoc system of ISDS. This future body would be open to all interested countries and adjudicate disputes under both existing and future investment treaties.[328] After completing a public consultation and impact assessment in 2016–2017, on 13 September 2017 the Commission made a recommendation to the European Council to start negotiations on a MIC.[329]

In June 2017, the Working Group III of UNCITRAL was mandated to explore whether there was sufficient support for multilateral approaches

---

[324] C. Titi, 'The European Commission's Approach to the Transatlantic Trade and Investment Partnership (TTIP): Investment Standards and International Investment Court System – An overview of the European Commission's draft TTIP text of 16 September 2015', *Transnational Dispute Management*, 12 (2015) at 1.

[325] S. S. Kho, A. Yanovich, B. R. Casey and J. Strauss, 'The EU TTIP Investment Court Proposal and the WTO Dispute Settlement System: Comparing Apples and Oranges?', *ICSID Review – Foreign Investment Law Journal*, 32 (2017), 326–45 at 327, 338–9.

[326] Titi, 'The European Commission's Approach to the Transatlantic Trade and Investment Partnership (TTIP)', 10.

[327] UNCTAD (ed.), *Reforming International Investment Governance* (United Nations, 2015), p. 152.

[328] European Commission, 'A Future Multilateral Investment Court' (December 2016).

[329] European Commission, 'A Multilateral Investment Court. State of the Union 2017' (September 2017).

to ISDS reform. The three-part mandate delegates the group to focus first on identifying concerns regarding ISDS, and then to consider whether reform is desirable and, if so, to develop any relevant solutions. First talks took place at UNCITRAL from 27 November to 1 December 2017, and continued throughout 2018.[330]

Until now, the only agreements that contain the feature of standing investment courts are the EU–Vietnam and EU–Singapore FTAs and CETA. Originally, the latter agreement only included several provisions to 'improve' ISA, similar to those provided for in the initial text of the EU–Singapore FTA (2014). However, after a revised or 'scrubbed' version of the agreement in 29 February 2016, an important change was made and now the investment chapter includes the establishment of an investment tribunal and an appellate tribunal for the resolution of disputes between investors and states, abandoning the system of ISA. The inclusion of this feature is also being debated in the process of the modernization of the EU FTAs with Mexico[331] and Chile,[332] and in the negotiation of an FTA with Japan, in which the only pending issue is investment protection, having the European Commission declared that, for the EU, 'ISDS is dead'.[333] Following the EU 'Trade for All' policy,[334] ICS will probably be under consideration in other future EU negotiations of FTAs (as with Philippines and Myanmar). Yet, the ongoing intra-EU discussion on trade agreements and investment protection, as an aftermath of the ECJ opinion of 16 May 2017, referred to in the preceding section, could have important effects on this policy.

The main features of the ICS in the three treaties that include it are described below.

---

[330] L. E. Peterson, 'UNCITRAL Meetings on ISDS Reform Get off to Bumpy Start, as Delegations Can't Come to Consensus on Who Should Chair Sensitive Process – Entailing a Rare Vote', September 2017: www.iareporter.com/articles/uncitral-meet ings-on-isds-reform-gets-off-to-bumpy-start-as-delegations-cant-come-to-consensus -on-who-should-chair-sensitive-process-entailing-a-rare-vote/ (accessed 23 February 2018).

[331] See: R. Torrent and R. Polanco, *Analysis of the Upcoming Modernisation of the Trade Pillar of the European Union-Mexico Global Agreement* (European Parliament, 2016).

[332] See: R. Polanco and R. Torrent, Analysis of the Prospects for Updating the Trade Pillar of the European Union-Chile Association Agreement (European Parliament, 2016).

[333] European Commission – Trade, 'A New EU Trade Agreement with Japan' (August 2017), p. 6.

[334] European Commission and Directorate-General for Trade, *Trade for All: Towards a More Responsible Trade and Investment Policy* (Publications Office, 2015), p. 21.

(a) Establishment of the Tribunal

The composition of the ICS differs in CETA and the EU–Vietnam and Singapore FTAs. In the case of the agreement with Vietnam the trade committee shall, upon the entry into force of the agreement, appoint *nine* members of the tribunal. Three of them shall be nationals of an EU member state, three shall be nationals of Vietnam and three shall be nationals of third countries. In the treaty with Singapore the tribunal consider six members, two appointed by the EU, two by Singapore and two by both parties who shall not be nationals of Singapore or an EU Member State. The trade committee may decide to increase or decrease the number of the members of the tribunal by multiples of three. In the EU–Vietnam FTA the members of the tribunal shall be appointed for a renewable four-year term, with the exception of five of the nine persons appointed after the entry into force of the agreement, to be determined by lot, whose terms shall extend to six years. In the EU–Singapore FTA the appointment term is 8 years, except for three initial members determined by lot, which will be 12 years.[335]

In the case of CETA, the joint committee shall, upon the entry into force of the agreement, appoint *fifteen* members of the tribunal. Five of them shall be nationals of an EU member state, five shall be nationals of Canada and five shall be nationals of third countries. The joint committee may decide to increase or decrease the number of the members of the tribunal by multiples of three. The members of the tribunal shall be appointed for a five-year term, renewable once, except that the terms of seven of the fifteen persons appointed after the entry into force of the agreement, to be determined by lot, shall extend to six years.[336]

In these agreements it is stipulated that the members of the investment tribunal shall possess the qualifications required in their respective countries for appointment to judicial offices, or shall be jurists of recognized competence. They shall have demonstrated expertise in public international law. It is also desirable that they have expertise, in particular, in international investment law, international trade law and the resolution of disputes arising under international investment or international trade agreements.[337]

---

[335] EU–Vietnam IPA (2018), Ch. 3, Art. 3.38; EU-Singapore IPA (April 2018), Art. 3.9.
[336] CETA, Art. 8.27.
[337] EU–Vietnam IPA (2018), Ch. 3, Art. 3.38.4; EU-Singapore IPA (April 2018), Art. 3.9; CETA, Art. 8.27.4.

The investment tribunal shall hear cases in divisions consisting of three members, of whom one shall be a national of an EU member state, one a national of Canada or Vietnam, and one a national of a third country, who will chair the division. This nationality requirement is not found in the EU-Singapore FTA. The disputing parties may agree that a case be heard by a sole member who is a national of a third country, to be selected by the president of the tribunal.[338]

(b)   Limited Scope

Only specific claims can be brought to the ICS. These claims relate to non-discriminatory treatment, in relation to the expansion, conduct, operation, management, maintenance, use, enjoyment and sale or disposal of a covered investment and investment protection. In the EU-Singapore IPA this does not include MFN.[339] As mentioned before, a filter mechanism is established for financial services to ensure that the parties can take legitimate prudential measures, as is also enshrined in the prudential carve-out.[340] Punitive damages are explicitly excluded.[341]

States reaffirm their 'right to regulate' and it is stipulated that the mere fact that laws are modified in a manner that negatively affects an investment or interferes with an investor's expectations does not amount to a breach of an obligation under the treaty.[342] Arbitral tribunals may award only monetary damages or restitution in property and, therefore, a decision by the tribunal cannot lead to the repeal of a measure adopted by the EU Parliament, an EU member state, Canada, Singapore or Vietnam.[343] In the EU–Vietnam IPA,[344] there is also a rule establishing that arbitral tribunals shall be bound by the interpretations of domestic law given by competent courts and authorities – rather than that the

---

[338] EU–Vietnam IPA (2018), Ch. 3, Art. 3.38.6-9; EU-Singapore IPA (April 2018), Art. 3.9; CETA, Art. 8.27.6-9.

[339] CETA Ch. 8, Section C and D, EU–Vietnam IPA (2018), Ch. 3, Art. 3.27; EU-Singapore IPA (April 2018), Art. 3.1.

[340] CETA, Arts. 13.16, 13.21, EU–Vietnam IPA (2018), Ch. 3, Art. 4.5; EU-Singapore IPA (April 2018), Art. 4.4.

[341] CETA, Art. 8.39.4, EU–Vietnam IPA (2018), Ch. 3, Art. 3.53.3; EU-Singapore IPA (April 2018), Art. 3.18.2.

[342] CETA, Art. 8.9; EU–Vietnam IPA (2018), Ch. 3, Art. 2.2; EU-Singapore IPA (April 2018), Art. 2.2.1.

[343] CETA, Art. 8.39; EU–Vietnam IPA (2018), Ch. 3, Art. 3.53; EU-Singapore IPA (April 2018), Art. 3.18.1.

[344] EU–Vietnam IPA (2018), Ch. 3. Art. 3.42.3.

'tribunal shall follow the prevailing interpretation' of these courts – included in CETA and the EU-Singapore IPA.[345]

(c) Regulation of Proceedings

A particular feature of these tribunals is that they rely on existing ISDS procedural rules, and a claim may be submitted under either the ICSID Convention and Rules of Procedure for Arbitration Proceedings, the ICSID Additional Facility Rules, the UNCITRAL Arbitration Rules or any other rules on agreement of the disputing parties.[346] These features give the proceedings a 'hybrid' nature: procedures are conducted before a permanent tribunal, but the decisions take the form of awards issued under arbitration rules.

However, both the EU–Vietnam IPA and CETA include special regulations of the proceedings that go beyond the arbitral rules mentioned previously Firstly, both agreements include rules to prevent fraudulent or manipulative claims, and an investor may not submit a claim to the tribunals when the investment was made through fraudulent misrepresentation, concealment, corruption or conduct amounting to an abuse of process.[347]

Secondly, a statutory limit of three years in which to bring a claim is introduced. This limit can be extended if a domestic court proceeding is pursued, up to two years after the investor exhausts or ceases to pursue claims or proceedings and, in any event, no later than seven or ten years.[348]

Thirdly, parallel proceedings are explicitly prohibited, and investors cannot simultaneously submit claims under CETA and another international agreement, unless the claimant withdraws the pending claim. This is in order to avoid divergent awards or overlapping compensation.[349]

Fourthly, both agreements provide for an expedited system for rejecting unfounded or frivolous claims. Investment tribunals can quickly dismiss frivolous claims (those 'manifestly without legal merit') and claims without legal basis ('those unfounded as a matter of law') as preliminary questions, even before deciding on the merits of the case. This feature is also considered in the EU-Singapore IPA.[350]

---

[345] CETA Art. 8.31; EU-Singapore IPA (April 2018), Art. 3.13.2 fn 7.
[346] CETA, Art. 8.23; EU–Vietnam IPA (2018), Ch. 3, Art. 3.33.2; EU-Singapore IPA (April 2018), Art. 3.6.
[347] CETA, Art. 8.18.3; EU–Vietnam IPA (2018), Ch. 3, Art. 3.27.2.
[348] CETA, Art. 8.19.6; EU–Vietnam IPA (2018), Ch. 3, Art. 3.30.2.
[349] CETA, Art. 8.24; EU–Vietnam IPA (2018), Ch. 3, Art. 3.34.
[350] CETA Arts. 8.32, 8.33; EU–Vietnam IPA (2018), Ch. 3, Arts. 3.44 and 3.45; EU-Singapore IPA (April 2018), Arts. 3.14 and 3.15.

Fifthly, a higher level of transparency of proceedings is provided for. Following the UNCITRAL Rules on Transparency,[351] almost all documents will be made publicly available on a website, including submissions by the parties and decisions of the tribunal. All hearings will be open to the public, and interested parties (such as non-governmental organizations (NGOs), trade unions and business associations) will be able to make submissions. A similar provision is included in the EU-Singapore IPA.[352]

Finally, in both CETA and in the IPAs with Singapore and Vietnam, the investment tribunals shall order that the costs of proceedings be borne by the unsuccessful disputing party.[353] This is a novelty for IIAs, which, in general, have no clear rules regarding the costs of arbitration treaty with such provisions. It is aimed at preventing a government from bearing all its costs even if it has successfully defended itself in arbitration.[354]

(d)   Appellate Tribunal

Although the 2004 US Model BIT and CAFTA–DR already included a provision for the possible establishment of an appellate body,[355] the EU–Vietnam FTA was the first IIA in which an appellate tribunal was created. CETA originally provided for only the possible creation of an appeal mechanism (Article X.42).[356] However, after the 'scrubbed' text of CETA, it also includes that feature, as well as the IPA with Singapore.

Now in the EU–Vietnam IPA, the appeal tribunal shall be composed of *six* members: two shall be nationals of an EU member state, two shall be nationals of Vietnam and two shall be nationals of third countries, all appointed by the trade committee, after proposals made by each contracting party (three candidates, two of whom shall be nationals of that party and one shall be a non-national). The trade committee may agree to

---

[351] UNCITRAL, 'Rules on Transparency in Treaty-based Investor–State Arbitration. UN Doc. A/RES/68/462' (April 2014).

[352] CETA, Art. 8.36; EU–Vietnam IPA (2018), Ch. 3, Art. 3.8; EU–Singapore IPA (April 2018), Annex 8.

[353] CETA, Art. 8.39.5; EU–Vietnam IPA (2018), Ch. 3, Art. 3.53.4; EU–Singapore IPA (April 2018), Art. 3.21.

[354] European Commission, Investment Provisions in CETA.

[355] US Model BIT (2004), Annex D; CAFTA–DR (2004); Chapter 10, Annex 10-F.

[356] This was in line with the European Commission's policy of 2010. European Commission, 'Communication from the Commission to the Council, the European Parliament, the European Economic and Social Committee and the Committee of the Regions Towards a Comprehensive European International Investment Policy' (July 2010).

increase the number of members of the appeal tribunal, by multiples of three. The appeal tribunal shall hear appeals in divisions consisting of three members, of whom one shall be a national of an EU member state, one a national of Vietnam and one a national of a third country. The division shall be chaired by the member who is a national of a third country. In the treaty with Singapore the tribunal consider six members, two appointed by the EU, two by Singapore and two by both parties who shall not be nationals of Singapore or an EU Member State.[357]

The number of members of the appellate tribunal in CETA is not pre-defined, and shall be decided by the CETA joint committee. A division of the appellate tribunal constituted to hear the appeal shall consist of three randomly appointed members of the appellate tribunal.[358]

In these agreements the appellate tribunal can hear appeals from the awards issued by the investment tribunal, and may uphold, modify or reverse that award, based on: (a) errors in the application or interpretation of the applicable law; (b) manifest errors in the appreciation of the facts, including the appreciation of relevant domestic law; and (c) the grounds set out in Article 52(1)(a)–(e) of the ICSID Convention, in so far as they are not covered by paragraphs (a) and (b).[359] In CETA, the appellate tribunal might also remand the case for adjustment of the award to the first-instance tribunal, if the joint committee decides to include such a feature in the adoption of the rules of functioning of the appellate tribunal, a feature that is already included in the agreements with Vietnam and Singapore.[360]

(e) Reception of the Investment Courts System

The question of whether an Investment Court System (or a multilateral investment court) is needed, desirable or politically feasible is of considerable policy salience. Even if one believes that a strong case can yet be

---

[357] EU–Vietnam IPA (2018), Ch. 3, Art. 3.39.8; EU–Singapore IPA (April 2018), Art. 3.10.

[358] CETA, Art. 8.28.

[359] CETA, Art. 8.28.2, EU–Vietnam IPA (2018), Ch. 3, Art. 3.54; EU–Singapore IPA (April 2018), Art. 3.19. ICSID Convention Art. 52(1) provides that either party may request annulment of the award on one or more of the following grounds: (a) that the tribunal was not properly constituted; (b) that the tribunal has manifestly exceeded its powers; (c) that there was corruption on the part of a member of the tribunal; (d) that there has been a serious departure from a fundamental rule of procedure; or (e) that the award has failed to state the reasons on which it is based.

[360] S. Lester, 'The New Investment Appellate Court Will Have Remand', International Economic Law and Policy Blog, 2 March 2016. http://worldtradelaw.typepad.com/. (accessed 25 March 2018)

made in favour of such courts, the question remains as to what kind of agreement should be proposed. Should countries seek an agreement on a relatively smaller scale (such as the OECD's failed Multilateral Agreement on Investment (MAI)), or should they aim to involve the larger number of countries that are members of the WTO or some other global bodies, such as the United Nations (UN)? Does the ICS properly address the shortcomings of ISDS? Or does it create another type of bias in favour of states?

This type of questions has informed the reactions to the ICS approach fostered by the EU. While some scholars have highlighted the positive aspects of this model as curing some of the legitimate problems of ISDS that stem from the fact that adjudication of investment disputes is an exercise of public authority,[361] others have pointed out the shortcomings of establishing an ICS (and eventually a MIC).

For Reinisch, the 'awards' issued by a hybrid between a court and an arbitral tribunal risk not being recognized as arbitral awards or being enforced as such pursuant to the specific rules of the ICSID Convention. However, they could be regarded as enforceable awards under the New York Convention,[362] but this is opinion is not shared by other commentators. Nappert has mentioned that, as the process as currently contemplated by the ICS is not arbitration, the decisions rendered by those courts are not arbitral 'awards' as contemplated by the New York Convention – regardless of the label that is put on them – and therefore will not be enforceable under either the ICSID Convention or the New York Convention.[363]

For Lavranos, the ICS deprives claimants of any role in the appointment of the judges, while giving the home and the host states the exclusive authority to do so, albeit in advance of a particular case and before knowing whether they will be respondents. The pre-selection of the judges of the investment tribunal and the appellate tribunal by the contracting parties carries the risk of selecting 'pro-state' individuals, in particular since they would be paid only by the states (or, more

---

[361] R. Howse, 'Courting the Critics of Investor–State Dispute Settlement: The EU Proposal for a Judicial System for Investment Disputes' (Fall 2015) p. 7 (citing von Bogdandy and Venzke).

[362] A. Reinisch, 'Will the EU's Proposal Concerning an Investment Court System for CETA and TTIP Lead to Enforceable Awards? – The Limits of Modifying the ICSID Convention and the Nature of Investment Arbitration', *Journal of International Economic Law*, 19 (2016), 761–86 at 785.

[363] S. Nappert, 'Escaping from Freedom? The Dilemma of an Improved ISDS Mechanism', *European Investment Law and Arbitration Review*, 1 (2015), 171–90 at 12.

accurately, their taxpayers).[364] Kho *et al.* also concur in this point, stressing that, while the ICS 'might appear to increase the level of arbitrator neutrality by creating a standing panel of arbitrators, in fact it may unintentionally create a system of arbitrator selection which is actually less balanced and fair than the current one'.[365]

Finally, other commentators consider that the ICS does not put an end to ISDS, as it still empowers foreign companies to circumvent domestic legal systems and courts, and sue governments in parallel tribunals. For them, ICS is a 'zombie' ISDS.[366]

As we saw in the first chapter of this work, the establishment of these types of courts is not something new and, in fact, is, in a way, a return to peaceful mechanisms of dispute settlement involving states that predate ISA. Some lessons learned from this experience could be useful to analyse the pitfalls and possible gains of the ICS (or MIC) approach, and will be presented later in this book.

3   Code of Conduct

Some recent IIAs include provisions for the establishment of a code of conduct for arbitrators or members of the tribunal, or set up a procedure allowing the contracting parties later to adopt such a code of conduct.

In the few cases in which this type of provision is provided for, a treaty body – a commission integrated with representatives of the contracting parties – is usually mandated with the mission of agreeing on a code of conduct for members of arbitral tribunals under the IIA.[367] Generally, these agreements do not provide a specific timeline for adoption of the code of conduct,[368] or parameters on the content of such code.

---

[364] N. Lavranos, 'The Shortcomings of the Proposal for an "International Court System" (ICS)' (February 2016).

[365] S. Kho, M. Bate, A. Yanovich, B. Casey and J. Strauss, 'The EU TTIP Investment Court Proposal and the WTO Dispute Settlement System: Comparing Apples and Oranges?' (2016), p. 17.

[366] P. Eberhardt, *The Zombie ISDS* (Corporate Europe Observatory, 2016).

[367] Canada–Honduras FTA (2013), Art. 10.26; Canada–Jordan BIT (2009), Arts. 29.2.c, 51.2.d; Canada–Peru FTA (2008), Art. 826.2; Colombia–Peru BIT (2007), Art. 24.3(c), Art. 37(d), 72.2; Canada–Peru BIT (2006), Art. 29.2.

[368] Canada–Honduras FTA (2013) mandates the adoption of a code of conduct by the Free Trade Commission at its first session following the entry into force of the agreement. Australia–China FTA (2015) includes a code of conduct in Annex 9A, but with no active role for the home state.

In CETA, there is more explicit guidance about the content of such a code of conduct for members of the investment tribunals. The agreement mandates a committee on services and investment, on the agreement of the contracting parties, to adopt a code of conduct that may include disclosure obligations, and provisions on the independence and impartiality of arbitrators and on confidentiality. The contracting parties endeavour to make their best efforts to ensure that the code of conduct is adopted no later than two years after the entry into force of CETA.[369] This code will supplement or replace the current 'default' code of conduct recognized in the treaty: the International Bar Association (IBA) Guidelines on Conflicts of Interest in International Arbitration.[370]

The fact that the CETA's code of conduct does not exist in the text of the agreement has been criticized, as it remains unknown whether the contracting parties have addressed the problems associated with arbitrators' impartiality and independence,[371] and because it does not spell out what sanctions, aside from removal from the case, would apply in the event of a breach (e.g. returning fees).[372]

Other treaties that already include a code of conduct provide for roles for the home and the host states in the implementation of that code. For example, in the EU–Singapore IPA, prior to his or her appointment as a member of a tribunal a candidate shall communicate matters concerning actual or potential violations of the code of conduct to the disputing parties and the non-disputing state party, for their consideration. The disclosure obligation is a continuing duty that requires the member of the tribunal to disclose in writing any such interests, relationships or matters that may arise during any stage of the proceeding at the earliest time that the arbitrator becomes aware of it.[373] A similar provision is found in the Korea–Vietnam FTA, but the arbitrator shall disclose any interests, relationships or matters that could create a conflict of interest in writing to the joint committee on the agreement, for consideration by both the host and the home states.[374] In the amended Australia–Singapore FTA, the obligation is to disclose conflicts of interest

---

[369] CETA, Arts. 8.30.1, 8.44.2.
[370] International Bar Association, *Guidelines on Conflicts of Interest in International Arbitration* (2014).
[371] Bernasconi-Osterwalder and Mann, 'A Response to the European Commission's December 2013 Document "Investment Provisions in the EU–Canada Free Trade Agreement (CETA)', p. 24.
[372] Nappert, 'Escaping from Freedom?', 18.
[373] EU–Singapore IPA (April 2018), Annex 7, 3-5.
[374] Korea–Vietnam FTA (2015), Annex 15-B, para. 3.

in writing to the parties – without clarification of whether that includes the contracting parties or the parties in the dispute.[375]

Although the EU–Vietnam IPA also includes a binding code of conduct for members of the investment and appellate tribunal, based on the IBA ethical guidelines, that code does not include an obligation to disclose conflicts of interest to the non-disputing parties (even to the home state).[376]

4   Adoption of Supplemental Rules of Procedure

Some investment agreements concluded in the last fifteen years also contain provisions that empower the contracting parties – including the home and the host states – to adopt supplemental rules of procedure that complement the arbitration rules previously established in an IIA.

The few agreements that include this type of provision – notably, several concluded by Canada – generally provide for the adoption of binding rules through a process of mutual consultation.[377] A similar provision is included in the EU–Singapore IPA, on fees and costs of legal representation.[378]

A more recent group of IIAs also provides for obligations of publicity to interested persons, establishing that the parties shall promptly publish the supplemental rules of procedure that they adopt, or otherwise make them available in such a manner as to facilitate knowledge of it.[379] An analogous provision is included in the Chile–Hong Kong Investment Agreement.[380]

A special case in this regard is the COMESA Investment Treaty. The COMESA Common Investment Area (CCIA) Committee shall establish Rules of Arbitration consistent with the provisions of the agreement before the COMESA Court of Justice – including the timelines for an appellate process – and may establish a specific form for this purpose and make it available through the Internet and other means. Until the adoption

---

[375] Australia–Singapore FTA (2016), Ch. 8, Art. 27.6, Annex 7.
[376] EU–Vietnam FTA. Ch. 8, Annex II IPA (2018), Annex 8.
[377] E.g. Canada–Mongolia BIT (2016), Art. 38.3; Canada–Tanzania BIT (2013), Art. 37; Canada–China BIT (2012), Arts. 18, 24.2.c.
[378] EU–Singapore IPA (April 2018), Arts. 3.21.5 and 4.1.4(e).
[379] Canada–Hong Kong (2016) BIT, Art. 23.3; Canada–Guinea BIT (2015), Art. 24.3; Burkina Faso–Canada BIT (2015), Art. 25.3; Canada–Côte d'Ivoire BIT (2014), Arts. 23.3, 38.3; Canada–Serbia BIT (2014), Art. 24.3, 39.3; Canada–Serbia BIT (2014), Art. 24.3, 39.3; Canada–Cameroon BIT (2014), Art. 23.3, 38.3; and Benin–Canada BIT (2013), Arts. 26.3, 48.3.
[380] Chile–Hong Kong Investment Agreement (2016), Art. 21.5.

of such rules, the ICSID Rules of Arbitration shall govern the arbitration except to the extent modified by the COMESA Investment Treaty, irrespective of whether the host and home states are parties to the ICSID Convention.[381]

5   The Nature of Regulating the Work of Tribunals in ISDS

The regulation of the work of tribunals in ISDS is becoming increasingly important in recent IIAs. Waibel believes that it is likely that states seeking to reassert control over IIAs will evolve towards rules that are not in the disposition of the disputing parties, either with all the appointments being drawn from a roster fully nominated by the contracting states, or even with a more pronounced shift towards the creation of standing investment tribunals, with state-appointed judges, that could dent the attractiveness of ISDS to investors.[382]

However, even if more active participation by the home state in the appointment of arbitrators on investment disputes is considered important for the overall impartiality and legitimacy of ISDS, this feature falls short of diplomatic protection, being a unilateral action that is not directly focused on determining the international responsibility of a state.

Similarly, codes of conduct can be used as control mechanisms of conflicts of interests, in order to reduce the 'agency slack' due to different preferences between states and arbitrators.[383] Although relevant to the overall participation of home states in the ISDS system, they are also far from being an example of diplomatic protection, as they are not directed towards determining the responsibility of another state due to a violation of international law.

Finally, although the adoption of supplementary rules of procedure could be relevant to improving ISDS or the ICS, if they are directed towards guaranteeing due process of law and equality of arms to the disputing parties, the role of the home state in its formulation is removed from the realm of diplomatic protection, being closer to the treaty- or rule-making powers of sovereign states.

---

[381] COMESA Investment Treaty (2007), Annex A, Arts. 2(3), 3.

[382] M. Waibel, 'Arbitrator Selection' in A. Kulick (ed.), *Reassertion of Control Over the Investment Treaty Regime* (2017), pp. 333–55 at p. 355.

[383] Van Aaken, 'Control Mechanisms in International Investment Law', 425–6.

V

Unilateral Home State Participation in ISDS

In this chapter we will examine the different mechanisms in which the home state can directly participate in investor–state arbitration, without requiring the joint intervention of the respondent host state. There are at least three mechanisms whereby this participation can take place: non-disputing party interventions and unilateral interpretations; consultation of draft awards; and enforcement of final awards.

A Non-Disputing State Party Interventions

Several investment treaties include provisions that allow for unilateral statements or interpretation of the international investment agreement, by a non-disputing state party (NDSP) to a pending investor–state dispute settlement, which includes the home state of the foreign investor. Depending on the text of the treaty, interventions of the home state in ISDS proceedings could include written or oral statements, access to evidence and documentation in general.

In the following section we will analyse the treaty-making practice and case law with respect to these two types of unilateral interpretations from the home state of the investor.

1 Regulated in the Treaty

Non-disputing state party interventions are not a new idea. The 1962 OECD Draft Convention on the Protection of Foreign Property included such a right for both investor-state and to state-to-state arbitration.[1] Even

---

[1] Organisation for Economic Co-operation and Development (OECD), 'Draft Convention on the Protection of Foreign Property', *International Legal Materials*, 2 (1963), 241–67,

the OECD's failed Multilateral Agreement on Investment[2] contained a provision allowing NDSP submissions.[3] It is also included in the Tribunal Rules of Procedure of the Iran–United States Claims Tribunal.[4]

Today, provisions allowing NDSP interpretations are mainly found in FTAs, being NAFTA,[5] the first treaty that formally included this procedural tool, and which recognized the systemic interest of each contracting party in the interpretation of the agreement.[6]

In the decade that followed the conclusion of NAFTA, its contracting parties continued to include this mechanism in FTAs negotiated with other states, such as the Mexican FTAs with Bolivia, Colombia and Venezuela, Nicaragua, and Uruguay;[7] in the United States' FTAs with Singapore, Chile and the Dominican Republic and Central America (CAFTA–DR), as well as in the Canada–Chile FTA[8] During that period, this procedural device is seldom found outside NAFTA members.[9]

According to an OECD survey on the basis of 1,660 investment treaties available by December 2011, only 25 IIAs include provisions on the

Annex 6(b)(i) allowed intervention by a contracting party with an interest that might be affected by the decision in the case.

[2] OECD, *The Multilateral Agreement on Investment Draft Consolidated Text* (1998), Art. D (12): 'The arbitral tribunal shall notify the Parties Group of its formation. Taking into account the views of the parties, it may give to any Contracting Party requesting it an opportunity to submit written views on the legal issues in dispute, provided that the proceedings are not unduly delayed thereby. Any Contracting Party requesting it within thirty days after receipt by the Parties Group of the notification of the tribunal's formation shall be given an opportunity to present its views on issues in dispute in which it has a legal interest.'

[3] W. Alschner, 'The Return of the Home State and the Rise of "Embedded" Investor–State Arbitration' in S. Lalani and R. Polanco (eds.), *The Role of the State in Investor–State Arbitration* (Brill/Martinus Nojhoff, 2014), pp. 309–10.

[4] Iran–United States Claims Tribunal, 'Tribunal Rules of Procedure' (1983). Note 5 to Article 15: 'The arbitral tribunal may, having satisfied itself that the statement of one of the two Governments – or, under special circumstances, any other person – who is not an arbitrating party in a particular case is likely to assist the tribunal in carrying out its task, permit such Government or person to assist the tribunal by presenting oral or written statements.'

[5] NAFTA, Arts. 1127–9.

[6] M. Kinnear, A. Bjorklund and J. F. G. Hannaford, *Investment Disputes under NAFTA. An Annotated Guide to NAFTA Chapter 11*, looseleaf edn (Kluwer Law International, 2006), pp. 1128–31.

[7] This was the first occurrence of non-disputing state party participation in a bilateral context.

[8] E.g. Mexico–Colombia–Venezuela FTA (1994), Annex 17–16, Rules 8, 9; Bolivia–Mexico FTA (1994), Arts. 15–28, 15–29, 15–30; Canada–Chile FTA (1996), Arts. G-29, G-30.

[9] Chile–Korea FTA (2003), Arts. 10.32, 10.33; Panama–Taiwan FTA (2003), Arts. 10. 28–10.30.

participation of NDSPs (together with the participation of *amici curiae*). Only seven countries had included such provisions in at least 12 per cent of their IIAs (Canada, Chile, Colombia, Japan, Mexico, Peru and the United States), almost exclusively in FTAs and much less often in bilateral investment treaties (BITs).[10]

This phenomenon has been explained by a different incentive structure, as dispute would appear more often in regional treaties and when a state expects to be a 'repeat player', it has a greater interest in influencing the interpretation of the agreement for future cases, besides its participation as a potential respondent state.[11] Such a rationale could be behind the increasing number of FTAs and BITs including this type of provision, as ISDS cases have risen steeply. In the last fifteen years, we find a total of 85 IIAs that include this interpretative device, being the majority investment chapters of FTAs, followed by BITs and a few regional investment treaties. Besides NAFTA members, countries such as Canada, Japan and Chile now regularly include these clauses in their IIAs.

(a) Different Types of Participation

In the agreements of the last fifteen years that allow the intervention of NDSPs, we find at least three distinct types of intervention in the arbitral procedure: limited participation, broad participation, and participation under *amicus curiae* rules. There is an important difference between both broad and limited participation and participation under *amicus* rules. While the former are expressed as a right of the NDSP and their submissions cannot be denied by the tribunal, the acceptance of the latter is in the discretion of the tribunal.[12]

Limited Participation In this type of clause, the right of the NDSP is restricted to making written or oral submissions to a tribunal on a question of interpretation of the IIA.[13] Many treaties also explicitly include the duty of the disputing party to deliver to the other parties written notice of a claim that has been submitted to arbitration

---

[10] J. Pohl, K. Mashigo and A. Nohen, *Dispute Settlement Provisions in International Investment Agreements* (2012), pp. 35–6.

[11] Alschner, 'The Return of the Home State', 310–11.

[12] M. Paparinskis and J. Howley, 'Article 5. Submission by a Non-Disputing Party to the Treaty' in D. Euler, M. Gehring and M. Scherer (eds.), *Transparency in International Investment Arbitration* (Cambridge University Press, 2015), pp. 196–226 at p. 203.

[13] Under some IIAs, at the request of a disputing party, the non-disputing party should resubmit its oral submission in writing: e.g.: Australia–Korea FTA (2014), Art. 11.20.4; Japan–Malaysia EPA (2005), Art. 85.13; Japan–Switzerland ECA (2009), Art. 94.10.

Table 5.1 *IIAs, including NDSP submissions*

	FTAs	BITs	RITs
Number of Treaties	47	35	3
% of Total Data Set	8	6	0.5

(usually no later than thirty days after the claim is submitted) and copies of all pleadings filed in the arbitration, at the cost of the requesting party. The state receiving information as an NDSP shall treat the information as though it were a disputing party, and thus respect the confidentiality of documents when it is required.[14] In some treaties, these provisions also include the right to receive from the disputing party a copy of the evidence that has been tendered to the tribunal and the written argument of the disputing parties.[15]

Article 1128 of NAFTA contains no procedural guidance on how these submissions operate, leaving the disputing parties and the arbitral tribunals almost with a 'blank sheet of paper' on important procedural aspects of this type of intervention.[16] Few treaties limit the right to present NDSP submissions for the consent of the disputing parties or the arbitral tribunal, such as the Canada–Czech Republic BIT, which also restricts the availability of the pleadings.[17]

Broad Participation   In some treaties, besides the right of the NDSP to make written and oral and submissions to the tribunal regarding the interpretation of the IIA, the respondent state shall 'promptly' transmit to the NDSP documents about the dispute, usually including the notices of intent and arbitration, pleadings, memorials, and briefs submitted to the tribunal, written submissions, minutes or transcripts of hearings of the tribunal, as well as orders, awards and decisions of the tribunal. There

---

[14] E.g. NAFTA, Arts. 1127–9; Mexico-Colombia-Venezuela FTA (1994), Annex 17–16, Rules 8, 9; Bolivia–Mexico FTA (1994), Arts. 15–28, 15–29, 15–30.

[15] Chile–Japan FTA (2007), Art. 95.

[16] Kinnear, Bjorklund and Hannaford, *Investment Disputes under NAFTA. An Annotated Guide to Nafta Chapter 11*, pp. 1128–32.

[17] Canada–Czech Republic BIT (2009), Annex B.II.1.

is also a general rule that the tribunal shall conduct hearings in a manner that is open to the public – which also would include the NDSP.[18]

Several of these agreements explicitly mention that NDSPs are allowed to attend hearings during the arbitration. In some of them, the respondent state has a specific period within which to deliver to the NDSP the abovementioned documents (usually thirty days), and the NDSP parties should bear some of the costs related to its interventions, such as for access to documents and evidence,[19] while on others there is not a specific timeframe to receive them or provisions on the costs of these interventions.[20]

This broad participation of NDSPs is also provided for in treaties recently concluded by the EU, such as CETA and the IPAs with Singapore and Vietnam. In these agreements, the respondent state shall, within thirty days of receipt, or promptly after any dispute concerning confidential or protected information has been resolved, deliver to the NDSP the basic documents of the dispute (e.g. request for consultations, claim to arbitration and request for consolidation). All other documents shall be delivered on request. The tribunal shall not draw any inference from the absence of any submission by an NDSP and ensure that any submission does not disrupt or unduly burden the proceedings, or unfairly prejudice any disputing party. It shall also ensure that the disputing parties are given a reasonable opportunity to present their observations on any submission by an NDSP.[21]

Participation under *Amicus Curiae* or Transparency Rules   In some of these agreements, there is no express provision for NDSP submissions, but home states could intervene in the arbitral proceedings as *amicus*

---

[18] E.g. Singapore–US FTA (2003), Arts. 15.19.2, 15.20.1–2; Chile–US FTA (2003), Arts. 10.19.2, 10.20.1–2; Morocco–US FTA (2004), Arts. 10.19.2, 10.20.1–2. This provision is also included in the US Model BITs (2004) (2012), Art. 28(2).

[19] E.g. Canada–Mongolia BIT (2016), Art. 28; Canada–Hong Kong BIT (2016), Art. 27; Canada–Guinea BIT (2015), Art. 29. The same provision is included in the 2004 Canadian Model FIPA, Arts. 33–35.

[20] E.g. Chile–Hong Kong Investment Agreement (2016), Art. 27; Canada–Korea FTA (2014), Arts. 8.29–31, 8.35. Canada–Honduras FTA (2013), Arts. 10.30–32.

[21] CETA, Art. 8.38; EU–Singapore IPA (April 2018), Art. 3.17 and Annex 8; EU–Vietnam IPA (2018), Ch. 3, Art. 3.46. In the latter agreement, documents may be made publicly available by communication to the repository referred to in the UNCITRAL Transparency Rules: UNCITRAL, 'Rules on Transparency in ISDS'.

curiae, considering the broad definition of that institution in certain IIAs.[22]

A clear disadvantage, as compared with explicit NDSP submissions, is that *amicus curiae* briefs cannot be filed as a right of the home state, and are accepted only at the discretion of the tribunal. However, once they are admitted they can actually be more extensive than NDSP submissions, which are limited to questions of interpretation of the IIA, while *amicus* briefs may comment on both law and fact.[23]

Although some treaties include transparency provisions, allowing the home state to receive copies of the notice of investment dispute and pleadings (usually within a timeframe of thirty days), there is not always a formal mechanism for making NDSP submissions.[24] This situation might change if, in the negotiation of IIAs, countries make reference to the UNCITRAL Rules on Transparency in treaty-based investor–state arbitration, which, in Article 5, provide for, as a general transparency rule, submissions by an NDSP to the treaty:[25]

> 1. The arbitral tribunal shall, subject to paragraph 4, allow, or, after consultation with the disputing parties, may invite, submissions on issues of treaty interpretation from a non-disputing Party to the treaty.

> 2. The arbitral tribunal, after consultation with the disputing parties, may allow submissions on further matters within the scope of the dispute from a non-disputing Party to the treaty.

> In determining whether to allow such submissions, the arbitral tribunal shall take into consideration, among other factors it determines to be relevant, the factors referred to in article 4, paragraph 3, and, for greater certainty, the need to avoid submissions which would support the claim of the investor in a manner tantamount to diplomatic protection.

> 3. The arbitral tribunal shall not draw any inference from the absence of any submission or response to any invitation pursuant to paragraphs 1 or 2.

> 4. The arbitral tribunal shall ensure that any submission does not disrupt or unduly burden the arbitral proceedings, or unfairly prejudice any disputing party.

---

[22] E.g. Nicaragua–Taiwan FTA (2006), ASEAN Comprehensive Investment Agreement (2009), Art. 39.6; ASEAN–Australia–New Zealand FTA (2009), Art. 26.6.

[23] Alschner, 'The Return of the Home State', 312.

[24] Chile–Argentina FTA (2017), Art. 8.32; Japan–Ukraine BIT (2015), Art. 18.8; Mexico–UAE BIT (2016); Colombia–Japan BIT (2011), Art. 32.

[25] UNCITRAL, 'Rules on Transparency in ISDS'.

5. The arbitral tribunal shall ensure that the disputing parties are given
a reasonable opportunity to present their observations on any submission
by a non-disputing Party to the treaty.

This provision borrows from the different IIAs examined before, and requires the tribunal to accept NDSP submissions if the respective state wishes to make them. This could help to avoid a 'one-sided' treaty interpretation affecting the scope of legal obligations of the other contracting states, even if they are not directly involved as a party to that specific dispute. In contrast, Article 4 of the same rules makes the acceptance of third person's submissions facultative to the respective tribunal, which *may* invite or allow such submissions.[26]

The use of these rules will help to embed NDSP submissions in IIAs, even if they do not explicitly provide for that right for NDSPs. However, adherence to these rules is still rather limited, with only forty-six IIAs having been concluded after 1 April 2014 making reference to or including provisional rules modelled on them, although the number of agreements that include such rules is increasing.[27]

(b)   Treaty Case Law

The case law on NDSP intervention is largely limited to NAFTA – where it has been used extensively – and CAFTA. Submissions under other agreements providing for this mechanism are still scarce. In the next section we will analyse the available case law on NDSP, with special focus on the intervention of the home state in ISDS.

NAFTA Case Law   NAFTA contracting parties have regularly exercised their right to make submissions as NDSPs. From all fifty-nine NAFTA Chapter 11 cases brought until 28 February 2018, Article 1128 submissions have been presented in thirty-two cases, with a total of ninety-five submissions. From this group, in twenty-seven cases the home state of the investor filed one or more submissions, with an overall total of forty-six submissions. While the United States has made thirty-four NDSP submissions as a home state in twenty-one cases, Canada has made twelve NDSP submissions as home states in six cases; Mexico is yet to present one of these submissions.

---

[26] Paparinskis and Howley, 'Submission by a Non-Disputing Party', 210–13.
[27] UNCITRAL, 'Status UNCITRAL Rules on Transparency in Treaty-based Investor–State Arbitration' (February 2018).

Table 5.2 *United States' NDSP submissions as home state in NAFTA*[28]

Cases	Number of NDSP Submissions	Subject Matter
1 *Metalclad* v. *Mexico*, ICSID Case No ARB(AF)/97/1	1	**Substantive:** expropriation
2 *Pope & Talbot* v. *Canada* (UNCITRAL)	8	**Substantive:** joint interpretations, most-favoured nation (MFN), national treatment (NT), fair and equitable treatment (FET), expropriation, performance requirements **Procedural:** prerequisites to bringing a claim
3 *S. D. Myers* v. *Canada* (UNCITRAL)	1	**Substantive:** definition of investment, damages
4 *Feldman* v. *Mexico*, ICSID Case No ARB(AF)/ 99/1	1	**Procedural:** prerequisites to bringing a claim
5 *UPS* v. *Canada* (UNCITRAL)	3	**Substantive:** NT, FET, international minimum standard (IMS), treaty interpretation. **Procedural:** prerequisites for bringing a claim, *amicus curiae*
6 *Fireman's Fund* v. *Mexico*, ICSID Case No ARB(AF)/02/1	1	**Procedural:** subject matter jurisdiction
7 *GAMI* v. *Mexico*, UNCITRAL	1	**Procedural:** subject matter jurisdiction

[28] These Art. 1128 submissions were obtained from the website US Department of State, 'NAFTA Investor–State Arbitrations' (February 2018). Although these submissions are usually available on the respective websites of NAFTA countries, in *Mesa* v. *Canada*, the claimant informed the tribunal that a document mentioned in the United States' Art. 1128 submission, namely the submission filed by Mexico in *Mercer International Inc.* v. *Canada*, did not appear to be available to the public, and requested the United States

Table 5.2 *cont.*

Cases	Number of NDSP Submissions	Subject Matter
8 *Bayview* v. *Mexico*, ICSID Case No ARB(AF)/ 05/1	1	**Substantive:** territoriality
9 *Merrill & Ring* v. *Canada*, (UNCITRAL) ICSID Administered Case	1	**Procedural:** limitation period
10 *Chemtura Corp.* v. *Canada*, UNCITRAL (formerly *Crompton* v. *Canada*)	1	**Substantive:** MFN, FET
11 *Mobil Investments and Murphy Oil* v. *Canada*, ICSID Case No ARB(AF)/07/4	2	**Substantive:** interpretation of annexes on non-conforming measures (NCMs)
12 *Clayton/Bilcon* v. *Canada* (PCA Case No 2009–04)	2	**Procedural:** Parallel proceedings **Substantive:** IMS, NT, reflective losses, damages
13 *Detroit International* v. *Canada* (UNCITRAL, PCA Case No 2012–25)	1	**Procedural:** waiver
14 *Mesa Power* v. *Canada*, (UNCITRAL, PCA Case No 2012–17)	2	**Procedural:** ISDS formalities, cooling-off period, treaty interpretation **Substantive:** FET, IMS, full protection and security (FPS), NT, government procurement
15 *KBR* v. *Mexico* (ICSID Case No UNCT/14/1)	1	**Procedural:** waiver

either to produce this document immediately or alternatively to delete the reference to it in its submission. Some days later, the United States submitted the 'secret' submission filed by Mexico: *Mesa Power* v. *Mexico*, Award, paras. 201, 203.

Table 5.2 *cont.*

Cases	Number of NDSP Submissions	Subject Matter
16 Mercer v. Canada, ICSID Case No ARB(AF)/ 12/3	1	**Procedural:** delegation of authority to state enterprises, limitation period **Substantive:** NT, MFN, IMS, reservations and exceptions
17 Windstream Energy v. Canada, PCA Case No 2013-22	1	**Substantive:** Indirect expropriation, IMS
18 Eli Lilly v. Canada (UNCITRAL, ICSID Case No UNCT/14/2)	2	**Procedural:** limitation period **Substantive:** FET, legitimate expectations, denial of justice
19 Lone Pine v. Canada (ICSID Case No UNCT/15/2)	1	**Substantive:** definition of investment, expropriation, IMS
20 RFP v. Canada (PCA Case No 2016-13)	1	**Procedural:** limitation period **Substantive:** 'Relating to' requirement, NT by states/ provinces, taxation measures
21 Mobil Investments v. Canada (ICSID Case No ARB/15/6)	1	**Substantive:** lack of good faith as breach of obligation

These interventions have been focused on a wide variety of treaty issues, both procedural and substantive. Procedural issues have included interpretations on preconditions for arbitration, waivers and *amicus curiae*. Submissions on substantive issues have dealt with the scope and coverage of the agreement, interpretations of treaty obligations (NT, FET, IMS, performance requirements, and expropriation), damages and reflective losses, among others.

Table 5.3 *Canada's NDSP submissions as home state in NAFTA*[29]

	Cases	Number of NDSP Submissions	Subject Matter
1	*Loewen* v. *US* (ICSID Case No ARB(AF)/98/3)	2	**Substantive:** NT, FET, FPS, treaty interpretation
2	*Methanex* v. *US* (UNCITRAL)	4	**Substantive:** definition of investment, NT, expropriation, causation, treaty interpretation **Procedural:** prerequisites to bringing a claim, *amicus curiae*
3	*Mondev* v. *US*, ICSID Case No ARB(AF)/99/2	2	**Procedural:** treaty interpretation, prescription, ISDS formalities; **Substantive:** NT, IMS, expropriation
4	*ADF* v. *US* (ICSID Case No ARB (AF)/00/1)	2	**Procedural:** treaty interpretation; **Substantive:** IMS
5	*Thunderbird* v. *Mexico* (UNCITRAL)	1	**Procedural:** Burden of proof; **Substantive:** NT
6	*Grand River* v. *US*, UNCITRAL	1	**Substantive:** IMS

Until now, home states have tended to use Article 1128 NDSP less than the other non-disputing contracting parties; and when home states make use of this right, normally they support the position of the host state either implicitly or explicitly, and not the position of its national investor. From all the existing NAFTA Chapter 11 arbitrations decided by 28 February 2018, in only two cases did the home state endorse the position of the claimant against the host state, although partially and only in certain issues.

[29] These submissions were obtained from the public website Foreign Affairs Trade and Development Canada Government of Canada, 'Cases Filed against the Government of Canada' (January 2018).

In *Metalclad* v. *Mexico*, the United States – the home state of the investor – sided with the claimant, supporting the view that the actions of local governments, including municipalities, were subject to the NAFTA standards, and that the term 'tantamount to expropriation' of Article 1110 addressed both measures that directly expropriate and measures equivalent to expropriation that indirectly expropriate investments. However, the United States sided also with the host state, rejecting the suggestion of the claimant that the term 'tantamount to expropriation' was intended to create a new category of expropriation not previously recognized in customary international law. The arbitral tribunal followed the views of the United States on both issues.[30]

In *Feldman* v. *Mexico*, the United States supported its investor's view, when it expressed the interpretation that NAFTA did not bar a claim by a natural person who was both an American citizen and a permanent resident of Mexico. Yet, on the issue of whether the three-year limitation period for making a claim under Article 1117(2) of NAFTA required the claimant simply to deliver a notice of intent or actually to submit a claim to arbitration, the United States favoured the interpretation of Mexico.[31] The tribunal dismissed the respondent state's preliminary defence pertaining to the claimant's lack of standing because of his permanent residence in Mexico. However, it rejected the interpretation of the United States that Article 1117(3) of NAFTA distinguished between 'making a claim' and 'submitting a claim to arbitration', for the purposes of commencement arbitration.[32]

In early NAFTA Chapter 11 cases, states exercised this right directly, without a previous procedural order from the tribunal. In fact, in the very first NDSP submission, in *Ethyl Corp.* v. *Canada*, because Mexico's notice was received only on the second and last day of the hearing on jurisdiction, the claimant raised the issue of timeliness, but the tribunal rejected it.[33] More recently, the United States' Article 1128 oral submissions during a hearing in *Eli Lilly* v. *Canada* were rejected by the claimant,

---

[30] *Metalclad* v. *Mexico*, Award, paras. 73, 102–12.

[31] G. Kaufmann-Kohler, 'Non-Disputing State Submissions in Investment Arbitration' in L. Boisson de Chazournes, M. G. Kohen and J. E. Viñuales (eds.), *Diplomatic and Judicial Means o Dispute Settlement* (Martinus Nijhoff Publishers, 2012), pp. 314–15.

[32] *Marvin Roy Feldman Karpa* v. *United Mexican States*, ICSID Case No ARB(AF)/99/1. Interim Decision on Preliminary Jurisdictional Issues, 6 December 2000, paras. 37, 59.

[33] *Ethyl Corp.* v. *Government of Canada*, UNCITRAL Award on Jurisdiction, 24 June 1998, para. 48, fn 15.

and the tribunal invited the United States to make a written supplemental submission to allow the parties to make observations on the United States' position.[34] In *S. D. Myers* v. *Canada, Feldman* v. *Mexico*, and in *Bayview Irrigation District* v. *Mexico*, the tribunal invited, by letter, the home state in these cases (the United States), and the other contracting party, to exercise their rights under Article 1128 of NAFTA and deliver the submissions on a specific date, on precise issues of treaty interpretation.[35] The same happened in *Mondev* v. *United States*, in which Canada – the home state of the investor – was invited by the tribunal to present a submission.[36] On occasion, tribunals have requested clarifications of submissions presented by NDSPs.[37] In more recent arbitrations; it is commonplace that tribunals are taking a more disciplined approach to the organization of the proceedings to accommodate these interventions,[38] with more control of the tribunal in specific procedural orders, including a timeframe within which to present these submissions.[39]

In NAFTA, home state NDPS submissions have often been selective in the issues addressed. For Coe, such an attitude of self-restraint is due to

[34] *Eli Lilly and Co.* v. *Government of Canada*, UNCITRAL, ICSID Case No UNCT/14/2, Award, 16 March 2017, para. 59.

[35] *S. D. Myers, Inc.* v. *Government of Canada*, UNCITRAL, Second Partial Award, 21 October 2002, para. 48; *Feldman* v. *Mexico*, Award, para. 32; *Bayview Irrigation District et al.* v. *United Mexican States*, ICSID Case No ARB(AF)/05/1, Award, 19 June 2007, para. 12.

[36] *Mondev* v. *US*, Award, para. 25.

[37] *Mobil Investments Canada Inc. and Murphy Oil Corp.* v. *Canada*, ICSID Case No ARB(AF)/07/4. Decision on Liability and on Principles of Quantum, 22 May 2012, para. 21

[38] M. Hunter and A. Barbuk, 'Procedural Aspects of Non-Disputing Party Interventions in Chapter 11 Arbitrations', *Asper Review of International Business and Trade Law*, 3 (2003), 163–5.

[39] For example, in *ADF Group* v. *US*, on 3 May 2001 the tribunal issued Procedural Order No 1 instructing the ICSID Secretariat to inform the governments of Canada and Mexico that any submission that they might wish to make pursuant to NAFTA, Art. 1128, should be filed within forty days after the service upon the Claimant of the Respondent's Counter-Memorial: *ADF Group* v. *US*, Award, para. 7. In *Canfor* v. *US*, a joint Order of the Costs of Arbitration and for the Termination of Certain Arbitral Proceedings holds that a letter from an official of one NAFTA party explaining the operation of an intergovernmental agreement with another NAFTA party did not purport to be an Art. 1128 submission. *Canfor Corp.* v. *United States of America; Tembec et al.* v. *United States of America; Terminal Forest Products Ltd* v. *United States of America*, UNCITRAL. Joint Order on the Costs of Arbitration and for the Termination of Certain Arbitral Proceedings, 19 July 2007, para. 111.

the fact that states must consider both the reciprocal and long-term implications of supporting certain interpretations of the treaty, and how those views interlock with past positions that they have taken, or future positions that they envisage taking as a possible respondent state.[40] Another explanation given is that the role of NAFTA parties as capital exporters, recipients of foreign investment, and sovereign states, transcends the merits of the specific cases.[41]

It is not unusual for a NAFTA respondent state to rely on views taken by one or both of the other two NAFTA states as an NDPS, either to suggest to the tribunal a subsequent state practice or to offer evidence of the concordant intent of the NAFTA parties.[42] In that context, NDSP submissions are often referenced in NAFTA awards and, in certain cases, are used as part of the basis of the decision. For example, in *Chemtura Corp. v. Canada*,[43] the Article 1128 submissions of Mexico and the United States are mentioned in the award as firmly opposing the possibility of using Article 1103 of NAFTA to import a FET clause from a BIT concluded by Canada.[44] Similarly, in *ADF v. United States*, the Article 1128 submissions of Canada and Mexico regarding IMS are explicitly referred to in the award.[45]

More recently, in the award in *Mesa v. Canada* – decided in favour of the respondent state – the tribunal cited Mexico's and the United States' Article 1128 submissions to support the conclusion that the challenged measure constituted procurement and could not be challenged under Article 1102 or 1103 of NAFTA.[46] In *Eli Lilly v. Canada*, the tribunal rejected the claim of denial of justice, largely following the reasoning of the United States' Article 1128 submission.[47]

In the same vein, NDSP submissions have been cited in arbitral awards, even in cases in which they have not been presented. In *Archer*

---

[40] J. J. Coe Jr, 'Taking Stock of NAFTA Chapter 11 in Its Tenth Year: An Interim Sketch of Selected Themes, Issues, and Methods', Vand. J. Transnat'l L., 36 (2003), 1381 at1410.

[41] M. Kinnear, 'Letter from Meg Kinnear to the Tribunal in Pope & Talbot Inc. v. Canada (NAFTA/UNICTRAL), 1 October 2011 – Exhibit A of the Submission of the United States of America in Chemtura Corporation v. Canada, 31 July 2009'.

[42] Coe Jr, 'Taking Stock of NAFTA Chapter 11 in Its Tenth Year', 1410.

[43] *Chemtura Corp. v. Canada*, Award, paras. 13–14, 61.

[44] A. Cate, 'Non-Disputing State Party Participation in Investor–State Arbitration under CAFTA–DR', July 2011: http://kluwerarbitrationblog.com/blog/2011/07/01/non-disputing-state-party-participation-in-investor-state-arbitration-under-cafta-dr/ (accessed 25 March 2018).

[45] *ADF Group v. US*, Award, paras. 57–60.

[46] *Mesa Power v. Canada*, Award, paras. 410, 430, 465–66.

[47] *Eli Lilly v. Canada*, Award, paras. 204–208, 218–225.

Daniels v. *Mexico*, the intervention pursuant to the Article 1128 submission of the United States during the *Loewen* case, and of Canada at the jurisdictional stage of *Methanex* are cited as one of the bases of the award.[48] Similarly, in *Glamis Gold* v. *United States*, and *Cargill* v. *Mexico*, both awards cite Article 1128 submissions made before other tribunals on the minimum standard of treatment (*ADF* v. *Mexico*, and *Pope & Talbot* v. *Canada*).[49]

CAFTA–DR Case Law

As in NAFTA, under CAFTA–DR, contracting parties have regularly exercised their rights to make submissions as NDSPs in ISDS arbitrations. So far, Article 10.20.2 of CAFTA–DR has been used by at least one NDSP in seven out of nine cases under Chapter 10 of CAFTA–DR, with a total of seventeen submissions. From that group, in six cases, the home state of the investor – the United States in all of them – filed one submission.

Table 5.4 *United States' NDSP submissions as home state in CAFTA–DR*[50]

	Cases	Number of NDSP Submissions	Subject Matter
1	*RDV* v. *Guatemala* (ICSID Case No ARB/ 07/23)	1	**Substantive:** IMS, FET
2	*Pac Rim* v. *El Salvador*, (ICSID Case No ARB/ 09/12)	1	**Substantive:** denial of benefits
3	*TECO* v. *Guatemala* (ICSID Case No ARB/ 10/23)	1	**Substantive:** IMS, FET

[48] *Archer Daniels* v. *Mexico*, Award, paras. 175–6.
[49] *Glamis Gold* v. *US*, Award, paras. 601, 612, 618; *Cargill* v. *Mexico*, Award, paras. 268, 275, 284–6.
[50] These submissions were obtained from the website US Department of State, 'CAFTA–DR Investor–State Arbitrations' (February 2018). The only cases in which there were NDSP submissions but not from the home state was *Commerce Group Corp. and San Sebastian Gold Mines, Inc.* v. *Republic of El Salvador*, ICSID Case No ARB/09/17, in which the home state was the United States.

Table 5.4 *cont.*

	Cases	Number of NDSP Submissions	Subject Matter
4	*Berkowitz* v. *Costa Rica* (formerly *Spence International and ors* v. *Costa Rica*) (ICSID Case No UNCT/13/2)	1	**Substantive:** scope and coverage, IMS, expropriation
5	*Corona Materials* v. *Dominican Republic* (ICSID Case No ARB(AF)/14/3)	1	**Procedural:** limitations period for bringing claims, the role of local litigation waiver **Substantive:** denial of justice
6	*Aven and ors* v. *Costa Rica* (ICSID Case No UNCT/15/3)	1	**Substantive:** IMS, expropriation, relation between treaty chapters

These interventions have focused on a variety of treaty interpretation issues, both substantive – such as the minimum standard of treatment, denial of justice, denial of benefits, expropriation – as well as procedural, such as the scope of application of CAFTA's dispute settlement provisions, waivers and limitation period for bringing claims.

Until now, the submissions presented by NDSPs have always been in line with the position of the host state, and they have generally been accepted by the arbitral tribunals.

In *Pac Rim Cayman* v. *El Salvador*, the tribunal expressly cited the NDSP submission of the home state – the United States – (together with that of Costa Rica), as the basis for its decision on denial of benefits, ruling that it had no jurisdiction to hear or decide the claim.[51] Similarly, in *TECO* v. *Guatemala*, the tribunal accorded weight to the submissions of the Dominican Republic, El Salvador and Honduras, under Article 10.20.2 of CAFTA–DR, while rejecting the claim on 'legitimate expectations'. In the eyes of the tribunal, it is clear 'that any investor has the expectation that the relevant applicable legal framework will not be disregarded or applied in an arbitrary manner. However, that kind of expectation is irrelevant to the

---

[51] *Pac Rim Cayman* v. *El Salvador*, Decision on the Respondent's Jurisdictional Objections, paras. 4.55–4.57.

assessment of whether a state should be held liable for the arbitrary conduct of one of its organs. What matters is whether the state's conduct has objectively been arbitrary, not what the investor expected years before the facts'.[52] Although it is not cited in the award, this position is, in substance, the same as that advanced by the United States in its NDSP submission.[53]

While deciding preliminary objections in *Corona v. Dominican Republic*, the tribunal agreed with the view expressed by the United States' NDSP submission in the case that a claimant cannot rely on the latest in a series of alleged breaches in order to frame its case as falling within the three-year limitation window.[54]

In an NDSP submission in *Spence International Investments v. Costa Rica*, the United States reiterated its interpretation that neither the concept of 'good faith' nor that of 'legitimate expectations' is a component element of FET under customary international law that gives rise to an independent host state obligation, citing extensively the NDSP submissions of Honduras and El Salvador in the cases *RDC Corp. v. Guatemala*, and *TECO v. Guatemala*.[55]

However, in *RDC Corp. v. Guatemala*, the tribunal rejected the strict standard of proof of the IMS, based on an analysis of state practice, advocated by the United States in its NDSP submission, and consequently declared a violation of the FET standard.[56]

As in NAFTA, in Article 10.20.2 of CAFTA–DR, it is explicitly recognized that NDSPs may make oral and written submissions to the tribunal regarding the interpretation of the agreement, and representatives of these states have regularly attended CAFTA–DR ISDS hearings. Probably benefiting from the experience of Article 1128 NAFTA submissions, ISDS tribunals under CAFTA–DR provide for basic procedures for NDSP submissions.[57]

---

[52] *TECO Guatemala Holdings, LLC v. Republic of Guatemala*, ICSID Case No ARB/10/23, Award, 19 December 2013, para. 621.

[53] *TECO Guatemala Holdings, LLC v. Republic of Guatemala*, ICSID Case No ARB/10/23, Submission of the United States of America, 23 November 2012, paras. 5–7.

[54] *Corona Materials LLC v. Dominican Republic*, ICSID Case No ARB(AF)/14/3, Award on the Respondent's Expedited Preliminary Objections in Accordance With Article 10.20.5 of the DR-CAFTA, 31 May 2016, paras. 172–5, 238.

[55] *Aaron C. Berkowitz, Brett E. Berkowitz and Trevor B. Berkowitz (formerly Spence International Investments and ors) v. Republic of Costa Rica*, ICSID Case No UNCT/13/2, US Article 10.20.2 Submission, 17 April 2015, paras. 17, fn 24.

[56] *Railroad Development Corp. v. Republic of Guatemala*, ICSID Case No ARB/07/23. Award, 29 June 2012, paras. 207–19.

[57] *TCW Group, Inc. and Dominican Energy Holdings, L.P. v. Dominican Republic*, UNCITRAL, Procedural Order N° 3, 16 December 2008, paras. 3.15, 3.5. However, in

Other IIAs

Besides NAFTA and CAFTA–DR, there is little public information on home states' NDSP submissions under other IIAs.[58] In contrast to the submissions referred to before, in these cases home state intervention has in occasions supported the investor's claims (at least partially).

In *Renco* v. *Peru*, a case brought under Article 10.20.2 of the Peru–US trade promotion agreement (TPA), by a procedural order, the arbitral tribunal invited the United States to comment on the interpretation of Article 10.20.4, within a period of 21 days.[59]

In a first NDSP submission, the United States advanced a narrower reading of the expedited review mechanism for claims under Article 10.20.4, in favour of the claimant, declaring that such provision requires tribunals to consider preliminary objections – other than objections as to the tribunal's competence – that a claim cannot succeed as a matter of law.[60]

In a second submission, the United States took an interpretation more favourable to the host state, declaring that a failure to make a claim under the appropriate provision and to comply with the conditions and limitations on consent of the treaty, including a waiver provision, 'results in lack of consent by the party and the concomitant lack of jurisdiction of the tribunal with respect to that claim'.[61] In a third submission, the United States explicitly agreed with Peru that the discretion whether to permit a claimant either to proceed under or to remedy an ineffective waiver 'lies with the respondent as a function of the respondent's general discretion to arbitration and not with a tribunal'. Furthermore, the submission states that the United States and Peru share the position that if all formal and material requirements are not met, the waiver contained in the treaty shall be deemed ineffective and the tribunal will lack jurisdiction, and that this constitutes 'the authentic interpretation of

---

this case finally there were no NDSP submissions, as TCW and the Dominican Republic settled the dispute as reflected in a Consent Award of 16 July 2009.

[58] Unless otherwise indicated, these submissions were obtained from the website US Department of State, 'NAFTA Investor–State Arbitrations'.

[59] Under the Peru–US TPA (2006), Art. 10.20.4, 'a tribunal shall address and decide as a preliminary question any objection by the respondent that, as matter of law, a claim submitted is not a claim for which an award in favour of the claimant may be made'.

[60] *The Renco Group, Inc.* v. *Republic of Peru*, ICSID Case No UNCT/13/1, Non-Disputing State Party Submission of the United States of America, 10 September 2014.

[61] *The Renco Group, Inc.* v. *Republic of Peru*, ICSID Case No UNCT/13/1, Second Non-Disputing State Party Submission of the United States of America, 1 September 2015, para. 16.

Article 10.18 and, under the Vienna Convention on the Law of Treaties, "shall be taken into account, together with the context"'.[62]

In a preliminary decision, the arbitral tribunal agreed with the claimant and the home state on a more limited reading of Article 10.20.4. In so doing, the tribunal concluded that the treaty does not mandate or require addressing and deciding objections as to competence in Article 10.20.4, concluding that that provision 'clearly and unambiguously excludes competence objections from its scope'.[63] Yet, in a later award, the tribunal found that the claimant had failed to establish the requirements for Peru's consent to arbitrate under the treaty, and its claims were dismissed for lack of jurisdiction.[64]

In *Aeroport Belbek LLC and Mr Igor Valerievich Kolomoisky* v. *Russian Federation*, PCA Case No 2014–30, Ukraine (the home state) made a submission as NDSP even though the 1998 Ukraine–Russia BIT does not include such provision. Using its inherent powers and prior consultation with the disputing parties, on 3 May 2016 the tribunal granted the Ukrainian application to make that submission, but denied a subsequent request from Ukraine to attend and make oral submissions at the hearing on 7 July 2016. In this case, the claimants submitted that Russia had breached its obligations under the abovementioned BIT by taking measures that deprived the claimants of their property, contractual and other rights to operate a commercial flight passenger terminal at Belbek Airport in Crimea.[65]

In *Bridgestone* v. *Panama*, a case initiated pursuant to Chapter 10 of the Panama–US TPA, claimants alleged that a decision by the Supreme Court of Panama related to trademark proceedings violated provisions of the TPA on NT, IMS and expropriation. The United States made two NDSP submissions on the expedited review mechanism for claims that lack of legal merit considered in Article 10.20.4–5 of the Panama–US TPA, as well as on the denial of benefits clause and the definition of

---

[62] *The Renco Group, Inc.* v. *Republic of Peru*, ICSID Case No UNCT/13/1, Third Non-Disputing State Party Submission of the United States of America, 11 October 2015, para. 8.

[63] *The Renco Group, Inc.* v. *Republic of Peru*, ICSID Case No UNCT/13/1. Decision as to the scope of the respondent's preliminary objections under Art. 10.20.4, 18 December 2014, para. 231.

[64] *The Renco Group, Inc.* v. *Republic of Peru*, ICSID Case No UNCT/13/1, Partial Award on Jurisdiction, 15 July 2016.

[65] Permanent Court of Arbitration (PCA), 'Arbitration between Aeroport Belbek LLC and Mr. Igor Valerievich Kolomoisky as Claimants and the Russian Federation' (August 2016).

investment.[66] Both submissions are explicitly cited by the tribunal, which follows the United States' interpretation that the TPA's benefits should not be denied to firms that have a real and continuous link with the country in which they are established – which supported the claimant's position. However, the decision does not follow the United States' interpretation that the definition of 'investment' explicitly excludes claims to payment that arise from commercial contracts for the sale of goods or services and that are not immediately due – which supported the host state's position.[67]

Finally, in *Italba* v. *Uruguay*, a case brought under the 2005 Uruguay–US BIT, the claimant alleged that Uruguay's telecommunications regulator failed to issue an updated licence to operate to a local subsidiary, and the United States presented one NDSP submission. The submission elaborates the United State' interpretation of licences and authorizations as investments, the meaning of control of an investment, denial of benefits, limitation periods, and expropriation, NT, MFN and IMS, taking positions that are more in line with the respondent host state's interpretation on the same issues.[68]

2 Unilateral Interpretations of Home States

In the event of lack of specific provision in an IIA on the introduction of NDSP submissions, a home state can simply issue a unilateral statement on interpretation, if it is dissatisfied with the interpretation of an arbitral tribunal.[69] This unilateral conduct may contribute to the formation of subsequent practice under Article 31(3)(b) of the Vienna Convention on the Law of Treaties, when it is explicitly agreed to or tacitly accepted by other treaty parties. If that is not the case, unilateral assertions might have

---

[66] *Bridgestone Licensing Services, Inc. and Bridgestone Americas, Inc.* v. *Republic of Panama*, ICSID Case No ARB/16/34, US Submission Pursuant to Article 10.20.2 of the US–Panama TPA, 28 August 2017; *Bridgestone Licensing Services, Inc. and Bridgestone Americas, Inc.* v. *Republic of Panama*, ICSID Case No ARB/16/34, US Supplemental Submission Pursuant to Article 10.20.2 of the US–Panama TPA, 25 September 2017.

[67] *Bridgestone Licensing Services, Inc. and Bridgestone Americas, Inc.* v. *Republic of Panama*, ICSID Case No ARB/16/34, Decision on Expedited Objections, 13 December 2017, paras. 151–152, 177, 282–285, 302.

[68] *Italba Corp.* v. *Oriental Republic of Uruguay*, ICSID Case No ARB/16/9, Submission of the US, 9 November 2017.

[69] For example, under ICSID Arbitration Rules, Rule 37, after consulting both parties, the tribunal may allow a person or entity that is not a party to the dispute (the 'non-disputing party') to file a written submission with the tribunal regarding a matter within the scope of the dispute.

limited value, especially if they are perceived as self-serving and deter-mined by the desire to influence the tribunal's decision in favour of the respondent state.[70] Unilateral interpretations by states could range from statements posted on official websites, or submissions made as respondent states in specific cases, or as formal interpretive submissions.

There have been a limited number of cases in which a home state has issued such unilateral interpretations. In *SGS* v. *Pakistan*, Switzerland, the home state of the investor, submitted a letter to the ICSID Secretariat as a non-disputing state, expressing its disagreement with and 'alarm' about the award's narrow interpretation of the umbrella clause included in Article 11 of the 1995 Pakistan–Switzerland BIT, which considered it to be 'counter' to the Swiss government's intent.[71] Although the letter was entitled 'Interpretation of Article 11 of the Bilateral Investment Treaty between Switzerland and Pakistan In the light of the Decision of the Tribunal on Objections to Jurisdiction of ICSID in Case No ARB/01/13 SGS Société Générale de Surveillance SA versus Islamic Republic of Pakistan', as it was submitted after the award on jurisdiction was issued, it did not influence the decision.

In *Aguas del Tunari* v. *Bolivia*, by letter dated 1 October 2004, the arbitral tribunal wrote to the Netherlands (the home state of the investor) regarding certain statements made by Dutch diplomats before their Parliament that apparently coincided with the Bolivian position. Using Rule 34 of the ICSID Arbitration Rules, and being mindful of not triggering diplomatic protection,[72] the tribunal requested only narrow comments from the Netherlands, with respect to specific documents.[73] Although the response, dated 29 October 2004, was entitled 'Interpretation of the Agreement on encouragement and reciprocal pro-tection of investments between the Kingdom of the Netherlands and the

---

[70] Kaufmann-Kohler, 'Non-Disputing State Submissions in Investment Arbitration', 316–19.

[71] L. Johnson and M. Razbaeva, 'State Control Over Treaty Interpretation' (2014), p. 7; E. Gaillard, 'Investment Treaty Arbitration and Jurisdiction Over Contract Claims – the SGS Cases Considered' in T. Weiler (ed.), *International Investment Law and Arbitration: Leading Cases from the ICSID, NAFTA, Bilateral Treaties and Customary International Law* (Cameron May, 2005), pp. 325–46 at p. 325; A. Newcombe and L. Paradell, *Law and Practice of Investment Treaties: Standards of Treatment* (Kluwer Law International, 2009), pp. 466–8. The letter is reprinted in M. Baldi, 'Letter from Swiss Secretariat for Economic Affairs to Antonio R. Parra, ICSID Deputy Secretary-General, 1 October 2003', *Mealey's International Arbitration Reports*, 19 (2004), E1–2.

[72] Kaufmann-Kohler, 'Non-Disputing State Submissions in Investment Arbitration', 314.

[73] *Aguas del Tunari* v. *Bolivia*, Decision on Respondent's Objections to Jurisdiction, Annex IV.

Republic of Bolivia', the tribunal eventually made no use of these commentaries, as it did not find subsequent practice establishing agreement of the parties regarding the interpretation of the BIT.[74]

On 1 May 2008, the United States made a submission to the ad hoc annulment committee in the case *Siemens* v. *Argentina*. In the document, the United States declared that it 'would not normally seek to make an unsolicited submission in an ICSID proceeding in which it is not a party'; it felt 'compelled to do so in this case . . . to correct the record in this case', regarding the United States' interpretation of Articles 53–54 of the ICSID Convention has been inaccurately characterized, which is 'important beyond the present case in a number of disputes by US investors against Argentina'. For the United States, a state is obligated to abide by and comply with an award rendered against it, 'irrespective of an investor's enforcement efforts'.[75] As the case was discontinued on 9 September 2009 pursuant to ICSID Arbitration Rule 43(1), the tribunal did not have the opportunity to decide on this issue.

In *Achmea* v. *Slovak Republic*, after consultation with the parties, by letter dated 10 May 2010, the tribunal invited the Netherlands – the home state – to provide any observations that it might have on the jurisdictional question before the tribunal, especially with respect to the validity of the 1991 Netherlands–Slovakia BIT, after the accession of Slovakia to the EU. On 10 June 2010, the Dutch government provided observations concluding that the BIT in question continued to be in force and that there was 'no reason to doubt the jurisdiction of the Arbitral Tribunal' in the dispute.[76] In a subsequent letter to the tribunal, dated 23 June 2010, the Dutch government attached a '*note verbale*' that it had received from the Slovak Ministry of Foreign Affairs, stressing that the BIT had not been formally terminated, leaving open the question of the validity and applicability of intra-EU BITs.[77] In the award, the tribunal dismissed the intra-EU jurisdictional objection and acknowledged the input from the Netherlands as 'helpful', although it spelled out that it did not rest any

---

[74] *Aguas del Tunari* v. *Bolivia*, Decision on Respondent's Objections to Jurisdiction, para. 260

[75] *Siemens AG* v. *Argentine Republic*, ICSID Case No ARB/02/8. Submission by the United States of America to the ad hoc Annulment Committee regarding Arts. 53 and 54, 1 May 2008.

[76] *Achmea BV* v. *Slovak Republic*, UNCITRAL, PCA Case No 2008-13 (formerly Eureko BV v. Slovak Republic). Award on Jurisdiction, Arbitrability and Suspension, 26 October 2010, paras. 155–163.

[77] *Achmea* v. *Slovak Republic*, Award on Jurisdiction, Arbitrability and Suspension, paras 164–6.

part of its decision upon the attitude of either contracting party, particularly that of the government of the Netherlands (or of the European Commission) to the question of the validity of the BIT or the existence, continuation or extent of the jurisdiction of the tribunal.[78]

3 The Nature and Value of Non-Disputing State Party Intervention

Clearly, interventions by non-disputing contracting submissions are not binding on tribunals in the same way as joint interpretations made by the contracting parties are. However, it has been argued that coinciding NDSP submissions can be demonstrative of an agreement between the contracting parties on the treaty's correct interpretation under Article 31(3)(a) of the VCLT, and some even consider these interventions a type of subsequent state practice for the effects of Article 31(3)(b) of the VCLT.[79] Tribunals and commentators generally appear comfortable with relying on them, where interventions by all the other treaty parties support interpretations by the respondent state. This constitutes good evidence of an agreement on interpretation and thus should be given considerable weight.[80] At the very least, one might expect that the concurrence of the contracting parties on a point of interpretation would be highly persuasive to a tribunal.[81]

According to UNCTAD, tribunals are likely to pay attention to statements made by NDSPs in order to find confirmation of subsequent agreement or practice between the contracting parties and, for instance, when all the non-disputing treaty parties intervene in support of the interpretation of the treaty by the respondent state, this could amount to an authoritative interpretation.[82] Coe believes that this type of intervention may serve a moderating function, either because the respondent state softens its position in anticipation of the potentially contradicting

[78] Kaufmann-Kohler, 'Non-Disputing State Submissions in Investment Arbitration', 316.
[79] Paparinskis and Howley, 'Submission by a Non-Disputing Party', 222.
[80] A. Roberts, 'Power and Persuasion in Investment Treaty Interpretation: The Dual Role of States', American Journal of International Law, 104 (2010), 179 at 219.
[81] Kinnear, Bjorklund and Hannaford, Investment Disputes under NAFTA. An Annotated Guide to NAFTA Chapter 11, pp. 1128–35.
[82] UNCTAD, 'Interpretation of IIAs: What States Can Do', 14.

views of other parties or because it does not, leaving differing views before the tribunal.[83]

Alschner points out that when a contracting state does not know on which side it is more likely to be in future litigation, it has more incentives to prevent 'extreme' interpretations by arbitral tribunals, and it will look more favourably to NDSP interventions aimed at preventing biased interpretations in support of the investor, and foster those more favourable to the state.[84]

However, some have expressed concern that occasional views expressed by state parties on the meaning of particular provisions of treaties are not a viable method of achieving uniformity in the interpretation of IIAs.[85] According to Schreuer, once a case is under way, the home state of the disputing investor might support restrictive interpretations of investor rights, as it 'is typically less interested in an interpretation favourable to its national in the pending dispute than in an interpretation that favours State respondents generally'.[86] For Roberts, the concern of a limited interpretation of the treaty by an NDSP because of its interest as actual or potential respondent in other cases is not persuasive. Contracting parties do not appear solely concerned about preventing future liability, and they also balance that interest with protection for their nationals as home states. If that were not the case, they would simply withdraw from their IIAs.[87] However, as the case law examined in the previous section evidences, it is in fact very much more likely that a home state makes NDSP submissions that are closer to the host state's position rather than that of its national investor.

Hunter and Barbuk have characterized the NDSP framework with respect to NAFTA arbitrations as being designed to make an 'intergovernmental business'.[88] In this context, home states are more likely to strike a balanced approach between the protection of their national

---

[83] Coe Jr, 'Taking Stock of NAFTA Chapter 11 in Its Tenth Year', 1419–20.

[84] Alschner, 'The Return of the Home State', 311.

[85] C, Schreuer and M. Weiniger, 'A Doctrine of Precedent?' in P. Muchlinski, F. Ortino and C. Schreuer (eds.), *The Oxford Handbook of International Investment Law* (Oxford University Press, 2008), pp. 1188–206 at p. 1200.

[86] C. Schreuer, 'Investment Protection and International Relations' in A. Reinisch and U. Kriebaum (eds.), *The Law of International Relations: Liber Amicorum Hanspeter Neuhold* (Eleven International Publishing, 2007), pp. 345–58 at p. 353.

[87] Roberts, 'Power and Persuasion', 220.

[88] Hunter and Barbuk, 'Procedural Aspects of Non-Disputing Party Interventions in Chapter 11 Arbitrations', 163.

investors and their own regulatory interests[89] or, in the words of Pierce and Coe:[90]

> A party's right to intervene may be a mixed blessing for a claimant. NAFTA Parties are unlikely to endorse interpretations and theories of recovery that enlarge their own exposure to claims. Their involvement in the process is nonetheless to be welcomed. [...] Party submissions that agree on an interpretative point will presumably be helpful to the tribunal. And such submissions may provide an important check upon fanciful theories of recovery or treaty interpretations proffered by only one NAFTA party.

Another objection against NDSP submission is that it prolongs the arbitration and involves the disputing parties in incurring additional costs, and can delay the procedure when they are not submitted in a timely fashion. Written submissions of NDSPs have often been repetitive.[91] For example, in a submission made in the *UPS* case, the United States merely reiterated its position in *Pope & Talbot* and *ADF*, materially attaching those documents.[92] In *Aven* v. *Costa Rica*, the United States also attached the NSDP submission presented by the same country in another CAFTA case – *Spence International Investments* v. *Costa Rica* – containing its interpretation on CAFTA–DR provisions on IMS and expropriation (Articles 10.5 and 10.7).[93]

In addition, these interventions are 'cost free' for the NDSP,[94] as generally, IIAs do not require them to bear the costs that disputing parties incur as a result and consequence of their interventions, and arbitral tribunals do not generally have the power to shift these costs to non-disputing parties. As we have seen, only certain IIAs provide that NDSP parties should bear some of the costs related to their interventions, such as access to documents and evidence. But, manifestly, the value of photocopies does not seem to be the highest cost in ISDS.

[89] Alschner, 'The Return of the Home State', 315.
[90] C. C. Pearce and J. J. Coe Jr, 'Arbitration under NAFTA Chapter Eleven: Some Pragmatic Reflections upon the First Case Filed against Mexico', *Hastings International and Comparative Law Review*, 23 (1999), 311 at 338.
[91] Hunter and Barbuk, 'Procedural Aspects of Non-Disputing Party Interventions in Chapter 11 Arbitrations', 154–5.
[92] *United Parcel Service of America, Inc.* v. *Government of Canada*, Third US 1128 Submission, 23 August 2002.
[93] *David R. Aven and ors* v. *Republic of Costa Rica*, ICSID Case No UNCT/15/3, US Article 10.20.2 Submission, 12 February 2016.
[94] Hunter and Barbuk, 'Procedural Aspects of Non-Disputing Party Interventions in Chapter 11 Arbitrations', 172–3.

For Alschner, home states have no incentive to use these submissions extensively, as it is time and resource intensive for its own interests, and may not want to engage in interpretative statements to pursue broad interpretations of an investment treaty that can affect them if they were subject to future ISA. NDSPs seem to choose the dispute and the topics that require intervention, rather than giving overall support to the other contracting parties of an IIA in ongoing ISDS arbitrations.[95] However, we must recall that this mechanism has been used in more than half of Chapter 11 NAFTA proceedings and in the majority of CAFTA investor–state disputes.

Another objection raised against this type of submission is that it can increase the likelihood that home states will exercise diplomatic protection. For Kaufmann-Kohler, there is a risk of covert return of diplomatic protection if these interventions are not directed to providing interpretation of the treaty, but to 'allow the investor's home state to run in aid of its national in an ongoing arbitration by pleading the facts in dispute'. She advances that tribunals should reject submissions that exceed those limits, either because there is an express prohibition on the use of diplomatic protection (as in Article 27(1) of the ICSID Convention or in certain IIAs), or in the absence of that prohibition, for the reason that such kinds of intervention would go against the general framework of ISDS.[96]

In fact, in the discussion of the UNCITRAL Rules on Transparency in ISDS there was special concern to avoid the use of these submissions supporting investors' claims in a manner tantamount to diplomatic protection. However, as Paparinskis and Howley point out, the right to exercise diplomatic protection still exists despite the presence of ISDS unless it has been waived or suspended by a unilateral act or a treaty. In the end, it will be for the tribunal to determine whether NDSP submissions correspond to diplomatic protection, and if they are not allowed under the applicable law and dispute settlement rules.[97]

Although, generally, when a state uses this kind of intervention to make the formulaic declaration that it 'takes no position on how the interpretive positions it offers apply to the facts of this case',[98] and that 'no inference

---

[95] Alschner, 'The Return of the Home State', 315–16.
[96] Kaufmann-Kohler, 'Non-Disputing State Submissions in Investment Arbitration', 323–5.
[97] Paparinskis and Howley, 'Submission by a Non-Disputing Party', 216, 218, 220.
[98] See, among others: *Feldman* v. *Mexico*, Canada's NAFTA Second Art. 1128 Submission; *Loewen* v. *US*, Mexico Third 1128 Submission; *Methanex* v. *US*, Second Submission of Canada Pursuant to NAFTA Art. 1128; *UPS* v. *Canada*, First Mexican 1128 Submission.

should be drawn from the absence of comment on any issue',[99] in reality, some of these interventions go beyond a merely legal interpretation and touch indirectly the specific facts of the case, through rejection of the claimant's position and generally supporting the position of the host state. As Hunter and Barbuk highlight, on several occasions, NDSPs appear to have forgotten that they were indeed non-disputing parties, addressing legal arguments and factual questions in specific cases.[100]

For example, in *Methanex*, Canada agreed with the United States in the interpretation of Article 1105 of NAFTA, and that 'the Investor's suggestion would broaden the requirement to provide full protection and security to foreign investors beyond that which is contemplated by the international minimum standard of treatment recognized by customary international law'.[101] In *UPS*, the United States agreed with Canada's position at the hearing – which Mexico also approved – that a breach of Article 1502(3)(a) of NAFTA 'may only occur wherever a referenced monopoly 'exercises' delegated 'governmental authority''.[102] Although Mexico has not been a home state in Chapter 11 NAFTA disputes, its NDSP submissions under that treaty follow the same pattern. For instance, in *Pope & Talbot*, Mexico submitted that the interpretation urged by the claimant on national treatment was 'simply wrong', and agreed with Canada that NAFTA did not create a *lex specialis* of expropriation.[103]

Alschner believes that fears of a return to diplomatic protection through this mechanism are overstated, because, aside from some technical differences – e.g. no exhaustion of local remedies is needed – these interventions occur as a part of 'structured, legal proceedings rather than discretionary and potentially politicized diplomatic consultations'.[104]

In my opinion, when it comes to NDSP, we are clearly facing a mechanism that has the ability to trigger diplomatic protection inside ISDS. The home state could theoretically advance an interpretation of the

---

[99] See *TECO* v. *Guatemala*, Submission of the US, para. 5–7; *Railroad Development Corp.* v. *Republic of Guatemala*, ICSID Case No ARB/07/23. Submission of the United States of America, 31 January 2012.

[100] Hunter and Barbuk, 'Procedural Aspects of Non-Disputing Party Interventions in Chapter 11 Arbitrations', 165.

[101] *Methanex Corp.* v. *US*, Second Submission of Canada.

[102] *United Parcel Service of America* v. *Government of Canada*. US Second 1128 Submission, 13 May 2002.

[103] *Pope & Talbot Inc.* v. *Government of Canada*, Supplemental Submissions of the United Mexican States, 25 May 2000.

[104] Alschner, 'The Return of the Home State', 314.

IIA in order to secure the responsibility of the host state for an injury caused to its national by violation of the investment treaty. But, in reality, that is not happening. For any of the abovementioned reasons, home states tend to side with host states with respect to interpretation of the treaty, and in the few cases in which they have sided with the investor, they usually do so only partially. In none of the cases analysed in this section have home states' interventions explicitly delved into the facts of the case, and even if they did, the value that the tribunal will give to an NDSP submission that is not consistent with those of other contracting parties is likely to be relative.

The analysis of the case law in NDSP submissions shows that, in the majority of the cases, the interventions of the home state of the investor cannot be considered an exercise of diplomatic protection, as they are favourable to the host state. In some cases, such as $GAMI^{105}$ and $Mondev,^{106}$ the home state has even presented submissions explicitly arguing that the tribunal has no jurisdiction to hear the claims of its own national, or supported the position that the claims of its national should be dismissed on the merits.[107] As Weiler mentions, '[t]he days when a government would lend its support for a claim made by its investor against another country appear to have passed into history'.[108]

However, in at least five cases in which the home state has taken a position in line with the claimant, this interpretation has been followed by the tribunal, as has previously been referred to in the analysis of *Metalclad* v. *Mexico*, *Feldman* v. *Mexico*, *Pac Rim Cayman* v. *El Salvador*, *TECO* v. *Guatemala*, and *Renco* v. *Peru*. On the other hand, unilateral interpretations in the absence of IIA provisions have largely been not decisive for the dispute, either because the issue was already decided (*SGS* v. *Pakistan*), or it was deemed not relevant (*Achmea* and *Aguas del Tunari*), or it was settled between the parties to the arbitration (*Sanum*).

In practice, home states seem not to be seeking to advance their investors' claims directly through NDSP, and in most cases are taking

---

[105] *GAMI Investments Inc.* v. United Mexican States, UNCITRAL. US 1128 Submission, 30 June 2003.

[106] *Mondev International Ltd* v. *United States of America*, Canada 1128 Submission, 6 July 2001.

[107] K. Parlett, 'Diplomatic Protection and Investment Arbitration' in R. Hofmann and C. J. Tams (eds.), *International Investment Law and General International Law: From Clinical Isolation to Systemic Integration?* (Nomos, 2011), pp. 211–29 at p. 215.

[108] T. Weiler, 'NAFTA Investment Law in 2001: As the Legal Order Starts to Settle, the Bureaucrats Strike Back', *International Lawyer*, 36 (2002), 345–53 at 348.

the opportunity to express general views on interpretation, even if doing so might indirectly affect their investors' claims.[109] More than diplomatic protection, this seems to be a way of regaining control as masters of the treaties.

B   Consultation of Draft Awards or Decisions

Certain IIAs stipulate that, before issuing a decision or award on liability, a disputing party can request that the arbitral tribunal send the draft decision or award for comment, not only to the disputing parties but also to the non-disputing contracting states including the home state of the investor.[110]

This feature was included in the 2004 US Model BIT and appeared for the first time in a treaty in the Morocco–US FTA of the same year.[111] By February 2018, only nineteen IIAs had provided for this mechanism – mostly those concluded by the United States, some Latin American countries and Korea.[112]

All these agreements provide for the same procedural framework for the consultation of draft awards or decisions. Within sixty days after the tribunal transmits its proposed decision or award, the home state (and any other NDSP) may submit written comments to the tribunal concerning any aspect of its proposed decision or award. The tribunal shall consider any such comments and issue its decision or award not later than forty-five days after the expiration of the sixty-day comment period. These agreements only exclude this consultation of draft awards in the hypothetical case in which an appeal procedure is available.

This *ex post* interpretation of the home state could potentially be another source of diplomatic protection, if the claimant or the respondent state requests this possibility, and the home state takes the bold approach of directly intervening in the final phase of the proceedings and siding with its national investor. However, there is little treaty-making and no case law in this regard, and experience in the use of other provisions that allow the intervention of home states in ISDS arbitrations suggests that contracting states will take a careful attitude before advancing interpretation of the agreement at such a later stage.

---

[109] *Cf.* Roberts, 'Power and Persuasion', 219.
[110] UNCTAD, 'Interpretation of IIAs: What States Can Do', 14.
[111] US Model BIT (2004), Art. 28.9; Morocco–US FTA (2004), Arts. 10.20.9–10.
[112] E.g. CAFTA–DR (2004), Arts. 10.20.9–10; Uruguay–US BIT (2005), Art. 28.9; Colombia–US FTA (2006) Arts. 10.20.9–10.

It could also be the case that, once the comments of the home state on the draft award of decision are required, such state decides to support the position of the host state, especially if it deems it necessary for the overall interpretation of the agreement – a situation that could affect the home state as a future respondent in investment claims. In this situation, instead of diplomatic protection we will be facing another example of reassertion of control of the investment treaties by the states – something that is not unlikely to happen, as has been shown by the experience on NDSP submissions that was analysed in the precedent section.

C   Enforcement of ISDS Awards

The recognition and enforcement of ISDS awards is different for ICSID and non-ICSID awards. In the case of ICSID Convention claims, the preamble already requires the contracting parties to comply with any arbitral award, and Article 53(1) mandates them to 'abide by and comply with the terms of the award'. Article 54(1) adds that 'Each Contracting State shall recognize an award rendered pursuant to this Convention as binding and enforce the pecuniary obligations imposed by that award within its territories as if it were a final judgment of a court in that State.'[113] This provision applies not only to the host state, but to all contracting states of the ICSID Convention.[114] Non-execution constitutes a violation of this specific obligation, enabling the use of dispute settlement mechanisms, including those before the International Court of Justice.[115]

With respect to non-ICSID awards, their recognition and enforcement is usually governed by the New York Convention,[116] as applied by the domestic courts of the state parties to that treaty. Here is one of the major differences with the ICSID system, as a local court may refuse to recognize and enforce non-ICSID awards on grounds provided in the Convention,[117] that are broad enough to admit of interpretation – such as the violation of a 'public policy',

---

[113] ICSID Convention, Arts. 53(1), 54(1).
[114] C. Schreuer, *The ICSID Convention: A Commentary* (Cambridge University Press, 2001), pp. 1123–4.
[115] A. Giardina, 'L'exécution des sentences du Centre international pour le règlement des différends relatifs aux investissements', *Revue critique de droit international privé*, 712 (1982), 273–93 at 291–2.
[116] Convention on the Recognition and Enforcement of Foreign Arbitral Awards, 10 June 1958, 21 UST 2517, T.I.A.S. No 6997, 330 U.N.T.S. 38 [hereinafter 'New York Convention'].
[117] P. Polášek and S. T. Tonova, 'Enforcement Against States' in J. A. Huerta Goldman, A. Romanetti and F. X. Stirnimann (eds.), *WTO Litigation, Investment Arbitration, and*

or the issuing of awards *ultra vires*.[118] Additionally, non-ICSID awards may be reviewed by the courts and under the laws of the seat in which arbitration took place.[119] In contrast, the ICSID system is independent of such domestic rules dealing with the enforcement of the arbitral awards, and also of the New York Convention.[120]

Host states' compliance with ISDS arbitration awards has generally been considered good. Schreuer points out that 'the consequences of non-compliance with an award for a state's reputation with private and public sources of international finance are such that States usually prefer to abide by decisions of tribunals'.[121] In 2007, Parra noted that, at that time, ICSID provisions on enforcement of awards had been tested in only four cases, in which execution was rejected in domestic courts due to sovereign immunity.[122] In 2008, Dugan *et al.* highlighted that voluntary compliance with ICSID awards was the norm and that around 95 per cent of arbitration awards by then – including commercial awards – were satisfied without enforcement.[123] An even more optimistic appraisal in March 2011 reported that the great majority of ICSID awards – more than 80 per cent – were complied with voluntarily: an estimate that rose to 90 per cent before Argentina 'started digging in its heels' in some cases.[124]

However, in recent years there have been some problems with compliance and enforcement of awards. Argentina was particularly criticized

Commercial Arbitration (Wolters Kluwer Law & Business, Kluwer Law International, 2013), pp. 357–87 at p. 372.

[118] T. Mizushima, 'The Role of the State after an Award Is Rendered in Investor–State Arbitration' in S. Lalani and R. Polanco Lazo (eds.), *The Role of the State in Investor–State Arbitration* (Brill/Martinus Nijhoff, 2014), pp. 380–404 at pp. 277–9.

[119] Polášek and Tonova, 'Enforcement Against States', 373.

[120] A. Broches, 'Awards Rendered Pursuant to the ICSID Convention: Binding Force, Finality, Recognition, Enforcement, Execution', *ICSID Review*, 2 (1987), 287–334 at 287, 308–9, 311.

[121] Schreuer, 'Investment Protection and International Relations', 348.

[122] A. R. Parra, 'The Enforcement of ICSID Arbitral Awards. 24th Joint Colloquium on International Arbitration. Paris, November 2007' (2007), p. 3. The cases were *SARL Benvenuti & Bonfant v. People's Republic of the Congo* (ICSID Case No ARB/77/2); *Liberian Eastern Timber Corp. v. Republic of Liberia* (ICSID Case No ARB/83/2); *Société Ouest Africaine des Bétons Industriels v. Republic of Senegal* (ICSID Case No ARB/82/1); and *AIG Capital Partners, Inc. and CJSC Tema Real Estate Co. v. Republic of Kazakhstan* (ICSID Case No ARB/01/6).

[123] C. F. Dugan, D. Wallace Jr., N. D. Rubins and B. Sabahi, *Investor–State Arbitration* (Oxford University Press, 2008), pp. 675–6.

[124] A. Ross, 'Nicosia: Investment Arbitration – A View from Cyprus', *Global Arbitration Review* (2011) 6.

for pushing the limits of the regime by 'proactively non-paying'.[125] A non-exhaustive investigation in early 2010 revealed that, for different reasons, at least six countries were declining to pay final awards rendered pursuant to an IIA.[126] In 2012, the OECD highlighted that, some problems had arisen regarding states' enforcement of ICSID and non-ISCID awards, with a number of refusals to comply with awards coming from Argentina, Kazakhstan, Russia, Thailand, Zimbabwe and the Kyrgyz Republic.[127] A similar finding was underscored by Polášek and Tonova in 2013, adding Zimbabwe to the list of 'non-compliant' countries.[128] A less optimistic view of the 'automatic' enforcement of ICSID awards is commented on in a more recent review of European, Middle Eastern and African arbitration.[129] In any case, these episodes of non-compliance are still not the rule in ISDS arbitration, and even Argentina settled five long outstanding awards in October 2013.[130]

But foreign investors are not entirely on their own in the event of non-payment or non-compliance by the host state, and among several options they might seek the help of their home state to enforce the award. Refusal to comply with the award and reliance on state immunity leads to revival of the right of diplomatic protection after the espousal of the claim: something that is fairly common in trade disputes.[131]

Diplomatic protection can then be an alternative or a supplement to the judicial enforcement of ISDS awards, especially in view of state immunity from execution,[132] which is preserved even at the ICSID Convention. Article 55 of that Convention states that nothing in it

---

[125] L. E. Peterson, 'Argentina by the Numbers: Where Things Stand with Investment Treaty Claims Arising out of the Argentine Financial Crisis' (February 2011).

[126] L. E. Peterson, 'How many States Are Not Paying Awards under Investment Treaties?' (May 2010).

[127] D. Gaukrodger and K. Gordon, 'Investor–State Dispute Settlement: A Scoping Paper of the Investment Policy Community', *OECD Working Papers on International Investment*, No 2012/3 (2012) p. 30.

[128] Polášek and Tonova, 'Enforcement Against States', 373–4.

[129] J. W. Barratt and M. N. Michael, 'The "Automatic" Enforcement of ICSID Awards: The Elephant in the Room?', *European, Middle Eastern and African Arbitration Review* 2014.

[130] By the end of 2013, Argentina had settled five ICSID cases with Vivendi, National Grid plc, Continental Casualty Co., Azurix and Blue Ridge Investments: L. E. Peterson, 'After Settling some Awards, Argentina Takes more Fractious Path in Bond-Holders Case, with New Bid to Disqualify Arbitrators' (December 2013).

[131] A. Joubin-Bret, 'Is There a Need for Sanctions in International Investment Arbitration?', *Proceedings of the Annual Meeting (American Society of International Law)*, 106 (2012), 130–3 at 132.

[132] Schreuer, 'Investment Protection and International Relations', 348.

'shall be construed as derogating from the law in force in any Contracting State relating to immunity of that State or of any foreign State from execution'.[133]

Although problems of state immunity from execution have been discussed, mainly in the context of the enforcement of judgments against a foreign state, in principle, the same rules would apply to arbitral awards.[134] Such immunity protects assets serving governmental purposes (*jure imperii*) and not those serving commercial purposes (*jure gestionis*). This immunity is rarely renounced – and if it is, the waiver is narrowly interpreted. Moreover, states often conduct *jure gestionis* activities through separate legal entities, making it difficult to enforce the award because we are not dealing with the state by itself.[135] According to Mizushima, recent practice suggests that there has been an expansion of the scope of foreign state immunity from execution in two respects: first, an expansive interpretation of what constitutes sovereign property that is immune from execution, and, second, a restrictive interpretation of a waiver of immunity.[136]

Other procedural and economic difficulties that investors face for the enforcement and execution of the ISDS awards are the potential disclosure of confidential information that the investor is keen to protect, the fact that such process could even further compromise future business relationships with the host state and, most importantly, the usual lengthy duration of these proceedings, that might imply high expenses.[137] An example of this is the famous *Sedelmayer* case,[138] in which Russia had persistently refused to pay the award since 1998. After protracted litigation, in which various targeted assets were protected by sovereign immunity (e.g. overflight rights paid by a German airline, merchandise and equipment presented by a Russian agency in a trade show) the claimant could partially collect

---

[133] ICSID Convention, Art. 55.
[134] Mizushima, 'The Role of the State after an Award Is Rendered', 280.
[135] J. E. Viñuales and D. Bentolila, 'The Use of Alternative (Non-Judicial) Means to Enforce Investment Awards against States' in L. Boisson de Chazournes, M. G. Kohen and J. E. Viñuales (eds.) *Diplomatic and Judicial Means of Dispute Settlement* (Martinus Nijhoff Publishers, 2012), pp. 254–6.
[136] Mizushima, 'The Role of the State after an Award Is Rendered', 282–6.
[137] Viñuales and Bentolila, 'The Use of Alternative (Non-Judicial) Means', pp. 257–8.
[138] D. Charlotin, 'Looking Back: German Investor, Franz Sedelmayer, Was Early-Adopter of Investment Treaty Arbitration, but Had to Engage in Decade-Long Assets Hunt against Russia' (August 2017).

in February 2014, after the seizure and auction of Russian property in Sweden and Germany.[139]

Additional enforcement problems might arise in the rare cases in which the investor requests provisional remedies, or claims specific performance and not pecuniary compensation, such as injunctions, annulment of governmental measures, declaration of the rights and obligations or of the illegality of the decision,[140] or even the restitution of the investment (as in *Arif* v. *Moldova*).[141] In those cases, the home state might have more leverage for the enforcement of such awards or decisions.

The exercise of diplomatic protection from the home state to enforce ISDS awards may potentially take the form of inter-state arbitration, inter-national adjudication or home state countermeasures or threats thereof.[142]

1   Inter-State Arbitration

Even in the IIAs in which diplomatic protection is expressly excluded during ISDS, the home state could become an 'enforcer' if the host state fails to abide by the arbitral award. From the sample of investment treaties concluded in the last fifteen years, we find that forty-eight IIAs (around 9 per cent of the sample), expressly provide for the possibility of state-to-state arbitration in the event of non-compliance by the respondent state.[143] This feature is also provided for in FTAs with investment chapters recently concluded by the EU, such as CETA, and the FTAs with Vietnam and Singapore,[144] as well as in the TPP.[145] The same provision is also included in the US and Canadian model BITs,[146] and in Article 11.36.5 of NAFTA.

Such a procedure can be triggered only by demand of the home state of the disputing investor, if the other contracting party fails to abide by or

---

[139] Federation of German Industries (BDI), *Background: Facts and Figures. International Investment Agreements and Investor-State Dispute Settlement* (2014), p. 20.

[140] Gaukrodger and Gordon, 'Investor–State Dispute Settlement: A Scoping Paper', 98.

[141] *Mr Franck Charles Arif* v. *Republic of Moldova*, ICSID Case No ARB/11/23. Award, 8 April 2013.

[142] Gaukrodger and Gordon, 'Investor-State Dispute Settlement: A Scoping Paper', 31.

[143] Twenty-nine are FTAs with investment chapters, seventeen are BITs and one is an RIT.

[144] CETA, Art. 8.42; EU–Vietnam FTA, Ch. 8; Art. 32; EU–Singapore FTA, Art. 9.28.

[145] TPP, Art. 9.28.8.

[146] US Model BIT (2004) (2012), Art. 34.8; Canada Model FIPA (2004), Art. 45.5.

comply with a final award rendered.[147] In the large majority of such proceedings, the home state may seek a determination that non-compliance with the final award is inconsistent with the obligations of the respective agreement; and a recommendation that the respondent state abide by or comply with the final award.[148]

If this mechanism of ISA is triggered, IIAs, almost without exception, refer such disputes to ad hoc arbitration of a panel of three members, providing that each party nominates one and the appointed arbitrators agree on the chair, as will be examined in detailed in the next chapter.

2 International Adjudication

The Statute of the International Court of Justice[149] provides that the jurisdiction of the ICJ 'comprises all cases which the parties refer to it and all matters specially provided for in the Charter of the United Nations or in treaties and *conventions in force*' (emphasis added). Therefore, the consent of the states is required as the basis of jurisdiction of the Court. This requirement appears to be fulfilled by Article 64 of the ICSID Convention, which stipulates that 'Any dispute arising between Contracting States concerning the interpretation or application of this Convention which is not settled by negotiation shall be referred to the International Court of Justice by the application of any party to such dispute, unless the states concerned agree to another method of settlement'.[150] A dispute over non-compliance of an ICSID award could, in principle, be a dispute concerning the application or interpretation of the Convention, and ending up with an ICJ judgment finding the host state to be in breach of its obligations under Article 53(1) of the ICSID Convention.[151] There is no similar provision for non-ICSID awards.

Mizushima has advanced another possible interpretation that would limit the possibility of using the adjudicatory powers of the ICJ as an enforcement mechanism of an ICSID award. If such an award originates

---

[147] E.g.: Mexico–Singapore BIT (2009), Art. 18.8; Belarus–Mexico BIT (2008), Art. 20.8; Colombia–Northern Triangle FTA (2007), Art. 12.29.7.

[148] E.g.: Argentina–Chile FTA (2017), Art. 8.40.10; Chile–Hong Kong Investment Agreement (2016), Art. 32.10; Australia–Singapore FTA (amended 2016), Art. 33.11.

[149] Statute of the International Court of Justice, 26 June 1945, 3 Bevans 1179; 59 Stat 1031; TS 993; 39 AJIL Supp 215 (1945), Art. 36(1).

[150] ICSID Convention, Art. 64.

[151] Polášek and Tonova, 'Enforcement Against States', 380.

from ISDS that was initiated in accordance with an IIA – as is often the case – it is then necessary to take into account the state-to-state dispute settlement provided for in that agreement. If such an IIA excludes the possibility of settling an inter-state dispute at the ICJ, the jurisdiction of that court may be denied if one adopts the line of reasoning that is limited by the phrase 'unless the states concerned agree to another method of settlement' of Article 64 of the ICSID Convention.[152]

Countries may also declare that they do not confer jurisdiction on the ICJ to settle any disputes arising concerning the interpretation or application of the treaty. Turkey has taken this position in several IIAs concluded in the last fifteen years, leaving only inter-state negotiation as the sole mechanism for settling such disputes.[153]

Schreuer has mentioned that the use of this type of diplomatic protection was considered an '*ultima ratio*' – a check designed to counterbalance the immunity of execution of states.[154] During the drafting of the ICSID Convention there was also concern that this might be used either to frustrate ISA proceedings, or that it would create an inequitable situation in favour of the investor, as there would be no corresponding right for the host state in the event that a foreign investor failed to comply with an award.[155] So far, no claim has been instituted before the ICJ under Article 64 of the ICSID Convention, with regard to the refusal of a state to comply with an ICSID award.[156]

3 Home State Countermeasures

Diplomatic protection may involve negotiation and a number of diplomatic means, including certain unilateral acts of self-help from the home state, such as diplomatic protest and countermeasures, though the latter can raise questions related to their legality.[157]

Non-compliance by a state with an ISDS award rendered under an IIA may be considered by the home state – another contracting party to the treaty – as an internationally wrongful act by the host state that causes injury. In that context, the home state could take temporal and non-

---

[152] Mizushima, 'The Role of the State after an Award Is Rendered', 289–90.
[153] E.g.: Gabon–Turkey BIT (2012), Art. 12.4.c; Pakistan–Turkey BIT (2012), Art. 10.4.(c); Cameroon–Turkey BIT (2012), Art. 10.4.d.
[154] Viñuales and Bentolila, 'The Use of Alternative (Non-Judicial) Means', 268.
[155] Schreuer, 'Investment Protection and International Relations', 349.
[156] Polášek and Tonova, 'Enforcement against States', 380.
[157] UNCTAD, *Dispute Settlement: State-State* (United Nations, 2003), p. 24.

forcible countermeasures with the intention of procuring its cessation and to obtain reparation for the injury.[158] Countermeasures can be used by the home state as a 'sword' to ensure the implementation of investment protection obligations.[159]

These measures are essentially temporary or reversible – limited for as long as the necessary conditions for taking them are satisfied – and must fulfil certain conditions for legitimacy, such as proportionality and not affecting certain fundamental international obligations.[160] Furthermore, applying countermeasures in this context does not mean that the underlying obligations of the investment treaty are suspended or terminated.

This issue becomes relevant if we believe that rights on IIAs are directly owed to the investor, or that they are delegated rights originally owed to the home state. If we follow the first theory, as the investor's rights are direct rights, the substantive investment protection rules should be excluded from applying to relations between states, unless that is explicitly allowed in the treaty. Therefore, the home state would not be entitled to engage in diplomatic protection over breaches of IIAs standards of treatment of investors and investment. As Douglas put it, as 'the contracting states have opted out of the inter-state secondary rules of state responsibility in relation to a limited group of wrongs causing damage to a particular sphere of private interests,' the home state of the investor 'has no immediate secondary rights within the investment treaty regime to challenge the commission of this breach of treaty; instead the new rights arising upon the breach of treaty vest directly in the investor'.[161]

Paparinskis lengthily contest this line of thought, stressing, among several reasons, that the parallel invocation of responsibility for the breach of the same primary rule is not unknown to the international law of responsibility, either historically or in the work of the International Law Commission on codification of the law on state responsibility. He

---

[158] ILC, 'Draft Articles on Responsibility of States for Internationally Wrongful Acts, with commentaries. Report of the International Law Commission, 53rd session (A/56/10)' (2008) II *Yearbook of the International Law Commission* 31–143 at I., Art. 22 and Part III.

[159] M. Paparinskis, 'Investment Arbitration and the Law of Countermeasures', *British Yearbook of International Law* (2008), 265–352 at 270.

[160] International Law Commission, 'Draft Articles on Responsibility of States for Internationally Wrongful Acts, with Commentaries. Report of the International Law Commission, 53rd Session (A/56/10)', *Yearbook of the International Law Commission*, II (2008), 31–143, Art. 22, Comm. 4 and 6.

[161] Z. Douglas, 'The Hybrid Foundations of Investment Treaty Arbitration', *British Yearbook of International Law*, 74 (2003), 151–289 at 190–1.

concludes that the legal entitlement to engage in diplomatic protection has not disappeared, 'even if for pragmatic reasons of efficiency the exercise of diplomatic protection has faded into the background'.[162]

But besides the general regime for invocation of responsibility by an injured state against another under international law,[163] virtually all the FTAs that provide for state-to-state arbitration, allow some kind of countermeasure, in the event that the responding party in those proceedings fails to comply with the arbitral award or panel ruling, within a reasonable period of time. In those cases, the complaining party is typically entitled to temporary remedies, such as the suspension of obligations undertaken under the treaty or to receive compensation.

Originally included in Article 2019 of NAFTA, this feature is also provided for in recently concluded agreements – such as CETA[164] – and almost every FTA with an investment chapter provides for countermeasures if the other party does not comply with an inter-state award declaring that such a party has generally failed to carry out its obligations under the agreement, or has adopted a measure inconsistent with the treaty.

From the group of IIAs concluded in the last fifteen years, seventy-three (14 per cent of the sample) include that possibility, being the large majority of the investment chapters of FTAs (sixty-one treaties)[165] with only twelve BITs including similar provisions, establishing that if the contracting parties fail to reach an agreement to implement the decision of the arbitral panel within sixty days of the decision, the party bringing the dispute shall be entitled to compensation or to suspend benefits of equivalent value to those awarded by the arbitral panel.[166] The Chile–Uruguay BIT only provides for suspension of benefits as a measure of retaliation and a timeframe of just thirty days for the non-compliant state to implement the decision of the arbitral panel.[167]

---

[162] Paparinskis, 'Investment Arbitration and the Law of Countermeasures', 288–92.

[163] See ILC, 'Draft Articles on Responsibility of States for Internationally Wrongful Acts, with commentaries', III.

[164] CETA, Art. 29.14.

[165] E.g. Australia–Singapore FTA (amended 2016), Ch. 16, Art. 10; Honduras–Peru FTA (2015), Art. 15.12-13; Canada–Korea FTA (2014), Arts. 21.2, 21.11.

[166] E.g. Canada–Côte d'Ivoire BIT (2014), Art. 37.9; Canada–Mali BIT (2014), Art. 37.9; Canada–Senegal BIT (2014), Art. 38.9.

[167] Chile–Uruguay BIT (2010), Annex F – Art. 11.

Although, until recently, there was no publicly available information about home states using countermeasures to ensure the implementation of IIAs' obligations,[168] in recent years we have seen some examples of measures to secure host states' compliance with investment treaty awards consisting in the withdrawal or suspension of trade benefits, or the non-support in loan requests to international financial institutions.[169]

(a)   Withdrawal or Suspension of Trade Benefits

A couple of years after winning an investment dispute against Argentina,[170] Azurix Corp. filed a petition with the United States Trade Representative (USTR) in order to review the eligibility of Argentina as a beneficiary of the US Generalized System of Preferences (GSP), a programme to promote economic growth in the developing world that provides preferential duty-free treatment for products from designated beneficiary countries and territories, including developing and least-developed countries.[171]

The basis for Azurix's request was the delay of the Argentinian government in paying the outstanding award. To be eligible for the GSP, countries must meet certain mandatory and discretionary criteria that are regularly reassessed, and any person may present a petition to the GSP Subcommittee to request modifications to the list of eligible countries, to be suspended or withdrawn.[172] The designation or removal of the list is made by the President, who could even confer such a designation waiving some mandatory criteria if is in the national economic interest of the United States and reports such determination to Congress with reasons therefor. Under the mandatory criteria of ineligibility we find that a country:[173]

---

[168] Paparinskis, 'The Limits of Depoliticisation in Contemporary Investor–State Arbitration', 276.

[169] C. B. Rosenberg, 'The Intersection of International Trade and International Arbitration: The Use of Trade Benefits to Secure Compliance with Arbitral Awards', Geo. J. Int'l L., 44 (2012), 503.

[170] *Azurix Corp.* v. *Argentine Republic* (ICSID Case No ARB/01/12). Award, 24 July 2006.

[171] United States Trade Representative, 'Office of the United States Trade Representative. Generalized System of Preferences (GSP): Notice Regarding the Announcement of Petitions Accepted for the 2009 Annual GSP Country Practices Review, Acceptance of Pre-Hearing Comments and Requests To Testify for the 2009 Annual GSP Country Practices Review Hearing, and the Initiation of the 2010 Annual GSP Country Practices Review'.

[172] Office of the United States Trade Representative, 'U.S. Generalized System of Preferences (GSP) Guidebook' (December 2012), pp. 20–1.

[173] United States Code, 2006, V. 12, Title 19, Customs Duties, Sections 1701-End to Title 20, Education, Sections 1–1482, p. 636.

(I) has nationalized, expropriated, or otherwise seized ownership or control of property, including patents, trademarks, or copyrights, owned by a United States citizen or by a corporation, partnership, or association which is 50 percent or more beneficially owned by United States citizens,

(II) has taken steps to repudiate or nullify an existing contract or agreement with a United States citizen or a corporation, partnership, or association which is 50 percent or more beneficially owned by United States citizens, the effect of which is to nationalize, expropriate, or otherwise seize ownership or control of property, including patents, trademarks, or copyrights, so owned, or ...

(E) Such country fails to act in good faith in recognizing as binding or in enforcing arbitral awards in favour of United States citizens or a corporation, partnership, or association which is 50 percent or more beneficially owned by United States citizens, which have been made by arbitrators appointed for each case or by permanent arbitral bodies to which the parties involved have submitted their dispute.

Azurix argued that Argentina had failed to comply with its obligations under the 1991 Argentina–US BIT, and that as a result it no longer met the requirements to be a beneficiary of the GSP. The company even pointed out that it had negotiated an agreement on the conditions for payment of the award, with significant advantages for Argentina, including a reduction of the payable amount and the interest, and assisting Argentina with credit rating agencies and international banks.[174]

After failing to obtain its annulment, the Argentinian government insisted that it was open to honouring the award,[175] and explained the delay of payment by saying that the claimant had not brought its rulings to a local court for collection.[176] Argentina held that it was in full compliance with the ICSID Convention, interpreting its Article 54 as saying that, in order to be enforced, ICSID arbitral awards must first be brought before domestic courts, and that if there is any disagreement on this point, it contemplated the case of submitting the case to the ICJ.[177] On that point, Azurix was wary of the Argentine judiciary and of the fees that those courts charged for the processing of such awards, especially if

---

[174] Viñuales and Bentolila, 'The Use of Alternative (Non-Judicial) Means', 271–2.
[175] *Azurix Corp.* v. *Argentine Republic* (ICSID Case No ARB/01/12), Decision on the Application for Annulment of the Argentine Republic, 1 September 2009.
[176] La Nación, 'Ofensiva argentina para frenar a EE.UU.' (2011).
[177] Viñuales and Bentolila, 'The Use of Alternative (Non-Judicial) Means', 272.

there is a risk that they would be overturned, or paid in bonds rather than cash.[178]

A second example of the use of the suspension of trade benefits to push the enforcement of an ISDS award is the *CMS/Blue Ridge* case. On 26 July 2001, CMS Gas Transmission Company ('CMS') filed an arbitration case against Argentina, concerning the suspension of a tariff adjustment formula for gas transportation. That action damaged TGN, an Argentinian gas transportation company in which CMS had an investment. The dispute was arbitrated under ICSID Arbitral Rules and, on 12 May 2005, an ICSID tribunal issued a final award in CMS's favour, in the amount of US$133.2 million, after finding that Argentina had breached its obligations to CMS, as a protected investor, under the 1991 Argentina–US BIT.[179]

On 8 September 2005, Argentina filed an application with the Secretary-General of ICSID, seeking annulment of the award. On 25 September 2007, the ICSID Annulment Committee 'confirmed Argentina's obligation to pay CMS $133.2 million plus interest in compensation, holding that payment by Argentina of the sum awarded is obligatory'.[180]

On 5 June 2008, Blue Ridge Investments – a Bank of America subsidiary – notified Argentina that it was the successor in interest to CMS as a purchaser and assignee of the CMS's award. As in *Azurix*'s case, Blue Ridge displayed aggressive diplomatic pressure before the USTR to exclude Argentina from the list of beneficiaries of the GSP.[181]

Under USTR recommendation, on 26 March 2012 President Barack Obama suspended the duty-free treatment Argentina that enjoyed under the GSP, and that country is no longer part of the list of beneficiaries designated by the United States.[182] The explicit basis of this decision was that Argentina had 'not acted in good faith in enforcing arbitral awards in favour of United States citizens or a corporation, partnership, or associa-

---

[178] The Economist, 'Foreign-Investment Disputes: Come and Get Me' (February 2012).
[179] *CMS Gas Transmission Co.* v. *Republic of Argentina*. Decision of the Tribunal on Objections to Jurisdiction, 1 July 2003.
[180] *CMS Gas Transmission Co.* v. *Argentine Republic*, ICSID Case No ARB/01/8. Decision of the ad hoc Committee on the Application for Annulment of the Argentine Republic, 25 September 2007.
[181] International Centre for Trade and Sustainable Development (ICTSD), 'US Suspends Argentina from Trade Preference Scheme', *Bridges Weekly Trade News Digest*, (2012) 16.
[182] United States Trade Representative (USTR), 'GSP in Use – Country Specific Information' (February 2018).

tion that is 50 percent or more beneficially owned by United States citizens'.[183] This was the first time that a GSP country's eligibility had been suspended on this basis.[184]

With US$477 million in exports of duty-free products to the United States, Argentina was the ninth-largest GSP beneficiary in 2011.[185] It has been reported that delisting Argentina could have had significant economic repercussions for its export industry, which amounted to an estimated US$500 million in benefits in 2010.[186]

Although *Azurix* and *Blue Ridge* were precisely two of the cases settled by Argentina in 2013, Argentina has not been listed again, as legal authorization of the GSP programme expired on 31 July 2013. Thus, products that were previously eligible for GSP duty-free benefits are now subject to regular duties.[187]

However, not all the attempts of investors to convince their host states to adopt these measures are successful. In 2012, in the context of a dispute between Chevron and Ecuador,[188] that company tried to persuade the USTR to exclude Ecuador from the trade preferences granted under the Andean Trade Preference Act (ATPA), due to its failure to comply with an ISDS award of US$77.70 million plus interest in favour of Chevron, and asked the United States to prevent the enforcement of a US$19 billion judgment against Chevron in Ecuadorian courts for pollution in the Ecuadorian Amazon[189] (the 'Lago Agrio' case).

Major American business groups – including the US Chamber of Commerce, the National Association of Manufacturers, the National Foreign Trade Council, the US Council for International Business, and the Emergency Committee for American Trade, pressured President Barack Obama's administration to suspend the ATPA benefits to

---

[183] B. Obama, 'Presidential Proclamation – To Modify Duty-free Treatment Under the Generalized System of Preferences and for Other Purposes' (March 2012).

[184] T. R. Posner and M. C. Walter, 'The Abiding Role of State–State Engagement in the Resolution of Investor–State Disputes' in J. E. Kalicki and A. Joubin-Bret (eds.), *Reshaping the Investor–State Dispute Settlement System* (Brill, 2015), pp. 381–93 at p. 385.

[185] Rosenberg, 'Intersection of International Trade and International Arbitration', 524.

[186] Viñuales and Bentolila, 'The Use of Alternative (Non-Judicial) Means', 271.

[187] United States Trade Representative, 'Generalized System of Preferences (GSP)' (January 2015).

[188] *Chevron Corp. (USA) and Texaco Petroleum Co. (USA) v. Republic of Ecuador* (PCA Case No 34877) Final Award, 31 Ago. 2011, paras. 141–2.

[189] Polášek and Tonova, 'Enforcement Against States', 379.

Ecuador, citing the Andean country's mistreatment of Chevron as proof of a deteriorating investment climate.[190] Finally, the United States did not exclude Ecuador from the ATPA, and remained the sole beneficiary country under that programme – Bolivia, Peru and Colombia ceased to be beneficiary countries in 2010 and 2012 – until it expired on 31 July 2013, although it was not renewed.[191] On the other hand, in March 2014, a New York Federal Court upheld Chevron's claim that the *Lago Agrio* judgment rendered by an Ecuadorian court was procured by corruption, in violation of the US Racketeer Influenced and Corrupt Organizations (RICO) Act.[192] The payment of the ISDS award by Ecuador is still pending.

(b) Voting against Loans

The lobbying efforts of Azurix and Blue Ridge led the US Government to an additional sanction against Argentina for unpaid arbitral awards by voting in the Inter-American Development Bank (IADB) and the World Bank to withdraw or suspend loans to Argentina.[193] Azurix's lawyers also petitioned the US government to withhold support for Argentina's request to restructure between US$8 billion and US$9 billion in defaulted debt owed to the Paris Club of wealthy creditor nations.[194]

In the cases of Azurix and CMS, the lobbying efforts of Azurix and Blue Ridge led the US government to levy an additional sanction on Argentina for the unpaid arbitral awards by voting in the IADB and the World Bank to withdraw or suspend loans to Argentina.[195]

On 14 September 2011, the United States, with its 30 per cent stock in the IADB, voted against granting Argentina a US$230 million loan. Although the loan was finally approved (even if Germany and Spain also voted against it),[196] it has been reported that the vote was aimed at sending a clear message that the United States is concerned with Argentina's attitude and that US diplomacy will take into account

---

[190] Reuters, 'U.S. Business Groups Urge Ecuador Trade Benefits Be Cut' (2012).
[191] P. O'Laughlin, 'ATPA's Impact on U.S. Economy, Drug Crop Eradication Still Negligible, Says USITC' (2014).
[192] J. Hepburn, 'As Merits Hearings Approach in Chevron v. Ecuador BIT Arbitration, Latest Legal Arguments Come into Focus' (December 2014).
[193] The Economist, 'Foreign-Investment Disputes: Come and Get Me'.
[194] MercoPress, 'US Decision to Vote against Loans for Argentina "will not affect funding for 2012"' (2011) *MercoPress*.
[195] Viñuales and Bentolila, 'The Use of Alternative (Non-Judicial) Means', 275.
[196] C. Burgueno, 'US, Spain and Germany Vote against Argentina at the IADB' (2012).

international fulfilments when discussing new cooperation or assistance programmes.[197]

Although Argentina came out declaring that US strategy had neutral impact for 2012 funding[198] and that the World Bank announced in the same year that it would deepen its support for social programmes in Argentina,[199] that situation could potentially change in the future. On 12 February 2013, the US decision was backed-up by the UK. As the UK Secretary of State for International Development pointed out:[200]

> I have instructed the UK's representatives at the Inter-American Development Bank and World Bank to vote against all new proposals for financial support to the Government of the Republic of Argentina presented by these institutions, while reserving the right to support proposals that can demonstrate exceptional benefits to the poorest people of Argentina. . . .
>
> The UK must ensure that the scarce resources of the MDBs are used as effectively as possible to foster development and economic growth. In light of recent actions by the Argentine Government I am no longer confident that further investments in Argentina would be consistent with these objectives. The actions include the failure to comply with the World Bank's International Centre for Settlement of Investment Disputes rulings . . . This position will be kept under review, subject to the future actions of the Government of the Republic of Argentina and its compliance with its international obligations.

Later, Canada, France, Spain, Denmark, Finland, Austria and Germany, also casted votes against multilateral development bank loans to Argentina.[201]

The examples previously referred to are some of the few available in which a clear measure has been adopted by a home state due to a host state's non-compliance with an ISDS award. Besides them, home states could also engage in other forms of diplomatic protection, including

---

[197] MercoPress, 'US Will Vote against Loans to Argentina in World Bank and IDB' (2011).
[198] Reuters, 'Argentina Unhurt in 2012 by U.S. Loan Hurdles-Source' (2011).
[199] World Bank, 'News & Broadcast – Argentina: World Bank to Deepen Its Support to Social Programs' (March 2012).
[200] House of Commons (UK), 'House of Commons Hansard Written Answers' (December 2013).
[201] American Task Force Argentina (AFTA), 'ATFA Applauds UK Government's Decision to Oppose Future Lending to Argentina' (February 2013).

negotiations, withholding payments due to the host state, offsetting the claim arising from the award against claims that the host state has against the home state, and freezing assets that belong to the host state.[202] However, it is difficult to assess the magnitude and effectiveness of such measures, there being few known cases and scarce public information about others.

---

[202] Schreuer, *The ICSID Convention*, p. 1109.

VI

Current and Future Roles of Diplomatic
Protection in Investment Disputes

Although diplomatic protection is today an institution of customary international law that is accepted by all countries, disputes between a foreign investor and a host state are not regularly settled using this mechanism. This is largely a consequence of the consolidation of investor–state dispute settlement for the international settlement of investment disputes.

It has even been suggested that diplomatic protection has become superfluous in investor–state disputes. In the *Diallo* case, the International Court of Justice declared inadmissible an application with regard to the violation of the rights of two companies registered under the laws of Zaire (now Democratic Republic of Congo), where Mr Diallo was manager and shareholder. The ICJ held that in 'contemporary international law, the protection of the rights of companies and the rights of their shareholders, and the settlement of the associated disputes, are essentially governed by bilateral or multilateral agreements for the protection of foreign investments and not by diplomatic protection'. Moreover, the Court declared that 'the role of diplomatic protection somewhat faded, as in practice recourse is only made to it in rare cases where treaty regimes do not exist or have proved inoperative'. Thus, protection 'by substitution' appears to be the very last resort for the defence of foreign investments, and would be admissible only if such companies could not rely on the benefit of an international treaty and no other remedy is available to them.[1]

Dugard has stated that, in the context of the dramatic changes in international law in recent years, whereby individuals are increasingly the subject of many primary rules, both through custom and under treaty, which protect them against their own governments and foreign ones, the

---

[1] *Case Concerning Ahmadou Sadio Diallo (Republic of Guinea v. Democratic Republic of the Congo)*, Preliminary Objections, Judgment of 24 May 2007, [2007] ICJ Rep. 582, pp. 614-615.

foreigner who does business abroad has now direct rights conferred by multilateral and bilateral investment treaties: 'In these circumstances it is possible to argue that the individual is now a subject of international law with standing to enforce his or her human rights at the international level . . .. Consequently, it may be suggested that the need for diplomatic protection by the national State has ceased to exist.'[2]

Diplomatic protection could also be less relevant if the foreign investor has its own leverage power vis-à-vis the host state. Poulsen believes that large multinationals have been able to bargain in investor–state disputes for similar or greater legal guarantees than those provided in international investment agreements.[3]

In practice, ISDS now overshadows recourse to diplomatic protection, which is perceived as a residual mechanism for the settlement of investment disputes, 'to be resorted to in the absence of other arrangements recognizing the direct right of action by individuals'.[4] Yet, even if the potential for the use of diplomatic protection for the settlement of investment disputes has been drastically reduced, it has not been eliminated entirely.[5] As we will analyse below, this residual character does not stem from the IIA regime, as very few treaties contain explicit exclusions of diplomatic protection. But in some cases the exclusion is explicit – notably in Article 27(1) of the ICSID Convention: 'No Contracting State shall give diplomatic protection, or bring an international claim, in respect of a dispute which one of its nationals and another Contracting State shall have consented to submit or shall have submitted to arbitration under this Convention.'

But if the home state agrees to intervene in the dispute, its claim would not have the same characteristics as an ISDS claim. It is generally accepted that investor–state arbitration claims are not diplomatic protection claims, as there are two basic differences between them: Firstly, ISDS claims are introduced directly by an investor without the consent of its home state of nationality, whereas diplomatic claims are submitted by

---

[2] J. Dugard, 'Diplomatic Protection', May 2009: http://opil.ouplaw.com/view/10.1093/law:epil/9780199231690/law-9780199231690-e1028 (accessed 20 August 2018).

[3] L. N. S. Poulsen, 'The Importance of BITs for Foreign Direct Investment and Political Risk Insurance: Revisiting the Evidence' in K. P. Sauvant (ed.), *Yearbook on International Investment Law & Policy 2009–2010* (Oxford University Press Inc., 2010), pp. 539–74 at p. 546.

[4] *CMS v. Argentina*. Decision of the Tribunal on Objections to Jurisdiction, p. 795.

[5] C. Schreuer, 'Investment Protection and International Relations' in A. Reinisch and U. Kriebaum (eds.), *The Law of International Relations: Liber Amicorum Hanspeter Neuhold* (Eleven International Publishing, 2007), pp. 345–58 at p. 354.

and at discretion of the home state that has functional control of the claim.[6] Secondly, when damages are awarded in ISDS they are calculated on the basis of the damage suffered by the investors and paid directly to them. This is unlike in diplomatic protection claims, in which eventual compensations are calculated by taking other considerations into account – such as the character of the international obligation that has been breached – and paid to the home state of the investor, who does not have a general obligation to distribute the sums perceived to its national.[7]

As these two types of claims are, in essence, different from each other, there is no general rule of international law that excludes the parallel use of diplomatic protection in the presence of an ISDS claim. Diplomatic protection and ISDS are, in principle, not mutually exclusive categories, unless there is an explicit exclusion in a treaty.[8]

Yet, in international law, a state has a *right* but not a *duty* to protect its nationals in an investment dispute,[9] so it might be the case that the investor's home state decides not to intervene in a conflict between its national investor and another state and therefore does not espouse all or some claims in this regard. Several reasons can lead a home state to take this position, but they can all be summarized as having other competing interests (i.e. political, economic or military) that collide with the investor's interest in 'politicizing' the dispute and trigger diplomatic protection.

Even if we accept that diplomatic protection has become residual, this does not mean that home states are completely excluded from the settlement of investment disputes outside ISDS. In the following sections we will examine the current role of diplomatic protection for the settlement of investment disputes, focusing on two different issues: the limited character of the exclusion of diplomatic protection on investment treaties; and the situations in which a home state can currently exercise diplomatic protection in favour of its nationals outside the framework of the ISDS system. It is important to note that this type of home state intervention is different from that taking place inside ISDS proceedings,

---

[6] Z. Douglas, 'The Hybrid Foundations of Investment Treaty Arbitration', *British Yearbook of International Law*, 74 (2003), 151–289 at 169.

[7] K. Parlett, 'Diplomatic Protection and Investment Arbitration' in R. Hofmann and C. J. Tams (eds.), *International Investment Law and General International Law: From Clinical Isolation to Systemic Integration?* (Nomos, 2011), pp. 211–29 at pp. 215–16.

[8] *Loewen Group, Inc. and Raymond L. Loewen* v. *United States of America*, ICSID Case No ARB(AF)/98/3, Reply of the United States of America to the Counter-Memorial of the Loewen Group, Inc. on Matters of Jurisdiction and Competence, 26 April 2002, p. 38.

[9] C. F. Amerasinghe, *Diplomatic Protection* (Oxford University Press, 2008), p. 87.

which were analysed in a preceding chapter, and which in general terms cannot be considered diplomatic protection, as the home state's intervention largely serves the purpose of regaining control of the investment treaty, as one of its 'masters'.

Yet, even if the possibilities for use of diplomatic protection are broad – and are not traditionally limited by IIAs – there is rarely public information about home states using such tools to protect their national investors, and the main reasons for home states not intervening – or being perceived as not doing so.

A Limited Exclusion of Diplomatic Protection in Investment Treaties

Contrary to what it might be believed the large majority of investment treaties do not exclude diplomatic protection in cases in which ISDS has been triggered by a foreign investor. With the important exception of the ICSID Convention, this exclusion is not found in other rules of arbitration applicable to investment disputes.

1 Limitations in the ICSID Convention

As mentioned previously, Article 27(1) of the ICSID Convention prohibits diplomatic protection once the investor has submitted or consented to submit the dispute to ICSID arbitration. But an absolute exclusion of diplomatic protection was not conceived of in the origins of the ICSID Convention.

Aron Broches' Working Paper of 1962 provided that nothing 'shall affect the right of a contracting state to give diplomatic protection or bring an international claim in respect of an alleged violation of another Contracting State of any of its obligations under this Convention with respect to the dispute'.[10]

The ICSID Preliminary draft of 15 October 1963, in Section 17(2), established:

> Nothing in this Section shall be construed as precluding a Contracting State from founding an international claim against another Contracting State upon the facts of a dispute which one of these Contracting State and a national of the other shall have consented to submit or shall have submitted to arbitration pursuant to this Convention, where those facts

[10] A. R. Parra, *The History of ICSID* (Oxford University Press, 2012), p. 332.

> also give rise to a dispute concerning the interpretation or application of an agreement between the states concerned; without prejudice, however, to the finality and binding character of any arbitral award rendered pursuant to this Convention as between the parties to the arbitral proceedings.[11]

After the regional discussions on the project, Broches decided to eliminate that part of the provision for being considered superfluous and confusing.[12]

A more restrictive rule providing for the suspension of diplomatic protection during ISA was finally included in Article 27(1) of the ICSID Convention, with only minor opposition of the Venezuelan and Canadian delegates, who argued that the rule was superfluous 'since diplomatic protection could only apply if the state had failed to comply with the arbitration agreement with the national'.[13] Broches considered a home state not being able to espouse a claim of its national an 'important innovation' and a corollary of the principle allowing an investor a direct and effective right to submit a claim against a foreign state without the intervention of the home state, giving international binding effect to the limitation of sovereignty inherent in the convention.[14]

But the ICSID Convention prohibits diplomatic protection only *after* the investor has submitted or consented to submit the dispute to arbitration. Thus, the suspension of diplomatic protection starts to apply only at the moment at which the consent of the parties to the dispute becomes mutual.[15] Only two exceptions to this rule are envisaged. Firstly, as we analysed in the previous chapter, under Article 27(1), the home state could resort to diplomatic protection if the other contracting states 'have failed to abide by and comply with the award rendered in such dispute'. Secondly, under Article 27(2), diplomatic protection 'shall not include informal diplomatic exchanges for the sole purpose of facilitating a settlement of the dispute'.

According to the Report of the Executive Directors on the ICSID Convention, the reasoning behind this is that 'when a host state consents to the submission of a dispute with an investor to the Centre, thereby

---

[11] Ibid., p. 365.

[12] M. Paparinskis, 'Investment Arbitration and the Law of Countermeasures', *British Yearbook of International Law*, (2008), 265–352 at 313.

[13] Ibid., 283.

[14] International Centre for Settlement of Investment Disputes (ICSID), *History of the ICSID Convention* (International Centre for Settlement of Investment Disputes, 1968), vol. ii p. 242. Summary Record of Proceedings, First Session, 16 December 1963 at 4.

[15] Paparinskis, 'Investment Arbitration and the Law of Countermeasures', 306.

giving the investor direct access to an international jurisdiction, the investor should not be in the position to ask his State to espouse his case and that State should not be permitted to do so'.[16]

The exclusion of diplomatic protection is thus inherent and essential to the logic of the ICSID system, precluding derogation by both parties of the dispute. As the tribunal in *Banro v. Congo* held: 'By consenting to ICSID arbitration, the host state knows that it will be protected from diplomatic intervention on the part of the state of which the investor is a national. Conversely, the state of which the investor is a national, by becoming a party to the ICSID Convention, knows that an investor who is a national and has consented to ICSID arbitration at the time of the investment in another Contracting State cannot seek assistance, and if such a request is made, it cannot grant it. Any method of combining diplomatic protection with ICSID arbitration is precluded.'[17]

Therefore, within the ICSID framework, there can be no duplication of an international claim brought through ISA and the espousal of the same claim by the home state through diplomatic protection. However, this is not the general rule outside the ICSID system. In fact, the overwhelming majority of IIAs are silent on an explicit prohibition of the use of diplomatic protection in parallel to ISDS proceedings,[18] as we will examine in the next section.

2 Limitations in Other Investment Treaties

A survey of bilateral investment treaties (BITs) conducted in 1991 concluded that only 32 out of about 400 treaties included rules similar to Article 27(1) of ICSID.[19] Similarly, Paparinskis cites that, of the thirty-four model BITs formulated from 1991 to 2007, only five prohibit diplomatic protection during investment arbitration in general, four

---

[16] R. Rayfuse (ed.), 'Report of the Executive Directors on the Convention on the Settlement of Investment Disputes between States and Nationals of Other States (18 March 1965)', *ICSID Reports: Volume 1: Reports of Cases Decided Under the Convention on the Settlement of Investment Disputes between States and Nationals of Other States, 1965* (Cambridge University Press, 1993), pp. 23–33 at p. 30.

[17] *Banro American Resources, Inc. and Société Aurifere du Kivu et du Maniema SARL v. Democratic Republic of the Congo* (ICSID Case No ARB/98/7), Award 1 Sep 2000 (2002) 17 ICSID Review 382–92, para. 21.

[18] G. Kaufmann-Kohler, 'Non-Disputing State Submissions in Investment Arbitration' in L. Boisson de Chazournes, M. G. Kohen and J. E. Viñuales (eds.), *Diplomatic and Judicial Means of Dispute Settlement* (Martinus Nijhoff Publishers, 2012), p. 322.

[19] P. Peters, 'Dispute Settlement Arrangements in Investment Treaties', (1991) 22 *Netherlands Yearbook of International Law*, 22 (1991), 91–161.

prohibit diplomatic protection during ICSID investment arbitration, and twenty-five do not address the issue at all.[20]

According to an OECD survey that analysed 1,660 IIAs available by December 2011, provisions prohibiting diplomatic protection once ISDS arbitration has begun first appeared in the 1975 Singapore–UK BIT[21] and were included in around 21 per cent of the treaties in that sample. Yet, almost all these treaties allow diplomatic protection when a contracting state fails to abide by and comply with an award or, more rarely, where the arbitral tribunal declares that the dispute falls outside its jurisdiction, or once arbitration has been concluded, or combinations of these exceptions. In the survey, most countries had at least one treaty that limits diplomatic protection, and four countries (Australia, Chile, Costa Rica and Malaysia) had included such language in more than two-thirds of their IIAs.[22]

In our data set of investment treaties signed in the last fifteen years that are publicly available, we find only sixty-five agreements (around 12 per cent of the sample) that restrict the use of diplomatic protection, Switzerland, Japan, Colombia, India and Singapore being the countries that have more often included this type of provision in their IIAs.

These treaties have a very similar wording to Article 27(1) of the ICSID Convention, meaning that contracting parties shall refrain from giving diplomatic protection in respect of matters related to disputes between a party and an investor of the other party that they have consented to submit or submitted to arbitration, unless that other contracting party has failed to abide by and comply with the award rendered in such investment dispute.[23] Some agreements give guidelines about the duration of an 'acceptable' delay for these purposes. For example, according to the Colombia–Spain BIT, diplomatic protection is admissible if the respondent state has not respected the decision of the arbitral tribunal or the ordinary court 'within the deadline provided for by the decision'.[24] The Italian BITs with Congo and Nicaragua add that such delay might be

---

[20] Paparinskis, 'Investment Arbitration and the Law of Countermeasures', 284–5.
[21] Singapore–UK BIT (1975), Art. 8.
[22] J. Pohl, K. Mashigo and A. Nohen, *Dispute Settlement Provisions in International Investment Agreements*, pp. 31–2.
[23] E.g. India–Slovenia BIT (2011), Art. 11.5; Colombia–UK BIT (2010), Art. IX.11; BLEU–Colombia BIT (2009), Art. XII.11.
[24] Colombia–Spain BIT (2005), Art. 10.12.

established on the basis of provisions of international or domestic law applicable in the case.[25]

Replicating Article 27(2) of the ICSID Convention, the majority of these treaties also add that, for the purposes of this paragraph, diplomatic protection shall not include informal diplomatic exchanges for the sole purpose of facilitating a settlement of the investment dispute.[26]

Some of these agreements even leave more space for the use of diplomatic protection and include a specific involvement in the settlement of disputes as part of the consultation mechanism that obviously is addressed to enhance the participation of the home state – as the host state would already be part of the dispute. This is notably included in several IIAs concluded by China, which provide that the representatives of the contracting parties may hold meetings for the purpose of 'addressing disputes arising out of investments'[27] or directly 'resolving disputes arising out of investments'.[28] A similar provision is found in some BITs concluded by Azerbaijan and in the India–Slovakia BIT to resolve any dispute 'in connection'[29] with the agreement, arising between the contracting parties,[30] or to achieve the 'mutual settlement of investment dispute'.[31]

Following the formula of the Singapore–UK BIT, in IIAs concluded by Australia, Bosnia and Herzegovina, as well as in the Guyana–Switzerland and Mozambique–UK BITs, the home state could pursue a dispute through diplomatic channels if the ICSID Secretary-General or the arbitral tribunal has decided that the dispute is not within its jurisdiction.[32]

In the India–Uruguay BIT and the Brunei–Japan economic partnership agreement (EPA), the exclusion of diplomatic protection also does not apply if the respondent state 'has contravened a rule of international

---

[25] Congo Democratic Republic–Italy BIT (2006), Art. X b; Italy–Nicaragua BIT (2004), Art. X.5.
[26] E.g. Jordan–Saudi Arabia BIT (2017), Art. 15.20; Nigeria–Singapore BIT (2016), Art. 17.2; Singapore–Turkey FTA (2015), Art. 12.19.2.
[27] Canada–China BIT (2012), Art. 18(d).
[28] E.g. Bahamas–China BIT (2009), Art. 12(c); China–Malta BIT (2009), Art. 12; China–Pakistan FTA (2006), Art. 56(c).
[29] Azerbaijan–Latvia BIT (2005), Art. 10; India–Slovakia BIT (2006), Art. 9.
[30] Azerbaijan–Syria BIT (2009), Art. 10.
[31] Azerbaijan–UAE BIT (2006), Art. 10.
[32] E.g. Bosnia and Herzegovina–India BIT (2006), Art. 9.5; Guyana–Switzerland BIT (2005), Art. 8 (4); Australia–Turkey BIT (2005), Art. 13.6.

law, including the denial of justice or the provisions of this Agreement'.[33]

More 'space' for diplomatic protection is also provided for in IIAs recently concluded by the European Union. In CETA and the IPAs with Singapore and Vietnam, the limitation of diplomatic protection shall not exclude the possibility of a contracting party having recourse to state to state dispute settlement procedures, not only in the traditional cases of facilitating a settlement of the dispute and when the respondent state has failed to abide by and comply with an ISDS award, but also in respect of a measure of general application even if that measure is alleged to have breached the agreement as regards a specific investment in respect of which a claim has been submitted, and is without prejudice to its rights as non-disputing party.[34]

3 Limitations in Other Arbitral Rules

As we have seen, the ICSID Convention restriction on diplomatic protection is not the general rule in IIAs. But this limitation is also largely absent in other ISDS arbitral rules.

Although the ICSID Arbitration Rules are the most used for the settlement of known investor–state disputes (55 per cent), other rules that are used extensively are those of the United Nations Commission on International Trade Law (UNCITRAL) (31 per cent), and followed to a much lesser extent by ICSID Additional Facility (6 per cent), the Stockholm Chamber of Commerce (SCC) (5 per cent) and the International Chamber of Commerce (ICC) (2 per cent).[35]

From those other arbitral rules, neither the ICC[36] nor the ICSID Additional Facility Arbitration Rules provide for such restriction. Furthermore, in relation to the latter, it is explicitly stated that no provisions of the ICSID Convention shall be applicable.[37]

Until recently, neither the UNCITRAL nor the SCC Arbitration Rules included such restrictions. But now UNCITRAL Rules on Transparency

---

[33] India–Uruguay BIT (2008) Art. 9 (6); Brunei–Japan EPA (2007), Art. 67.22.
[34] CETA Art. 8.42.2; EU–Singapore IPA (April 2018), Art.3.23.1; EU–Vietnam IPA (2018), Ch. 3, Art. 3.58.
[35] United Nations Conference on Trade and Development (UNCTAD), 'Investment Dispute Settlement Navigator' (February 2018).
[36] International Chamber of Commerce (ICC), 'ICC Rules of Arbitration' (January 2012).
[37] ICSID, 'ICSID Additional Facility Rules (2006)', April 2006: https://icsid.worldbank.org /en/Pages/icsiddocs/ICSID-Additional-Facility-Rules.aspx (accessed 5 January 2018), Art. 3.

applicable to treaty-based ISAs initiated pursuant to a treaty concluded after 1 April 2014, do include them. As we have discussed before, under Article 5 of these rules the arbitral tribunal needs to avoid non-disputing state party submissions that would support the claim of the investor in a manner tantamount to diplomatic protection.[38] Basically, the same provision is included in the 2017 SCC Arbitration Rules.[39]

4 Implied Limitations

As we have examined, the large majority of IIAs and arbitral rules do not explicitly exclude diplomatic protection when ISDS arbitration is taking place. However, some scholars seem to believe that this limitation is somehow ingrained in the investment treaties. Kaufmann-Kohler has implied that, as a matter of principle, the limitation of diplomatic protection should apply to any investment arbitration, otherwise that would be contrary to the 'obligation to respect' the ISA dispute settlement framework.[40] Similarly, Amerasinghe believes that it would be 'reasonable' to infer that, once the ISA is initiated, the IIA does not permit the resort of diplomatic protection by the home state.[41] Potestà has suggested that, even if an IIA lacks a provision excluding diplomatic protection during ISDS procedures, if both contracting parties of the applicable treaty are members of the ICSID Convention, it can be given effect to under the binding obligation of Article 27(1), in accordance with Article 31(3)(c) of the Vienna Convention on the Law of Treaties, even if the ISA at hand is not under ICSID rules.[42] Juratowitch has submitted that 'a state would be *estopped* under customary international law from initiating a diplomatic protection action concerning rights covered by an investment treaty to which it was party where the relevant investor and the host state had both consented to arbitration'.[43]

---

[38] UNCITRAL, 'Rules on Transparency in Treaty-based Investor–State Arbitration. UN Doc. A/RES/68/462', April 2014: www.uncitral.org/uncitral/en/uncitral_texts/arbitra tion/2014Transparency.html (accessed 14 February 2018).

[39] Arbitration Institute of the Stockholm Chamber of Commerce, '2017 Arbitration Rules' (January 2017). Appendix III, Art. 4.

[40] Kaufmann-Kohler, 'Non-Disputing State Submissions in Investment Arbitration', 322.

[41] Amerasinghe, *Diplomatic Protection*, p. 341.

[42] M. Potestà, 'Towards a Greater Role for State-to-State Arbitration in the Architecture of Investment Treaties?' in S. Lalani and R. Polanco Lazo (eds.), *The Role of the State in Investor–State Arbitration* (Brill/Martinus Nijhoff, 2014), p. 269.

[43] B. Juratowitch, 'The Relationship between Diplomatic Protection and Investment Treaties', *ICSID Review*, 23 (2008), 10–35 at 22.

But, as Paparinskis points out, there is no sufficient state practice to justify the existence of some type of 'fork-in-the-road' customary law rule, between ISDS and diplomatic protection.[44] As we have seen, the exclusion of diplomatic protection from ISDS cases founded on investment treaties is a practice included in only a minority of IIAs, which is not sufficiently widespread across states to create an international customary rule. On arbitral rules, until very recently, this exclusion was particular to ICSID Convention arbitration. Therefore, in the absence of a specific provision in an investment treaty or the applicable arbitral rules, there should be no limitation on having both ISA and diplomatic protection claims in parallel.

Yet, there are some cases in which diplomatic protection should not be encouraged, regardless of the fact that diplomatic protection has been explicitly excluded or not in a particular IIA. Roberts has pointed out as examples, cases when it is aimed as a form of 'appeal' or a 'collateral attack' on existing investor–state awards.[45] In some circumstances the recourse to diplomatic protection would be unavailable for other reasons, like the non-compliance with diplomatic protection requirements. Kulick explains that if an investor brings a non-ICSID ISA, without previously exhausting local remedies (something that is rather likely to happen), that circumstance would bar access to state-to-state arbitration.[46]

Finally, even if there is definitely room for the potential use of diplomatic protection on investment disputes, this right has seldom been used, for the reasons explained elsewhere in this book.

B   Current Mechanisms of Diplomatic Protection in Investment Disputes

Although diplomatic methods have been criticized for being long, cumbersome and generally ineffectual,[47] they have also been hailed as the most frequently used, as 'the vast majority of disputes between States are

---

[44] Paparinskis, 'Investment Arbitration and the Law of Countermeasures', 281.

[45] A. Roberts, 'State-to-State Investment Treaty Arbitration: A Hybrid Theory of Interdependent Rights and Shared Interpretive Authority', Harv. Int'l L.J. 55, (2014), 1 at 29.

[46] Andreas Kulick, 'State-State Investment Arbitration as a Means of Reassertion of Control. From Antagonism to Dialogue', in A. Kulick (ed.), *Reassertion of Control Over the Investment Treaty Regime* (2017), pp. 128–52 at p. 134.

[47] C. F. Dugan, D. Wallace Jr, N. D. Rubins and B. Sabahi, *Investor–State Arbitration* (Oxford University Press, 2008), pp. 27–8.

settled by direct diplomatic negotiations'.[48] However, as Echandi points out, today, there not enough data is available to assess the rate of success or failure of preliminary amicable consultations in investment disputes.[49]

In the following sections we will examine the existing mechanisms of diplomatic protection and their effective (or potential) use on investment disputes.

1 Consular Assistance/Diplomatic Action

Home states regularly get involved in actions to assist their nationals in doing economic activities in foreign states, through the use of consular assistance and diplomatic action, that could include their assistance in matters related to investment such as purchase of property, grant of concessions, and the arrangement of legal defences, among other actions.

There are important differences between consular assistance and diplomatic protection. The former has traditionally been distinguished from diplomatic protection, as it has a preventive nature, does not necessarily depend on a violation of international law, and is not adversarial when directed against a state.[50] As diplomatic protection is of a remedial nature, it has often been considered as involving judicial proceedings, and interventions on behalf of nationals outside the judicial process are generally regarded as consular assistance. Yet, international legal doctrine, judicial decisions (at both international and national levels), and the work of the International Law Commission shows that diplomatic action is not limited to international judicial or arbitral proceedings.[51]

However, those differences are not always easy to identify. According to the Vienna Convention on Diplomatic Relations (VCDR),[52] one of the functions of a diplomatic mission is to protect, in the receiving state, the interest of the sending state and its nationals. This is also considered as part of the consular function in the Vienna Convention on Consular

---

[48] P. Malanczuk, *Akehurst's Modern Introduction to International Law* (Routledge, 1997), p. 275.

[49] R. Echandi, 'Complementing Investor–State Dispute Resolution: A Conceptual Framework for Investor–State Conflict Management': Prospects in International Investment Law and Policy (Cambridge University Press, 2013), pp. 277–8.

[50] Amerasinghe, *Diplomatic Protection*, pp. 45–6.

[51] A. M. H. Vermeer-Künzli, *The Protection of Individuals by Means of Diplomatic Protection: Diplomatic Protection as a Human Rights Instrument* (Department of Public International Law, Faculty of Law, Leiden University, 2007), pp. 67–9.

[52] Vienna Convention on Diplomatic Relations, 18 April 1961, 23 U.S.T. 3227, 500 U.N.T.S. 95, Art. 3(1)(b).

Relations (VCCR),[53] together with help and assistance for nationals a – concept that also comprises legal entities ('bodies corporate'). The lines are further blurred in practice, as a diplomatic mission can exercise both consular assistance and diplomatic protection. The problem is not to determine what constitutes consular assistance, but to define which actions are comprised in diplomatic protection to the exclusion of consular assistance,[54] as there is no consensus about which actions taken by one state against another are considered diplomatic protection or not.[55]

According to Dugard, diplomatic protection could include consular action,[56] and other scholars are of the opinion that diplomatic protection comprises the 'helping and protecting of nationals abroad in the pursuance of their rights and other lawful activities by consular or diplomatic organs'.[57]

ILC Draft Article 1 on Diplomatic Protection defines it as 'the invocation by a State, through diplomatic action or other means of peaceful settlement, of the responsibility of another State for an injury caused by an internationally wrongful act of that State to a natural or legal person that is a national of the former State with a view to the implementation of such responsibility'.

The commentary to ILC Draft Article 1 explains that the term 'diplomatic action' covers 'all the lawful procedures employed by a state to inform another state of its views and concerns, including protest, request for an inquiry or for negotiations aimed at the settlement of disputes'.[58] Therefore, diplomatic action, for the purpose of diplomatic protection, encompasses more than just adjudication, and includes demarches and all other kinds of diplomatic protests beyond the stage of consular assistance.[59]

---

[53] Vienna Convention on Consular Relations, 24 April 1963, 21 U.S.T. 77, 596 U.N.T.S. 261, Art. 5(a) and (e).

[54] Vermeer-Künzli, *The Protection of Individuals by Means of Diplomatic Protection*, pp. 68 and 80.

[55] C. Forcese, 'Shelter from the Storm: Rethinking Diplomatic Protection of Dual Nationals in Modern International Law', *George Washington International Law Review*, 37 (2005), 469 at 473.

[56] J. Dugard, 'First Report of the Special Rapporteur on Diplomatic Protection', *Yearbook of the International Law Commission 2000 (United Nations Publications, 2000)*, pp. 35–72 p. 39.

[57] A. Randelzhofer, 'Nationality' in E. Biglieri and G. Prati (eds.), *Encyclopedia of Public International Law* (Elsevier, 2014), pp. 416–24 at pp. 420–1.

[58] ILC, 'Draft Articles on Diplomatic Protection, with Commentaries', 27.

[59] Vermeer-Künzli, *The Protection of Individuals by Means of Diplomatic Protection*, pp. 77–8.

Consular assistance could then evolve into diplomatic protection, depending on the escalation of measures adopted by the home state. But, again, the dividing line is not always clear. For example, informal diplomatic exchanges 'for the sole purpose of facilitating a settlement of the dispute' are excluded from the limitation of diplomatic protection of Article 27(2) of the ICSID Convention, but they could easily become diplomatic protection, especially if such diplomatic action takes place in parallel with ISA.

The following examples will illustrate the different levels of consular assistance and diplomatic action given by home states.

(a)   To Facilitate the Settlement of a Dispute

Diplomatic exchanges might be used to 'facilitate' the settlement of an investment dispute, if the interest of the host state is in line with the claims of its investor abroad.

We find one example of this, in the cases brought against India by the controversial Dabhol Power Corporation – owned by three major American companies (Enron, General Electric and Bechtel). After the project collapsed following several disputes with respect to the construction of natural-fired gas electricity plants,[60] the US government actively participated in facilitating the settlement of the dispute, with the use of diplomatic exchanges. In parallel to the arbitrations initiated under contracts and BITs concluded by India with other third countries (Mauritius, UK, Austria, France, Switzerland and Netherlands),[61] high-level talks in favour of the company took place, and an inter-agency 'Dabhol Working Group' was even instituted. The combined effects of arbitration and diplomatic presume came into fruition and all the cases were settled in July 2005, on confidential terms.[62]

---

[60] G. van Harten, 'TWAIL and the Dabhol Arbitration', *Comparative Research in Law & Political Economy. Research Report No 19/2011*.

[61] *Bechtel Enterprises Holdings, Inc. and GE Structured Finance (GESF) v. Government of India; Standard Chartered Bank v. Republic of India; Offshore Power Production CV, Travamark Two BV, EFS India-Energy BV, Enron BV, and Indian Power Investments BV v. Republic of India; Erste Bank Der Oesterreichischen Sparkassen AG v. Republic of India; Credit Suisse First Boston v. Republic of India; Credit Lyonnais SA (Calyon SA) v. Republic of India; BNP Paribas v. Republic of India; ANZEF Ltd v. Republic of India; and ABN Amro NV v. Republic of India.*

[62] G. Gertz, 'The International Investment Regime Is Stronger Than You Think. GEG Working Paper 2015/96' (2015) *The Global Economic Governance Programme, University of Oxford*, 15–18.

We find one example of this, in an interesting turn about what 'facilitate the settlement of a dispute' might mean, in *Fraport* v. *Philippines*, in early 2011, the German government decided to withhold US$61 million in development aid to fight HIV/AIDs and tuberculosis in Philippines until the dispute was solved.[63] The claim was brought by the German company that held rights under a concession for building and operating an airport terminal. At the time of the reported intervention by Germany, an initial award by an ICSID arbitral tribunal, declining jurisdiction, had been annulled.[64] A new case was submitted in April 2011 and another award of December 2014 also found that the tribunal lacked jurisdiction over Fraport's claims.[65]

On 17 April 2012, Argentina's President, Cristina Fernández, announced the expropriation by law of 51 per cent of the total of 57.4 per cent of shares belonging to the company Repsol-YPF SA, controlled by the Spanish energy corporation Repsol. The Argentinian government declared that it took over the corporation because Repsol had not developed energy in Argentina but, instead, had used its profits to invest overseas. Repsol countered that the decline in development of energy exploration projects and oil production in Argentina derived from government controls on the price of domestic oil and gas, and restrictions on exports.[66] Describing the expropriation as an aggression against its own interests, the Spanish government threatened to retaliate against Argentina directly, and also to involve the EU.[67] Spain curtailed biodiesel shipments from Argentina for some eight months, using trade to send a clear message of its disapproval of the expropriation.[68] After suggesting, in April 2012, the filing of an EU complaint against Argentina before the World Trade Organization,[69] in December 2012, Spain and the EU reportedly urged the members of the OECD to hold that Argentina was in non-compliance with the national treatment provisions of the OECD Declaration on International Investment and Multinational

---

[63] *Fraport AG Frankfurt Airport Services Worldwide* v. *Republic of the Philippines*, ICSID Case No ARB/03/25, Award, 16 August 2007.

[64] *Fraport AG Frankfurt Airport Services Worldwide* v. *Republic of the Philippines*, ICSID Case No ARB/03/25. Decision on the Application for Annulment of Fraport AG Frankfurt Airport Services Worldwide, 23 December 2010.

[65] *Fraport AG Frankfurt Airport Services Worldwide* v. *Republic of the Philippines* (ICSID Case No ARB/11/12), Award, 10 December 2014.

[66] S. A. Aaronson, 'A Fresh Approach to International Investment Rules' (2011), p. 3.

[67] F. Ortiz, 'Spain Has few Ways to Pressure Argentina over YPF' (2012).

[68] Aaronson, 'A Fresh Approach to International Investment Rules', 3–4.

[69] Ortiz, 'Spain Has few Ways to Pressure Argentina over YPF'.

Enterprises. This created some controversy, about the appropriateness of the exercise of diplomatic protection by Spain, at the same time that Repsol had filed before ICSID a request for arbitration against Argentina.[70]

Although formal talks to achieve a settlement began in June 2012, an agreement between the disputing parties was reached only in April 2014, with Repsol receiving for its lost shareholding US$5 billion in denominated bonds and agreeing that any dispute arising from, or in connection with, the settlement agreement would be resolved exclusively through arbitration in conformity with UNCITRAL Rules.[71] The settlement was reached right after the constitution of the arbitral tribunal in *Repsol* v. *Argentina*,[72] following several efforts from Argentina to disqualify two arbitrators due to alleged lack of independence.[73]

(b)   Diplomatic Pressure

Some foreign investors can rely on diplomatic pressure from their home state to assist in the settlement of investment disputes in the shadow of a potential ISA.

In *Foresti* v. *South Africa* it was reported that, in 2004, prior to the initiation of the arbitration proceedings, the Italian Embassy in South Africa served an 'aide memoire' in relation to the Black Economic Empowerment (BEE) legislation that led to the arbitration. In that document, Italy warned South Africa of the adverse effects that BEE would have on foreign investors and the likelihood of provoking several investment disputes.[74]

In *Nykomb* v. *Latvia*,[75] there is evidence of a home state pressuring a host state for the fulfilment of contractual obligations by a state-owned enterprise, which failure was later acknowledged in ISA. In March 1997, Latvenergo (a Latvian stated-owned electricity distribution company) entered into a contract with Windau (a private Latvian company) to

---

[70] L. E. Peterson, 'As Repsol Files Arbitration against Argentina,Row Erupts over Alleged "diplomatic protection" by Spain and the EU – Investment Arbitration Reporter (IAReporter)' (2012).

[71] Investment Arbitration Reporter (IAReporter), 'Repsol–Argentina Settlement Agreement, April 2014' (April 2014).

[72] *Repsol, SA and Repsol Butano, SA v. Argentine Republic* (ICSID Case No ARB/12/38).

[73] F. Fortese and L. E. Peterson, 'Full Light Is Shed on the Reasons for ICSID's Rejection of Argentine Efforts to Remove Arbitrators in Repsol Case' (2013).

[74] L. E. Peterson, 'South Africa Mining Arbitration Sees Another Amicus Curiae Intervention' (February 2009).

[75] Stockholm Chamber of Commerce, Nykomb Synergetics Technology Holding AB v. Republic of Latvia, SCC. Arbitral Award, 16 December 2003.

build a cogeneration plant in the town of Bauska, which was to produce electric power and heat on the basis of natural gas. The electric power would be purchased by Latvenergo and distributed over the national grid, with the heat to be purchased and distributed by the Bauska municipality.

At the time, Latvian law entitled Windau to receive a 'double average sales tariff' for the electricity produced by the plant to the national grid, as a way of inducing the development of natural gas power plants. In June 1997 – and after a ruling of the Latvian Constitutional Court – the Latvian legislature modified the law limiting the double tariff and, in October 1998, the legislature officially repealed it. In March 1999, Nykomb (a Swedish company), purchased a majority stake in Windau, and in September 2000 it became 100 per cent owner. Although the cogeneration plant was finished in September 1999 and started production in February 2000, Latvenergo refused to pay the double tariff, unilaterally declaring the contract void, and did not pay despite pressure to do so from the Swedish government.[76] Later, Nykomb initiated an ISDS case before the SCC, claiming expropriation and treatment in violation of the Energy Charter Treaty. The tribunal ordered Latvia to pay Nykomb compensation for damages and costs, and furthered ordered, as specific performance, that Latvia should ensure the payment of the double tariff until 2007.[77]

In a more extreme display of diplomatic pressure, Lithuania blocked Serbia's accession to the EU, after the cancellation of the privatization of Serbia's beer maker Belgrade Beer Industry (Beogradska Industrija Piva (BIP)), being the 52 per cent of shares in BIP purchased by a consortium of AB Alita, a Lithuanian brewing company and United Nordic Beverages AB of Sweden, in July 2007.[78]

An alleged breach of the contractual obligations by the buyers – failing to carry out their investment commitments and not performing their obligations to purchase the company's remaining shares (48 per cent) – led the Serbian Privatization Agency (SPA) to terminate the share purchase agreement in February 2010. Serbia not only took over the shares of the plant and refused to return the purchase price, but also went to the Serbian Court of Arbitration, demanding compensation from foreign

---

[76] Association for International Arbitration, *Alternative Dispute Resolution in the Energy Sector* (Maklu, 2009), p. 47.

[77] M. D. Slater, 'The Energy Charter Treaty: A Brief Introduction to Its Scope and Initial Arbitral Awards' in Association for International Arbitration (ed.), *Alternative Dispute Resolution in the Energy Sector* (Maklu, 2009), pp. 15–54 at p. 48.

[78] InSerbia News, 'Dacic: I Expect Lithuania to Ratify SAA' (April 2013).

investors (mainly Alita) and claimed payment of around €68.3 million in liquidated damages. Following a partial award concerning jurisdiction issued on 15 November 2011, the Serbian Foreign Trade Court of Arbitration, on 17 September 2012, awarded to SPA around €17.1 million in damages. At the same time, Alita initiated a procedure before the Commercial Court of Belgrade, requesting the setting aside of the partial arbitral award on jurisdiction, and later initiated a similar proceeding to set aside the award on damages.[79]

By August 2012, all other EU member states had ratified Serbia's stabilization and association agreement (SAA) with the EU, with the exception of Lithuania. Several negotiations took place to disentangle the ratification of Serbia's SAA by Lithuania, with reports of both countries having 'tense' relationships after the unsuccessful privatization of the BIP brewery.[80] The Lithuanian Congress finally ratified the agreement on 18 June 2013, and it entered into force on 1 September 2013.[81]

Another type of diplomatic pressure is not directed at the payment of a claim, but at pushing the host state to consent to arbitration. In *Compañía del Desarrollo Santa Elena* v. *Costa Rica*, the investor's home state (the United States) pressed Costa Rica to consent to arbitration, invoking the 'Helms amendment', which prohibited foreign aid to any country that had expropriated property of US citizens or corporations owned at least at 50 per cent by US citizens, unless a remedial action had been taken by that state.[82] The United States requested the delay of a loan of

---

[79] G. L. Nouel, 'Arbitration Due to the Failed Privatisation Process of Belgrade Beer Industry (BIP)', *The Brief* (2013) March, 6–7.

[80] b92.net, 'Lithuania won't block Serbia's EU pathway', March 2013: www.b92.net/eng/news /politics.php?yyyy=2013&mm=03&dd=28&nav_id=85396 (accessed 19 January 2018); Balkan Insight, 'Lithuania Ratifies Serbia's EU Stability Agreement', June 2013: www.balk aninsight.com/en/article/lithuania-ratifies-serbia-s-saa (accessed 19 January 2018).

[81] Government of the Republic of Serbia. European Integration Office, 'Ratification of the SAA' (January 2015).

[82] The Helms Amendment, prohibits US foreign aid, including US approval of financing by international financial institutions, to a country that has expropriated the property of a US citizen or corporation at least 50 per cent owned by US citizens, where the country in question has not: '(A) returned the property, (B) provided adequate and effective compensation [...] as required by international law, (C) offered a domestic procedure providing prompt, adequate and effective compensation in accordance with international law, or (D) submitted the dispute to arbitration under the rules of the [ICSID Convention] or other mutually agreeable binding international arbitration procedure.' The same US Code explicitly allows the President of the US to instruct the US Executive Directors of each multilateral development bank and international financial institution

US$175 million to Costa Rica by the Inter-American Development Bank (IADB), until that country consented to ICSID jurisdiction,[83] which Costa Rica finally did. Startlingly, this fact is acknowledged in the final award.[84]

It is highly likely that home states have had several other interventions of this type, and some have suggested that the vast majority of disputes are settled diplomatically.[85] However, public awareness of diplomatic means is limited and therefore the scarcity of data makes it difficult to assess. That would explain why the empirical analysis of this diplomatic or consular assistance has received little academic attention, as political pressure in informal dispute settlement procedures is rarely observed, unless it is particularly intense and reported in media outlets. Some researchers have embarked on the analysis of non-traditional sources – such as Wikileaks – to get a more complete context of this phenomenon.[86]

Thus, the creation of ISDS might not necessarily replace diplomatic protection, but rather has complemented it. It is just that we are not aware of most of these diplomatic or consular actions of 'assistance' or 'pressure'.

For the intervention of the home state to qualify as consular assistance or diplomatic protection, seems to be an issue of degree. There might be a spectrum that goes from weaker forms of assistance (meetings, letters and calls) closer to consular assistance, to stronger diplomatic pressure, closer to diplomatic protection. The magnitude may vary, depending on

---

'to vote against any loan or other utilization of the funds of such bank or institution for the benefit of any country to which assistance is prohibited', unless such assistance is directed specifically to programs which serve the basic human needs of the citizens of that country (§2370a(b)). United States Code, 2000, V. 12: Title 22, Foreign Relations and Intercourse, p. 722.

[83] J. E. Viñuales and D. Bentolila, 'The Use of Alternative (Non-Judicial) Means to Enforce Investment Awards against States' in L. Boisson de Chazournes, M. G. Kohen and J. E. Viñuales (eds.), *Diplomatic and Judicial Means of Dispute Settlement* (Martinus Nijhoff Publishers, 2012), pp. 248–77 at p. 270.

[84] *Compañía del Desarrollo de Santa Elena SA v. Republic of Costa Rica*, ICSID Case No ARB/96/1, Final Award, 17 February 2000, paras. 24–6.

[85] L. N. S. Poulsen, 'Sacrificing Sovereignty by Chance: Investment Treaties, Developing Countries, and Bounded Rationality', London School of Economics and Political Science (LSE) 2011, p. 177.

[86] G. Gertz, S. Jandhyala and L. S. Poulsen, 'Conference "The Political Economy of International Investment Agreements"', Deutsches Institut für Entwicklungspolitik – World Trade Institute. Bonn, 8–9 December 2014' (2014).

the strength of the political relations and the level of economic dependence between the home and the host state.[87]

2   State-to-State Dispute Settlement

Today, ISA is seen as essential to the system of IIAs, but, historically, this has not been the case. As Montt points out, these agreements were originally designed to provide protections to foreign investors, in the traditional setting of dispute settlement under international law, and not with the purpose of giving direct cause of action to investors. In fact, BITs including exclusively state-to-state dispute settlement mechanisms, comprised the majority of treaties concluded before 1986.[88] In a survey of 1,660 investment treaties, the OECD reported that although 96 per cent of the reviewed agreements included ISDS, countries that began early BIT programmes have a large number of treaties that do not include ISA (e.g. around 32 per cent of Germany's BITs and 28 per cent of Switzerland's BITs do not provide for ISDS).[89]

Even the first agreements that provided for ISA did not exclude state-to-state dispute settlement. For example, Article VII.1 of the 1958 Abs–Shawcross Draft Convention provided that any dispute as to the interpretation or application of the Convention may, with the consent of the interested parties, be submitted to an arbitral tribunal under the provisions of the Annex to that Convention. In the absence of such consent or of agreement for settlement by other means, the dispute may be submitted by either party to the ICJ.[90]

Similarly, the 1962 OECD Draft Convention provided for state-to-state dispute settlement, but only with reference to arbitral procedures according to the Annex of the Convention.[91]

The ICSID Convention provides that any dispute arising between the contracting states concerning the interpretation or application of the Convention that is not settled by negotiation 'shall be referred to the International Court of Justice by the application of any party to such dispute, unless the states concerned agree to another method of

---

[87]   Gertz, 'The International Investment Regime', 5.
[88]   Montt, S. *State Liability in Investment Treaty Arbitration: Global Constitutional and Administrative Law in the BIT Generation* (Hart Publishing, 2009), p. 64.
[89]   Pohl, Mashigo, and Nohen, *Dispute Settlement Provisions in IIAs*, p. 8.
[90]   G. Schwarzenberger, 'The Abs–Shawcross Draft Convention on Investments Abroad: A critical Commentary', *Journal of Public Law*, 9 (1960), 147 at 162.
[91]   OECD Draft Convention on the Protection of Foreign Property, Annex 6(b)(i).

settlement'.[92] While this provision is couched in general terms, it does not confer jurisdiction on the ICJ to review a decision of an arbitral tribunal in an investor–state dispute, since such proceedings would contravene the provisions of Article 27 of ICSID, unless the other contracting state had failed to abide by and comply with the award rendered in that dispute.[93]

Espousal of private claims is a precondition of triggering ISDS mechanisms in investment disputes. As a general rule, under customary international law, states may espouse claims after the exhaustion of local remedies and only from nationals, and conversely, they may not protect or espouse claims of non-nationals.[94] Beyond that, most of the countries do not have general policies on this issue, and seem to operate on a case-by-case basis.

However, some countries have public policies on espousal of claims. For example, Canada has published guidelines on governmental espousal of investment claims, declaring as principles that: (a) such claims must have belonged to Canadian citizens from the events that gave rise to them until the moment of presentation of the claim; (b) normally, the Canadian government would not espouse claims against a foreign state without previous exhaustion of local remedies, except in cases of denial of justice; and (c) in the case of claims made by corporations, Canada cannot espouse claims related to assets expropriated or confiscated abroad, unless the claims originate from a company formed under the laws of Canada or a Canadian province before the date of the claim.[95]

Similarly, the United States has declared that it does not formally espouse claims on behalf of its nationals unless the claimant provides persuasive evidence demonstrating that 'was at the time the claim arose and remains a US citizen, that all local remedies have been exhausted or the claimant has demonstrated that attempting to do so would be futile, and that the claim involves an act by the foreign government that is considered wrongful under international law'.[96]

In Switzerland, a 1980 federal law on claims for compensation towards foreign countries sets the frame of reference in which diplomatic protection can be requested and granted, stipulating that the Swiss Federal Department of Foreign Affairs (FDFA) shall verify whether the

---

[92] ICSID Convention, Art. 64.

[93] Rayfuse, 'Report of the Executive Directors on the Convention on the Settlement of Investment Disputes between States and Nationals of Other States (18 March 1965)', 30.

[94] Amerasinghe, *Diplomatic Protection*, pp. 91–2.

[95] Dugan et al., *Investor–State Arbitration*, pp. 19–20.

[96] US Department of State, 'Bilateral Investments, Other Bilateral Claims and Arbitrations' (January 2015).

requirements of diplomatic protection are fulfilled. Moreover, the Swiss government may exclude cases of minor importance from protection.[97]

It must be noted that, after the espousal of a claim, the home state gains complete control over it, meaning that it may abandon the claim, submit it to arbitration, compromise it or release it with or without reduced compensation, settle it or make any other disposition that it deems expedient in the public interest, as may in its opinion appear reasonable under the circumstances.[98]

In IIAs, state-to-state dispute settlement provisions are found more often than ISA.[99] However, there is an important difference of scope between them, as inter-state mechanisms are usually conceived for the interpretation or application of the agreement, while ISA is commonly used to obtain compensation for the breach of investment treaty obligations.

From the IIAs concluded in the last fifteen years, state-to-state dispute settlement mechanisms are provided for in almost all treaties included in the sample: only the 2015 Palestine–Venezuela BIT does not consider such feature.[100]

The large majority of state-to-state dispute settlement provisions in IIAs consider recourses to diplomatic methods and jurisdictional methods, including either ad hoc arbitration between the contracting parties or adjudication to the ICJ.[101]

---

[97] V. Jentsch, *The Role of Bilateral Investment Treaties (BITs) in Switzerland: Importance and Alternatives from an Entrepreneurial Perspective* (2009), p. 6.

[98] E. Borchard, *The Diplomatic Protection of Citizens Abroad: Or, The Law of International Claims* (Banks Law Publishing Co., 1915) pp. 366 and 369.

[99] Interestingly, the Italy–Chad BIT (1969), Art. 7 – reportedly the first BIT providing for unconditional offer to investor–state arbitration – does not consider state-to-state adjudication or arbitration and leaves the settlement of disputes between the two contracting parties to diplomatic means: M. Potestà, 'State-to-State Dispute Settlement Pursuant to Bilateral Investment Treaties: Is There Potential?' in N. Boschiero, T. Scovazzi, C. Pitea and C. Ragni (eds.), *International Courts and the Development of International Law* (T. M. C. Asser Press, 2013), pp. 753–68 at p. 753.

[100] There is also no inter-state dispute settlement provision in the Korea–Turkey Investment Agreement (2015), but the 2012 framework agreement between both parties, would be applicable, which includes arbitration.

[101] Yet, there are some IIAs in which the inter-state settlement of disputes does not include arbitration or adjudication. Under the China–Taiwan BIT, Art. 15, dispute resolution is limited to amicable settlement in the Cross-Straits Economic Cooperation Committee (ECC). Under the Australia–New Zealand Investment Protocol (2011), Art. 25, dispute settlement only includes consultations between the states. In the Netherlands–Oman BIT (2009), Art. 8, diplomatic negotiations are the only mechanism provided for inter-state settlement of disputes. It is similar in the Azerbaijan–UAE BIT (2006), Art. 12, in which such disputes can also be settled by a joint committee.

But despite the prevalence of provisions on ISDS in IIAs, they have been tested in a limited number of cases, as we will examine in the following sections.

(a) Diplomatic Methods

There are some situations in which diplomatic protection through diplomatic means is not residual, but is the main mechanism for the settlement of investment disputes.

Firstly, diplomatic methods can be used *in the absence of investment treaties*. For example, in October 2003 a dispute arose in the company Cora de Comstar, a mobile telephone operator in Côte d'Ivoire that had two main American investors. The dispute started when an Ivorian former investor managed to seize the company's offices and assets, with support from the local police. Although the company reportedly threatened the host state with international arbitration, in the absence of an investment treaty with Côte d'Ivoire, the United States applied diplomatic methods to pressure the host state. This action that was finally successful, and both sides agreed to a deal in which the Ivorian government paid the Cora de Comstar American investors US$5 million.[102]

Secondly, diplomatic protection could be used *to enforce rights that are recognized to foreign investors in international agreements that are not investment treaties*. Recanati has described in detail the dispute between Italy and Switzerland after the latter decided to impose restrictions on the acquisition of immovable property by foreigners in 1983 ('Lex Koller'), which provided for a limited number of authorizations to non-resident foreigners to acquire property in Switzerland.[103] The canton of Grissons decided effectively to implement this law in the late 1980s, and succeeded in judicial proceedings confiscating assets that were the property of Italian nationals. In June 1991, Italy accepted to grant diplomatic protection to them, invoking breach of the 1868 Italy–Switzerland Establishment Convention – a treaty that granted full rights of property to nationals of both countries in Italy and Switzerland on reciprocity

---

[102] Gertz, 'The International Investment Regime', 12–14.

[103] The 1983 Swiss Federal Act on Acquisition of Real Estate by Persons Abroad (or 'Lex Koller') restricts the acquisition of Swiss residential and other non-commercial real estate by non-Swiss persons. In 2002, liberalization was introduced to EU nationals with permanent residence in Switzerland, who are treated as Swiss nationals due to the Swiss bilateral agreements with the EU: W. Muller and A. Vogel, 'The Swiss Lex Koller before Its Next Revision?', January 2017: https://uk.practicallaw.thomsonreuters.com/8-551-2765? transitionType=Default&contextData=(sc.Default)&firstPage=true&bhcp=1 (accessed 25 February 2018).

basis. On 14 April 1992 an agreement was announced between Italy, Switzerland and Grissons, allocating an extra number of authorizations to that canton so that they could be distributed, with retroactive effect, between the affected Italian owners, who, in exchange, should pay 'compensation for administrative costs' of about 12 per cent of the value of each property.[104]

Thirdly, although it is uncommon, in some IIAs the use of diplomatic protection is *the only available mechanism* for the settlement of investment disputes. A minor number of investment agreements make no provision for ISDS – as some of the early BITs signed between EU members, such as Germany, France, Italy and the Netherlands and African, Middle East or Asian countries.[105] Of the IIAs concluded in the last fifteen years, a small group of agreements do not include ISA.[106] A few IIAs provide that the right to use ISDS is lost or limited in the event of subrogation, when a governmental agency has made payment of a guarantee reimbursing losses incurred by the investor. In these cases, the home state that has been subrogated to the rights of the investor may not submit the case to ISDS, although this does not impair engagement in direct negotiations between both contracting parties of the IIA.[107]

Fourthly, diplomatic protection can be considered a *subsidiary dispute settlement mechanism*, in the event of waiver of ISDS agreed between the host state and the foreign investor. Even if we consider that investors are pursuing their own rights directly conferred by an IIA when initiating

---

[104] M. Recanati, 'Diplomatic Intervention and State-to-State Arbitration as Alternative Means for the Protection of Foreign Investments and Host States' General Interests: The Italian Experience' in G. Sacerdoti, P. Acconci, A. D. Luca and M. Valenti (eds.), *General Interests of Host States in International Investment Law* (Cambridge University Press, 2014), pp. 422–44 at pp. 426–30.

[105] See, by way of example, the France–China BIT (1985) and the Netherlands–Benin BIT (2001); S. Woolcock, *The EU Approach to International Investment Policy after the Lisbon Treaty* (Directorate-General for External Policies of the Union, 2010) p. 43.

[106] This is the case in all Brazilian IIAs concluded in 2015–18; the PACER Plus Agreement (2017) between Australia, the Forum Islands and New Zealand; Hong Kong–ASEAN Investment Agreement (2017); China–Hong Kong CEPA Investment Agreement (2017); China–Taiwan Cross-Strait BIT (2012), Netherlands–Oman BIT (2009); Australian FTAs with Japan (2014), Malaysia (2012) and the United States (2004), and in the Investment Protocol with New Zealand (2011); EFTA FTAs with Hong Kong (2011), Serbia (2009), Albania (2009) and Colombia (2008). In the Japan–Philippines EPA (2006), Art. 150, in the absence of the ISDS, the resort to international arbitration is subject to the mutual consent of the parties to the dispute.

[107] Gabon–Turkey BIT (2012), Art. 13.8; Kazakhstan–Serbia BIT (2010), Art. 8; India–Mexico BIT (2007), Arts. 9.10, 21–27; Australia–Mexico BIT (2005), Arts. 10.2, 21; COMESA Investment Treaty (2007), Art. 9.10.

arbitration against host states, that does not mean that they have the capacity to waive diplomatic protection in advance, as it is a right of the home state, and not of the investor. As Schreuer mentions, 'In situations of egregious violations of investors' rights, their home states would most probably resume diplomatic protection despite any prior waiver of investment arbitration secured by the host state.'[108]

Fifthly, some aggravated investors would have no choice but diplomatic protection, as the injury suffered may not qualify for protection under an investment treaty, or because *not every dispute that arises under IIAs has the ability to trigger ISDS*, providing for relationships that are not covered or are excluded by the treaty.[109] Besides the inclusion of exceptions, carve-outs and non-conforming measure – where there is not a legal violation of the treaty, several IIAs concluded in the last fifteen years have explicit exclusions from the ISA.[110] For example, in all Canadian IIAs (even CETA), a decision by Canada following a review under the Investment Canada Act, with respect to whether to permit an investment that is subject to review, is not subject to the ISDS provisions.[111] Mexico regularly includes the same type of provision in its IIAs.[112] The Pacific Alliance Additional Protocol includes exclusions from both Mexico and Chile, in relation to decisions adopted by their respective investment agencies.[113] In all these cases, the only applicable mechanism of dispute settlement is the one considered between states, if the home state espouses the claim of its investor.

Sixthly, there are other reasons why investors might want to leave the option of diplomatic protection open, even when ISDS is permitted. This would be the case when the *claim is not focused on obtaining pecuniary remedies,* but in specific performance from the host state, such as the

---

[108] Schreuer, 'Investment Protection and International Relations', 357.

[109] L. Reed, 'Observations on the Relationship between Diplomatic and Judicial Means' in L. Boisson de Chazournes, M. G. Kohen and J. E. Viñuales (eds.), *Diplomatic and Judicial Means of Dispute Settlement* (Martinus Nijhoff Publishers, 2012), pp. 291–305 at pp. 299–301.

[110] Mexico–Panama FTA (2014), Art. 10.2.4 excludes the application of the investment chapter to measures adopted for national security reasons and public order. The FTAs of Colombia with Israel (2013) and Panama (2013) in Annex 14-D also exclude those measures related to health, safety, the environment and labour rights.

[111] CETA, Art. 8.45, Annex 8-C; Canada–Korea FTA (2014), Art. 8.44, Annex 8-F; Canada–Honduras FTA (2014), Annex 10.44; Benin–Canada BIT (2013), Annex IV; Canada–China BIT (2012), Art. 34 and Annex D.34; Canada–Kuwait BIT (2011), Annex 3.

[112] Mexico–Peru FTA (2011), Art. 11.35.2; NAFTA, Art. 1138.2.

[113] PAAP (2014), Chapter 10, Annexes from Mexico and Chile.

reversal of governmental decisions or regulations, where the home state would probably be better placed to discuss these topics, via consultations and other inter-state mechanisms provided for in the treaty.[114]

Seventhly, another situation in which the most efficient hope for redress might be diplomatic protection, is when *an entire class of investors is damaged by a broad measure adopted by a host state.*[115] For example, in *Abaclat* v. *Argentina* the question was posed whether ICSID was able to handle effectively a mass claim of 60,000 claimants purporting to have ownership interest in Argentine sovereign bonds in one single proceeding.[116] A member of the arbitral tribunal highlighted these problems in a couple of dissenting statements on procedural orders, opposing the decision of the majority to examine only some and not all claimants (eight 'claimant witnesses' chosen by the legal representatives of the claimants).[117] Maybe, in these cases, state-to-state dispute settlement could help to overcome procedural problems derived from mass claims, handling such disputes in a way similar to ancient binational claims commissions.

Eighthly, a claim by the home state could also make sense when *injuries are individually small but collectively large.* In these *class action* cases, the home state could seek a ruling that the host state violated the treaty in relation to that class. Roberts has advanced that this approach would help to counter some of the problems that states currently face in fighting arbitral battles on multiple fronts and in being bound by conflicting rulings. For example, it would permit common issues of law or fact, such as liability and defences, to be determined in a consistent, streamlined way. Future investor–state claims could then build on

---

[114] D. Gaukrodger and K. Gordon, 'Investor–State Dispute Settlement: A Scoping Paper of the Investment Policy Community', *OECD Working Papers on International Investment*, No 2012/3 (2012), p. 28.

[115] Reed, 'Observations on the Relationship between Diplomatic and Judicial Means', pp. 299–301.

[116] D. F. Donovan, 'Abaclat and Others v Argentine Republic as a Collective Claims Proceeding', *ICSID Review*, 27 (2012), 261–7; H. van Houtte and B. McAsey, 'Abaclat and others v Argentine Republic ICSID, the BIT and Mass Claims', *ICSID Review*, 27 (2012), 231–6.

[117] *Abaclat and others* v. *Argentine Republic*, ICSID Case No ARB/07/5 (formerly Giovanna a Beccara and others v. Argentine Republic). Statement of Dissent of Dr Santiago Torres Bernárdez to Procedural Order No 27, 30 May 2014; *Abaclat and others* v. *Argentine Republic*, ICSID Case No ARB/07/5. Statement of Dissent of Dr. Santiago Torres Bernárdez to Procedural Order No 32, 1 August 2014.

these awards by establishing jurisdiction and damages on an individualized basis.[118]

Finally, another case in which diplomatic protection may be favoured is *when the injured investors are individuals or small companies*, who might welcome their case being brought by their home state to avoid the expense of bringing a direct claim themselves. Similarly, diplomatic mechanisms might be preferred when investors fear retaliation or discrimination by the host state in the event of launching ISA, if their intention is to continue to have business in that country.[119]

(b)   Treaty Review

Almost all investment treaties provide that one contracting party may initiate a treaty review about the interpretation or application of the treaty.[120] As defined by UNCTAD, *interpretation* is 'the determination of the meanings of particular provisions of an agreement in concrete or proposed situations', while *application* relates 'to the extent to which the actions or measures taken or proposed by the contracting parties comply with the terms of an agreement, its object and purpose'.[121]

As we have seen in previous sections, the scope of the review of an investment agreement, either by the contracting parties or by a treaty body, is, in principle, broad, and could play a role not only in the prevention of investment disputes, but also in their settlement. Some IIAs are even explicit on this goal. BITs concluded by the United States in the 1980s specifically provide that the parties 'agree to consult promptly, on the request of either, to resolve any disputes in connection with the treaty'.[122]

Certain IIAs provide that the review mechanism can be used to seek or endeavour to resolve, or contribute to resolving, disputes regarding any

---

[118] Roberts, 'State-to-State Investment Treaty Arbitration', 29.

[119] Ibid., 14–15.

[120] Although this is the typical formulation, some IIAs use the terminology 'differences', 'divergences', 'matters' or 'questions'. Some IIAs use the formula 'interpretation *and* application': see UNCTAD, *Dispute Settlement*, pp. 14–15. A few IIAs have an even broader scope, adding 'implementation' to the mix – a notion related to the execution of the treaty obligation, or how the contracting parties have put their treaty commitments into effect. See SADC Investment Protocol (2006), Art. 24; Portugal–Qatar BIT (2009), Art. 10; Libya–Slovakia BIT (2009), Art. 9.

[121] UNCTAD, *Dispute Settlement*, p. 14.

[122] E.g. Haiti–US BIT (1983), Art. VI; Democratic Republic of Congo (Zaire)–US BIT (1984), Art. VI; Cameroon–US BIT (1986), Art. VI.

matter arising under the agreement,[123] the application of the treaty,[124] or unambiguous investment disputes. For example, the Sub-Committee on Investment of the Australia–Japan EPA has the function of considering any issues brought by either party concerning investment agreements between a party and an investor of the other party.[125] This dispute resolution function is sometimes exercised through the state-to-state settlement procedures of the same treaty,[126] but in most cases it could be implemented by the treaty body without using those mechanisms.

Treaty review clauses can also be included, together with the provisions on state-to-state dispute settlement. For example, CAFTA–DR establishes that the parties shall at all times endeavour to agree on the interpretation and application of the agreement, and 'make every attempt through cooperation and consultations to arrive at a mutually satisfactory resolution of any matter that might affect its operation'.[127] In that context, any party 'may request in writing consultations with any other Party with respect to any actual or proposed measure or any other matter that it considers might affect the operation of this Agreement'.[128]

The review of IIAs can also be linked with the provisions on state-to state dispute settlement. For example, under the Jordan–Singapore BIT, among the functions of the joint committee established by the treaty are assessing the functioning and results of the treaty and reviewing any claim by a party pursuant to a 'letter exchange' procedure, found in Article 5 of the said BIT, that allows parties to adopt or maintain limitations to national treatment in relation to any sectors or matters.[129]

In the absence of explicit state-to-state dispute settlement procedures, the role of the treaty bodies is crucial for dispute resolution. For example, the China–Taiwan BIT does not provide for any arbitration mechanisms, but refers to the Cross-Straits Economic Cooperation Committee (ECC),[130] which shall establish an investment dispute settlement

---

[123] E.g. Canada–Korea FTA (2014), Art. 20.1.2(f); Mexico–Panama FTA (2014), Art. 17.1.2 (d); EFTA–Costa Rica–Panama FTA (2013), Art. 11.1(e).

[124] E.g. Australia–Malaysia FTA (2012), Art. 19.1.3(b); India–Malaysia ECA (2011), Art. 15.1.3(e); Costa Rica–Singapore FTA, Art. 16.1.2(c).

[125] Australia–Japan EPA (2014), Art. 14.18(e).

[126] E.g. Australia–Korea FTA (2014), Art. 21.3.2(d); PAAP (2014), Art. 16.2.1(c); Australia–Malaysia FTA (2012), Art. 19.1.3(b).

[127] CAFTA–DR, Art. 20.1.

[128] Ibid., Art. 20.4.1.

[129] Jordan–Singapore BIT (2004), Art. 8.1.2(e).

[130] Cross-Strait Bilateral Investment Promotion and Protection Agreement (2012), Art. 15. The ECC is a mechanism established under the 2010 Cross-Strait Economic Cooperation

mechanism, although its dispute resolution is limited to amicable settlement, and decision-making procedures are consensus based.[131]

(c) State-to-State Adjudication

Nowadays, the adjudication of investment disputes by international courts is rather unusual. The ICJ has decided only a handful of investment cases, and other regional courts have adjudicated another few. But this scenario could change if the proposal of the EU (which is also endorsed by Canada) of establishing a standing investment tribunal and an appellate court is successful.

In the following section we will examine the existing case law on investment dispute settlement by these international and regional tribunals.

(i) International Court of Justice (ICJ)   The ICJ was established by the United Nations Charter in June 1945, as its principal judicial organ, and all its members are automatically parties to the Statute, although non-members are also allowed to become parties to it.[132]

Since the beginning of its work in April 1946, the ICJ has only four leading cases addressing foreign investment disputes on the merits: *Nottebohm*, *Barcelona Traction*, *ELSI*, and *Diallo*, but only in the latter was the investor's claim partially accepted, with considerably lower compensation for material injuries in relation to personal property. Although the number of investment cases decided by the ICJ is low, it has created relevant jurisprudence in issues such as seizure and requisition of property owned or controlled by foreign investors, and governmental decisions affecting foreign shareholders of a company.

While ICSID tribunals (and other investment tribunals) often refer to the jurisprudence of the ICJ, showing a particular deference to it, the World Court has never referred to ICSID's (and other investment tribunals') decisions or awards. Pellet believes that the ICJ's indifference comes from the fact that the Court regards itself as the supreme public international law tribunal, and that the cases that are put before the ICJ do not lend themselves to references to specific ISDS jurisprudence,

Framework Agreement (ECFA), an interim treaty intended to foster the establishment of a free trade area between China and Taiwan. C.-H. Wu, 'The Many Facets of States in International Investment Law' in S. Lalani and R. Polanco (eds.), *The Role of the State in Investor–State Arbitration* (Brill/Martinus Nijhoff, 2014), pp. 405–29 at p. 419.

[131] Wu, 'The Many Facets of States in International Investment Law', p. 419.
[132] Malanczuk, *Akehurst's Modern Introduction to International Law*, pp. 281–2.

although he also notes that investment tribunals implement general principles that go far beyond the investment law alone.[133]

Seizure and Requisition of Property Claims   In the *Nottebohm* case, Liechtenstein espoused the claims of Mr Friedrich Nottebohm, an alleged citizen of Liechtenstein, who claimed restitution and compensation from Guatemala, based on his arrest, detention and expulsion from that country, and also the seizure of his property. In a famous decision, the ICJ declared the claim inadmissible, under the 'effective nationality' principle,[134] considering that Liechtenstein was not entitled to extend its diplomatic protection to Mr Nottebohm – who had been born a German citizen and had applied for naturalization only after the outbreak of World War II, having settled in Guatemala for 34 years – and finding that he had no effective bond of attachment with Liechtenstein.[135]

In the *ELSI* case, the United States espoused the claims of two American corporations – Raytheon Company and Machlett Laboratories Inc. – that wholly owned the Italian company Elettronica Sicula SpA (ELSI), against Italy, pleading a violation of certain provisions of the 1948 Italy–US friendship, commerce and navigation agreement, which provided in Article XXVI that 'Any dispute between the High Contracting Parties as to the interpretation or the application of this Treaty, which the High Contracting Parties shall not satisfactorily adjust by diplomacy, shall be submitted to the International Court of Justice, unless the High Contracting Parties shall agree to settlement by some other pacific means.'[136]

The claim was motivated by the requisition, in March 1968, of ELSI's plant in Sicily, by resolution of the major of Palermo, on the ground of 'grave public necessity', after Raytheon decided that ELSI would cease operations, as it was not economically self-sufficient, and started the dismissal of staff who were no longer required.[137] The proceedings before the ICJ were instituted in 1987, after several years of diplomatic negotiations between Italy and the United States. The Court's judgment, 21 years after the disputed events, rejected the claim on the ground that

---

[133] A. Pellet, 'The Case Law of the ICJ in Investment Arbitration', *ICSID Review – Foreign Investment Law Journal*, 28 (2013), 223–40 at 225.

[134] Dugan *et al.*, *Investor–State Arbitration*, pp. 292–4.

[135] *Nottebohm case (Liechtenstein v. Guatemala)*, Judgment 6 April 1955 [1955] ICJ Reports 4, pp. 25–6.

[136] Treaty of Friendship, Commerce and Navigation between the United States of America and the Italian Republic. Signed at Rome, 2 February 1948.

[137] *Elettronica Sicula SPA* (ELSI) *(United States of America v. Italy)*, Judgment 20 July 1989 [1989] ICJ Rep. 1, pp. 12–41.

the United States had not proven neither that the ELSI plant in Palermo had a substantial value before the requisition, or that had the main shareholder – Raytheon – been damaged by such seizure.[138]

Shareholders' Claims   In the *Barcelona Traction* case, Belgium initiated proceedings before the ICJ against Spain, on behalf of Barcelona Traction, Light and Power Ltd, a company incorporated in Toronto, Canada, which was in charge of developing a system to produce and distribute electric power in Barcelona, and which was declared bankrupt by a Spanish Court, after defaulting on payments of bonds secured by mortgages of several subsidiaries in Spain.[139]

Belgium espoused the claim to seek reparation for damage allegedly sustained by the Belgian national's shareholders in the company, as a result of acts committed by Spain against Barcelona Traction that ultimately resulted in the bankruptcy of the company. The Court found that Belgium lacked *locus standi* to exercise diplomatic protection of shareholders in a Canadian company in relation to measures taken against that company in Spain, because, even if the company operated in another country and was controlled by foreign shareholders, the state whose nationality the company possessed still had a right to make claims on its behalf.[140] Canada did exercise diplomatic protection on behalf of the company, but the ICJ had no compulsory jurisdiction between Canada and Spain, in an issue that did not confer standing on Belgium.[141] Additionally, the ICJ held that 'an act directed against and infringing only the company's rights does not involve responsibility towards the shareholders, even if their interests are affected'.[142]

This differs from the *ELSI* case because, in that decision, the Court did not delve into the issue of shareholder standing, although implicitly recognized that the United States had interests in exercising diplomatic protection covering indirect ownership, probably due to the fact that in *ELSI* the Court was dealing with a corporation in the respondent state and not in a third country, as in *Barcelona Traction*.[143]

The *Diallo* case, between Guinea and the Democratic Republic of the Congo (DRC), refers to the claim of Mr Ahmadou Sadio Diallo,

---

[138] A. F. Lowenfeld, *International Economic Law* (Oxford University Press, 2003), p. 436.
[139] Ibid., p. 433.
[140] Malanczuk, *Akehurst's Modern Introduction to International Law*, p. 266.
[141] Lowenfeld, *International Economic Law*, p. 434.
[142] *Barcelona Traction*, Judgment Second Phase, p. 36.
[143] Dugan *et al.*, *Investor–State Arbitration*, p. 310.

a Guinean national who was the manager of and a shareholder in two companies registered under the laws of Zaire ('Africom-Zaire' and 'Africontainers-Zaire'), now called DRC. In 1995, Mr Diallo was arrested and deported from Zaire, on the basis that his presence and conduct had breached 'public order'.[144]

In a judgment of 24 May 2007 on preliminary objections, the ICJ declared the application of Guinea admissible, but only as far as it concerned the protection of Mr Diallo's rights as an individual and as a shareholder, excluding the protection of both companies, as it was considered that such protection was governed by bilateral or multilateral agreements for the protection of foreign investments and not by diplomatic protection.[145]

In a judgment on the merits on 30 November 2010, the Court found that, with the arrest, detention and expulsion of Mr Diallo, DRC had violated the International Covenant on Civil and Political Rights (ICCPR) and the African Charter on Human and Peoples' Rights (ACHPR).[146] In a subsequent judgment on 19 June 2012, the ICJ fixed the amount of compensation due from the DRC to the Republic of Guinea for the injuries suffered by Mr Diallo, assigning a clear higher value to non-material injury (US$85,000), vis-à-vis material injury in relation to his personal property (US$10,000), and rejecting claims of compensation concerning material injury allegedly suffered by Mr Diallo as a result of a loss of professional remuneration during his unlawful detentions and expulsion, and as a result of a deprivation of potential earnings.[147]

Cases Declining Jurisdiction   There have been other cases before the ICJ relating to foreign investments, but they were not decided on the merits as the Court declined jurisdiction. These cases referred to diverse issues such as nationalization, public debt and freezing of assets.

The *Interhandel* case related to a company incorporated in Switzerland (Société international pour participations industrielles et commerciales – Interhandel) that pursued litigation before the US courts to unblock its assets in that country (90 per cent of shares in the General Aniline and Film Corporation), ordered in the application of US laws on enemy

---

[144] Ibid., p. 310.
[145] *Diallo*, Preliminary Objections, pp. 614–15.
[146] *Case Concerning Ahmadou Sadio Diallo (Republic of Guinea v. Democratic Republic of the Congo)*, Merits, Judgment 30 November 2010 [2010] ICJ Rep 639, pp. 667, 687, 692.
[147] *Case Concerning Ahmadou Sadio Diallo (Republic of Guinea v. Democratic Republic of the Congo)*, Compensation, Judgment of 19 June 2012 [2012] ICJ Rep 324, pp. 344–6.

property, as it was deemed that the company was controlled by a German company (IG Chemie). Switzerland espoused the claim of Interhandel and brought a claim against the United States before the ICJ in 1957.[148] The Court dismissed the case, admitting a preliminary objection on the ground that the claimant had not exhausted local remedies, even if Interhandel litigated its claim in American courts during ten years.[149]

In the *Certain Norwegian Loans* case, France instituted proceedings against Norway on behalf of French nationals, asking the court to adjudicate that in certain bonds stipulated in gold and issued between 1896 and 1909 by the Norwegian government and other Norwegian institutions, on the French market and other foreign markets, the borrower could discharge the substance of his debt only by the payment of the gold value. The Norwegian government had suspended convertibility to gold in 1914, in 1920 and since 1931.[150]

The ICJ found that it had no jurisdiction to adjudicate upon the dispute, because it considered that, by virtue of the condition of reciprocity, the Norwegian government was entitled to invoke the reservation contained in the French Declaration of 1 March 1949, accepting the compulsory jurisdiction of the Court; and such reservation excluded from the jurisdiction of the ICJ the dispute that was referred by the application of the French government.[151]

Finally, another investment dispute in which jurisdiction was denied by the ICJ was the *Anglo–Iranian Co.* case. This case, brought by Great Britain against Iran, claiming that the 1951 Iranian Oil Nationalization Act – which nationalized the oil industry and created a National Iranian Oil Company – expropriated the sixty-year-old concession granted in 1933 to the Anglo–Persian Oil Co. (later Anglo–Iranian Oil Co., and British Petroleum) by the Imperial Government of Persia (then Iran).[152] The Court decided that the consent of Iran to the jurisdiction of the Court, contained in a Declaration of 1930, was limited to disputes related to the application of treaties accepted by Iran after that date, and not to a concession contract signed later, rejecting also the use of the most-

---

[148] *Interhandel case (Switzerland v. United States of America)*, Preliminary Objections, Judgment 21 March 1959 [1959] ICJ Rep 6, pp. 19–29.

[149] Dugan *et al.*, *Investor–State Arbitration*, p. 352.

[150] B. MacChesney, 'Case of Certain Norwegian Loans (France v. Norway)', *American Journal of International Law*, 51 (1957), 777–83.

[151] *Case of Certain Norwegian Loans (France v. Norway)*. Judgment, 6 July 1957 [1957] ICJ Rep 9, p. 27.

[152] *Anglo–Iranian Oil Co. case (United Kingdom v. Iran)* Jurisdiction, Judgment, 22 July 1952 [1952] ICJ Rep. 93, p. 113.

favoured nation clauses of other Iranian treaties concluded after Iran's acceptance of the ICJ jurisdiction.[153]

(ii) **Regional Courts**   In a few IIAs, the treaty provides for referral to an external adjudicatory body of a regional nature. From our survey of the past fifteen years, we find this feature in only four treaties: (1) the Agreement on the EEU, which provides for inter-state dispute settlement at the Eurasian Economic Union Court;[154] (2) the Lebanon–Syria BIT, which refers to the Unified Agreement for the Investment of Arab Capital in the Arab States, which in Chapter VI provides for arbitration to the Arab Investment Court;[155] (3) the Common Market for Eastern and Southern Africa (COMESA) Investment Agreement, which provides for the settlement of inter-state disputes that cannot be resolved by mediation, negotiation or other amicable means, or international arbitration, to the COMESA Court of Justice;[156] and (4) the Southern African Development Community (SADC) Investment Protocol, that refers the settlement of the disputes to the SADC Tribunal, for the interpretation, application and implementation of the protocol, if parties could not resolve them using negotiations.[157]

But an older agreement with similar provisions has been recently the object of debate: the 1997 Convention on the Protection of the Rights of Investors (the 'Moscow Convention') which provides for the Economic Court of the Commonwealth of Independent States (CIS) as one of the fora for the settlement of disputes with regard to the implementation of investments within the framework of the Moscow Convention.[158] In three ISAs against Kyrgyzstan, submitted

---

[153] Lowenfeld, *International Economic Law*, pp. 432–3.
[154] Under the Agreement on the Eurasian Economic Union (2014), Art. 112, disputes related to interpretation and/or application of the provisions of the treaty are settled by consultations and negotiations. If no agreement is achieved within three months, any of the parties can submit a dispute to the Court of the Union, unless the parties have agreed otherwise. Article 10 of the Treaty of the Eurasian Economic Community (EEC) (2008) provided for the settlement of the dispute by the Court of the EEC. Both were respectively replaced by the Agreement on the EEU and the Eurasian Economic Union Court from 1 January 2015.
[155] Lebanon–Syria BIT (2010), Art. 7.
[156] COMESA Investment Agreement (2007), Arts. 26, 27.
[157] SADC Investment Protocol (2006), Art. 24.
[158] The Convention on Protection of the Rights of the Investor (1997), Art. 11 provides that 'disputes concerning implementation of investments within the framework of the present Convention are to be resolved by courts or arbitration courts of the state-parties, the Economic Court of the Commonwealth of Independent States and/or other

before the Arbitration Court at the Moscow Chamber of Commerce and Industry under the basis of the Moscow Convention, the tribunals agreed that this agreement included the Kyrgyz Republic's consent to submit any investment disputes to international arbitration on the choice of the investor.[159]

In disagreement with these awards, the Kyrgyz Republic applied to the Moscow Commercial Court to have them set aside and, more importantly, requested an authoritative interpretation from the CIS Economic Court on whether its consent under Article 11 of the Moscow Convention constituted consent to jurisdiction of an international arbitral tribunal.[160] On 23 September 2014, the CIS Economic Court ruled that the Moscow Convention did not, in fact, contain any consent to arbitration, and that the provision merely set out possible forms of arbitration that the disputing investor and host state might consider. The CIS Economic Court found that any binding consent to arbitration would need to be contained in some other instrument, such as a treaty, contract or national legislation. Although the investors have downplayed the effect of the CIS Economic Court ruling, as being merely advisory, and considered that it could not affect the tribunal's jurisdiction or the enforceability of its award, its concrete effects are yet to be seen, as the CIS Economic Court issued a binding judgment rather than an advisory opinion, at the request of Kyrgyzstan, citing powers granted to it under its founding statutes.[161]

(d) State-to-State Arbitration

The large majority of IIAs include provisions on state-to-state dispute settlement, usually using international arbitration. According to

international courts or international arbitration courts'. S. Usoskin, 'Kyrgyz Republic's Mixed Fortunes in Investment Arbitration' (May 2014).

[159] The cases are: *Lee John Beck and Central Asian Development Corp. v. Kyrgyz Republic*, in which the tribunal awarded US$118 million against Kyrgyzstan; *OKVV et al. v. Kyrgyz Republic*, in which the tribunal awarded US$23 million against Kyrgyzstan; and *Stans Energy v. Kyrgyz Republic*, in which the tribunal awarded US$2.2 million against Kyrgyzstan. See J. Hepburn, 'CIS Economic Court Issues Authoritative Interpretation of Investment Treaty at Root of Series of Investor–State Arbitrations' (September 2014).

[160] S. Usoskin, 'Kyrgyz Republic's Mixed Fortunes in Investment Arbitration', May 2014: www.cisarbitration.com/2014/05/14/kyrgyz-republics-mixed-fortunes-in-investment -arbitration/ (accessed 9 February 2018).

[161] J. Hepburn, 'CIS Economic Court Issues Authoritative Interpretation of Investment Treaty at Root of Series of Investor–State Arbitrations', September 2014: www.iareporter .com/articles/20140923_2 (accessed 9 February 2018).

Posner, there is a basic difference between BITs and investment chapters of FTAs in this regard.[162] On the one hand, BITs usually follow the traditional inter-state model for the settlement of disputes, providing for the submission to ad hoc arbitration of any dispute between the parties concerning the interpretation or application of the treaty, for a binding decision of a tribunal.[163] On the other hand, FTAs usually follow the WTO model, referring the settlement of claims to a panel that issues a report, based on which the parties have to agree on the final resolution of the dispute, which could include modification of the challenged measure to conform with the obligations of the treaty, and not direct compensation for the investor. The scope of disputes included in investment chapters of FTAs also usually be wider, including not only differences concerning the interpretation or application of the agreement, but also disputes concerning measures inconsistent with the treaty or failure to carry out obligations established under the agreement. This model is found in NAFTA[164] and in several FTAs concluded by its members.[165]

Yet, not all FTAs follow this model. In agreements concluded notably by the EU, Japan and Australia, the final panel report is binding on the parties and the scope of the dispute is limited to the interpretation and application of the agreement.[166] Some agreements preserve a wider scope of disputes, but provide that the award is binding on the parties.[167] Other treaties keep the scope limited to the interpretation

---

[162] T. Posner, 'The Role of Non-Disputing States in Investment Dispute Settlement, 22nd Investment Treaty Forum (ITF), British Institute of International and Comparative Law (BIICL), 8 May 2014'.

[163] The large majority of the BITs concluded in the last fifteen years stipulate that inter-state awards are binding on the parties. E.g.: Serbia–UAE BIT (2013), Art. 10.6; China–Japan–Korea trilateral investment agreement (2012), Art. 17.5; Moldova–Qatar BIT (2012), Art. 10.4.

[164] NAFTA, Arts. 2006–2008 and 2018, also follows the WTO model, although the scope of disputes broadly includes 'any actual or proposed measure or any other matter that it considers might affect the operation of this Agreement'.

[165] E.g. Honduras–Peru FTA (2015), Art. 15.10; Korea–New Zealand FTA (2015), Art. 19.13; Canada–Korea FTA (2014), Arts. 21.2, 21.10.

[166] E.g. PACER Plus (2017), Ch. 14, Art. 15; CETA, Arts. 29.2, 29.10. In the EU–Singapore IPA Arts. 3.33 to 3.37, the ruling shall be complied in good faith, and non-compliance remedies are considered. In the EU–Vietnam FTA (2018), Ch. 15, Art. 15.22 the reports and rulings of the arbitration panel shall be 'unconditionally accepted' by the parties.

[167] E.g. Australia–Japan FTA (2014), Arts. 19.1, 19.4, 19.12.8; Mexico–Panama FTA (2014), Arts. 18.3, 18.16; PAAP (2014), Arts. 17.3, 17.16.

or application of the treaty, with a final report that is not directly binding.[168]

A few other FTAs follow a completely different trend, regulating the settlement of disputes between the contracting parties on the interpretation or application of the investment chapter, in that section of the treaty, separately from the regular state-to state dispute settlement mechanism of the FTA.[169] This procedure is modelled on BITs, providing for submission to an ad hoc tribunal only after the failure of a consultation period of six months that is held directly between the contracting parties or through a treaty body.[170] If no agreement is reached within that timeframe, after receipt through diplomatic channels of the request for arbitration, each party shall appoint one member to the arbitral panel. Typically, the two members shall then select a national of a third state, who, upon approval by the two parties, shall be appointed chair of the arbitral panel. In the event of disagreement between the parties the President of the ICJ is considered the appointing authority in the large majority of IIAs.

However, certain BITs provide for a 'conditional' binding effect for inter-state awards, closer to the WTO model. This the case in a number of Canadian BITs, which, although initially providing that state-to-state awards are final and binding, allow the contracting parties to meet within sixty days of the decision of an arbitral tribunal, and decide on the manner in which to implement the decision of the arbitral tribunal. If they fail to reach a decision, the contracting party bringing the dispute 'shall be entitled to receive compensation of equivalent value to the arbitral tribunal's award'.[171]

There is another important difference between BITs and FTAs when it comes to inter-state dispute settlement. As we have seen in the preceding

---

[168] E.g. EFTA–Bosnia and Herzegovina FTA (2013), Art. 45; EFTA–Hong Kong FTA (2011), Arts. 10.1, 10.19; Panama–Singapore FTA (2006), Arts. 15.2, 15.3, 15.15.

[169] China–Peru FTA (2009), Art. 138; China–Pakistan FTA (2006), Art. 53.

[170] In China–Hong Kong CEPA Investment Agreement (2017), Arts. 17, 18, the joint committee is in charge of dispute settlement through consultations. Intra-MERCOSUR Investment Facilitation Protocol (2017), Art. 24, refers to MERCOSUR dispute settlement mechanisms. Chile–Hong Kong Investment Agreement (2016), Art. 23, refers to Chile–Hong Kong FTA (2012), Ch. 17, for dispute settlement. Under Burkina Faso–Canada BIT (2015), Art. 39.2, the joint commission can meet 'by any technological means available'.

[171] E.g. Canada–Côte d'Ivoire BIT (2014), Art. 37.9; Canada–Mali BIT (2014), Art. 37.9; Canada–Senegal BIT (2014), Art. 38.9.

section several FTAs with an investment chapter include state-to-state arbitration (even in the absence of ISA), that could eventually trigger countermeasures, such as suspension of concessions, in the event of non-compliance with the award. This feature is less common in inter-state dispute settlement provisions in BITs.

Finally, certain IIAs – mostly FTAs – provide for reference to another treaty for the settlement of state-to-state disputes. This is the case of agreements that have been concluded to supplement a previous FTA,[172] or trade agreements that made explicit reference to previous BITs signed between the same (or some) contracting parties.[173]

(i) Scope of State-to-State Dispute Settlement   Even though inter-state dispute settlement in investment disputes rarely happens in practice, some authors have sketched a typology of state-to-state arbitration. Roberts distinguishes three main categories: (1) diplomatic protection claims, in which the home state brings a diplomatic protection claim on behalf of its investors for an IIA violation; (2) purely interpretive disputes, in which the home or the host state seeks a pure interpretation of the IIA, on either an abstract or a concrete dispute; and (3) requests for declaratory relief, in which either the home or the host state brings a claim on an issue that has arisen or may arise in an ISDS claim.[174]

Kulick proposes four different categories of state-to-state arbitration: (1) inter-state treaty violation claims, on abstract application claims, either related to a specific ISDS dispute (e.g. when the host state refuses

---

[172] E.g. Hong Kong-ASEAN Investment Agreement (2017), Art. 21, refers to ASEAN–Hong Kong FTA (2017), Ch. 13; Chile–China Supplementary Agreement on Investment (2012), Art. 26, references Chapter X of the Chile–China FTA (2005). China–Taiwan BIT refers its dispute settlement to the Cross-Straits ECC, established under the Cross-Strait ECFA (2010).

[173] E.g. China–Costa Rica FTA (2010), Art. 89, reaffirms the commitments between the same parties under a 2007 BIT; the ASEAN Comprehensive Investment Agreement (2009), Art. 27, makes applicable the ASEAN Protocol on Enhanced Dispute Settlement Mechanism (2004) for the settlement of disputes. China–Singapore FTA (2008), Art. 84, makes applicable the dispute settlement provisions of the ASEAN–China Investment Agreement (2009), that were under negotiation at the time of signature of the China–Singapore FTA. In CEFTA (2006), Art. 30.3, any dispute related to the interpretation or application of the investment provisions of the FTA, shall not be submitted to the arbitral procedure set out in that agreement, if that dispute can be presented to the arbitration procedures provided for one of the previous BITs between CEFTA states (Albania, Bosnia and Herzegovina, Moldova, Montenegro, Serbia and Kosovo), which are set out in Annex 6 to that FTA.

[174] Roberts, 'State-to-State Investment Treaty Arbitration'.

to honour the award), or not linked to another dispute (e.g. on issues related to denunciation of the IIA); (2) diplomatic protection claims, in which the home state introduces state-to-state dispute settlement on behalf of the investor for violation of the IIA; (3) abstract interpretation claims, in which the home state resorts to inter-state dispute settlement to obtain a type of 'pre-emptive' interpretation of the IIA; and (4) concrete interpretation claims, in which the dispute over the interpretation of an IIA is related to a specific dispute between the investor of a contracting party and the other contracting party as a host state. Here, he distinguishes three sub-categories: where inter-state proceedings conclude before the ISDS proceedings; where inter-state proceedings are introduced after the ISDS proceedings have concluded; and where both inter-state and ISDS proceedings take place in parallel.[175]

Having those typologies in mind, for our purposes we will make a simpler distinction as to whether, in IIAs, state-to-state dispute settlement mechanisms exist as a complement to ISA or in lieu of it,[176] focusing on the role that the home state has in these proceedings.

(1) Complementing Investor–State Arbitration The complementarity could be explicitly considered in the IIA, typically in the event of non-compliance with an arbitral award triggering state-to-state dispute settlement provisions. But complementarity could also come from an 'abstract' dispute initiated by a state with a view to resolving questions of interpretation or application of the treaty, without claiming any specific breach on the part of the other contracting party,[177] that would clarify substantive and procedural rights granted to investors ('pure interpretive' disputes).

In principle, there seems to be no reason against an 'abstract' interpretation of a treaty provision using inter-state arbitration, besides the problem of proving the existence of a dispute. Yet, some have pointed out that 'an authoritative interpretation in the absence of a concrete treaty violation may blur the line between judicial and advisory functions'.[178]

---

[175] Kulick, 'State-State Investment Arbitration'.

[176] Posner, 'The Role of Non-Disputing States in Investment Dispute Settlement, 22nd Investment Treaty Forum (ITF), British Institute of International and Comparative Law (BIICL), 8 May 2014'.

[177] Potestà, 'Towards a Greater Role for State-to-State Arbitration', pp. 249–50.

[178] See C. J. Trevino, 'State-to-State Investment Treaty Arbitration and the Interplay with Investor–State Arbitration Under the Same Treaty', *Journal of International Dispute Settlement*, (2014) 5, 199–233 at 206.

Inter-state arbitration for 'abstract' interpretations might also be questioned if it is initiated while ISDS arbitration is pending, or with the purpose of challenging the enforcement of awards previously rendered by ISDS tribunals.

Conceding that 'interpretive disputes are unlikely to be purely abstract',[179] Roberts has advanced the idea that, for the purposes of limiting future damages and costs, home states could also initiate 'declaratory claims', seeking a declaration that the host state has violated the investment treaty, without identifying particular investors that have been harmed or seeking compensation on their behalf.[180] The effects of these awards in future ISDS proceedings is highly debatable, as we will analyse later.

In any case, as state-to-state arbitration has rarely been used for this purpose, the existence of such conflicts has hardly been tested. One of the few reported cases is the inter-state arbitration initiated by Peru pursuant to the 2000 Chile–Peru BIT, while a previous ISA was taking place under the same BIT, between a Chilean investor and the Republic of Peru (*Peru* v. *Chile* case). Based on the existence of the state-to-state arbitration, Peru requested suspension of the ISDS proceedings in which it was the respondent, arguing that interpretative priority should be given to inter-state proceedings.[181] Without providing any reasoning for it, the request was denied by the investor–state arbitral tribunal merely holding that 'the conditions for a suspension of the proceedings were not met'.[182] The inter-state arbitration was not pursued further by Peru.

(2) Instead of Investor–State Arbitration   Additionally, state-to-state dispute settlement could take place instead of ISA ('diplomatic protection claims'), in the few IIAs in which such arbitration is not included, or in disputes under IIAs that are not included in the scope of ISDS, either because they are explicitly excluded from the treaty (e.g. taxation measures, or pre-establishment rights), or also in the rare cases in which investors have decided not to use ISA.

---

[179] Roberts, 'State-to-State Investment Treaty Arbitration', 54.
[180] Ibid., 66–8.
[181] R. Dolzer and C. Schreuer, *Principles of International Investment Law* (Oxford University Press, 2012), p. 214.
[182] *Empresas Lucchetti, SA and Lucchetti Peru, SA* v. *Republic of Peru*, ICSID Case No ARB/03/4 (also known as: Industria Nacional de Alimentos, AS and Indalsa Perú SA v. Republic of Peru), Award, 7 February 2005, para. 9

According to Posner, these reasons could include fears of retaliation by the host state, the cost involved in the procedures in relation to multiple and relatively small investments affected by the same measure, or because the main objective is not to obtain compensation, but to have measures modified and removed in order to continue doing business in the host state.[183] In these 'concrete' disputes, the home state espouses the claim of its national and uses state-to-state arbitration exercising diplomatic protection.[184]

Examples of inter-state arbitration in lieu of ISA are the Brazilian IIAs concluded since 2015, which are a clear revival of traditional diplomatic protection, as they refuse to allow investors to initiate or participate in the resolution of the investment dispute, which depends on the espousal of their home state. Some authors have criticized this feature, fearing that the new Brazilian IIAs might become 'toothless lions' if private parties are deprived of proper enforcement mechanisms if the home state does not bring the claim.[185] It is interesting to note that while the cooperation and facilitation investment agreements with Latin American agreements safeguard Brazil from facing ISA procedures, by expressly stating that MFN obligations shall not extend to dispute settlement provisions that these countries have in IIAs with other partners;[186] CFIAs with some African countries leave an open door for Brazilian investors to invoke ISA in any future dispute with Mozambique, Angola and Malawi – as the agreements with those countries that did not limit MFN obligations in their CFIAs.[187]

---

[183] Posner, 'The Role of Non-Disputing States in Investment Dispute Settlement, 22nd Investment Treaty Forum (ITF), British Institute of International and Comparative Law (BIICL), 8 May 2014'.

[184] Potestà, 'Towards a Greater Role for State-to-State Arbitration', pp. 249–50.

[185] J. P. Muniz and L. A. S. Peretti, 'Brazil Signs New Bilateral Investment Treaties with Mozambique and Angola: New Approach to BITs or "toothless lions"?', April 2015: https://globalarbitrationnews.com/20150407-brazil-signs-new-bilateral-investment -treaties/ (accessed 15 January 2018).

[186] Brazil–Chile CFIA (2015), Art. 6(3)(a)(i); Brazil–Colombia CFIA (2015), Art. 5.3a)(i); Brazil–Mexico CFIA (2015), Art. 5.3a)(i); Brazil–Peru ETEA (2016), Art. 2.6.3; Intra-MERCOSUR Investment Facilitation Protocol (2017), Art. 24; and Brazil-Suriname CFIA (2018), Art. 6.3.

[187] F. Morosini and M. Ratton Sánchez-Badin, 'The New Brazilian Agreements on Cooperation and Facilitation of Investments (ACFI): A New Formula for International Investment Agreements?', August 2015: www.iisd.org/itn/2015/08/04/the-brazilian -agreement-on-cooperation-and-facilitation-of-investments-acfi-a-new-formula-for -international-investment-agreements/ (accessed 11 January 2018), p. 23.

The joint committees set forth in the new Brazilian BITs are charged with reaching for consensus and resolving amicably any questions or disputes regarding investment from the contracting parties. Dispute resolution provisions provide for state-to-state arbitration only in the event that an investment dispute cannot be resolved through the joint committees. Nonetheless, in some agreements there is no regulation of the procedure for such arbitration.[188]

Although all Brazilian IIAs concluded since 2015 include a state-to-state arbitration clause, the ones negotiated early with African states have vague wording on this.[189] The CFIAs with Latin American states and Ethiopia advance the issue, gradually including more detailed provisions on the procedure for the arbitration.[190] Morosini and Ratton believe that the difference in approach is due to two interrelated factors: Firstly, African states seemed to have accepted the CFIA proposed by Brazil without much bargaining or demands, either for lack of negotiating capacity, or for believing that the agreements met their internal demands: Secondly, the well-developed negotiating capacity and previous experience of Chile, Colombia, Mexico and Peru on IIAs with detailed ISDS and state-to-state arbitration make it reasonable to believe that that they would demand a similar approach in their agreements with Brazil.[191]

The only known case of a home state invoking the inter-state dispute settlement mechanism contained in an IIA is *Italy v. Cuba*, in which Italy brought arbitration proceedings against Cuba in May 2003, espousing the claims of injuries suffered by a group of sixteen Italian investors operating in Cuba, for alleged breaches of the 1993 Italy–Cuba BIT, invoking the ad hoc arbitration in Article 10 of the same treaty.[192] After an interim award in March 2005, the

---

[188] J. P. Muniz, K. A. N. Duggal and L. A. S. Peretti, 'The New Brazilian BIT on Cooperation and Facilitation of Investments: A New Approach in Times of Change', *ICSID Review – Foreign Investment Law Journal*, 32 (2017), 404–17 at 415.

[189] 'If the dispute cannot be resolved, the Parties to the exclusion of the investors may resort to arbitration mechanisms between States, which are to be agreed upon by the joint committee, whenever the Parties find it appropriate': Angola–Brazil CFIA (2015), Art. 15.6; Brazil–Malawi CFIA (2015), Art. 13.6; Brazil–Mozambique CFIA (2015), Art. 15.6.

[190] Brazil–Chile CFIA (2015), Art. 25; Brazil–Colombia CFIA (2015), Art. 23; Brazil–Mexico CFIA (2015), Art. 19; Brazil–Peru ETEA (2016), Art. 2.21; Brazil–Suriname CFIA (2018), Art. 25; and Brazil–Ethiopia CFIA (2018), Art. 24.

[191] Morosini and Ratton Sánchez-Badin, 'The New Brazilian Agreements on Cooperation and Facilitation of Investments (ACFI)', p. 27.

[192] Trevino, 'State-to-State Investment Treaty Arbitration', 206.

inter-state arbitral tribunal issued a final award in March 2008, rejecting all the claims made by Italy, both on jurisdictional grounds or on their merits.[193] This case gave the opportunity to analyse the applicability of two basic principles of diplomatic protection in the context of an investment treaty: the nationality rule and the exhaustion of local remedies.

Nationality Rule

In relation to nationality, difficulties may arise if a state uses inter-state dispute settlement to provide diplomatic protection to its nationals, particularly in the cases of corporations and its shareholders. Article 9 of the ILC Draft Articles on Diplomatic Protection declares:[194]

> For the purposes of the diplomatic protection of a corporation, the state of nationality means the state under whose law the corporation was incorporated. However, when the corporation is controlled by nationals of another State or States and has no substantial business activities in the state of incorporation, and the seat of management and the financial control of the corporation are both located in another State, that State shall be regarded as the state of nationality.

In contrast to this traditional rule, several IIAs provide for a different understanding of corporate nationality, considering that a company could be considered a national of a state merely because of its incorporation, without any requirement for a 'genuine link', such as the fact that the seat of management and substantial business activities are located in another state.[195] The question here is to determine which rule applies when diplomatic protection is exercised in the context of an IIA.

In *Italy v. Cuba*, the majority of the tribunal rejected Italy's diplomatic protection claim on behalf of two companies controlled by Italian nationals but registered in Panama (Cristal Vetro SA) and Costa Rica (Pastas y Salsas Qué Chévere), considering that Italy lacked standing to espouse those claims, on the basis that since the investment protected under Article 1 of the Cuba–Italy BIT is 'the one realized by natural or legal persons of one Contracting party', and therefore in the case of legal persons 'the nationality of shareholders or, more generally, of the holders

---

[193] M. Potestà, 'Republic of Italy v. Republic of Cuba', *American Journal of International Law*, 106 (2012), 341–7.
[194] ILC, 'Draft Articles on Diplomatic Protection', Art. 9.
[195] D. Gaukrodger, 'Investment Treaties as Corporate Law: Shareholder Claims and Issues of Consistency', *OECD Working Papers on International Investment* (2013) at 32.

of capital, should not be taken into consideration'.[196] The dissenting arbitrator, Attila Tanzi, criticized the 'overly restrictive reading' of Article 1, noting that the same agreement broadly defined both 'investor' and 'investment' in a way that included the control of companies by foreign shareholders, beyond the rule of the place of incorporation – something that is also acknowledged in Article 9 of the ILC Draft Articles on Diplomatic Protection.[197] In Tanzi's view, these wide-ranging definitions create a special agreement between the contracting parties that constitutes a departure from the customary nationality 'rules'.[198] This interpretation is consistent with the ICJ's rulings in *Barcelona Traction*,[199] *ELSI*[200] and *Diallo*,[201] and thus home states who are not authorized to bring diplomatic protection claims under customary international law may be entitled to do so if an IIA confers on them standing in inter-state arbitration proceedings.[202]

Exhaustion of Local Remedies

In relation to the customary rule on exhaustion of local remedies, generally, IIAs dispense with such a requirement for investors, allowing them to resort to international arbitration directly. However, there is no such provision in relation to state-to-state dispute settlement in IIAs, and the question arises whether this rule is applicable. According to

[196] *Italian Republic* v. *Republic of Cuba*, Ad hoc State-State Arbitration, Final Award, 1 January 2008, paras. 203, 206, 208, 211.
[197] *Italian Republic* v. *Republic of Cuba*, Ad hoc State-State Arbitration, Dissenting Opinion of Attila Tanzi, 1 January 2008, paras. 31–7.
[198] Trevino, 'State-to-State Investment Treaty Arbitration', 208.
[199] In *Barcelona Traction*, the lack of standing of Belgium is decided in the light of the general rules of diplomatic protection, 'in the absence of any treaty on the subject between the Parties'. *Barcelona Traction*, Judgment Second Phase, p. 33.
[200] In the *ELSI* case, the respondent held that the Italy–United States FCNA was essentially irrelevant to the claims of the United States, since the measures taken by Italy directly affected not American nationals or corporations but an Italian corporation (ELSI), whose shares were owned by American corporations. 'The Chamber did not accept this argument. Nor did it accept the contention that the right to organize, control and manage a corporation was limited to the founding of a Company and the election of its directors and did not include its continuing management.' *Elettronica Sicula SPA (ELSI) (United States of America* v. *Italy)*, Dissenting Opinion of Judge Schwebel, 20 July 1989 [1989] ICJ Rep. 1, pp. 94–5.
[201] In *Diallo*, the ICJ held that the *ELSI* judgment was based not on customary international law but on an FCNA between the two countries 'directly granting to their nationals, corporations and associations certain rights in relation to their participation in corporations and associations having the nationality of the other State': *Diallo*, Preliminary Objections, para. 87.
[202] Trevino, 'State-to-State Investment Treaty Arbitration', 208.

Dugard, the rule on exhaustion of local remedies in principle applies only to cases in which the claimant state has been injured 'indirectly', meaning through its national. It does not apply where the claimant state is directly injured by another state, as the claimant state has a distinct reason of its own for bringing an international claim. 'In practice it is difficult to decide whether the claim is "direct" or "indirect" where it is "mixed", in the sense that it contains elements of both injury to the state and injury to the nationals of the state.'[203]

In the preliminary phase of the *Italy* v. *Cuba* arbitration, Cuba raised the objection that local remedies had not been exhausted by the Italian investors, and therefore that Italy was barred from resorting to diplomatic protection.[204] The tribunal found that the exhaustion rule was not applicable to the claim that Italy brought in its own name but that it was a prerequisite for the claims brought on behalf of its nationals.[205] Potestà points out that the tribunal could have found that the two claims could not be separated and that they should be treated as a whole, applying the exhaustion rule because the injury to the nationals would have been the one 'preponderant'.[206] This would be in line with the *Interhandel* and *ELSI* judgments, as in neither case did the claimant state succeed in avoiding the 'local remedies' rule.[207] In *Interhandel* the ICJ held that the claim by Switzerland adopted the cause of its national 'for the purpose of securing the restitution to that company of assets vested by the Government of the United States',[208] while in *ELSI* the ICJ held that it had 'no doubt that the matter which colours and pervades the United States claim as a whole, is the alleged damage to [its nationals] Raytheon and Machlett, said to have resulted from the actions of the Respondent'.[209]

On the same issue, Italy also submitted that the rule on exhaustion of local remedies had been waived by the contracting parties to the BIT, as the only precondition for submitting the dispute to arbitration was

---

[203] J. Dugard, 'Second Report of the Special Rapporteur on Diplomatic Protection', *Yearbook of the International Law Commission 2001* (United Nations, 2009), pp. 97–114, paras. 18–19.

[204] Potestà, 'Towards a Greater Role for State-to-State Arbitration', p. 261.

[205] *Italian Republic* v. *Republic of Cuba*, Ad hoc State-State Arbitration, Interim Award, 15 March 2005, para. 89.

[206] Potestà, 'Towards a Greater Role for State-to-State Arbitration', p. 262.

[207] Dugard, 'Second Report of the Special Rapporteur on Diplomatic Protection', para. 28.

[208] *Interhandel case*, Judgment Preliminary Objections, pp. 28–29.

[209] *ELSI case*, Judgment, para. 52.

a period of amicable settlement.[210] Although the tribunal did not address this issue, according to Potestà, it would not seem that the presence of such a negotiation period can be taken as amounting to an express waiver, considering that reference is required of the parties to the BIT and does not affect what is required of the investor.[211] Furthermore, Italy also submitted that since, under Article 9 of the Italy–Cuba BIT, the investors have only the choice – and not the obligation – to resort to domestic courts, it would be illogical to require Italy to respect the exhaustion of local remedies.[212] The arbitral tribunal did not agree with this view, holding that nothing in Article 9 implied a waiver of the rule on exhaustion of local remedies.[213] For Trevino, it seems paradoxical to hold that this rule does not apply when the home state brings a direct claim, or when the investor brings a claim against the host state, but that it is still relevant when the home state brings a diplomatic protection claim under the same set of facts.[214] Potestà holds a similar view, although stressing that there is ample authority that a waiver of this type must not be freely implied.[215]

(ii) Existence of the Dispute

As Trevino points out, the contracting party invoking state-to-state arbitration will have to demonstrate the existence of a 'dispute' as a necessary condition for establishing the jurisdiction of the tribunal. This could raise questions about the burden of proof of the existence of a dispute, and the value that is given to situations less obvious than affirmative disagreement, such as silence or failure to respond a question posed by the other state.[216]

This question has been tested in very few cases in relation to investment treaties. On 28 June 2011, Ecuador initiated state-to-state proceedings against the United States, under the 1993 Ecuador–US BIT, seeking to overturn the interpretation of Article II(7) of the same treaty, which stipulates that each party shall provide 'effective means' of asserting

---

[210] *Italy* v. *Cuba*, Interim Award, para. 41. According to the Cuba–Italy BIT (1993), Art. 10.1: 'Disputes between the Contracting parties relating to interpretation and application of this Agreement shall, as far as possible, be settled amicably through diplomatic means.'
[211] Potestà, 'Towards a Greater Role for State-to-State Arbitration', p. 263.
[212] *Italy* v. *Cuba*, Interim Award, para. 41.
[213] *Italy* v. *Cuba*, Interim Award, para. 90.
[214] Trevino, 'State-to-State Investment Treaty Arbitration', 210.
[215] Potestà, 'Towards a Greater Role for State-to-State Arbitration', pp. 263–4.
[216] Trevino, 'State-to-State Investment Treaty Arbitration', 201–2.

claims and enforcing rights with respect to investment, investment agreements, and investment authorizations. The Permanent Court of Arbitration acted as registry in this arbitration.

An interpretation of that particular clause had been adopted earlier, by an investor–state tribunal in the *Chevron* v. *Ecuador* case, concerning a delay of over thirteen years by Ecuadorian courts in deciding seven separate contract claims against that country. The *Chevron* v. *Ecuador* tribunal held that to find a failure by domestic courts to enforce rights 'effectively', a distinct and 'potentially less-demanding' test is applicable under the Ecuador–US BIT, as compared with denial of justice under customary international law.[217] By diplomatic note dated 8 June 2010, Ecuador informed the United States that it disagreed with that interpretation, explaining its view that it was the parties' intention to incorporate into the BIT pre-existing obligations under customary international law relating to the prohibition against denial of justice. The note gave notice that, if no confirming note was received or if the United States did not otherwise agree with the said interpretation, an unresolved dispute must be considered to exist between both governments concerning the interpretation and application of the investment treaty.[218] No such confirming note was received by Ecuador, and on 24 August 2010 the United States sent a diplomatic note to Ecuador merely answering that it was 'currently reviewing the views expressed in your letter and considering the concerns that you have raised' and that it looked forward 'to remaining in contact'.[219]

Once Ecuador had initiated inter-state arbitration against the United States for the interpretation of Article II(7) of the Ecuador–US BIT – almost one year after the exchange of diplomatic notes – the United States denied the existence of a dispute, arguing that in order to find jurisdiction, 'the claimant must demonstrate that the disputing parties put themselves in positive opposition to one another arising from a concrete situation regarding the performance of their treaty obligations'.[220] As Ecuador was not claiming a breach of a specific treaty

---

[217] *Chevron Corp. (USA) and Texaco Petroleum Co. (USA)* v. *Republic of Ecuador*, UNCITRAL, PCA Case No 34877. Partial Award on Merits, 30 March 2010, para. 244.

[218] *Republic of Ecuador* v. *United States of America* (PCA Case No 2012-5). Request for Arbitration, 28 June 2011, paras. 7, 8 and 12.

[219] *Republic of Ecuador* v. *United States of America* (PCA Case No 2012-5), Statement of Defense, 29 March 2012, para. 6.

[220] *Ecuador* v. *US*, Statement of Defense, para. 9.

provision by the United States, it had not advanced a 'positive opposition' regarding the meaning of the standard of 'effective means'.[221]

On 29 September 2012, the arbitral tribunal issued an award (although the decision was not made public until four years later). The majority of the tribunal favoured the United States, holding that its silence could not be taken to mean that it rejected Ecuador's stated view on its preferred interpretation of Article II(7) of the Ecuador–US BIT, and that might be reasonably explained as it wished to avoid interfering with a prior tribunal's decision.[222]

A dissenting minority opinion by the arbitrator, Raul Vinuesa, held that international case law did not support the majority's view that a 'positive opposition' could be inferred only when there was no other reasonable explanation for a party's silence, adding that the ruling would have practical consequences for both Ecuador and the United States, bringing 'juridical certainty' to the legal relations between the two states. For Mr Vinuesa, the phrase 'interpretation or application' found in the state-to-state arbitration clause was stated in a 'disjunctive manner', and evidenced that disputes concerning interpretation of the treaty could be submitted to arbitration 'without also requiring the application of the Treaty' to be at issue.[223]

Nevertheless, the dissenting opinion appeared to agree with the majority in relation to the potential breadth of the state-to-state arbitration clause on the ISA clause. Rejecting the United States' narrower view of the clause, which was deemed to marginalize and subordinate the role of the state-to-state mechanism in comparison with the investor–state mechanism, Mr Vinuesa stressed that 'neither the text nor the context of the Treaty allow a restrictive and partial interpretation of Article VII, let alone the dependence or subordination thereof to the mechanism provided for by Article VI of the Treaty'.[224]

(iii) Conditions Previous to Adjudication or Arbitration   In the large majority of IIAs concluded in the past fifteen years, state-to-state arbitration or adjudication is triggered after a previous phase that provides for consultations or diplomatic negotiations during a given period of time.

---

[221] Trevino, 'State-to-State Investment Treaty Arbitration', 203.

[222] J. Hepburn and L. E. Peterson, 'US-Ecuador Inter-State Investment Treaty Award Released to Parties; Tribunal Members Part Ways on Key Issues' (October 2012).

[223] *Republic of Ecuador* v. *United States of America* (PCA Case No 2012-5). Dissenting Opinion of Professor Raul Emilio Vinuesa, 29 September 2012, para. 30.

[224] *Ecuador* v. *US*, Dissenting Opinion of Raul Emilio Vinuesa, para. 31.

The usual duration of consultations in BITs is six months or 180 days,[225] although in several cases there is no specific timeframe,[226] and in a few others the period is shorter[227] or longer.[228] A substantially shorter time for consultations is generally provided for in FTAs, with enormous variations between treaties, ranging from ten to ninety days, or any other period on which the contracting parties might agree.[229]

Under the large majority of the treaties examined, the request for consultations is a necessary precondition for allowing a contracting party to initiate state-to-state arbitration. In fact, the lack of this preliminary phase was one of the arguments that the United States used to deny jurisdiction in *Ecuador* v. *United States*. Although Article VII of the Ecuador US–BIT provides for the submission to an arbitral tribunal of a dispute between the parties concerning the interpretation or application of the treaty 'which is not resolved through consultations or other diplomatic channels', Ecuador commenced the arbitral proceedings without formally requesting prior consultation with the United States, as established in Article V of the same treaty.[230] For the United States, Ecuador had merely announced its views on the BIT and demanded confirmation by the United States, which in fact considered Ecuador's request 'a decree, not a good-faith invitation to consultations under the Treaty'.[231]

Several IIAs include an additional phase after consultations and before resorting to inter-state arbitration, referring the dispute to a joint com-

---

[225] E.g. Iraq–Jordan BIT (2013), Art. 10; Guatemala–Russia BIT (2013), Art. 9; Colombia–Singapore BIT (2013), Art. 22.

[226] E.g.: Canada–Côte d'Ivoire BIT (2014), Art. 37; Japan–Papua New Guinea (2011), Art. 15; Austria–Tajikistan BIT (2010), Art. 20.

[227] In the Chile–Uruguay BIT (2010), Annex F, Art. 2.5, it is only thirty days.

[228] Under Cameroon–Turkey BIT (2012), Art. 11, the duration of the consultation is twelve months. In the Kenya–Slovakia BIT (2011), Art. 10, it is nine months.

[229] E.g. Indonesia–Japan EPA (2007), Art. 142, provides for ninety days if the party complained against does not enter into consultations, or sixty days if the parties fail to resolve the dispute through consultation. Colombia–Northern Triangle FTA (2007), Art. 18.11, provides for ten days, if the party complained against does not respond a request for consultation, or does not enter into consultations within thirty days after such request, or if the parties fail to resolve the matter through the consultation within sixty days.

[230] Under Ecuador–US BIT (1993), Art. V: 'The Parties agree to consult promptly, on the request of either, to resolve any disputes in connection with the Treaty, or to discuss any matter relating to the interpretation or application of the Treaty.'

[231] *Ecuador* v. *US*, Statement of Defense, para. 3.

mission or other treaty body instituted under the treaty,[232] or allowing the use of alternative methods of dispute resolution, such as good offices, conciliation or mediation, on a voluntary basis.[233]

(iv) Establishment of Panel/Arbitral Tribunals Almost without exception, IIAs refer inter-state disputes to ad hoc arbitration by a panel of three members, providing generally that each party nominate one and the appointed arbitrators agree on the chair,[234] with most of them having the President of the ICJ as the appointing authority,[235] in the event that there is no agreement on that matter after a given period of time (usually two months or sixty days).[236] Certain FTAs provide for a variation without an appointing authority: each party shall appoint one panel member, within a short period of time (from twenty to thirty days of the request of the establishment of the panel) and propose a list of candidates (from three to five) to serve as chair of the panel. If a party

---

[232] E.g. Israel–Myanmar BIT (2014), Art. 9; Australia–Korea FTA (2014), Art. 20.7; PAAP (2014), Art. 17.6.

[233] E.g. Canada–Korea FTA (2014), Art. 21.5; Australia–Japan FTA (2014), Art. 19.5; Mexico–Panama FTA (2014), Art. 18.7; EU–Singapore IPA (April 2018), Art. 3.4.

[234] E.g. in Israel–Myanmar BIT (2014), Art. 9, both arbitrators appointed by the parties, shall select the Chairman with the approval of the contracting parties. In Japan–Saudi Arabia BIT (2013), Art. 13, the President is agreed by the two arbitrators chosen by the parties within thirty days. In Morocco–Vietnam BIT (2012), Art. 10, two arbitrators, appointed by the parties within three months, shall agree upon a national of a third state to be appointed as Chairman, within five months.

[235] In some IIAs the appointing authority is the Secretary General of the PCA, e.g.: ECT, Art. 27. Israel–Japan BIT (2017), Art. 23; Japan–Kenya BIT (2016), Art. 14; EFTA–Costa Rica–Panama FTA (2013), Art. 12.4. In others, it is the Secretary General of the Latin American Integration Association (ALADI), e.g. Mexico–Panama FTA (2014), Art. 18.10; Chile–Uruguay BIT (2010), Annex F, Art. 5; Chile–Peru FTA (2006), Art. 16. In some others, it is the Director-General of the WTO, e.g. New Zealand–Malaysia FTA (2009), Art. 16.9; ASEAN–Australia–New Zealand FTA (2009), chap. 17, Art. 11; Peru–Singapore FTA (2008), Art. 17.9. Mauritius–Zambia BIT (2015), Art. 9, as well the US Model BITs (2004) (2012), Art. 27 provide for the Secretary-General of ICSID. The Madagascar–Mauritius BIT (2004), Art. 11(d) provides for the President of the ICC. In the PAAP (2014), Art. 17.3, the Pro-Tempore President of the Pacific Alliance would make the appointment by lot. The France Model BIT (2006), Art. 10.4 specifies the Secretary General of the United Nations.

[236] E.g. in Palestine–Russia BIT (2016), Art. 9, it is six months; in Morocco–Rwanda BIT (2016), Art. 9, it is five months; in Canada–Nigeria BIT (2014), Art. 38, it is four months; and in Gambia–Morocco BIT (2006), Art. 9, the arbitrators shall be appointed within three months and the Chairman within five months. The Colombia–Singapore BIT (2013), Art. 22, does not provide for an appointing authority or a period in which to nominate the arbitrators.

fails to appoint a panel member or to propose its chair candidates, the panel member or the chair shall be selected from the chair candidates of the other party.[237] Some merely decide the appointments by lot from an 'indicative' or 'contingent' list, or a roster of arbitrators previously nominated by the parties.[238] A few do not even provide for an appointment authority in the event of disagreement between the disputing parties or the arbitrators.[239]

In the vast majority of cases, these treaties prescribe that the arbitral tribunal shall determine its own rules of procedure, and in the rare cases in which a set of rules is specified, they usually follow the traditional framework of inter-state public international law arbitrations,[240] or make a referral to existing rules.[241]

Some IIAs have special provisions for inter-state disputes relating to financial services, stipulating that where a party submits to arbitration a state-to-state dispute involving financial services, each party shall, in the appointment of all arbitrators, take appropriate steps to ensure that the tribunal has expertise or experience in financial services law or practice. In the same vein, a process of consultation with the competent financial authorities of both parties is usually considered. When a dispute arises that involves financial services, the competent financial authorities of one party shall provide written notice to the competent financial authorities of the other party, and both authorities have 180 days to transmit a report on their consultations to the contracting parties, which, in turn, are not allowed to submit the dispute to arbitration until the expiration of that period. If a report on the consultations is

---

[237] E.g. Canada–Korea FTA (2014), Art. 21.7; Australia–Japan FTA (2014), Art. 19.6; Australia–Korea FTA (2014), Art. 20.8.

[238] E.g. Colombia–Israel FTA (2013), Art. 12.8, 12.11; Colombia–Costa Rica FTA (2013), Art. 18.9; Colombia–Korea FTA (2013), Art. 20.7.

[239] India–Malaysia ECA (2011), Art. 14.9; Malaysia–Pakistan CEPA (2007), Art. 118; Australia–Thailand FTA (2004), Art. 1805. In Oman–US FTA (2006), Art. 20.7, if the parties are unable to agree on the chair within thirty days, the party chosen by lot shall select as chair an individual who is not a national of that party, within five days.

[240] Douglas, 'The Hybrid Foundations of Investment Treaty Arbitration', 158–9.

[241] In the Israel–Japan BIT (2017), Art. 23, Israel–Myanmar BIT (2014), Art. 9, Argentina–Qatar BIT (2016), Art. 15, Iran–Slovakia BIT (2016), Art. 23; and China–Japan-Korea Trilateral Investment Treaty (2012), Art. 17, unless otherwise agreed, arbitration shall be conducted under UNCITRAL Arbitration Rules. According to Austria–Kyrgyzstan BIT (2016), Art. 23; EFTA–Costa Rica–Panama FTA (2013), Art. 12.5; EFTA–Bosnia and Herzegovina FTA (2013), Art. 45, arbitration shall be conducted under the PCA Optional Rules for Arbitrating Disputes between Two States.

issued, either party may make it available to the tribunal dealing with the inter-state dispute, but it does not have a binding character.[242]

(v) Interplay with Investor–State Arbitration   Some commentators think that we might have situations where an investor brings some claims directly against a state, and in parallel the home state may be able to bring other claims on behalf of the investor under diplomatic protection.[243] However, as mentioned in the *Diallo* case, the ICJ has taken a different approach, finding that the home state had standing to assert claims involving a person of its nationality regarding allegedly unlawful acts that infringed their direct rights, but not with respect to the rights of companies by substitution, considering this sort of protection as a last resort available to foreign shareholders who cannot rely on the benefit of an international treaty and to whom no other remedy is available.[244]

But that does not exclude an interaction between ISA and inter-state arbitration. There are at least three basic scenarios of interplay between them; (1) inter-state dispute settlement has concluded before ISA has started; (2) both dispute settlement mechanisms exist in parallel; and (3) state-to-state dispute settlement starts after ISA has concluded. In the next sections, we will analyse the main problems that can arise in the relationship between these two dispute settlement mechanisms.

(1)   Inter-State   Dispute   Settlement   before   Investor–State Arbitration   In this scenario, a state-to-state tribunal issues an award or a judgment before ISA has started. While several IIAs specify that an inter-state award is binding on the contracting parties, they do not explicitly address the issue of whether such a decision is also binding on an ISDS tribunal.

Advancing a theory of 'shared interpretive authority', Roberts submits that home states should be allowed to seek rulings from inter-state tribunals on disputes about the proper interpretation of IIAs, with the goal of promoting certainty and consistency in a decentralized ISDS system. Therefore, state-to-state awards or judgments should be considered binding on the treaty parties and future investor–state tribunals, or

---

[242] US Model BIT (2004) (2012), Art. 20.4–5, Uruguay–US BIT (2005), Art. 20.4–5; Rwanda–US BIT (2008), Art. 20.4–5.

[243] Reed, 'Observations on the Relationship between Diplomatic and Judicial Means', pp. 300–1.

[244] *Diallo*, Preliminary Objections, pp. 614–15

at least 'highly persuasive' with respect to the latter. If inter-state tribunals have jurisdiction over interpretive disputes, giving that award binding effect only as regards the instant dispute would deprive the award of practical effect.[245]

In the same line of thought, Potestà rightly points out that if the inter-state award is binding on the contracting parties, 'it is difficult to see why it should not be binding on the investor-State tribunal which has been established by the Contracting parties to resolve certain types of disputes'.[246] Trevino believes that, as a general rule, the investor–state arbitral tribunal should follow a previous interpretive inter-state award, unless it finds such interpretation 'manifestly incompatible or irreconcilable with the treaty text and/or the treaty parties' intended meaning'.[247] For Kulick, if the state-to-state's tribunal's interpretation was introduced first, that interpretation should prevail, as an expression of the contracting parties' agreement on how the IIAs should be interpreted, and should enjoy the same effect as the joint interpretations made by the contracting parties. Although he elaborates on the reasons for this equivalence, it is at least debatable whether the settlement of an interpretive dispute between the states has the same value as a joint agreement between them.[248]

An example of how this scenario operates in practice is given by the NAFTA inter-state case *In the Matter of Cross-Border Trucking Services*, which was a state-to-state claim brought by Mexico under Chapter 20 of NAFTA, seeking a declaration that the United States was in breach of its NT and MFN obligations for cross-border services, by failing to lift a moratorium on the processing of applications by Mexican-owned trucking firms for authority to operate in the US border states, and by refusing to permit Mexican investment in companies in the United States that provide transportation of international cargo.[249] The final report of the panel, issued in February 2001, unanimously upheld Mexico's claim that the United States was in breach of its pertinent NAFTA obligations and rejected the United States' argument that Mexico could not make

---

[245] Roberts, 'State-to-State Investment Treaty Arbitration', 29, 60.
[246] Potestà, 'Towards a Greater Role for State-to-State Arbitration', p. 267.
[247] Trevino, 'State-to-State Investment Treaty Arbitration', 226.
[248] Kulick, 'State-State Investment Arbitration', 147–8.
[249] *In the Matter of Cross-Border Trucking Services* (Secretariat File No USA-MEX-98-2008-01), Final Report of the Panel, 6 February 2001, para. 1. Although this is not formally an investment dispute, it is the only NAFTA Chapter 20 arbitration that interprets provisions of the investment chapter (Chapter 11) in order to determine breaches of the treaty with respect to cross-border services.

a claim on behalf of potential or unidentified Mexican investors. However, in spite of that outcome, the United States failed to lift the moratorium.[250]

In April 2009, CANACAR (Cámara Nacional del Autotransporte de Carga), a Mexican trade association representing individual trucking carriers, brought an ISA against the United States, claiming its failure to comply with the abovementioned Chapter 20 of NAFTA arbitral decision, and the violation of NT and MFN treatment against Mexican carriers by the US Department of Transportation.[251] While there is no public information that the claim has continued beyond the notice of arbitration, if an arbitral tribunal is constituted, it will have to rule on how much weight it will attribute to the previous inter-state award and not merely overlook it. This because, even if there is no direct *res judicata* effect (there being different parties in dispute) a subsequent investor–state tribunal should decide the issues in dispute *in accordance* with the NAFTA agreement,[252] which precisely provides for an inter-state mechanism as one of the avenues to settle a dispute on the interpretation and application of its treaty provisions.

(2) Inter-State Dispute Settlement and Investor–State Arbitration in Parallel   However, we can also ponder the question whether ISA and state-to-state dispute settlement could also exist in parallel. As we have seen, BITs and FTAs with investment chapters typically include provisions on the two types of dispute settlement. Although, in principle, proceedings running alongside do not necessarily compete with each other, as they involve different parties and a different scope, they could have conflicting decisions on the interpretation of the same legal provisions or the assessment of the same set of facts.

According to Schreuer, such parallel proceedings are undesirable and inter-state arbitration should neither interfere in investor–state cases nor affect the finality of awards.[253] But what can be done in the absence of specific treaty provisions in this regard? As the same author mentions, provisions in the BITs excluding state-to-state arbitration where ICSID arbitration had started or was available were contained in some older

---

[250] Roberts, 'State-to-State Investment Treaty Arbitration', 9.
[251] *CANACAR v. United States of America*. Notice of Arbitration, 2 April 2009.
[252] NAFTA, Art. 1131.1.
[253] Schreuer, 'Investment Protection and International Relations', 349–50.

German and US BITs,[254] but they are not common in investment law treaty-making.

In the same line of reasoning, another possibility is to adopt a narrow reading of the scope of inter-state dispute settlement clauses. Reisman submits that these provisions constitute a 'separate track' to ISDS provisions, with each track having exclusive jurisdiction on IIA issues. Interpretation of substantive rights and guarantees is reserved exclusively for ISA, and state-to-state dispute settlement provisions encompass only issues of failure by the host state to enforce the award, or the interpretation of certain matters that do not include specific investor's claims,[255] such as the effects of a denunciation or a termination of the treaty.[256]

However, there are several arguments to support the conclusion that an inter-state dispute settlement clause in an IIA should not be given an overly limited scope. Firstly, there is nothing in the language of IIAs that suggests that states agreed to limit their arbitration rights radically.[257] In fact, it could be the contrary, as the broad language of the dispute settlement clauses in IIAs, extending not only to the 'interpretation' of the treaty but also to the 'application' of the agreement.[258] Some agreements go beyond this and explicitly confirm a broad scope for the state-to-state clause. The Colombia–China BIT includes 'a claim alleging that the other Contracting party has breached an obligation of the present Agreement and has consequently generated damages to an investor'.[259] The BITs of Austria with Ethiopia, Kazakhstan, Tajikistan and Nigeria include as forms of relief 'pecuniary compensation for any loss or damage to the requesting Contracting party's investor or its investment; or ... any other form of relief to which the Contracting party against whom the award is made consents, including restitution in kind to an investor'.[260]

Secondly, certain treaties have a clause whereby state-to-state arbitration is excluded from the moment an investor brings ISA, but that limitation expires under certain circumstances. For example, in some

[254] Ibid., 350.

[255] W. M. Reisman, *Republic of Ecuador v. United States of America (PCA Case No 2012-5). Expert Opinion with Respect to Jurisdiction, Prof. W. Michael Reisman*, paras. 24–32.

[256] Potestà, 'Towards a Greater Role for State-to-State Arbitration', p. 255.

[257] Roberts, 'State-to-State Investment Treaty Arbitration', 11.

[258] Potestà, 'Towards a Greater Role for State-to-State Arbitration', p. 257.

[259] China–Colombia BIT (2008), Art. 8.1; also in the Colombia Model BIT (2007), Art. X.1.

[260] E.g. Austria–Ethiopia BIT (2004), Art. 20(1)(c),(d); Austria–Kazakhstan BIT (2010), Art. 23(1)(c),(d); Austria–Tajikistan BIT (2010), Art. 24(1)(c),(d).

IIAs the home state could pursue a diplomatic protection claim if an ISDS tribunal has decided that the dispute is not within its jurisdiction[261] or if the host state has contravened a rule of international law (including denial of justice)[262] or if the claim is in respect of a measure of general application, even if it is alleged to have breached the IIA as regards a specific investment in respect of which an ISDS claim has been submitted.[263] Such provisions indirectly confirm that the exclusion of diplomatic protection is only from a certain moment on, and not as a general rule.[264]

Thirdly, the home state could also be claiming its own right. In *Italy v. Cuba*, Italy explicitly claimed a 'double standing' to protect not only the rights of its nationals but also its own rights arising out of the Cuba–Italy BIT[265] – something that was not even contested by Cuba in relation to the interpretation or application of the agreement.[266] Italy requested as relief the cessation of violations of the treaty, a guarantee as to the future respecting of international obligations, and even a symbolic compensation payment of €1, for considering that Cuba had violated the letter, spirit and finality of the BIT, the norms of international law on the treatment and protection of foreigners, *and* because of the Cuban refusal to settle in an amicable way disputes relating to Italian investors.[267] Analysing Cuba's preliminary exceptions on jurisdiction, the tribunal considered that, as long the investors have not consented to international arbitration with the host state or submitted the dispute to arbitration, their right to obtain diplomatic protection from the home state remains.[268]

Fourthly, as Kulick recalls, if the states, as masters of the investment treaties, decided to keep including broad provisions on inter-state arbitration together with provisions on ISA, surely it was for a clear

---

[261] Bosnia and Herzegovina–India BIT (2006), Art. 9.5; Guyana–Switzerland BIT (2005), Art. 8 (4); Australia–Turkey BIT (2005), Art. 13.6; Belarus–Bosnia BIT (2004), Art. 8.3; Australia–Thailand FTA (2004), Art. 917.4; Mozambique–United Kingdom BIT (2004), Art. 8(4). Also found in Malaysia Model BIT (1998), Art. 7(4); Switzerland Model BIT (1995), Art. 8(4); and UK Model BIT (1991), Art. 8(4).

[262] India–Uruguay BIT (2008) Art. 9 (6); Brunei–Japan EPA (2007), Art. 67.22.

[263] CETA, Art. 8.42; EU–Singapore IPA (April 2018), Art. 3.23.2; EU–Vietnam IPA (2018), Ch. 3, Art. 3.58.

[264] Potestà, 'Towards a Greater Role for State-to-State Arbitration', p. 258.

[265] Potestà, 'Republic of Italy v. Republic of Cuba', 342.

[266] *Italy* v. *Cuba*, Interim Award, paras. 47, 63.

[267] *Italy* v. *Cuba*, Final Award, para. 139.

[268] *Italy* v. *Cuba*, Interim Award, para. 65.

reason: to retain a certain level of control in the interpretation or application of a treaty, in both abstract or concrete disputes that could be settled state to state. Therefore, parallel state-to-state and investor–state arbitration are perfectly possible, even if they pertain to the same interpretation issue.[269]

A realistic scenario is, then, one in which both mechanisms can exist at the same time. But how should they be coordinated in a way that respects both states' rights and the investors' legitimate expectations? In the framework of her 'hybrid theory', Roberts supports a 'symmetrical sequencing approach'. In this scenario, if a home state brings a state-to-state claim, a prohibition on duplicative claims from its investors would kick in, unless investors argue that their right to bring an ISDS claim should not be pre-empted because of bad faith on the part of their home state or collusive attempts between home and host states to avoid legitimate claims. This would have the advantage of preventing duplication and inconsistency, protecting host states from multiple cases arising from the same facts, and preventing a situation in which they would be subjected to legal claims and diplomatic pressure simultaneously.[270] However, this solution puts the burden of proof on the investor's side, with the additional problem that the large majority of IIAs do not allow investors to participate in state-to-state proceedings.

In order to protect the rights of investors, procedural mechanisms should be adopted, giving interested investors the opportunity to make submissions in inter-state arbitrations, in the same way that NDSPs have an opportunity to make submissions on treaty interpretation in ISAs.[271] However, few IIAs provide for such a possibility in inter-state disputes, even for contracting parties. Certain investment treaties allow a state that is not a party to the dispute to make submissions to an inter-state arbitration panel on a question of the interpretation of the treaty. Some require that third parties must have a 'substantial interest in the dispute',[272] and previous delivery of a written request to the parties to the

---

[269] Kulick, 'State-State Investment Arbitration', 143–4, 147.

[270] Roberts, 'State-to-State Investment Treaty Arbitration', 46, 48, 51. However, Roberts also acknowledges that it might have the disadvantage of creating a 'race to arbitration' between home states and investors, competing to bring claims in order to pre-empt claims by the other.

[271] Ibid., 28–9.

[272] China–Japan–Korea Trilateral Investment Treaty (2012), Art. 17; ASEAN–Australia–New Zealand FTA (2009), chap. 17, Art. 10. Strangely, Colombia–US FTA (2006), and Peru–US FTA (2006), Art. 21.11, also allows 'third-

dispute.[273] Although usually this type of participation is limited to written submissions, selected treaties include additional rights. In CAFTA–DR and the Colombia–Northern Triangle FTA, NDSPs are entitled to attend all hearings, to make written and oral submissions to the panel, and to receive written submissions by the disputing parties.[274] There are no similar rights for investors that are disputing parties in ISDS arbitrations, although some participation could be granted following the *amicus curiae* model, depending on the applicable rules of procedure of the inter-state dispute.

A limited number of IIAs include a process of coordination between investor–state tribunals, the contracting parties and state-to-state tribunals. As we examined before, the IIAs contained technical referrals to domestic authorities in financial services disputes, if the contracting parties cannot agree on the validity of the defences invoked by the host state, they may submit the issue to the decision of an arbitral panel established in accordance with the state-to-state dispute settlement procedures of the IIA.

Trevino suggests that a certain degree of deference should be given to inter-state proceedings. This would imply that, in practice, in the case of a parallel proceeding brought by an investor *after* an interpretive claim has been brought by a treaty party, a strong case can be made to suggest that the investor–state tribunal should stay proceedings and await the decision of an already constituted inter-state tribunal.[275] Similarly, if a treaty party initiates an inter-state arbitration after an ISDS proceeding has been instituted on the interpretation of the same provision, the investor–state tribunal should stay its proceedings if the meaning of the disputed clause is dispositive of its own decision, although, as we have seen in the *Peru* v. *Chile* case, investor–state tribunals are not bound to stay proceedings in these cases.[276]

---

party participation' from another contracting party that is not a disputing party in a state-to-state dispute!

[273] EFTA–Bosnia and Herzegovina FTA (2013), Art. 45.3.

[274] CAFTA–DR (2004), Art. 20.11; Colombia–Northern Triangle FTA (2007), Art. 19-11.

[275] Trevino, 'State-to-State Investment Treaty Arbitration', 226. The tribunal's power to grant a stay of the proceedings can derive from the applicable rules of arbitration. For example, under ICSID Arbitration Rules, Art. 19, 'The Tribunal shall make the orders required for the conduct of the proceeding'.

[276] Trevino, 'State-to-State Investment Treaty Arbitration', 228. Trevino bases this standard on the stay of proceedings issued by the tribunal in *SGS* v. *Philippines*, pending the determination of an issue relevant to its own decision by another judicial body.

A more optimal solution would be to include in the investment treaty rules on stay on these two types of claims, in a similar way as is considered today in certain IIAs in relation to consolidation of claims that have a question of law or fact in common.[277] CETA provides that when two or more claims that have been submitted separately pursuant to its investment chapter, and which have a question of law or fact in common and arise out of the same events or circumstances, a disputing party, or the disputing parties jointly, may seek the establishment of a separate division of the investment tribunal and request that such division issue a consolidation order. This is particularly important if there is potential for overlapping compensation orders, or one claim could have a significant impact on the resolution of the other. A tribunal appointed shall cede jurisdiction in relation to the claims, or parts thereof, over which a consolidating division of the tribunal has assumed jurisdiction.[278]

But in the absence of treaty provisions, the timing of these parallel proceedings seems to be of the essence, as we discussed in relation to joint treaty interpretations by the contracting parties. However, here we do not have both contracting parties agreeing on de jure or de facto amendments to an investment treaty. If there is a dispute, we have, by definition, two contradictory positions.

Although investors have the knowledge that state-to-state dispute settlement is part of the general regulatory framework of the investment treaty, they can legitimately expect that a change in their treaty right, as a consequence of the use of this mechanism, will be something exceptional, as the current case law evidences. In the absence of specific treaty provisions that deal with the interplay between ISDS and state-to-state dispute settlement, a strong argument may be made against inter-state arbitrations or adjudications that alter investors' legitimate expectations, particularly pending or after investor–state arbitration on the same substantive issues. In any case, it would be for the ISDS tribunal to manage the arbitral proceedings in a way that does not affect the due process of law. For example, if an inter-state award interpreting an IIA provision is rendered after the parties to ISA have already made their submissions, it would be reasonable to allow the disputing parties to

---

[277] See Canada–Honduras FTA (2013), Annex 10.29.9; Mexico–Slovakia BIT (2007), Art. 16; Belarus–Mexico BIT (2008), Art. 16.
[278] CETA, Art. 8.43.

submit their views on such interpretation, and its effect on the case in dispute.[279]

(3) Inter-State Dispute Settlement after Investor–State Arbitration   A third scenario of interplay would take place when an inter-state arbitral tribunal is called to interpret a treaty clause, *after* an investor–state arbitral tribunal has made a decision concerning the same provision, as in the *Ecuador* v. *US* case. The question here is whether the inter-state award could prevail over a previous ISDS award.

Some authors reject the possibility of a having a later state-to-state award superseding a prior ISA decision, on the basis of exclusive jurisdiction or *res judicata*. Reisman believes that where a dispute has already been adjudicated in ISA, the jurisdiction over that dispute is exclusive.[280] For Trevino, in such cases, once an investor–state award is rendered and applicable remedies are exhausted, it becomes *res judicata* and therefore cannot be affected by a subsequent conflicting decision by an inter-state tribunal.[281] As we have discussed previously, it is difficult to argue ISDS exclusive jurisdiction in the absence of any provision of the IIA barring inter-state arbitration. Additionally, can we consider the effect of *res judicata* if there is no absolute identity of the parties? For that, we would have to interpret either that the home state's claim is a reflection of the investor's right or, conversely, that the investor's claim is just a proxy of the home state and not its own.

Other authors are focused on more practical reasons for rejecting the effects of a later state-to-state against an ISDS prior decision. For Roberts, inter-state awards should have only prospective effects, not being able to function as an appeal from investor–state awards, nor should they be permitted to be used as a 'collateral attack' against them.[282]

Wong has suggested that a more coherent approach would be to treat the two arbitral regimes as mutually exclusive, and disallow inter-state arbitration of any issue that may properly be resolved by ISA. In this way, duplicative arbitral proceedings are eliminated and, with that, the

---

[279] Potestà, 'Towards a Greater Role for State-to-State Arbitration', p. 268. As we examined earlier, a similar solution was adopted by the *Pope & Talbot* tribunal, allowing the parties, and the NDSP, to comment on the interpretation made by NAFTA's FTC.

[280] *Republic of Ecuador* v. *United States of America* (PCA Case No 2012-5). Expert Opinion with Respect to Jurisdiction, Professor W. Michael Reisman, 24 April 2012, para. 29.

[281] Trevino, 'State-to-State Investment Treaty Arbitration', 229–30.

[282] Roberts, 'State-to-State Investment Treaty Arbitration', 63–64.

potential for conflicting awards is averted. He believes that state-to-state arbitration of any dispute (whether initiated by the home or the host state) should be barred if that dispute is on any issue over which the investor–state arbitral tribunal would have jurisdiction, even if the investor has yet to consent to arbitration.[283] Rejecting this argument, Kulick proposes a clear distinction based on the timing of the dispute that should be implemented through judicial dialogue. If ISA precedes state-to-state arbitration, the ISDS tribunal incidental interpretation should prevail in relation to that specific dispute. Judicial dialogue should lead the inter-state tribunal either to stay the proceedings under the conclusion of the ISDS procedures, or to refuse jurisdiction if there is evidence of bad faith or abuse of process.[284] Conversely, if state-to-state arbitration was introduced before ISA, the inter-state tribunal's interpretation shall be binding on all subsequent ISDS tribunals, regardless of whether the state-to-state arbitration pertained to an abstract or a concrete interpretation. Judicial dialogue, in this situation, should lead the ISDS tribunal to order stay of proceedings until the inter-state tribunal issues its award.[285]

But these interpretations analyse the interplay between state-to-state arbitration and ISA in a single setting. What would happen if a number of cases are introduced for the same underlying reasons and at around the same time (e.g. as in the 2001 Argentinian economic crisis)? If we consider that inter-state awards should have only prospective effects, would this interpretation apply only to the (un)lucky ISDS cases that came afterwards? Even if we believe that ISDS arbitration should always be given priority, how could an ISDS tribunal disregard an inter-state interpretation by an arbitral tribunal that is issued before a claim was formally introduced? Can we define the proper 'timing' of both state-to-state and investor–state arbitrations focusing only on a specific case? Would the interpretation of an IIA be restricted on a 'first come, first served' basis?

There seems to be no obvious or clear-cut answer for all these scenarios, and in my view an IIA clause providing for state-to-state arbitration could not be interpreted in a way that would excessively restrict its

---

[283] J. Wong, 'The Subversion of State-to-State Investment Treaty Arbitration', Colum. J. Transnat'l L., 53 (2014), 6–48 at 34–46.
[284] Kulick, 'State-State Investment Arbitration', pp. 149, 151.
[285] Ibid., p. 151.

application or render it useless. Yet, we also have to consider that the obligation to comply with investor–state awards is explicitly stated in several IIAs, as we have detailed before, and also in the ICSID Convention.[286] The obligation to comply with non-ICSID awards will arise out of other international conventions, such as the New York or Panama Conventions,[287] although under their provisions a domestic court may refuse the enforcement of an award on the ground of 'public policy'[288] – a notion that might be interpreted as including obligations derived from inter-state awards.

[286] ICSID Convention, Art. 53(1).

[287] Inter-American Convention on International Commercial Arbitration, 30 January 1975, 1438 U.N.T.S. 245; O.A.S.T.S. No 42; 14 I.L.M. 336 [hereinafter 'Panama Convention'].

[288] New York Convention, Art. V.2(b); and Panama Convention, Art. 5.2(b).

VII

Home State Limitations on Diplomatic Protection

A Why Home States Do Not Intervene

Developing and protecting public policies is part of a state's basic mission. Why would a home state not be able to protect private interests under international law if those interests also represent state public policies? As the World Trade Organization dispute settlement system shows, a state could effectively uphold both state and private interests. Greater involvement by the foreign investor's home state when the defence of a public interest is needed would not necessarily come at the expense of diplomatic relations with the host state. In fact, leaving control of the settlement of disputes to investors alone could create the opposite effect, as they are not likely to take into consideration other variables in the relationship between the home and the host states beyond the specific aspects in dispute.

But, as we have seen throughout this book, home states rarely intervene in favour of their national investors in disputes with host states – at least publicly. There are several reasons that might explain the reluctance of home states to participate openly in investor–state disputes even if there is a complete legal framework that entitles them to do so. In this chapter, we will examine four possible reasons for this behaviour: firstly, the difficulties related to determining who the home state is for a particular investment dispute; secondly, the limitations inherent in diplomatic protection; thirdly, the existence of competing interests with investors abroad; and fourthly, the very reserved nature of several types of diplomatic intervention, which makes it difficult to acknowledge its existence.

1 Who Is the Home State?

One problem with the intervention of the home state in investor–state disputes comes from the fact that, occasionally, it is not easy to identify who the home state of a specific investor is, as in some cases it is problematic to ascertain the nationality of investor-claimants,[1] which also has consequences for the purposes of exercising diplomatic protection. Actually, there could be cases in which the 'nominal' nationality of an investor for the purposes of an investment claim is different to the one that they are considered as having for the purposes of diplomatic protection.

Sauvant explains that several firms have moved towards an international division of labour, functions and competences at intra-firm level, using foreign and domestic affiliates to build corporate networks that specialize in the production of various parts that are assembled in any location worldwide that is best suited for this purpose: 'the emergence of such complex networks coordinated by headquarters makes it difficult at times to identify the boundaries of a particular firm, assigning origin for purposes of determining eligibility for preferential treatment or to determine liability in case of, for instance, gross negligence. It also means that the distinction between host and home countries is losing its sharpness'.[2]

This problem does not appear as evident at first glance. If we examine UNCTAD's database – Investment Dispute Settlement Navigator (ISDN) – of the total number of 904 known investor–state dispute settlement cases by July 2018, all have information on the home state,[3] which is a conclusion that might be explained if we plainly qualify as a home state that of the nationality of the non-disputing contracting party of the treaty invoked in each investor–state arbitration. Yet, UNCTAD itself has highlighted the difficulties of mapping direct shareholders to ultimate owners, due to the complex corporate structures that are more frequently found in larger multinational

---

[1] D. Gaukrodger and K. Gordon, 'Investor–State Dispute Settlement: A Scoping Paper of the Investment Policy Community', *OECD Working Papers on International Investment*, No 2012/3 (2012), pp. 17–18.

[2] K. P. Sauvant, *The Evolving International Investment Law and Policy Regime: Ways Forward. E15 Task Force on Investment Policy – Policy Options Paper. E15 Initiative* (International Centre for Trade and Sustainable Development (ICTSD) and World Economic Forum, 2016), p. 14.

[3] UNCTAD, 'Investment Dispute Settlement Navigator'.

enterprises (MNEs), and has labelled this problem the 'investor nationality conundrum'.[4]

UNCTAD also reports that nationality mismatch cases are highly relevant in ISDS. On the cases for which the relevant information is available, about one third of the claims since 2010 were filed by claimant entities that were ultimately owned by a parent in a third country, or even in the host state. The share of intermediate entities increases significantly in cases based on international investment agreements (IIAs) with countries that are major offshore and ownership hubs, where up to 75 per cent of claimant companies are ultimately foreign owned.[5]

According to the ISDN database, only seventeen countries are considered home states in more than ten ISDS cases, representing 88 per cent of the cases in the sample (904 arbitrations), with the United States being the largest home state for ISDS disputes (166 arbitrations; 18 per cent), followed by the Netherlands (107 arbitrations; 12 per cent), and the UK (78 arbitrations; 9 per cent).

It is also possible that are several home states in one dispute, as claimants may use different investment treaties in a particular case. This phenomenon seems to have been more recurrent in recent years, notably in intra-EU disputes.

But who are these investors? According to a 2012 survey carried out by the OECD (only on fifty ICSID cases and forty-five UNCITRAL cases), a third of the cases in the sample were brought by investors about which little or no public information is available, besides that extracted from documents of the arbitration case itself – including the memorial, the briefs and the award. This category appears to contain two types of investor: holding companies specifically formed around the asset or activity that is the subject of the arbitration, and small investors who are not obliged to report publicly and do not maintain extensive websites. In the sample, twenty of the fifty ICSID cases were brought by this category of investor, as were twelve of the forty-five UNCITRAL cases.[6]

This situation could also be explained by the extensive use of a 'nationality of convenience' – a merely formal link in order to gain access

---

[4] UNCTAD, *World Investment Report 2016. Investor Nationality: Policy Challenges* (United Nations, 2016), pp. 144–58.

[5] Ibid., p. 171.

[6] Gaukrodger and Gordon, 'Investor–State Dispute Settlement: A Scoping Paper', p. 17.

Table 7.1 *Home countries in more than ten ISDS cases*

No	Name	Cases as Home State
1	United States of America	166
2	Netherlands	107
3	United Kingdom	78
4	Germany	61
5	Canada	49
6	Spain	48
7	France	48
8	Luxembourg	40
9	Italy	36
10	Turkey	31
11	Switzerland	28
12	Cyprus	24
13	Austria	22
14	Belgium	19
15	Russian Federation	18
16	Greece	14
17	Ukraine	11

Source: UNCTAD, Investment Dispute Settlement Navigator

to international fora[7] – through 'forum shopping' or 'nationality planning' techniques that allow foreign investors to benefit from an investment treaty of a third country by routing their investment through that country.[8] Regardless of the reasons behind this phenomenon, one thing is clear: if we are not able to identify where claimant-investors really come from, it will be difficult to identify their home states. What would happen if two states claim to be the host state? What if the investor disagrees with a state

[7] M. Casas, 'Nationalities of Convenience, Personal Jurisdiction, and Access to Investor–State Dispute Settlement', *New York University Journal of International Law and Politics*, 49 (2016), 63–128 at 66.

[8] M. Skinner, C. A. Miles and S. Luttrell, 'Access and Advantage in Investor–State Arbitration: The Law and Practice of Treaty Shopping', *Journal of World Energy Law & Business*, 3 (2010), 260–85 at 260–1.

Table 7.2 *ISDS cases with several home states (2003–2017)*

Year	Cases with Several Home States	Cases	Home States
2006	1	*Rail World* v. *Estonia* (ICSID Case No ARB/ 06/6)	Netherlands, US
2007	0		
2008	1	*Itera* v. *Georgia* (ICSID Case No ARB/08/7)	Netherlands, US
2009	0		
2010	4	*Flughafen Zürich* v. *Venezuela* (ICSID Case No ARB/10/19)	Switzerland and Chile
		von Pezold and ors v. *Zimbabwe* (ICSID Case No ARB/10/15)	Germany and Switzerland
		Ascom and ors v. *Kazakhstan* (SCC Case No 116/2010)	Moldova, Romania, and Gibraltar
		Guaracachi v. *Bolivia* (PCA Case No 2011–17)	UK, US
2011	2	*Tenaris SA and Talta* v. *Venezuela* (I) (ICSID Case No ARB/ 11/26)	Portugal, Luxembourg
		The PV Investors v. *Spain*	Denmark, Germany, Ireland, Luxembourg, Netherlands, UK
2012	4	*Emmis* v. *Hungary* (ICSID Case No ARB/ 12/2)	Netherlands, Switzerland
		Slovak Gas v. *Slovakia* (ICSID Case No ARB/ 12/7)	France, Germany, Netherlands
		Tenaris and Talta v. *Venezuela* (II) (ICSID Case No ARB/ 12/23)	Portugal, Luxembourg

Table 7.2 *cont.*

Year	Cases with Several Home States	Cases	Home States
		Charanne and Construction Investments v. *Spain* (SCC Case No 062/ 2012)	Luxembourg, Netherlands
2013	4	*Antin* v. *Spain* (ICSID Case No ARB/13/31)	Luxembourg, Netherlands
		Eiser and Energía Solar v. *Spain* (ICSID Case No ARB/13/36)	Luxembourg, UK
		RREEF v. *Spain* (ICSID Case No ARB/13/30)	Luxembourg, UK
		Natland v. *Czech Republic*	Cyprus, Luxembourg, Netherlands, UK
2014	5	*Uzan* v. *Turkey* (SCC Case No 2014/023)	France, UK
		Highbury International v. *Venezuela* (ICSID Case No ARB/11/1)	Netherlands, Panama
		EuroGas v. *Slovakia* (ICSID Case No ARB/ 14/14)	Canada, US
		Dagher v. *Sudan* (ICSID Case No ARB/14/2)	Jordan, Lebanon
		Blusun v. *Italy* (ICSID Case No ARB/14/3)	Belgium, France, Germany
2015	11	*Watkins Holdings* v. *Spain* (ICSID Case No ARB/15/44)	Luxembourg, Netherlands
		OperaFund v. *Spain* (ICSID Case No ARB/ 15/36)	Malta, Switzerland
		MMEA and AHSI v. *Senegal* (ICSID Case No ARB/15/21)	UK, Netherlands
			UK, Netherlands

Table 7.2 *cont.*

Year	Cases with Several Home States	Cases	Home States
		JKX Oil & Gas and ors v. *Ukraine*	
		Hydro Energy 1 and Hydroxana v. *Spain* (ICSID Case No ARB/ 15/42)	Luxembourg, Sweden
		Hourani v. *Kazakhstan* (ICSID Case No ARB/ 15/13)	UK, US
		Greentech and Novenergia v. *Italy*	Denmark, Luxembourg
		Gabriel Resources v. *Romania* (ICSID Case No ARB/15/31)	Canada, UK
		Cube Infrastructure v. *Spain* (ICSID Case No ARB/15/20)	France, Luxembourg
		Álvarez y Marín Corporación and ors v. *Panama* (ICSID Case No ARB/15/14)	Costa Rica, Netherlands
		Adamakopoulos and ors v. *Cyprus* (ICSID Case No ARB/15/49)	Greece, Luxembourg
2016	8	*Infracapital* v. *Spain* (ICSID Case No ARB/ 16/18)	Luxembourg, Netherlands
		Grot and ors v. *Moldova* (ICSID Case No ARB/ 16/8)	US, Poland
		Eurus Energy v. *Spain* (ICSID Case No ARB/ 16/4)	Japan, Netherlands
		ESPF and ors v. *Italy* (ICSID Case No ARB/ 16/5)	Austria, Germany

Table 7.2 cont.

Year	Cases with Several Home States	Cases	Home States
		ENGIE and ors v. *Hungary* (ICSID Case No ARB/16/14)	France, Netherlands
		CIC Renewable and ors v. *Italy* (ICSID Case No ARB/16/39)	Germany, UK, Luxembourg
		Astro and South Asia Entertainment v. *India*	UK, Mauritius
		Alhambra v. *Kazakhstan* (ICSID Case No ARB/16/12)	Netherlands, Canada
2017	2	*Itisaluna Iraq and ors* v. *Iraq* (ICSID Case No ARB/17/10)	Jordan, UAE
		OHL and ors v. *Kuwait* (ICSID Case No ARB/17/8)	Spain, Italy

Source: UNCTAD, Investment Dispute Settlement Navigator

that claims to be the home state, or vice versa? The following examples will illustrate the problems that might derive from this situation.

In *Aucoven* v. *Venezuela*, the exercise of diplomatic protection from one country had a 'boomerang' effect in relation to the jurisdiction of the arbitral tribunal. In this case, Autopista Concesionada de Venezuela, CA (Aucoven), a Venezuelan company, initially owned 99 per cent by a Mexican corporation (ICA Holding), had entered into a concession agreement with Venezuela for the design, construction, operation, preservation and maintenance of the Caracas–La Guaira highway system. On 7 April 1997, at the start of Aucoven's operation of the highway system, the company requested authorization from the Venezuelan Ministry of Transportation and Communication to transfer 75 per cent of Aucoven's shares to Icatech, a company incorporated in the state of Florida, in the United States, but also a wholly owned subsidiary of the Mexican company ICA Holding.

Only 15 months later – on 30 June 1998 – and after several requests, the transfer of 75 per cent of Aucoven's shares to Icatech was authorized.[9]

Some months after Hugo Chávez took office as President of Venezuela, in October 1999, the newly established Venezuelan Ministry of Infrastructure initiated administrative proceedings to review the award of the concession and the concession agreement, and later initiated a procedure to have them declared null and void. In June 2000, Aucoven unilaterally terminated the concession agreement and informed the Ministry that it was willing to continue performing 'in good faith' the routine maintenance and toll-collection activities. At the same time, Aucoven filed a request for arbitration before ICSID. After violent protests in August 2002, in which protestors prevented Aucoven from collecting tolls, the company ceased the performance of routine maintenance and abandoned the highway in September 2002.[10]

Mexico took a number of diplomatic steps to facilitate an amicable solution of the dispute, such as writing letters to the Venezuelan Ministry of Foreign Affairs, and held meetings with government officials to explore a viable and mutually acceptable solution, before awards were rendered.[11] There is no record of any similar activity on the part of the United States – the 'home state' of Icatech.

In its submission on jurisdiction, Venezuela pointed out that Aucoven was, in fact, controlled by a Mexican holding, and therefore it could not initiate ICSID arbitration, since Mexico was not a contracting state under the ICSID Convention. Venezuela further argued that, since Mexican officials had sent written communications and held meetings with Venezuelan officials, this amounted to Mexico's diplomatic intervention that confirmed the direct interest of ICA Holding in Aucoven.[12] Aucoven argued that Mexico had not filed a formal protest with Venezuela or

---

[9] *Autopista Concesionada de Venezuela, CA* v. *Bolivarian Republic of Venezuela*, Decision on Jurisdiction. 27 September 2001, 16 ICSID Review 469–514, paras. 1–31.

[10] *Autopista Concesionada de Venezuela, CA* v. *Bolivarian Republic of Venezuela* (ICSID Case No ARB/00/5) Award of the Tribunal, 23 September 2003, paras. 44–50.

[11] J. E. Viñuales and D. Bentolila, 'The Use of Alternative (Non-Judicial) Means to Enforce Investment Awards against States' in L. Boisson de Chazournes, M. G. Kohen and J. E. Viñuales (eds.), *Diplomatic and Judicial Means of Dispute Settlement* (Martinus Nijhoff Publishers, 2012), p. 269.

[12] G. Álvarez Ávila, 'Autopista Concesionada de Venezuela, CA v. Bolivarian Republic of Venezuela (ICSID Case No ARB/00/5): Introductory Note', *ICSID Review* (2001), 16, 465–8 at 467.

espoused a claim in any other way, and that therefore an international dispute had arisen between Mexico and Venezuela.[13]

In its decision on jurisdiction, the arbitral tribunal examined the significance of the intervention by Mexican officials, concluding that as Mexico was not at the time a contracting state of the ICSID Convention, it was not bound by Article 27(1) prohibition on exercising diplomatic protection. In any case, the tribunal considered that the intervention of Mexico as an attempt to settle a dispute did not constitute prohibited diplomatic protection in the sense of the ICSID Convention, there being no indication that Mexico had espoused Aucoven's claim. If that were the case, a denial of jurisdiction was not a remedy available in the context of Article 27(1).[14]

In *Banro American Resources* v. *Democratic Republic of Congo*, the arbitrators' decision on whether or not the claimant qualified as an American investor under the 1990 Democratic Republic of Congo–US BIT, or if it was, in reality, a Canadian company, was influenced by the fact that the Canadian government intervened diplomatically to support Banro.[15] The majority of the arbitral tribunal ruled that it had no competence, declaring that it could not allow the requirements of nationality imposed by the ICSID Convention to be neutralized 'by investors who are seeking to avail themselves, depending on their own interests at a given point in time, simultaneously or successively, of both diplomatic protection and ICSID arbitration, by playing on the fact that one of the companies of the group does not have the nationality of a Contracting State party to the Convention, and can therefore benefit from diplomatic protection by its home state, while another subsidiary of the group possesses the nationality of a Contracting State to the Convention and therefore has standing before an ICSID tribunal'.[16]

IIAs do not usually include provisions to clarify who the home state is for the purposes of a treaty. To our knowledge, only the IISD Model International Agreement on Investment for Sustainable Development includes a provision whereby investors are obliged promptly to declare

---

[13] *Aucoven* v. *Venezuela*, Decision on Jurisdiction, para. 73.
[14] *Aucoven* v. *Venezuela*, Decision on Jurisdiction, paras. 48–9.
[15] G. Gertz, S. Jandhyala and L. S. Poulsen, 'Has Investor–State Arbitration Depoliticized Investment Disputes?', p. 10.
[16] *Banro American Resources, Inc. and Société Aurifère du Kivu et du Maniema SARL* v. *Democratic Republic of the Congo* (ICSID Case No ARB/98/7), Award, 1 September 2000 (2002) 17 ICSID Review 382–92, para. 24.

their home state, which should be accepted by the host state. This choice shall be based on its principal place of business, or a major centre of effective and sustained links with the home-state economy, and from which effective control over the investment is exercised. Subject to prior notification and consultation with the investor, within ninety days of the notice given by the investor, a host state may deny the benefits of the IIA to an investor that does not meet the requirements of ownership, control or substantial business activities in the territory of the other contracting party.[17]

2 Home State and Its Nationals May Have Competing Interests

We could assume that a home state will always have an interest in protecting its nationals from violations of international law by other sovereign states. However, in several cases the interests of the home state and those of its investors might differ, or even be in contradiction. A home state has, at the same time, an interest in the protection of its nationals, but it also has an interest in the proper interpretation of the investment treaty.[18] Thus, the home state also has common interests with the host state. Before deciding to intervene in ISA or to exercise diplomatic protection, a home state will have to weigh its interest in protecting the rights of its nationals against its other interests. In fact, what is more likely to happen is that home states will have common interests with the host states.

These different interests could lead to divergent positions in ISA. For example, in *Metalclad* v. *Mexico*, the United States rejected the interpretation of its national claimant that the term 'tantamount to expropriation' in Article 1110 of NAFTA was intended to create a 'new category of expropriation not previously recognized in customary international law'.[19] Similarly, in *Feldman* v. *Mexico*, the United States presented a non-disputing state party submission that on one issue was in favour of the host state – its position was that the submission of a claim to arbitration, and not the delivery of the notice

---

[17] IISD Model IAISD, Art. 2(I).
[18] A. Roberts, 'State-to-State Investment Treaty Arbitration: A Hybrid Theory of Interdependent Rights and Shared Interpretive Authority', Harv. Int'l L.J. 55 (2014), 49.
[19] *Metalclad Corp.* v. *United Mexican States*, ICSID Case No ARB(AF)/97/1. Submission of the Government of the United States of America, 9 November 1999.

of intent, must fall within the three-year limitation period of Article 1117(2) of NAFTA.[20]

The use of 'treaty shopping' or 'nationality planning' could make this conflict of interests even more patent. Investment disputes might arise between a 'foreign investor' and a host state that, under customary international law, would normally qualify as the home state of the claimant. For example, in *Tokios Tokelés*, a Lithuanian company controlled by Ukrainian interests brought an ISDS claim against Ukraine. In his famous dissenting opinion as Chairman in that arbitration, Weil held that the dispute, 'while formally meeting the condition of being between a Contracting State and a national of another Contracting State, is in fact between a Contracting State and a corporation controlled by nationals of that State'.[21] We find a similar situation in the *Yukos* cases against Russia under the Energy Charter Treaty. Russia argued that the tribunal lacked jurisdiction because the claimants did not qualify as 'investors', given the fact that they were nominally foreign companies with no substantial business activity in their countries of incorporation ('shell companies') owned and controlled by nationals of Russia – the host state in the dispute.[22] On a plain reading of Article 1(7) of the ECT, the arbitral tribunal held that the claimants were protected investors organized under the laws of Cyprus and the Isle of Man, irrespective of the nationality of their controllers or owners.[23]

Sometimes, a policy on non-intervention will be regarded as more optimal by home states if they do not have settled views on issues of interpretation of the investment treaty, as such views may be costly or time consuming to develop, especially in countries with an extensive inter-agency process.[24]

---

[20] *Marvin Roy Feldman Karpa v. United Mexican States*, ICSID Case No ARB(AF)/99/1. Submission of the United States on Preliminary Issues. 6 October 2000.

[21] *Tokios Tokelés v. Ukraine*, ICSID Case No ARB/02/18. Decision on Jurisdiction. Dissenting Opinion Chairman Prosper Weil, 29 April 2004, para. 10.

[22] *Yukos Universal Ltd (Isle of Man) v. Russian Federation*, UNCITRAL, PCA Case No AA 227 Interim Award on Jurisdiction and Admissibility, 30 November 2009, paras. 42–53; *Hulley Enterprises Ltd (Cyprus) v. Russian Federation*, UNCITRAL, PCA Case No AA 226, Interim Award on Jurisdiction and Admissibility, 30 November 2009, paras. 42–53; *Veteran Petroleum Ltd (Cyprus) v. Russian Federation*, UNCITRAL, PCA Case No AA 228. Interim Award on Jurisdiction and Admissibility, 30 November 2009, paras. 42–53.

[23] *Yukos v. Russia*, Interim Award; paras. 411–17; *Veteran Petroleum v. Russia*, Interim Award, paras. 411–17; *Hulley Enterprises v. Russia*, Interim Award, paras. 411–17.

[24] Roberts, 'State-to-State Investment Treaty Arbitration', 57.

There are broader interests outside the investment agreements that might influence home state actions, in either the international or the domestic arena. For example, in the case of comprehensive nationalizations effected on a non-discriminatory basis, in the process of large scale social reforms undertaken under exceptional circumstances of revolution, war and similar, foreign investors might be interested in settling an investment dispute with the host state in the most expedited way available for them, using ISA directly – if such a possibility is provided for in the respective IIA. Considering the difficult economic situation that a country faces in such dire circumstances, the home state of those investors may be more inclined to start diplomatic negotiations in order to determine compensation, and only failing this resort to international arbitration. This possibility is expressly provided for in the 1992 World Bank Guidelines on the Treatment of Foreign Investment, which, in the event of expropriation, provide for unilateral alterations an termination of contracts in the abovementioned extraordinary circumstances.[25]

Additionally, a confrontation with an expropriating government that has important economic consequences might cause that government to collapse, and a developed home state could end up participating in expensive aid flows in order to stabilize its successor.[26] In these circumstances a home state may also wish to take over the claims of its national investors for other compelling reasons, such as the protection of the essential security interests of the home state.[27]

Home states could also envisage limiting the future use of tools of diplomatic protection, if their national investors do not abide by principles that are supported by that state. For example, although corporate social responsibility instruments are largely of a voluntary nature, some investment disputes also entangle core CSR topics, even triggering parallel dispute proceedings based on the same set of facts. For example, the *Renco v. Peru* case[28] had a US company bringing an ISDS case against Peru, while, at the same time, that country was facing a claim before the Inter-American Commission on Human Rights (IACHR) on the

---

[25] World Bank, *Report to the Development Committee and Guidelines on the Treatment of Foreign Direct Investment* (1992), vol. II p. 43.

[26] N. Maurer, *The Empire Trap: The Rise and Fall of U.S. Intervention to Protect American Property Overseas, 1893–2013* (Princeton University Press, 2013), pp. 8–9.

[27] Roberts, 'State-to-State Investment Treaty Arbitration', 50.

[28] *The Renco Group, Inc.* v. *Republic of Peru*, ICSID Case No UNCT/13/1, Award, 9 November 2016.

damaging effects of La Oroya complex.[29] Home states could declare beforehand that they would not espouse investment claims of its nationals or companies that do not comply with certain policies considered in CSR principles and standards. Sornarajah believes that the rights under IIAs cannot be exercised in a manner that violates the principles of human rights law, which is globally binding because it generally constitutes customary international law, concluding that the home state 'cannot protect the rights of nationals who have violated human rights either through diplomatic intervention or through means of a treaty'.[30]

Domestically, a home state could be faced with the need to decide between protecting regulatory freedom of states, and its interest in protecting the rights of its nationals. In this regard, Roberts proposes the example of the claim in *Philip Morris* v. *Australia* for regulation on the plain packaging of cigarettes, under the 1993 Australia–Hong Kong BIT.[31] Hong Kong – or China – might wish to enact similar plain packaging legislation due to health concerns and therefore might not welcome an adverse arbitral award in the ISDS case, even if it would not be a binding precedent for a potential future arbitration involving Hong Kong for enacting plain packaging regulations.[32] Following the same example, several other disputes over Australia's plain packaging regulations have been brought before the WTO dispute settlement body, which have referred, inter alia, to breaches of obligations under the Agreement on Trade-Related Aspects of Intellectual Property Rights (TRIPs Agreement) and the Agreement on Technical Barriers to Trade (TBT Agreement) that correspond to correlative obligations in the Australia–Hong Kong BIT, as the same set of facts may trigger both type of claims in relation to substantive rights, under different trade and investment treaties.[33] This could have been an occasion on which to test the interest of Hong Kong in the effects of this particular public policy in international trade. However, Hong Kong is not found among the five

---

[29] *Community of La Oroya* v. *Peru*, Inter-American Commission on Human Rights, Report No 76/09, Petition 1473-06, Admissibility, 5 August 2009.

[30] M. Sornarajah, *Resistance and Change in the International Law on Foreign Investment* (Cambridge University Press, 2015), p. 319.

[31] This case was finally dismissed on jurisdictional grounds, with the tribunal declaring that Philip Morris committed abuse of rights as it changed its corporate structure to gain BIT protection: *Philip Morris Asia Ltd* v. *Commonwealth of Australia*, UNCITRAL, PCA Case No 2012-12, Award on Jurisdiction and Admissibility, 17 December 2015.

[32] Roberts, 'State-to-State Investment Treaty Arbitration', 49–50.

[33] R. Alford, 'The Convergence of International Trade and Investment Arbitration', *Santa Clara Journal of International Law*, 12 (2014), 35 at 44.

complainant against Australia, nor has it reserved its third-party rights – as China did – in all these cases.[34]

Interventions by the home state can also bear domestic political costs. National voters may oppose intervention for ideological reasons if they do not believe that the interests of private investors are the same as those of the country. Some others could oppose intervention because it fails a cost–benefit test.[35] In that context, home states may welcome ISA not because it effectively 'depoliticizes' the dispute – it can be argued that a conflict involving a government will always have a political side – but because it insulates the home state from having to be involved in costly and unwanted disputes.[36]

Many home states may be reluctant to espouse the claims of its investors if they can benefit from ISA as a main remedy, even if the investment treaty is silent on the point of the coexistence of diplomatic protection with an investor–state claim.[37] Maurer has described how the intervention of the American government on behalf of its investors abroad was extraordinarily successful at extracting compensation from host states between the 1890s and the 1980s, particularly in relation to natural resources, through the extensive use of threats of economic sanctions, aid withdrawals and military action. However, those interventions came with a cost, as US domestic interests repeatedly trumped strategic concerns for small economic gains relative to the American economy – returns from foreign direct investments were not a significant part of its national income – and added potential strategic losses, such as the animosity of the states in which American intervention was taking place, pushing that nation to ally with a hostile power.[38] This situation created a virtual 'empire trap', in which the promise made by one American administration to intervene on behalf of its investors in the

---

[34] The disputes against Australia, about certain measures concerning trademarks and other plain packaging requirements applicable to tobacco products, are the DS434 (Complainant: Ukraine), initiated on 13 March 2012; the DS435 (Complainant: Honduras), initiated on 4 April 2012; DS441 (Complainant: Dominican Republic), initiated on 18 July 2012; DS458 (Complainant: Cuba), initiated on 3 May 2013; and DS467 (Complainant: Indonesia), initiated on 20 September 2012. With the exception of the dispute brought by Ukraine (the authority for the panel in which lapsed on 30 May 2016) all the other disputes are pending. See World Trade Organization (WTO), 'Dispute Settlement – Index of Disputes Issues' (February 2018).

[35] Maurer, *The Empire Trap*, p. 8.

[36] Roberts, 'State-to-State Investment Treaty Arbitration', 57.

[37] N. S. Kinsella and N. Rubins, *International Investment, Political Risk, and Dispute Resolution: A Practitioner's Guide* (Oxford University Press, 2005), p. 415.

[38] Maurer, *The Empire Trap*, pp. 2–4.

protection of their property abroad, makes it harder for future American administrations to refrain from such intervention, repeatedly dragging the United States into conflict with foreign states.[39]

We should also consider that a home state's participation in investment disputes could clash with the interests of the foreign investor. If the participation of the home state in the dispute takes the form of state-to-state arbitration or adjudication, it would almost certainly not provide direct compensation to foreign investors,[40] because the international wrong is construed as having been suffered by the home state. This is relevant because compensation is the main remedy claimed by investors in ISA.[41]

Finally, even if a home state and its investors share common interests in a dispute, we should still expect that ISA will remain the primary mechanism for the settlement of investment disputes, as investors usually have the best economic incentive to take up claims if they have available resources.[42]

3 The Reserved Nature of Diplomatic Intervention

Another reason for diplomatic protection or other forms of home state intervention in investment disputes, such as consular assistance or diplomatic pressure, being perceived as not having been widely used, is because of the reserved nature of the majority of the diplomatic mechanisms. Although a distinction is usually made between 'open' and 'secret' diplomacy, 'much of modern diplomacy is in practice conducted on the basis of secrecy'.[43] Negotiations are secret almost by nature and several former negotiators have acknowledged that the lack of secrecy makes diplomacy even more difficult.[44] The French diplomat Jules Cambon famously observed that 'The day secrecy is abolished, negotiation of any kind will become impossible'[45] and that, on the day on which there would be no secrecy in negotiation, 'there would be no negotiations at all'.[46]

---

[39] Ibid., pp. 7–8.

[40] C. F. Amerasinghe, *Diplomatic Protection* (Oxford University Press, 2008), p. 319.

[41] B. Sabahi, *Compensation and Restitution in Investor–State Arbitration: Principles and Practice* (Oxford University Press, 2011), p. 46.

[42] Roberts, 'State-to-State Investment Treaty Arbitration', 49.

[43] R. P. Barston, *Modern Diplomacy* (Routledge, 2014), p. 11.

[44] J. Calvet de Magalhães, *The Pure Concept of Diplomacy* (Greenwood Publishing Group, 1988), pp. 69–70. See also C. L. Sulzberger, 'Lack of Secrecy Makes Diplomacy Even More Difficult' (1975).

[45] F. W. Matson, 'In Defense of Compromise', *The Pacific Spectator*, IX (1955), 264–71 at 270.

[46] J. Bovey, 'Secret Diplomacy Is the Best Kind' (1990).

However, the reserved nature of certain types of diplomacy does not mean absolute secrecy for the whole process. Again, Cambon reportedly observed that 'If there is secrecy in negotiation, this secrecy ends in the very hour when these negotiations lead to a convention'.[47]

There is ample evidence that home states have an interest in the defence of the interests of their investors abroad. Traditionally, part of the consular service is devoted to representing the commercial and economic interests of the sending state and its nationals in relations with the receiving state.[48] In that context, as was discussed previously, consular functions include protection, help and assistance in the receiving state with the interests of its nationals, both individuals and bodies corporate, within the limits permitted by international law.[49]

Diplomatic missions also have as functions, inter alia, the promotion and development of economic relations between the sending and the receiving states,[50] and embassies regularly include commercial services or attachés with the mission of facilitating the relationship of its nationals and companies with the economic authorities of the host state. These activities have been labelled 'commercial diplomacy', as they are conducted 'by state representatives with diplomatic status in view of business promotion between a home and a host country'.[51] Sometimes these activities are performed by different state agencies. For example, in the United States there are 'commercial diplomacy' activities of the US Commercial Service,[52] while the US Department of State prepares 'investment climate statements'.[53]

However, the existence of a system to support or assist national investors abroad, and even diplomatic or consular assistance in order to facilitate the settlement of investment conflicts with the host state, is

---

[47] Calvet de Magalhães, *The Pure Concept of Diplomacy*, p. 70.
[48] VCCR, Art. 5(b) and (c).
[49] Ibid., Art. 5(a) and (e).
[50] VCDR, Art. 3(e).
[51] O. Naray, 'Commercial Diplomacy: A Conceptual Overview', 7th World Conference of TPOs, The Hague, The Netherlands (2008), p. 2.
[52] These commercial diplomacy functions include services to overcome trade obstacles to accessing international markets, coordinated engagement with foreign governments to protect American business interests, and access to trade advocacy by the US government for government procurement bids. See US Commercial Service, 'Services for U.S. Companies' (February 2018).
[53] These statements are prepared annually by US embassies and diplomatic missions abroad, providing country-specific information and assessments of the investment climate in foreign markets. See US Department of State, 'Investment Climate Statements' (February 2018).

not equal to diplomatic protection, as it involves actions that are not necessarily directed towards obtaining a declaration on the responsibility of the host state for the breach of an international obligation. This kind of activity may be about domestic problems in the home state but that does not necessarily mean that it is a breach of an investment treaty, or that it is directed towards facilitating investment activities or preventing investment disputes.

Unfortunately, there is little research about this type of state intervention. As mentioned, Maurer has documented that the rise of ISA has facilitated a more restrictive approach on the part of the US government with respect to the espousal of investment claims from its nationals, producing little evidence that the United States uses coercive diplomacy in the contemporary period, as the government no longer needs to espouse the claims of its nationals, and companies could directly choose arbitration.[54] Gertz et al. have examined the investment disputes discussed in the Wikileaks cables, and concluded that threats of explicit sanctions against host state are few and far between.[55] More research on this subject is clearly needed, as the lack of public information in this regard makes it difficult to assess the intervention or non-intervention of home states in investment conflicts, using diplomatic or consular channels.

B   Lessons Learned: The Relevance of Peaceful Diplomatic Protection

As we have seen in the early part of this book, diplomatic protection does not have such a long history in the protection of foreigners and their property in international law. The first state practice involving diplomatic protection came only in the late eighteenth and early nineteenth centuries, and it was not easily accepted as a principle of international law by independent host states, notably in Latin America, where most of the countries claimed the existence of another principle: the equality of treatment of foreigners as a maximum standard, as was reflected in the Calvo doctrine and the Calvo clause and in general the preference for domestic courts in the settlement of foreign investment disputes.

---

[54] Maurer, The Empire Trap, p. 432.
[55] Gertz, Jandhyala and Poulsen, 'Has Investor-State Arbitration Depoliticized Investment Disputes?', p. 17.

Therefore, from a historical perspective, it is inaccurate to affirm that, before ISA, only diplomatic protection was available as a dispute settlement mechanism of investment disputes. Other means were also available, such as the use of domestic courts of either the host state, or sometimes the home state – in the cases of treaties that recognized foreign or special jurisdiction for aliens. It is also not accurate to declare that diplomatic protection was mostly exercised by force and 'gunboat diplomacy' was the main method of settlement of investment disputes. The documented work of binational claims commissions, international ad hoc arbitrations and tribunals is usually disregarded in contrast to well-known episodes of use of force.

Hence, contrary to what is sometimes affirmed, diplomatic protection was not always equivalent to the use of force from a powerful developed state against a developing country. Although it is true that unjustified military and forceful intervention took place, this anecdotal evidence blinds us to the fact that, most of the time, diplomatic protection was used through peaceful means, and that the settlement of disputes in those cases was not always in favour of the foreign investor.

In fact, one can affirm that, before the rise of ISA, no other method was more important to settle investment disputes than binational claims commissions: they decided the largest number of individual claims (more than any other peaceful mechanism, and certainly more than international adjudication).

Not every claim presented before binational claims commissions or mixed arbitral tribunals was about foreign investment. However, today, thousands of them would still qualify as 'investment claims' (including property rights, loans and concession contracts), even if we consider that the majority of the claims in certain commissions had no direct relationship with foreign investment, but with damages or injuries derived from torts, illegal detention, deaths or other crimes. As in other methods of peaceful dispute settlement, claims commissions dealt with the claims of both natural persons and legal entities.

As we are currently witnessing the return of mechanisms that imply a large involvement by the home state together with the host state in the settlement of investment disputes, through the overall reassertion of control over investment treaties, and the establishment of its corresponding fora (such as the Investment Court System, or eventually a multilateral investment court). In that context, I believe that several lessons can be drawn from the early experience of binational claims commissions and mixed arbitral tribunals that were commonplace in the nineteenth century until the aftermath of World War II.

1 Jurisdictional Issues

As we have mentioned before, the use of diplomatic protection has the general limitation of requiring the exhaustion of local remedies. Although this requirement is part of customary international law, it could well be waived by a treaty, if the contracting parties prefer this type of settlement of disputes. Some claims commission expressly did that, like the 1923 US-Mexico General Claims Commission, where it was explicitly declared that 'no claim shall be disallowed or rejected by the Commission by the application of the general principle of international law that the legal remedies must be exhausted as a condition precedent to the validity or allowance of any claim'.[56] The need to exhaust local remedies has not been highlighted as a relevant issue in the EU's ICS or in the MIC proposal, because of the direct access that investors would have before it. But it might be relevant for other types of dispute settlement involving the home state, and notably the use of inter-state dispute settlement or other tools of diplomatic protection.

Although similar to inter-state ad hoc arbitration, claims commissions had two basic differences from that mechanism, in relation to the number of claims that were decided and regarding the standing of private parties. First, ad hoc arbitrations normally settle one specific claim or group of claims, whereas claims commissions deal with several cases arising from the same issues or in a given period of time. In that sense, claims commissions provide a unique opportunity to have a systematized approach to settlement of several disputes, including those relating to foreign investment.[57] This is type of 'coherence' is precisely something that has been criticized as lacking in ISDS, and it is the aim of new proposals such as the ICS and the MIC.

Secondly, in inter-state ad hoc arbitration, the home state was taking the claim of its national against the host state where the alleged injury or damage took place, and kept control of the arbitration. Only in some cases were private claimants allowed to appoint their own lawyers.[58]

---

[56] General Claims Commission (Agreement 8 September 1923) (United Mexican States, United States of America), IV UNRIAA 11-14, Art. V.

[57] M. Paparinskis, *The International Minimum Standard and Fair and Equitable Treatment* (Oxford University Press, 2013), pp. 32–3.

[58] G. Guyomar, 'L'arbitrage concernant les rapports entre Etats et particuliers', *Annuaire français de droit international* (1959), 333–54 at 345.

Binational claims commissions reached different outcomes on the question of whether the consent of individual claimants was a precondition to jurisdiction. The 1923 US–Mexico General Claims Commission held that there was no requirement in this regard, and that only proof of nationality was required. The Italian–Mexican Commission, on the other hand, held that, in order to have jurisdiction, it was required that the private claimant initiate the claim.[59]

However, the majority of claims commissions gave *locus standi* only to home states, and even if individuals were allowed to access the proceedings, it was at times subject to express permission of the commission (Great Britain–Venezuela Commission) or from the home state government (US–Chile Commission), and in some cases it was required that evidence was received only through the government.[60] The question of access of nationals was the subject of controversy in the 1839 US–Mexico Commission, in which the position of the United States to grant direct access to private claimants was rejected by the Mexican government,[61] and in the 1923 US–Mexico General Claims Commission, where cases were presented either by the United States or by Mexico on behalf of its nationals.[62]

But this was not an absolute trend. In several binational claims commissions, home states allowed legal and natural persons to present their claims directly, to appoint lawyers of their choice and sometimes even to introduce evidence. That happened in the claims commissions between the US and Colombia (1857), Paraguay (1859), Costa Rica (1860), Chile (1862), Ecuador (1862) and Colombia (1864), and in the Mixed Claims Commission between Venezuela and Great Britain (1903) and the Netherlands (1903).[63] In those cases, these bodies are usually named 'mixed commissions' or 'mixed arbitral tribunals', which is a notion that entails one of the most important and radical characteristics for that time: that not only states but also private individuals may appear before them as parties.[64]

In this sense, the current ICS fostered by the EU resembles a mixed arbitral tribunal, because of the direct access that investors would have

---

[59] Parlett, *The Individual in the International Legal System*, p. 82.
[60] Ibid., p. 56.
[61] Ibid., p. 55.
[62] Mexico–US, Agreement 8 September 1923, Art. VI.
[63] Guyomar, 'L'arbitrage concernant les rapports entre Etats et particuliers', 347–52.
[64] P. D. Auer, 'The Competency of Mixed Arbitral Tribunals', *Transactions of the Grotius Society*, 13 (1927), xvii–xxx at 2.

before this 'hybrid' investment tribunal and appellate tribunal, which would be established with standing members but following arbitral procedural rules.

2 The Appointment of Decision-Makers

Claims commissions and mixed arbitral tribunals were conducted very similarly to inter-state ad hoc arbitration, with members appointed by each country – home and host states – and a third 'neutral' member usually acting as umpire in the event of disagreement by the commissioners. Sometimes members of the commissions acted as judges, supporting their decisions with reference to the rules and principles of international law,[65] and often the titles of 'arbitrators' or 'commissioner' were used as synonyms.

While Latin American countries were sometimes forced to submit disputes to arbitrators whose predispositions 'did not always inspire confidence among developing countries',[66] normally, arbitration took place under arbitrators freely appointed by the parties.

Ralston mentions that because, in some of the earlier arbitrations, each party paid their own arbitrators directly, an arbitrator was almost 'compelled to be the particular representative of his country rather than a judge'.[67] Umpires were occasionally selected by lot – a method that was criticized as being random and likely to lead to injustice and dissatisfaction. Later arbitrations showed substantial improvement, with the appointment of 'neutral' or independent arbitrators and umpires.[68] Yet, there was rarely a Latin American acting as an arbitrator, and countries from the region preferred European arbitrators, even in intra-Latin American disputes.[69]

---

[65] Amerasinghe, *Diplomatic Protection*, p. 16.

[66] G. Aguilar Álvarez and W. W. Park, 'The New Face of Investment Arbitration: NAFTA Chapter 11', Yale J. Int'l L., 28 (2003), 365 at 367 mentions that Latin American countries were forced to submit disputes to European sovereigns such as Britain's Queen Victoria, Russia's Tsar Alexander II, Germany's Kaiser Wilhelm II and King Léopold I of Belgium.

[67] J. H. Ralston, *International Arbitration from Athens to Locarno* (Stanford University Press, 1929), p. 224.

[68] Ibid., p. 225.

[69] L. M. Summers, 'Arbitration and Latin America', California Western International Law Journal, 3 (1972), 8. offers an explanation for this unbalance: 'Latin American nations themselves preferred European sovereigns as arbiters to their own presidents, even in intra-American disputes. There were more North Atlantic nationals and investments in Latin America than Latin American citizens and investments in Europe and the US. Also, the continual revolutions and upheavals in Latin America did cause considerable damage to persons and property.'

Again, this feature of binational claims commissions and mixed arbitral tribunals is very similar to the appointment process established in the EU's ICS, which has judges designated by each contracting party and from third countries, who serve as chairs of the respective divisions of the tribunal. Yet the ICS approach does not identify these decision-makers as arbitrators (as binational claims commissions and mixed arbitral tribunals did), even if they will use arbitral rules to conduct the proceedings and reach an outcome. This different denomination is probably due to political reasons, as a way of differentiating the ICS from the now-vilified ISDS.

However, using a different name does not guarantee that the main characteristics of the system have disappeared. Appointing an arbitrator or a judge is not only a technical matter but also a political one. States would tend to appoint judges that they expect to comply with certain fundamental values that, consciously or subconsciously, are closer to the interest of the state. This is could also work as a defence if the other state does not appoint judges (or arbitrators) with the same criteria. A state could effectively block the functioning of the tribunal, just by refusing to appoint judges. Neither CETA nor the EU–Vietnam and Singapore IPAs have rules for this situation – something that is commonly foreseen in arbitration, with the designation of an appointing authority.

3 A Balanced or a Biased Mechanism?

Amerasinghe mentions that binational claims commissions were regarded by Latin America – the region with most reported cases of this kind – as being prejudiced in favour of home states.[70] However, a more detailed analysis of the output of these peaceful mechanisms of dispute settlement shows that they were far from being merely 'victor's justice'. This discussion could help to inform the future implementation of the EU's ICS that has been criticized as being eventually 'biased' in favour of states.

In the beginning, binational claims commissions were essentially 'one sided', with Latin American states always being the respondent state.[71]

---

[70] Amerasinghe, *Diplomatic Protection*, p. 191.
[71] One of the few exceptions in this regard is the 1903 Mexican–Venezuelan Claims Commission. In this commission, besides a *Martínez del Río Hermanos* claim awarded in favour of Mexico, claims on behalf of Venezuela against Mexico were also allowed, without the signature of a specific protocol. Four claims were submitted, and only one was accepted. The total sum claimed amounted to US\$296,434.22 and only US\$12,112.50 was

A likely explanation for this imbalance is that there were more European and US investments in Latin America than the other way around, and that those investors were affected by disturbances that caused substantial damage to persons and property.[72] Later binational commissions were created to settle the claims of nationals of both sides, although Latin American countries were subject to far more cases, which were also financially more significant for their budgets. In any case, decisions of these commissions were not 'one sided' and, in the large majority of cases, were unanimous, resorting to umpires only exceptionally.

The commissions that were established to deal with disputes between Mexico and the United States provide an example of this evolution. The first binational claims commission between both countries was established under the Treaty of 11 April 1839, for claims involving hundreds of American citizens and millions of dollars in damage to their property, mainly during the Mexican War of Independence.[73] After almost one and a half year's work, the commission awarded a total of US$2,026,139.68 in favour of American claimants. A later US–Mexico General Claims Commission was constituted in 1923, to settle disputes between both countries from 1868, and including claims against one government by nationals of the other, for losses or damages originating from acts of officials or others acting for *either* government. The commission worked from 1924 to 1931 and from 1934 to 1937, reaching a final agreement in 1941.[74] A total of 3,617 claims were filed with the General Claims Commission, of which 2,781 claims were against Mexico and 836 against the United States.[75]

Other examples of the bidirectional nature of claims commission were the 1863 US–Peru and 1892 US–Chile General Claims Commissions that covered the claims of the citizens of either country against the government of the other state. In the former, the awards against the United

---

awarded, including interest. See J. H. Ralston and W. T. S. Doyle, *Venezuelan Arbitration of 1903* (US Government Printing Office, 1904), p. 888.

[72] Summers, 'Arbitration and Latin America', 8.

[73] P. M. Jonas, 'United States Citizens vs. Mexico, 1821–1848', unpublished PhD thesis, Marquette University (1989), pp. 1–2.

[74] A. F. Lowenfeld, *International Economic Law* (Oxford University Press, 2003), pp. 401, 402.

[75] United Nations, 'U.S.–Mexico General Claims Commission', Reports of International Arbitral Awards (United Nations, 2006), pp. 1–769 at p. 3.

States aggregated US$25,300 and those against Peru US$57,196.23.[76] In the latter, the commission awarded US$28,062.29 in favour of US citizens and US$3,000 in favour of Chilean citizens.[77]

It has also been pointed out that the total amount of the awards in claims commissions was disproportionately in favour of the United States and Europe.[78] But we should also compare the sums awarded with the amounts claimed. For example, the blockade and bombing of Venezuelan ports in 1902 by Germany, England and Italy, after the failure of Venezuela to pay unsettled debts and damages to foreigners,[79] ended with a subsequent agreement to arbitrate with the 'enforcing powers' and with other countries that had not participated in the forceful intervention but held similar claims against Venezuela (Belgium, France, the Netherlands, Spain, Mexico, the United States and Sweden–Norway).[80] The outcomes of such arbitrations were far from the amounts claimed by the investors. For example, the American claimants were awarded around 3 per cent of their claims; the Germans around 27 per cent; and the English 63 per cent (an outcome that might be explained by the fact that Great Britain had decided to filter the claims submitted to arbitration, allowing only those considered to be of 'good character').[81]

The 1923 Mexico–US General Claims Commission is also a good example of the amounts effectively awarded by these commissions. On 30 August 1931, the Commission disposed of 148 claims, with awards favourable to American claimants in eighty-nine cases (in total amounting to US$4,607,926.59) and favourable to Mexican claimants in five cases (in total amounting to US$39 million).[82] By a convention that came into force on 19 November 1941, Mexico agreed to pay, in instalments, a total of US$40 million in an en bloc settlement of the claims brought before the Commission, and other previous outstanding

---

[76] J. H. Ralston, *International Arbitration from Athens to Locarno* (Stanford University Press, 1929), pp. 215–16.

[77] Ibid., p. 209. Some cases are reported in United Nations, 'Commission for the Settlement of Claims under the Convention of 7 August 1892 concluded between the United States of America and the Republic of Chile', *Reports of International Arbitral Awards*, 29 (2011), 299–326.

[78] Summers, 'Arbitration and Latin America', 8.

[79] Amerasinghe, *Diplomatic Protection*, p. 191.

[80] Ralston, *International Arbitration from Athens to Locarno*, p. 223.

[81] Ibid., p. 224.

[82] United Nations, 'U.S.–Mexico General Claims Commission', p. 3.

claims.[83] This sum was distributed to the claimants by a US commission established in 1942, which worked until 1947 and considered 1,397 cases, rendering final awards on the claims of American nationals against Mexico in a total sum of US$37,948,200.05, and charging no interest even in some disputes dating back to the nineteenth century.[84]

However, there are strong arguments for considering that this mechanism was not absolutely balanced in favour of host states. Maurer has recently provided more information about the actual value of the compensation paid by Mexico, concluding that, even though foreign investors obtained less than what was claimed, in order to avoid American economic sanctions, Mexico paid far more than the market value of the assets.[85] A similar criticism has been formulated in relation to ISDS awards, with some awards to developing countries being financially more significant for them, even if they are far from the sums originally claimed.[86]

Sometimes the decisions of these commissions were revised after claims of bias in favour of the home state. One example is the work of the French–Mexican Claims Commission. After being established in 1924, its duration was extended in 1927, but Mexico did not appoint a new commissioner, considering that the jurisdiction of the commission had expired. In June 1929, the remaining two members of the commission decided twenty-three claims in the absence of a Mexican commissioner – a process that was finally suspended in the same month, until a tribunal could be regularly constituted.[87] On 2 August 1930, a new convention was signed, providing for a two-member arbitral commission composed of a representative of each country, with an umpire to be appointed by members of the Permanent Court of Arbitration in the event of disagreement.[88] This new commission reviewed the claims previously decided *in absentia* of a Mexican commissioner, concluding, by agreement of both commissioners, that only two of those awards were binding,

---

[83] United Mexican States, United States of America, Convention of 19 November 1941, IV UNRIAA 765-769.
[84] United Nations, 'U.S.–Mexico General Claims Commission', p. 4.
[85] Maurer, *The Empire Trap*, pp. 22–3.
[86] K. P. Gallagher and E. Shrestha, 'Investment Treaty Arbitration and Developing Countries: A Re-Appraisal', *Global Development and Environment Institute. Working Paper No 11–01* (2011), 9–10.
[87] United Nations, 'French–Mexican Claims Commission (France, United Mexican States)', Reports of International Arbitral Awards, pp. 307–560 p. 309.
[88] Ibid., pp. 318–21.

without requiring an umpire.[89] Similarly, after the integrity of the 1866 US–Venezuela Claims Commission was questioned by Venezuela due the large amounts awarded by it in favour of American citizens, a new commission was appointed by a Convention of 5 December 1885, in order to re-examine the work of the previous commission, and awarded a substantially lesser sum in favour of the claimants (US$980,572.60 instead of US$1,253,310.30),[90] in the total of fourteen cases decided.[91]

In certain cases, binational claims commissions even reviewed the work of previous inter-state ad hoc arbitrations. In the *Antoine Fabiani* case,[92] one of the claims reviewed by the 1902 French–Venezuelan Claims Commission had previously been referred to arbitration by the President of the Swiss Federation, by a Convention of 24 February 1891. After the arbitrator declined jurisdiction over a large part of the claims, Mr Fabiani presented the claim before the 1902 Claims Commission, contesting that the previous arbitration and award were conclusive, as the Swiss arbitrator had eliminated arbitrary acts imputable to the Venezuelan executive ('*faits du prince*'), and had only awarded in relation to the rest.[93] As the commissioners could not reach an agreement on the case, it was submitted to an umpire who finally rejected the claim, holding that there were no claims unsettled and that the Swiss arbitrator did not acknowledge lack of jurisdiction but simply decided against certain claims by Fabiani. In addition, the umpire held that Fabiani's claims were no longer private: 'When France intervened in behalf of her national, the claims of Fabiani were no longer individual and private claims; they became national. The right to intervene exists in the indignity to France through her national. Thenceforward it is national interests, not private interests that are to be safeguarded. It is the national honour which is to be sustained.'[94]

---

[89] A. H. Feller, *The Mexican Claims Commissions, 1923–1934: A Study in the Law and Procedure of International Tribunals* (Macmillan, 1935), p. 76.

[90] Ralston, *International Arbitration from Athens to Locarno*, pp. 220–1.

[91] United Nations, 'Claims Commission established under the Convention concluded between the United States of America and Venezuela on 5 December 1885', *Reports of International Arbitral Awards*, 29 (2011), 223–98.

[92] The claims presented by Mr Fabiani aggregated 46,994,563.17 francs, extended from 1878 to 1893, and were assembled under the general term of denial of justice imputable to the judicial and administrative authorities of Venezuela, and to damages suffered by him through the fault of its public powers, claiming for him both the direct and indirect damages. See *Antoine Fabiani* Case (1902 French–Venezuelan Commission), 31 July 1905, X UNRIAA 83-139.

[93] Ralston, *International Arbitration from Athens to Locarno*, pp. 232–3.

[94] *Antoine Fabiani Case*, p. 127.

In certain cases the decisions of the claims commissions were even considered as being 'biased' in favour of the host state. For example, in the *Gentini* case[95] brought before the 1903 Italy–Venezuela Claims Commission, to seek compensation on behalf of an Italian national whose store was looted by Venezuelan soldiers in 1871, the umpire denied the claim, based on the number of years for which the claimant had neglected his rights – almost thirty years – affirming that 'the claimant has so long neglected his supposed rights as to justify a belief in their nonexistence'.[96] This case has been criticized because the umpire did not express a source of international law to bar such a claim, and expressly excluded the use of municipal statutes of limitation, leaving the basis of his decision unclear.[97]

4 The Shortcomings and Legacy of Claims Commissions and Mixed Arbitral Tribunals

Binational claims commissions and mixed arbitral tribunals were not a perfect dispute settlement mechanism. One of the main problems they had to face was that, in general, the work of the commission extended beyond the original term, and had to be renewed by subsequent agreements, negotiations or even interpretations. In the case of the US–Mexico Claims Commission, this delay was considered 'unconscionable', even if the international responsibility of Mexico was recognized and claimants were in a position to receive substantial justice.[98] Some have pointed out that, despite its repeated extensions, the General Claims Commission decided only a small fraction of the claims before it, and that as the Mexican authorities failed to make any payments of awards to US beneficiaries, its outcome was finally replaced by a lump-sum settlement – an agreement that was probably influenced by the 'good neighbour policy' advanced by the Roosevelt administration and by the then upcoming World War II.[99] This can serve as a cautionary tale for the EU proposal for an ICS or the MIC. The political will to appoint members of

---

[95] *Gentini Case* (1903 Mixed Claims Commission Italy–Venezuela) X RIAA 551–561.

[96] *Gentini Case*, p. 561.

[97] C. F. Dugan, D. Wallace Jr, N. D. Rubins and B. Sabahi, *Investor–State Arbitration* (Oxford University Press, 2008), pp. 37–8.

[98] H. W. Briggs, 'The Settlement of Mexican Claims Act of 1942', *American Journal of International Law*, 37 (1943), 222–32 at 232.

[99] O. T. Johnson Jr and J. Gimblett, 'From Gunboats to BITs: Evolution of Modern International Investment Law', *Yearbook on International Investment Law & Policy 2010–2011* (2012), 666–7.

the tribunals and to finance their functioning that would be present today may not necessarily be present tomorrow. Besides the eventual financial constraints, states could later decide to not appoint judges, or to delay this process, effectively blocking the functioning of the tribunals. This is not a far-fetched idea, as the recent impasse over unfilled vacancies at the WTO's appellate body through US opposition teaches us.[100]

When compensation was awarded, both in binational claims commissions and in mixed arbitral tribunals (and also in inter-state arbitration), it was paid to the home state, which took the claim on behalf of its nationals.[101] For example, the treaty establishing the 1926 US–Panama Claims Tribunal expressly stipulated that any award was payable directly to the states.[102] Although we find that decisions of ad hoc arbitrations in which a monetary award was directly granted to the investor,[103] as a general rule, no money was directly attributed to the investors. This issue was debated in the United States regarding two awards that were obtained by fraud in the 1869 Mexican–US Claims Commission,[104] and it was explicitly established in the 1923 US–Mexico General Claims Commission.[105]

---

[100] Inside Trade, 'U.S. Rejects Proposal Brought by 58 Members to Fill WTO Appellate Body Slots' (January 2018).

[101] K. Parlett, *The Individual in the International Legal System: Continuity and Change in International Law* (Cambridge University Press, 2011), p. 57.

[102] Ibid., pp. 71–2.

[103] *Affaire des biens britanniques au Maroc espagnol* (*Spain* v. *United Kingdom*), Judgment, 1 May 1925 II UNRIAA 615-742; and *Walter Fletcher Smith Claim* (*USA* v. *Cuba*), Award, 2 May 1929, II UNRIAA 913-918, after the expropriation of parcels of land to an American citizen in Marianao Beach, by the Cuban government. The 1794 Jay Treaty also considered direct payment of claimants, although finally the claims were settled by a lump-sum agreement. See also Parlett, *The Individual in the International Legal System*, pp. 51–7.

[104] In these two cases, *Weil* and *La Abra*, individual claimants tried to compel the US Secretary of State to distribute the payment received from the Mexican government before the charges of fraud were decided, but the Supreme Court rejected such petition, on the basis that citizens of the United States were not party to the convention and the adjudication was deemed between the two states. After the fraud was considered founded by the US Court of Claims, the United States refunded the payments to Mexico. See Parlett, *The Individual in the International Legal System*, pp. 57–8.

[105] Mexico–US, Agreement 8 September 1923, Art. IX: 'The total amount awarded in all the cases decided in favour of the citizens of one country shall be deducted from the total amount awarded to the citizens of the other country and the balance shall be paid at Washington or at the City of Mexico, in gold coin or its equivalent to the Government of the country in favour of whose citizens the greater amount may have been awarded.'

After the rise of ISA, the use of binational claims commissions, mixed arbitral tribunals and diplomatic protection in general was deemed increasingly unworkable as a mechanism for protecting the interests of foreign investors in the context of contemporary international economic life,[106] disregarding them as valuable methods for settling investment disputes, and this system was gradually replaced by ISDS.

However, that does not mean that the outcome of peaceful diplomatic protection has been forgotten. Certain claims commissions or international adjudication cases are often cited in current ISDS disputes. The United States expressly recognized that fact in the *Loewen* case, pointing out that, in reality, 'investment-protection cases – including the great majority of those cited by the parties in the written and oral proceedings on liability and competence in this case – have often been decided in the context of claims espoused by States'.[107] For example, in *Asian Agricultural Products* v. *Sri Lanka*, the final award cites various tribunals and claims commissions, including those between Mexico and the United States; Greece and Turkey; and the United States and Venezuela.[108]

Two cases decided by the US–Mexico Claims Commission – although almost unrelated to foreign investment – have become relevant in current investment law, and are considered by some tribunals as 'leading cases' in determining the international minimum standard in claims arising from administrative or legislative acts of governments: the *Neer* case[109] and the *Roberts* case.[110] However, the use of the former case for such purposes has been questioned, deeming it relevant only 'in cases of failure to arrest and punish private actors of crimes against aliens'.[111]

---

[106] J. Paulsson, 'Arbitration without Privity', *ICSID Review*, 10 (1995), 232–57 at 255.

[107] *Loewen* v. *US*, Reply of the US to the Counter-Memorial of Loewen, para. 38.

[108] *Asian Agricultural Products Ltd (AAPL)* v. *Republic of Sri Lanka*, ICSID Case No ARB/ 87/3, Final Award, 27 June 1990, para. 40.

[109] *L. F. H. Neer and Pauline Neer (United States of America* v. *United Mexican States)*, 15 October 1926, IV UNRIAA 60-66, p. 61. Among many other cases, it has been cited in *Pope & Talbot.* v. Canada, Award in Respect of Damages, paras. 60, 61, 63 and *Mondev* v. *US*, Award, paras. 114-116.

[110] *Harry Roberts (United States of America* v. *United Mexican States)*, 2 November 1926, IV UNRIAA 77-81, p. 80. It has been cited in *Joseph Charles Lemire* v. *Ukraine*, ICSID Case No ARB/06/18, Award, 28 March 2011, paras. 248-249; and *SAUR International SA* v. *Republic of Argentina*, ICSID Case No ARB/04/4, Decision on Jurisdiction and Liability, 6 June 2012, para. 493, among others.

[111] J. Paulsson and G. Petrochilos, 'Neer-Ly Misled?', *ICSID Review – Foreign Investment Law Journal*, 22 (2007), 242–57.

Several discussions have taken place on whether the *Neer* 'outrageous treatment' standard developed by the US–Mexico Claims Commission in 1926 is relevant to modern-day ISA. Some tribunals have held that the minimum standard of treatment is not the *Neer* standard,[112] while others continue to hold that such a standard is relevant to the interpretation of the minimum standard of treatment, and that the threshold for finding a violation of that standard remains high.[113]

Although it is true that ISA has been a significant step towards providing individuals with access to international dispute settlement,[114] it has not been exempt from criticism. An updated role for peaceful diplomatic protection could help to improve the overall functioning of the current ISDS, working in a complementary way,[115] or provide an alternative to that system, through initiatives such as the ICS or the MIC, which could benefit from the lessons learned from similar mechanisms in previous eras.

Today, diplomatic protection is a recognized institution of customary international law that is used in a wide range of disputes, from international trade to human rights. ISA cannot be considered the sole mechanism for the settlement of investment disputes. To conclude this, would be to characterize this process for its more salient feature – the tip of the iceberg – and home states probably play a larger role in the settlement of investment disputes that take place before or instead of claims submitted to ISA. Further research is needed in those fields in order to have a clearer picture of how foreign investors truly settle investment disputes with host states on a regular basis.

[112] *Pope & Talbot. v. Canada*, Award on the Merits of Phase 2, para. 118; *Mondev v. US*, Award, paras.114-117; *ADF Group v. US*, Award, paras. 180-181; *Waste Management Inc. v. United Mexican States* [II], ICSID Case No ARB(AF)/00/3, Final Award, 30 April 2004, para. 93; *GAMI Investments, Inc. v. Government of the United Mexican States*, UNCITRAL, Final Award, 15 November 2004, para. 95; *Merrill & Ring v. Canada*, Award, para. 213; *Chemtura Corp. v. Canada*, Award, para. 215; *Gold Reserve Inc. v. Bolivarian Republic of Venezuela*, ICSID Case No ARB(AF)/09/1, Award, 22 September 2014, para. 567, among others.

[113] *Waste Management v. US* [II], Final Award, paras. 93, 98; *Thunderbird v. Mexico*, Award, para. 194; *Glamis Gold v. US*, Award, paras. 22, 612-616, 627; and *Cargill v. Mexico*, Award, para. 272, among others.

[114] F. Orrego Vicuña, *International Dispute Settlement in an Evolving Global Society: Constitutionalization, Accessibility, Privatization* (Cambridge University Press, 2004), pp. 64–5.

[115] D. Leys, 'Diplomatic Protection and Individual Rights: A Complementary Approach', *Harvard International Law Journal Online*, 57 (2016).

Yet, for all the good things that greater intervention by home states can bring to the settlement of investment disputes, it also has several short-comings. As we have seen, states have used these tools largely for their own benefit, in order to regain control as 'masters' of the IIAs, and to minimize their exposure to claims brought by foreign investors, instead of protecting them.

~

Conclusion

A Bringing Back the Home State to Investment Disputes

Possible solutions to criticisms against investor–state dispute settlement could be achieved through different 'roads', as they have been described elsewhere.[1] However, they might be troublesome (tailoring or limiting the system implies renegotiation of investment agreements) or difficult to accomplish (like negotiating a multilateral investment agreements). It is therefore worthwhile looking into other possibilities for settlement or prevention of investment disputes within the current framework of international investment law.

With more than 3,400 international investment agreements currently signed, any chance of a fundamental change in the present system in the short term seems unrealistic.[2] Plus, even countries that have exited the treaty-based arbitration system – such as Bolivia, Ecuador and Venezuela – are not returning to declare the exclusive jurisdiction of their domestic courts over investment disputes, admitting the use of regional or contract-based international arbitration for foreign investment disputes.[3]

In that sense, the larger role of home states that is provided for in existing investment agreements could be an opportunity to help to prevent investment disputes, to provide more clarity about the

---

[1] UNCTAD, 'Reform of Investor–State Dispute Settlement: In Search of a Roadmap', *IIA Issues Note* 2 (2013).

[2] M. E. Schneider, 'The Role of the State in Investor–State Arbitration: Introductory Remarks' in S. Lalani and R. Polanco Lazo (eds.), *The Role of the State in Investor–State Arbitration* (Brill/Martinus Nijhoff, 2014), p. 7.

[3] R. Polanco Lazo, 'Is There a Life for Latin American Countries after Denouncing the ICSID Convention?', *Transnational Dispute Management* 11 (2014).

interpretation of treaty provisions, to regulate the work of arbitrators, or to assist in the enforcement of ISDS awards.

As we have seen in the previous chapters, an increasing majority of IIAs give room for more active participation by the home state in investment disputes, through mechanisms of review of investment treaties, filtering of claims, joint interpretation of treaty provisions by the contracting parties, technical referrals to domestic authorities, nondisputing state party interventions and the overall regulation of the work of arbitrators or tribunals. Although most of these mechanisms would not qualify as 'diplomatic protection', as they are not triggered unilaterally by the home state, or do not focus directly on the purpose of implementing state responsibility, they have the potential to advance positions that are favourable for its national investors.

Home states will have an interest in intervening in investor–state arbitrations if they are concerned about the outcome of the dispute, because the interpretation of a particular provision of an IIA might affect its ability to implement its current or future public policies, or if it could affect a pending or parallel case based on the same grounds in another forum – such as the World Trade Organization dispute settlement system.

As we have detailed in this book, currently, the foreign investor's home state has increased its ability to participate in several stages of the dispute settlement proceedings between its national investor and the host state. However, it is rare for home states to use these mechanisms, even if they are progressively provided for in international investment agreements, besides the traditional tools of diplomatic protection provided by customary international law. When they do, home states tend to advance arguments along the same lines as or closer to the position of the host state, and not of its national investor. In some cases, states have even agreed to cooperate in investor–state controversies, promoting training in ISDS.[4]

With respect to diplomatic protection, although home states could decide to exercise this right in several ways that complement ISA, such as facilitating the settlement of the dispute via diplomatic negotiations, or assisting in the enforcement of awards through diplomatic pressure or even countermeasures, they rarely do so. Likewise, although almost every

---

[4] Colombia–Northern Triangle FTA (2007), Art. 20.3; Chile–Colombia FTA (2006), Art. 9.14.2.

investment treaty provides for a state-to-state dispute settlement mechanism over the interpretation or application of the agreement, home states do not use them and tend to not espouse investment claims when IIAs provide for the direct access of investors to ISA.

B There Is No 'Return' of Diplomatic Protection

From the analysis of the investment treaty-making and related case law of the past fifteen years, and considering the most probable reasons for the majority of home states not intervening – at least publicly – in ISDS proceedings, we can conclude that the bigger role that current IIAs provide for home states is not a 'return' of diplomatic protection in investment disputes: not even in the form of peaceful inter-state dispute settlement. This phenomenon is most likely to be explained as a way for states to regain control as the 'masters' of investment treaties, especially in matters of treaty interpretation. As Kulick has graphically depicted, today, the antagonism against the investment regime is no longer between developed or capital-exporting countries versus developing or capital-importing countries, but rather 'Contracting Parties vs. investor and the investor-state tribunal'.[5]

In the same vein, Klabbers mentions that whoever controls the process of interpretation of a treaty controls the 'truth', or at least the meaning to be given to the text subject to interpretation: 'Interpretation therewith equals power, and being able to decide on how to interpret would be tantamount to dictating the terms of a legal instrument.'[6] In that sense, 'interpretation is the continuation of treaty negotiations by other means'[7] as the meaning of a treaty is not fixed at the moment of its signature and debate on its meaning continues, even if longer provisions are drafted in order to avoid 'expansive' or unintended interpretations by the contracting parties.

New developments in this field, such as the establishment of standing investment tribunals or ombudspersons, excluding the resort to ISDS, extend this reassertion of control of states over the IIAs, limiting the

---

[5] Andreas Kulick, 'Reassertion of Control: An Introduction' in A. Kulick (ed.), *Reassertion of Control Over the Investment Treaty Regime* (2017), p. 13.

[6] J. Klabbers, 'Virtuous Interpretation' in M. Fitzmaurice, O. A. Elias and P. Merkouris (eds.), *Treaty Interpretation and the Vienna Convention on the Law of Treaties: 30 Years On* (Brill, 2010), p. 20.

[7] J. E. Alvarez, 'The Return of the State', Minn. J. Int'l L., 20 (2011), 223–64 at 234.

choice of dispute settlement and indirectly affecting their decision-making process – for example, through the appointment of judges or focal points.

The delegation made by states to arbitral tribunals on the meaning of provisions on investment standards and dispute settlement is currently being questioned even by the very states that established the investment regime, 'which are having second thoughts about the amount of sovereign "policy space" they have ceded'.[8] Many of these changes can be read as part of the pushbacks against investment liberalization that are also now advanced, not only by critics of the system (such as the Bolivarian Alliance for the Peoples of Our America (ALBA) countries), but also by former champions of it, such as Germany.[9]

Although some states are exiting the ISDS system – either totally or partially – the large majority of states are negotiating new investment treaties that give to home states more capacity to exercise some of their 'voice' options,[10] either together with host states – e.g. through joint review of the functioning of IIAs, joint interpretations and filtering of claims – or unilaterally, via non-disputing state party submissions, consultation and enforcement of awards and ISDS.

Roberts believes that we are witnessing a new era of the investment treaty system 'in which the rights and claims of both investors and treaty parties are recognized and valued, rather than one being reflexively privileged over the other'.[11] I am not so optimistic about the dawn of such a balanced novel era, but it is nevertheless undisputed that current IIAs provide for mechanisms on treaty interpretation and application that contain important investor protections while at the same time maintaining a meaningful degree of state sovereignty that can be exercised by home and host states in cases of agreement (joint interpretations and filtering of claims) or disagreement (ISDS and non-disputing state party submissions).[12]

---

[8] Ibid.

[9] Kulick, 'Reassertion of Control', 12.

[10] For a detailed application of Albert O. Hirschman's 'Exit, Voice, and Loyalty' rubric in investor–state disputes, see A. T. Katselas, 'Exit, Voice, and Loyalty in Investment Treaty Arbitration', Nebraska Law Review, 93 (2014), 313–69.

[11] A. Roberts, 'State-to-State Investment Treaty Arbitration: A Hybrid Theory of Interdependent Rights and Shared Interpretive Authority', Harv. Int'l L.J., 55 (2014), 1 at 5.

[12] Ibid., 27–8.

Although Roberts is right to affirm that the system of settlement of investment disputes is a hybrid one, in which ISDS and the state-to-state disputes settlement system coexist, more than striking a balance between both sides of the system with the purpose of respecting both state sovereignty and investment protection, home and host states seems to be more interested in 'damage control', focused on limiting the situations in which a state might be held internationally responsible in future investment disputes due to breaches of the same investment treaties, and keeping a wider margin for states to use their 'right to regulate'.

Maybe this is the clearest example of what the intention of states really is. The 'right to regulate' has been subject of several academic studies and is increasingly included in investment treaties (notably by EFTA and the EU),[13] as one of the ways of counterbalancing the seemingly excessive rights that the IIAs have granted to foreign investors.[14] But behind this well-intended idea, there is also an important risk that states use that 'extra' space not for legitimate regulatory purposes, or even in violation of individual rights. I believe that a more balanced approach would be to consider that states have the 'duty' and not a 'right' to regulate. A 'duty' implies that a state has to regulate when needed, and shall refrain from it when unnecessary. However, most importantly, a state can be held accountable for not fulfilling a duty, whereas a state could, as a matter of sovereignty, decide to exercise a right or not, as happens with diplomatic protection.

An alternative explanation would be that states are 'fixing' the system in response to criticisms against the investment regime formulated by civil society. In fairness, several improvements in transparency and partial access to the dispute through *amicus* briefs have been introduced in recent years, but they do not have the depth or breadth of the

---

[13] CETA, Art. 8.9; Guatemala–Trinidad and Tobago BIT (2013), Art. 2; New Zealand–Taiwan Province of China ECA (2013), Ch. 12, Art. 1; Bosnia and Herzegovina–EFTA FTA (2013), Art. 35; EFTA–Costa Rica–Panama FTA (2013), Art. 5.6; EFTA–Montenegro FTA (2011), Art. 33; EFTA–Hong Kong FTA, Art. 4.6; EFTA–Peru FTA (2010), Art. 5.6; EFTA–Ukraine FTA, Art. 4.8; Senegal–Turkey BIT (2010), Art. 4; Colombia–EFTA FTA (2008), Art. 5.6; SADC Investment Protocol (2006), Art. 14; France–Uganda BIT (2003), Art. 1.6. It is also provided for in the EU–Singapore IPA (April 2018), Art. 2.2.1, and the EU–Vietnam IPA (2018), Ch. 3, Art. 2.2.

[14] See C. Titi, *The Right to Regulate in International Investment Law* (Beck/Hart, 2014); L. W. Mouyal, *International Investment Law and the Right to Regulate: A Human Rights Perspective* (Routledge, 2016).

mechanisms that states now have, and local populations largely remain unheard.[15]

Thus, the current development of inter-state mechanisms in investment disputes might be also explained by the more selfish interest of states in regaining control over their treaties or, more precisely, by the interest that they have in limiting the delegation given to investor–state arbitral tribunals on the interpretation of those agreements. As Kulick pointed out, one of the main factors of the reassertion of control by states is that 'old' home states are now becoming 'new' respondent states in ISDS and some 'old' host states have experienced a change in position and will increasingly find themselves being 'new' home states.[16]

This phenomenon cannot be analysed in isolation. Evidence of this operation of 'recovery' of investment treaties from states can be found in other tools of treaty-making, such as the detailed definition of standards of protection, carve-outs, exceptions and exclusion of claims. Several investment treaties are now longer than before and, as Álvarez rightly points out, 'the length of a treaty is often inversely related to the rights that it accords'.[17] Even countries that led the movement in favour of wide international protection of investors and investment – such as the United States, the EU, Canada or Germany – now appear to be driving in the opposite direction, especially when investment treaties are agreed between developed countries, where a virtual return to the Calvo doctrine might take place, as was evidenced in the debate between the EU and the United States on the inclusion of ISA in the Transatlantic Trade and Investment Partnership (TTIP).[18]

I believe that, more than a return to diplomatic protection in investor–state disputes, we are witnessing a return of inter-state protection, restricting the space of arbitral tribunals to interpret investment agreements, or directly replacing this system for another one with larger state space and control – such as the Investment Court System approach. This phenomenon is not necessarily negative, but we must consider its potential implications in the current discussion about the transformation and reform of the investment regime. In its more common connotation, 'balance' means an even distribution of weight, enabling something to

---

[15] N. M. Perrone, 'The International Investment Regime and Local Populations: Are the Weakest Voices Unheard?', *Transnational Legal Theory*, 7 (2016), 383–405.

[16] Kulick, 'Reassertion of Control', 14.

[17] Alvarez, 'The Return of the State', 234.

[18] R. Polanco Lazo, 'The No of Tokyo Revisited: Or How Developed Countries Learned to Start Worrying and Love the Calvo Doctrine', *ICSID Review*, 30 (2015), 172.

remain upright and steady. We need to consider what we have in both sides of the balance, before changing the scales.

We can also think about other ways of balancing. With its imperfections, it is important to underscore the role of investment treaty arbitration in recognizing the right of foreign investors to present claims not only for alleged failures in the judicial system of the host state but also for any alleged failures in administrative decision-making.[19] Instead of pointing out the different treatment that this implies for foreign investors in relation to domestic investors, perhaps we should also consider recognizing for domestic investors, citizens and groups within the host state the same opportunities to file complaints about how their government treats them.[20]

---

[19] C. McLachlan, 'Investment Treaties and General International Law', *International & Comparative Law Quarterly*, 57 (2008), 362.

[20] K. Nadakavukaren Schefer, 'State Powers and ISDS' in S. Lalani and R. Polanco Lazo (eds.), *The Role of the State in Investor–State Arbitration* (Brill/Martinus Nijhoff, 2014), p. 3.

BIBLIOGRAPHY

Aaronson, S. A., 'A Fresh Approach to International Investment Rules' (2011)

Adriaensen, J., 'The Future of EU Trade Negotiations: What Has Been Learned from CETA and TTIP?', November 2017: http://blogs.lse.ac.uk/europpblog/ (accessed 28 February 2018)

Aguilar Álvarez, G. and W. W. Park, 'The New Face of Investment Arbitration: NAFTA Chapter 11', Yale J. Int'l L., 28 (2003), 365

Alford, R., 'The Convergence of International Trade and Investment Arbitration', *Santa Clara Journal of International Law*, 12 (2014), 35

Alschner, W., 'The Return of the Home State and the Rise of "Embedded" Investor–State Arbitration' in S. Lalani and R. Polanco (eds.), *The Role of the State in Investor–State Arbitration* (Brill/Martinus Nijhoff, 2014)

Alvarez, J. E., 'The Return of the State', Minn. J. Int'l L., 20 (2011), 223–64

Álvarez Ávila, G., 'Autopista Concesionada de Venezuela, C.A. v. Bolivarian Republic of Venezuela (ICSID Case No. ARB/00/5): Introductory Note', *ICSID Review*, 16 (2001), 465–8

Amerasinghe, C. F., *Diplomatic Protection* (Oxford University Press, 2008)

American Task Force Argentina (ATFA), 'ATFA Applauds UK Government's Decision to Oppose Future Lending to Argentina', February 2013: www.atfa.org /category/homepage/page/2/ (accessed 14 March 2018)

Antonietti, A., 'The 2006 Amendments to the ICSID Rules and Regulations and the Additional Facility Rules', *ICSID Review – Foreign Investment Law Journal*, 21 (2006), 427–48

Arbitration Institute of the Stockholm Chamber of Commerce, '2017 Arbitration Rules', January 2017: www.sccinstitute.com/media/168084/arbitration-rule s_eng_17_final.pdf (accessed 5 January 2018)

Association for International Arbitration, *Alternative Dispute Resolution in the Energy Sector* (Maklu, 2009)

Auer, P. D., 'The Competency of Mixed Arbitral Tribunals', *Transactions of the Grotius Society*, 13 (1927), xvii–xxx

b92.net, 'Lithuania Won't Block Serbia's EU Pathway', March 2013: www.b92 .net/eng/news/politics.php?yyyy=2013&mm=03&dd=28&nav_id=85396 (accessed 19 January 2018)

Baldi, M., 'Letter from Swiss Secretariat for Economic Affairs to Antonio R. Parra, ICSID Deputy Secretary-General, 1 October 2003', *Mealey's International Arbitration Reports*, 19 (2004), E1–2

Balkan Insight, 'Lithuania Ratifies Serbia's EU Stability Agreement', June 2013: www.balkaninsight.com/en/article/lithuania-ratifies-serbia-s-saa (accessed 19 January 2018)

Bank, R. and F. Foltz, 'Lump Sum Agreements', January 2009: http://opil.ouplaw .com/view/10.1093/law:epil/9780199231690/law-9780199231690-e842? rskey=2mFiG0&result=1&prd=EPIL (accessed 15 May 2018)

Bantekas, I., 'Corporate Social Responsibility in International Law', B.U. Int'l L.J., 22 (2004), 309

Barratt, J. W. and M. N. Michael, 'The "Automatic" Enforcement of ICSID Awards: The Elephant in the Room?', *The European, Middle Eastern and African Arbitration Review* (2014)

Barreiro Lemos, L. and D. Campello, 'The Non-Ratification of Bilateral Investment Treaties in Brazil: A Story of Conflict in a Land of Cooperation', *Review of International Political Economy*, 22 (2015), 1055–86

Barston, R. P., *Modern Diplomacy* (Routledge, 2014)

Bello, A., *Principios de derecho de jentes* (Imprenta de la Opinión, 1832; Reimpresión Valentín Espinal, 1837)

Ben Hamida, W., 'The First Arab Investment Court Decision', *Journal of World Investment & Trade*, 7 (2006), 699–721

Bernasconi-Osterwalder, N. and H. Mann, 'A Response to the European Commission's December 2013 Document "Investment Provisions in the EU–Canada Free Trade Agreement (CETA)"' (2014)

Bernasconi-Osterwalder, N. and D. Rosert, *Investment Treaty Arbitration: Opportunities to Reform Arbitral Rules and Processes* (2014)

Bhattacharya, U., N. Galpin and B. Haslem, 'The Home Court Advantage in International Corporate Litigation', *Journal of Law and Economics*, 50 (2007), 625–60

Bishop, R. D., J. Crawford and W. M. Reisman, *Foreign Investment Disputes: Cases, Materials, and Commentary* (Kluwer Law International, 2005)

Borchard, E., *The Diplomatic Protection of Citizens Abroad* (New York, 1914)

Borchard, E., *The Diplomatic Protection of Citizens Abroad: Or, The Law of International Claims* (Banks Law Publishing Company, 1915)

Bottini, G., *Extending Responsibilities in International Investment Law. E15 Initiative* (Geneva: International Centre for Trade and Sustainable Development (ICTSD) and World Economic Forum, 2015)

Bovey, J., 'Secret Diplomacy Is the Best Kind' (1990)

Briggs, H. W., 'The Settlement of Mexican Claims Act of 1942', *American Journal of International Law*, 37 (1943), 222–32

Broches, A., 'Awards Rendered Pursuant to the ICSID Convention: Binding Force, Finality, Recognition, Enforcement, Execution', *ICSID Review*, 2 (1987), 287–334

Brower, C. N. and S. Blanchard, 'What's in a Meme? The Truth about Investor–State Arbitration: Why It Need Not, and Must Not, Be Repossessed by States', Colum. J. Transnat'l L. 52 (2014), 689–896

Brower, II, C. H., 'Investor–State Disputes Under NAFTA: The Empire Strikes Back', Colum. J. Transnat'l L., 40 (2002), 43–88

Brower, II, C. H., 'Why the FTC Notes of Interpretation Constitute a Partial Amendment of NAFTA Article 1105', *Virginia Journal of International Law*, 46 (2005), 347

Brower, II, C. H., 'Obstacles and Pathways to Consideration of the Public Interest in Investment Treaty Disputes' in K. P. Sauvant (ed.), *Yearbook on International Investment Law & Policy* (Oxford University Press, 2009), pp. 347–78

Brown, C., *Commentaries on Selected Model Investment Treaties* (Oxford University Press, 2013)

Burgueno, C., 'US, Spain and Germany Vote against Argentina at the IADB' (2012)

Calvet de Magalhães, J., *The Pure Concept of Diplomacy* (Greenwood Publishing Group, 1988)

Calvo, C., *Derecho Internacional Teórico y Práctico de Europa y América* (D'Amyot, 1868), vol. i

Canada, 'Statement of Canada on Open Hearings in NAFTA Chapter Eleven Arbitrations' (2003)

Canada–Chile Free Trade Commission, 'Notes of Interpretation of Certain Chapter G Provisions', October 2002: www.international.gc.ca/trade-agreements -accords-commerciaux/agr-acc/chile-chili/ccftacommission.aspx?lang=eng (accessed 13 January 2018)

Canada–Chile Free Trade Commission, 'Declaration of the Free Trade Commission on Non-Disputing party participation', November 2004: www .international.gc.ca/trade-agreements-accords-commerciaux/agr-acc/chile-chili/CCFTA-decla-ALECC.aspx?lang=eng (accessed 13 January 2018)

Canada–Chile Free Trade Commission, 'Decision of the Canada-Chile Free Trade Commission, Interpretation of Article G-10', April 2010: www.international.gc .ca/trade-agreements-accords-commerciaux/agr-acc/chile-chili/interpreta tion-indirect.aspx?lang=eng (accessed 13 January 2018)

Canada, EU, 'Joint Interpretative Declaration on the Comprehensive Economic and Trade Agreement (CETA) between Canada and the European Union and Its Member States', October 2016: http://data.consilium.europa.eu/doc/docu ment/ST-13541-2016-INIT/en/pdf (accessed 16 January 2018)

Casas, M., 'Nationalities of Convenience, Personal Jurisdiction, and Access to Investor–State Dispute Settlement', *New York University Journal of International Law and Politics*, 49 (2016), 63–128

Cate, A., 'Non-Disputing State Party Participation in Investor–State Arbitration under CAFTA–DR', July 2011: http://kluwerarbitrationblog.com/blog/2011/07/01/non-disputing-state-party-participation-in-investor-state-arbitration-under-cafta-dr/ (accessed 25 March 2018)

Charlotin, D., 'Looking Back: German Investor, Franz Sedelmayer, Was Early-Adopter of Investment Treaty Arbitration, but Had to Engage in Decade-Long Assets Hunt against Russia', August 2017: www.iareporter.com/articles/looking-back-german-investor-franz-sedelmayer-was-early-adopter-of-investment-treaty-arbitration-but-had-to-engage-in-decade-long-assets-hunt/ (accessed 21 February 2018)

Clermont, K. M. and T. Eisenberg, 'Xenophilia in American Courts', *Harvard Law Review*, 109 (1996), 1120–43

Clermont, K. M. and T. Eisenberg, 'Xenophilia or Xenophobia in US Courts? Before and After 9/11', *Journal of Empirical Legal Studies*, 4 (2007), 441–64

Coe Jr, J. J., 'Taking Stock of NAFTA Chapter 11 in Its Tenth Year: An Interim Sketch of Selected Themes, Issues, and Methods', *Vand. J. Transnat'l L.*, 36 (2003), 1381

Cottier, T., P. Aerni, B. Karapinar, S. Matteotti, J. de Sépibus and A. Shingal, 'The Principle of Common Concern and Climate Change', *Archiv des Völkerrechts*, 52 (2014), 293–324

Cotula, L., *Foreign Investment, Law and Sustainable Development: A Handbook on Agriculture and Extractive Industries* (2016)

Coyle, J., 'The Treaty of Friendship, Commerce, and Navigation in the Modern Era', *Columbia Journal of Transnational Law*, 51 (2013), 302

Crawford, J., *Brownlie's Principles of Public International Law*, 8th edn (Oxford University Press, 2012)

Cuthbert, Joseph, *Diplomatic Protection and Nationality: The Commonwealth of Nations* (Northumberland Press, 1968)

Dawson, F. G., 'The Influence of Andres Bello on Latin-American Perceptions of Non-Intervention and State Responsibility', *British Yearbook of International Law*, 57 (1987), 253–315

de Vattel, E., *The Law of Nations, or, Principles of the Law of Nature, Applied to the Conduct and Affairs of Nations and Sovereigns, with Three Early Essays on the Origin and Nature of Natural Law and on Luxury* (Liberty Fund, 2008)

Desierto, D. A., 'Joint Decisions by State Parties: Fair Control of Tribunal Interpretations?', June 2012: http://arbitrationblog.kluwerarbitration.com/2012/06/08/joint-decisions-by-state-parties-fair-control-of-tribunal-interpretations/ (accessed 17 February 2018)

Dolzer, R. and C. Schreuer, *Principles of International Investment Law* (Oxford University Press, 2012)

Dolzer, R. and M. Stevens, *Bilateral Investment Treaties* (Martinus Nijhoff Publishers, 1995)

Donovan, D. F., 'Abaclat and Others v Argentine Republic as a Collective Claims Proceeding', *ICSID Review*, 27 (2012), 261–7

Douglas, Z., 'The Hybrid Foundations of Investment Treaty Arbitration', *British Yearbook of International Law*, 74 (2003), 151–289

Douglas, Z., *The International Law of Investment Claims* (Cambridge University Press, 2009)

Dugan, C. F., D. Wallace Jr, N. D. Rubins and B. Sabahi, *Investor–State Arbitration* (Oxford University Press, 2008)

Dugard, J., 'Diplomatic Protection', May 2009: http://opil.ouplaw.com/view/10.1093/law:epil/9780199231690/law-9780199231690-e1028 (accessed 20 August 2018)

Dugard, J., 'First Report of the Special Rapporteur on Diplomatic Protection', *Yearbook of the International Law Commission 2000* (New York: United Nations Publications, 2000), pp. 35–72

Dugard, J., 'Second Report of the Special Rapporteur on Diplomatic Protection', *Yearbook of the International Law Commission 2001* (New York: United Nations, 2009), pp. 97–114

Dumberry, P., *The Fair and Equitable Treatment Standard: A Guide to NAFTA Case Law on Article 1105* (Kluwer Law International, 2013)

Dunn, F. S., *The Protection of Nationals: A Study in the Application of International Law* (The Johns Hopkins Press, 1932)

Eberhardt, P., *The Zombie ISDS* (Corporate Europe Observatory, 2016)

Eberhardt, P. and C. Olivet, *Profiting from Injustice. How Law Firms, Arbitrators and Financiers Are Fuelling an Investment Arbitration Boom* (Corporate Europe Observatory (CEO) and the Transnational Institute (TNI), 2012)

Echandi, R., 'Complementing Investor–State Dispute Resolution: A Conceptual Framework for Investor–State Conflict Management': Prospects in International Investment Law and Policy (Cambridge University Press, 2013)

Energy Charter Secretariat, *The Energy Charter Treaty and Related Documents* (Energy Charter Secretariat, 2004)

Energy Charter Secretariat, 'About the Charter', https://energycharter.org/process/energy-charter-treaty-1994/energy-charter-treaty/ (accessed 23 February 2018)

Esquirol, J. L., 'Latin America' in B. Fassbender, A. Peters (eds.), *The Oxford Handbook of the History of International Law* (Oxford University Press, 2012), pp. 553–77

European Commission, 'A Future Multilateral Investment Court', December 2016: http://europa.eu/rapid/press-release_MEMO-16-4350_en.htm (accessed 20 January 2018)

European Commission, 'A Multilateral Investment Court. State of the Union 2017', September 2017: http://trade.ec.europa.eu/doclib/docs/2017/september/tradoc_156042.pdf (accessed 23 February 2018)

European Commission, 'Communication from the Commission to the Council, the European Parliament, the European Economic and Social Committee and the Committee of the Regions towards a Comprehensive European

International Investment Policy', July 2010: http://trade.ec.europa.eu/doclib /docs/2010/july/tradoc_146307.pdf (accessed 3 February 2018)

European Commission, 'Fact sheet on investment provisions in the EU–Singapore Free Trade Agreement' (2014)

European Commission, 'Online Public Consultation on Investment Protection and Investor-to-State Dispute Settlement (ISDS) in the Transatlantic Trade and Investment Partnership Agreement (TTIP)' (2014)

European Commission and Directorate-General for Trade, *Trade for All: Towards a More Responsible Trade and Investment Policy* (Publications Office, 2015)

European Commission – Trade, 'A New EU Trade Agreement with Japan', August 2017: http://trade.ec.europa.eu/doclib/docs/2017/july/tradoc_155684.pdf (accessed 23 February 2018)

European Commission – Trade, 'Singapore', September 2017: http://ec.europa.eu /trade/policy/countries-and-regions/countries/singapore/ (accessed 19 February 2018)

Ewing-Chow, M. and J. J. Losari, 'Which Is to Be the Master?: Extra-Arbitral Interpretative Procedures for IIAs', *Transnational Dispute Management*, 11 (2014), 1–20

Fach Gómez, K., 'Latin America and ICSID: David versus Goliath?' (2010)

Fauchald, O. K., 'The Legal Reasoning of ICSID Tribunals – An Empirical Analysis', *European Journal of International Law*, 19 (2008), 301–64

Federation of German Industries (BDI), Background: Facts and Figures. International Investment Agreements and Investor–State Dispute Settlement (2014)

Feldman, M., 'Joint Interpretation under a Divided TPP Investment Chapter' in W. Shan and J. Su (eds.), *China and International Investment Law: Twenty Years of ICSID Membership* (Martinus Nijhoff Publishers, 2014), pp. 408–28

Feller, A. H., *The Mexican Claims Commissions, 1923–1934: A Study in the Law and Procedure of International Tribunals* (Macmillan, 1935)

Forcese, C., 'Shelter from the Storm: Rethinking Diplomatic Protection of Dual Nationals in Modern International Law', *George Washington International Law Review*, 37 (2005), 469

Foreign Affairs Trade and Development Canada Government of Canada, 'Cases Filed against the Government of Canada', January 2018: www.international .gc.ca/trade-agreements-accords-commerciaux/topics-domaines/disp-diff /gov.aspx?lang=eng (accessed 20 February 2018)

Fortese, F. and L. E. Peterson, 'Full Light Is Shed on the Reasons for ICSID's Rejection of Argentine Efforts to Remove Arbitrators in Repsol Case' (2013)

Gaillard, E., 'Investment Treaty Arbitration and Jurisdiction Over Contract Claims – the SGS Cases Considered' in T. Weiler (ed.), *International Investment Law and Arbitration: Leading Cases from the ICSID, NAFTA, Bilateral Treaties and Customary International Law* (Cameron May, 2005), pp. 325–46

Gallagher, K. P. and E. Shrestha, 'Investment Treaty Arbitration and Developing Countries: A Re-Appraisal', *Global Development and Environment Institute. Working Paper No 11–01* (2011), 1–12

Garcia-Bolivar, O. E., 'Sovereignty vs. Investment Protection: Back to Calvo?', *ICSID Review*, 24 (2009), 464–88

Garcia-Mora, Manuel R. 'The Calvo Clause in Latin American Constitutions and International Law', Marq. L. Rev., 33 (1949) 205

Garner, B. A., *Black's Law Dictionary, Standard Ninth Edition*, 9th edn (West, 2009)

Gaukrodger, D., 'Investment Treaties as Corporate Law: Shareholder Claims and Issues of Consistency', *OECD Working Papers on International Investment* (2013)

Gaukrodger, D. and K. Gordon, 'Investor–State Dispute Settlement: A Scoping Paper of the Investment Policy Community', *OECD Working Papers on International Investment*, No 2012/3 (2012)

Gazzini, T., 'Nigeria and Morocco Move Towards a "New Generation" of Bilateral Investment Treaties', May 2017: www.ejiltalk.org/nigeria-and-mor occo-move-towards-a-new-generation-of-bilateral-investment-treaties/ (accessed 17 January 2018)

Gertz, G., 'The International Investment Regime Is Stronger Than You Think. GEG Working Paper 2015/96', *The Global Economic Governance Programme, University of Oxford* (2015)

Gertz, G., S. Jandhyala and L. S. Poulsen, 'Conference "The Political Economy of International Investment Agreements", Deutsches Institut für Entwicklungspolitik – World Trade Institute. Bonn, 8–9 December 2014' (2014)

Gertz, G. S. Jandhyala and L. S. Poulsen, 'Has Investor–State Arbitration Depoliticized Investment Disputes?', p. 10.

Gharavi, H. G., *The International Effectiveness of the Annulment of an Arbitral Award* (Kluwer Law International, 2002)

Giardina, A., 'L'exécution des sentences du Centre international pour le règlement des différends relatifs aux investissements', *Revue critique de droit international privé*, 712 (1982), 273–93

Gordon, K. and J. Pohl, *Investment Treaties over Time – Treaty Practice and Interpretation in a Changing World* (2015)

Government of the Republic of Serbia. European Integration Office, 'Ratification of the SAA', January 2015: www.seio.gov.rs/serbia-and-eu/ratification-of-the -saa.61.html (accessed 9 February 2018)

Grewe, W. G., *The Epochs of International Law*, revised edn (De Gruyter, 2000)

Guyomar, G., 'L'arbitrage concernant les rapports entre Etats et particuliers', *Annuaire français de droit international*, 5 (1959), 333–54

Guzman, A. T., 'Why LDCs Sign Treaties That Hurt Them: Explaining the Popularity of Bilateral Investment Treaties', *Virginia Journal of International Law*, 38 (1998), 639–88

Hepburn, J., 'As Merits Hearings Approach in Chevron v. Ecuador BIT Arbitration, Latest Legal Arguments Come into Focus', December 2014: www.iareporter.com/articles/20141229_1 (accessed 6 February 2018)

Hepburn, J., 'CIS Economic Court Issues Authoritative Interpretation of Investment Treaty at Root of Series of Investor–State Arbitrations', September 2014: www.iareporter.com/articles/20140923_2 (accessed 9 February 2018)

Hepburn, J. and L. E. Peterson, 'US–Ecuador Inter-State Investment Treaty Award Released to Parties; Tribunal Members Part Ways on Key Issues', October 2012: www.iareporter.com/articles/20121030_1 (accessed 13 February 2018)

Hershey, A. S., 'The Calvo and Drago Doctrines', *American Journal of International Law*, 1 (1907), 26–45

Hindelang, S. and M. Krajewski (eds.), *Shifting Paradigms in International Investment Law: More Balanced, Less Isolated, Increasingly Diversified*, 1st edn (Oxford University Press, 2016)

Hindelang, S. and C.-P. Sassenrath, *The Investment Chapters of the EU's International Trade and Investment Agreements in a Comparative Perspective* (Publications Office, 2015)

Holtzman, H. M. and B. E. Shifm, *Permanent Court of Arbitration* (United Nations, 2003), vol. 1, 3

Hooge, N. T., *Responsibility to Protect (R2P) as Duty to Protect?: Reassessing the Traditional Doctrine of Diplomatic Protection in Light of Modern Developments in International Law* (University of Toronto, 2010)

House of Commons (UK), 'House of Commons Hansard Written Answers', December 2013: www.publications.parliament.uk/pa/cm201213/cmhansrd/cm130212/text/130212w0004.htm#13021285002895 (accessed 14 March 2018)

Howse, R., 'Courting the Critics of Investor–State Dispute Settlement: The EU Proposal for a Judicial System for Investment Disputes', Fall 2015: https://cdn-media.web-view.net/i/fjj3t288ah/Courting_the_Criticsdraft1.pdf (accessed 20 January 2018)

Huerta Goldman, J. A., A. Romanetti and F. X. Stirnimann, 'Cross-Cutting Observations on Compositions of Tribunals' in J. A. Huerta Goldman, A. Romanetti and F. X. Stirnimann (eds.), *WTO Litigation, Investment Arbitration, and Commercial Arbitration* (Wolters Kluwer Law & Business, Kluwer Law International, 2013), pp. 129–34

Hunter, M. and A. Barbuk, 'Procedural Aspects of Non-Disputing Party Interventions in Chapter 11 Arbitrations', *Asper Review of International Business and Trade Law*, 3 (2003), 151

ILC, 'Draft Articles on Diplomatic Protection, with Commentaries. Report of the International Law Commission, 58th Session (A/61/10)', *Yearbook of the International Law Commission*, II (2006), 22–100

ILC, 'Draft Articles on Responsibility of States for Internationally Wrongful Acts, with commentaries. Report of the International Law Commission, 53rd session (A/56/10)', *Yearbook of the International Law Commission*, II (2008), 31–143

Indlekofer, M., *International Arbitration and the Permanent Court of Arbitration* (Kluwer Law International, 2013)

InSerbia News, 'Dacic: I Expect Lithuania to Ratify SAA', April 2013: http://inserbia.info/today/2013/04/dacic-i-expect-lithuania-will-ratify-saa/ (accessed 9 February 2018)

Inside Trade, 'U.S. Rejects Proposal Brought by 58 Members to Fill WTO Appellate Body Slots', January 2018: https://insidetrade.com/daily-news/us-rejects-propo sal-brought-58-members-fill-wto-appellate-body-slots (accessed 26 February 2018)

International Bar Association, *Guidelines on Conflicts of Interest in International Arbitration* (2014)

International Centre for Settlement of Investment Disputes (ICSID), 'Contracting States and Measures Taken by Them for the Purpose of the Convention. ICSID/ 8. Notifications Concerning Classes of Disputes Considered Suitable or Unsuitable for Submission to the Center', June 2017: https://icsid.worldbank .org/en/Documents/icsiddocs/ICSID%208-Contracting%20States%20and% 20Measures%20Taken%20by%20Them%20for%20the%20Purpose%20of% 20the%20Convention.pdf (accessed 26 February 2018)

International Centre for Settlement of Investment Disputes (ICSID), *History of the ICSID Convention* (International Centre for Settlement of Investment Disputes, 1968), vol. ii

International Centre for Settlement of Investment Disputes (ICSID), 'ICSID Additional Facility Rules (2006)', April 2006: https://icsid.worldbank.org/en /Pages/icsiddocs/ICSID-Additional-Facility-Rules.aspx (accessed 5 January 2018)

International Centre for Settlement of Investment Disputes (ICSID), 'Members of the Panels of Conciliators and Arbitrators', February 2018: https://icsid.world bank.org/en/Documents/icsiddocs/ICSID%2010%20-%20Latest.pdf (accessed 18 February 2018)

International Centre for Settlement of Investment Disputes (ICSID), 'Model Clauses Relating to the Convention on the Settlement of Investment Disputes Designed for Use in Bilateral Investment Agreements [September 1969]', *International Legal Materials*, 8 (1969), 1341–52

International Centre for Trade and Sustainable Development (ICTSD), 'US Suspends Argentina from Trade Preference Scheme', *Bridges Weekly Trade News Digest*, 16 (2012)

International Chamber of Commerce (ICC), 'ICC Rules of Arbitration', January 2012: www.iccwbo.org/Products-and-Services/Arbitration-and-ADR /Arbitration/Rules-of-arbitration/Download-ICC-Rules-of-Arbitration/ICC -Rules-of-Arbitration-in-several-languages/ (accessed 5 January 2018)

International Court of Justice, *The Permanent Court of International Justice, 1922– 2012* (United Nations, 2015)

International Institute for Sustainable Development, H. L. Mann, K. von Moltke, L. E. Peterson and A. Cosbey, 'IISD Model International Agreement on Investment for Sustainable Development' (2005)

International Labour Organization (ILO), 'Translating the 2030 Agenda for Sustainable Development into Action: Integrating Trade, Investment and Decent Work Policies. Background Note' (Nairobi, Kenya, 2016)

International Labour Organization (ILO), 'Tripartite Declaration of Principles concerning Multinational Enterprises and Social Policy (MNE Declaration, 5th ed.)', 2017: www.ilo.org/empent/areas/mne-declaration/lang–en/index .htm (accessed 9 February 2018)

International Organization for Standardization, 'ISO 26000 – Social Responsibility', 2010: www.iso.org/iso/home/standards/iso26000.htm (accessed 18 January 2018)

Investment Arbitration Reporter (IAReporter), 'Repsol–Argentina Settlement Agreement, April 2014', April 2014: www.iareporter.com/downloads /20140430 (accessed 20 August 2017)

Iran–United States Claims Tribunal, 'Tribunal Rules of Procedure' (1983)

Ishikawa, T., 'Keeping Interpretation in Investment Treaty Arbitration "on Track": The Role of States Parties', *Transnational Dispute Management*, 11 (2014)

Jacob, M., 'Investments, Bilateral Treaties', May 2011: http://opil.ouplaw.com /view/10.1093/law:epil/9780199231690/law-9780199231690-e1061 (accessed 13 January 2018)

Japan Bank for International Cooperation (JBIC), 'Japan Bank for International Cooperation Annual Report 2016': www.jbic.go.jp/wp-content/uploads/page /2016/12/53051/2016E_00_full.pdf (accessed 15 May 2018)

Jenča, M., 'The Concept of Preventive Diplomacy and Its Application by the United Nations in Central Asia', *Security and Human Rights*, 24 (2013), 183–94

Jentsch, V., *The Role of Bilateral Investment Treaties (BITs) in Switzerland: Importance and Alternatives from an Entrepreneurial Perspective* (2009)

Johnson, L. and M. Razbaeva, 'State Control Over Treaty Interpretation' (2014)

Johnson, O. T. and C. H. Gibson, 'The Objections of Developed and Developing States to Investor–State Dispute Settlement and What They Are Doing about Them' in A. W. Rovine (ed.), *Contemporary Issues in International Arbitration and Mediation: The Fordham Papers 2013* (2014), pp. 253–69

Johnson Jr, O. T. and J. Gimblett, 'From Gunboats to BITs: Evolution of Modern International Investment Law', *Yearbook on International Investment Law & Policy 2010–2011* (2012), 649–92

Jonas, P. M., 'United States Citizens vs. Mexico, 1821–1848', unpublished PhD thesis, Marquette University (1989)

Joubin-Bret, A., 'Is There a Need for Sanctions in International Investment Arbitration?', *Proceedings of the Annual Meeting (American Society of International Law)*, 106 (2012), 130–3

Juratowitch, B., 'The Relationship between Diplomatic Protection and Investment Treaties', *ICSID Review*, 23 (2008), 10–35

Katselas, A. T., 'Exit, Voice, and Loyalty in Investment Treaty Arbitration', *Nebraska Law Review*, 93 (2014), 313–69

Kaufmann-Kohler, G., 'Interpretive Powers of the Free Trade Commission and the Rule of Law' Fifteen Years of NAFTA (JurisNet, LLC, 2011), pp. 175–94

Kaufmann-Kohler, G., 'Non-Disputing State Submissions in Investment Arbitration' in L. Boisson de Chazournes, M. G. Kohen and J. E. Viñuales (eds.), *Diplomatic and Judicial Means of Dispute Settlement* (Martinus Nijhoff Publishers, 2012), pp. 307–26

Kho, S., M. Bate, A. Yanovich, B. Casey and J. Strauss, *The EU TTIP–Investment Court Proposal and the WTO Dispute Settlement System: Comparing Apples and Oranges?* (Cambridge, MA, 2016)

Kho, S. S., A. Yanovich, B. R. Casey and J. Strauss, 'The EU–TTIP Investment Court Proposal and the WTO Dispute Settlement System: Comparing Apples and Oranges?', *ICSID Review – Foreign Investment Law Journal*, 32 (2017), 326–45

Kinderman, D., 'Global and EU-Level Corporate Social Responsibility: Dynamism, Growth, and Conflict' in H. Backhaus-Maul, M. Kunze and S. Nährlich (eds.), *Gesellschaftliche Verantwortung von Unternehmen in Deutschland* (Springer Fachmedien Wiesbaden, 2018), pp. 101–13

Kinnear, M., 'Letter from Meg Kinnear to the Tribunal in Pope & Talbot Inc. v. Canada (NAFTA/UNICTRAL), 1 October 2011 – Exhibit A of the Submission of the United States of America in Chemtura Corporation v. Canada, 31 July 2009'

Kinnear, M., A. Bjorklund and J. F. G. Hannaford, *Investment Disputes Under NAFTA. An Annotated Guide to NAFTA Chapter 11*, looseleaf edn (Kluwer Law International, 2006)

Kinsella, N. S. and N. Rubins, *International Investment, Political Risk, and Dispute Resolution: A Practitioner's Guide* (Oxford University Press, 2005)

Klabbers, J., 'On Rationalism in Politics: Interpretation of Treaties and the World Trade Organization', *Nordic Journal of International Law*, 74 (2005), 405

Klabbers, J., 'Virtuous Interpretation' in M. Fitzmaurice, O. A. Elias and P. Merkouris (eds.), *Treaty Interpretation and the Vienna Convention on the Law of Treaties: 30 Years on* (Brill, 2010), pp. 17–37

Kluwer Law International, 'Kluwer Arbitration', February 2018: www.kluwerarbitration.com/ (accessed 28 February 2018)

Knudsen, J. S., *Bringing the State Back In? US and UK Government Regulation of Corporate Social Responsibility (CSR) in International Business* (2014)

Kolo, A., 'Tax "Veto" as a Special Jurisdictional and Substantive Issue in Investor-State Arbitration: Need for Reassessment?', *Suffolk Transnational Law Review*, 32 (2009), 475

Kovick, D. and C. Rees, 'International Support for Effective Dispute Resolution Between Companies and Their Stakeholders: Assessing Needs, Interests, and Models. Working Paper No. 63', June 2011: www.hks.harvard.edu/m-rcbg /CSRI/publications/workingpaper_63_rees%20kovick_june%202011.pdf (accessed 18 January 2018)

Kriebaum, U., 'The PCIJ and the Protection of Foreign Investments' in C. J. Tams, M. Fitzmaurice (eds.), *Legacies of the Permanent Court of International Justice* (Nijhoff, 2013), pp. 145–73

Kulick, A. (ed.), *Reassertion of Control Over the Investment Treaty Regime* (2017)

Kulick, A., 'Reassertion of Control: An Introduction' in A. Kulick (ed.), *Reassertion of Control Over the Investment Treaty Regime* (2017), pp. 1–29

Kulick, A., 'State–State Investment Arbitration as a Means of Reassertion of Control. From Antagonism to Dialogue' in A. Kulick (ed.), *Reassertion of Control Over the Investment Treaty Regime* (2017), pp. 128–52

La Nación, 'Ofensiva argentina para frenar a EE.UU.' (2011)

Lauterpacht, E., *Aspects of the Administration of International Justice* (Cambridge University Press, 1991)

Lavranos, N., 'The Shortcomings of the Proposal for an "International Court System" (ICS)', February 2016: https://efilablog.org/2016/02/02/the-shortcomings-of-the-proposal-for-an-international-court-system-ics/ (accessed 20 January 2018)

Lester, S., 'The New Investment Appellate Court Will Have Remand', International Economic Law and Policy Blog, 2 March 2016. http://worldtradelaw.typepad .com/. (accessed 25 March 2018)

Leys, D., 'Diplomatic Protection and Individual Rights: A Complementary Approach', *Harvard International Law Journal Online*, 57 (2016)

Lopez, C., M. Gotsi and C. Andriopoulos, 'Conceptualising the Influence of Corporate Image on Country Image', *European Journal of Marketing*, 45 (2011), 1601–41

Lowenfeld, A. F., *International Economic Law* (Oxford University Press, 2003)

MacChesney, B., 'Case of Certain Norwegian Loans (France v. Norway)', *American Journal of International Law*, 51 (1957), 777–83

Malanczuk, P., *Akehurst's Modern Introduction to International Law* (Routledge, 1997)

Mann, H., 'The Free Trade Commission Statements of October 7, 2003, on NAFTA's Chapter 11: Never-Never Land or Real Progress?' (2003)

Martini, P., 'Brazil's New Investment Treaties: Outside Looking ... Out?', June 2015: http://kluwerarbitrationblog.com/2015/06/16/brazils-new-investment -treaties-outside-looking-out-2/ (accessed 19 August 2018)

Matson, F. W., 'In Defense of Compromise', *The Pacific Spectator*, IX (1955), 264–71

Maurer, N., *The Empire Trap: The Rise and Fall of U.S. Intervention to Protect American Property Overseas, 1893–2013* (Princeton University Press, 2013)

McLachlan, C., 'Investment Treaties and General International Law', *International & Comparative Law Quarterly*, 57 (2008), 361–401

MercoPress, 'US Decision to Vote against Loans for Argentina "will not affect funding for 2012"' (2011)

MercoPress, 'US Will Vote against Loans to Argentina in World Bank and IDB' (2011)

Methymaki, E. and A. Tzanakopoulos, 'Masters of Puppets? Reassertion of Control through Joint Investment Treaty Interpretation' in A. Kulick (ed.), *Reassertion of Control Over the Investment Treaty Regime* (2017), pp. 155–81

Miles, K., *The Origins of International Investment Law: Empire, Environment and the Safeguarding of Capital* (Cambridge University Press, 2013)

Mistelis, L. A. and C. M. Baltag, 'Denial of Benefits and Article 17 of the Energy Charter Treaty', *Penn St. L. Rev.*, 113 (2008), 1301

Mitchener, K. J. and M. Weidenmier, 'How Are Sovereign Debtors Punished? Evidence from the Gold Standard Era', *Santa Clara University, Department of Economics Working Paper* (2004)

Mizushima, T., 'The Role of the State after an Award Is Rendered in Investor–State Arbitration' in S. Lalani, R. Polanco Lazo (eds.), *The Role of the State in Investor-State Arbitration* (Brill/Martinus Nijhoff, 2014), pp. 380–404

Monebhurrun, N., 'Novelty in International Investment Law: The Brazilian Agreement on Cooperation and Facilitation of Investments as a Different International Investment Agreement Model', *Journal of International Dispute Settlement* (2016), 79–100

Montt, S., *State Liability in Investment Treaty Arbitration: Global Constitutional and Administrative Law in the BIT Generation* (Hart Publishing, 2009)

Moore, K. A., 'Xenophobia in American Courts', *Northwestern University Law Review*, 97 (2003), 1497

Morosini, F. and M. Ratton Sánchez-Badin, 'The Brazilian Agreement on Cooperation and Facilitation of Investments (ACFI): A New Formula for International Investment Agreements?', August 2015: www.iisd.org/itn/2015 /08/04/the-brazilian-agreement-on-cooperation-and-facilitation-of-invest ments-acfi-a-new-formula-for-international-investment-agreements/ (accessed 11 January 2018)

Morosini, F. and M. Ratton Sánchez-Badin, 'The New Brazilian Agreements on Cooperation and Facilitation of Investments (ACFIs): Navigating between Resistance and Conformity with the Global Investment Regime', 2015: www.law .nyu.edu/sites/default/files/upload_documents/Morosini%20-%20Global% 20Fellows%20Forum.pdf (accessed 19 January 2018)

Mouyal, L. W., *International Investment Law and the Right to Regulate: A Human Rights Perspective* (Routledge, 2016)

Muchlinski, P. *et al.*, 'Statement of Concern about Planned Provisions on Investment Protection and Investor–State Dispute Settlement (ISDS) in the Transatlantic Trade and Investment Partnership (TTIP)', July 2014: www.kent .ac.uk/law/isds_treaty_consultation.html (accessed 4 August 2018)

Muller, W. and A. Vogel, 'The Swiss Lex Koller before Its Next Revision?', January 2017: https://uk.practicallaw.thomsonreuters.com/8-551-2765? transitionType=Default&contextData=(sc.default)&firstPage=true&bhcp=1 (accessed 25 February 2018)

Muniz, J. P., K. A. N. Duggal and L. A. S. Peretti, 'The New Brazilian BIT on Cooperation and Facilitation of Investments: A New Approach in Times of Change', *ICSID Review – Foreign Investment Law Journal*, 32 (2017), 404–17

Muniz, J. P. and L. A. S. Peretti, 'Brazil Signs New Bilateral Investment Treaties with Mozambique and Angola: New Approach to BITs or "toothless lions"?', April 2015: https://globalarbitrationnews.com/20150407-brazil-signs-new -bilateral-investment-treaties/ (accessed 15 January 2018)

Nadakavukaren Schefer, K., 'State Powers and ISDS' in S. Lalani and R. Polanco Lazo (eds.), *The Role of the State in Investor–State Arbitration* (Brill/Martinus Nijhoff, 2014)

Nadakavukaren Schefer, K. and T. Cottier, 'Responsibility to Protect (R2P) and the Emerging Principle of Common Concern', *NCCR Working Paper No 2012/29* (2012)

NAFTA Free Trade Commission, '2004 NAFTA Commission Meeting – Joint Statement, San Antonio 16 July 2004', July 2004: www.international.gc.ca /trade-agreements-accords-commerciaux/agr-acc/nafta-alena/JS-SanAntonio .aspx?lang=en (accessed 14 January 2018)

NAFTA Free Trade Commission, 'Statement of the Free Trade Commission on Non-Disputing Party Participation' (2004)

NAFTA Free Trade Commission, 'Statement of the Free Trade Commission on Notices of Intent to Submit a Claim to Arbitration' (2003)

Nappert, S., 'Escaping from Freedom? The Dilemma of an Improved ISDS Mechanism', *European Investment Law and Arbitration Review*, 1 (2015), 171–90

Naray, O., 'Commercial Diplomacy: A Conceptual Overview', 7th World Conference of TPOs, The Hague, The Netherlands (2008)

New Zealand Ministry of Foreign Affairs and Trade, 'Comprehensive and Progressive Agreement for Trans-Pacific Partnership', February 2018: www .mfat.govt.nz/en/about-us/who-we-are/treaties/cptpp/ (accessed 23 February 2018)

Newcombe, A. and L. Paradell, *Law and Practice of Investment Treaties: Standards of Treatment* (Kluwer Law International, 2009)

Nolte, George, 'First Report on Subsequent Agreements and Subsequent Practice in Relation to Treaty Interpretation', UN Doc. A/CN.4/660 (19 March 2013) *International Law Commission Sixty-fifth session*

North American Free Trade Agreement (NAFTA) – Free Trade Commission, 'Notes of Interpretation of Certain Chapter 11 Provisions', July 2001: www .international.gc.ca/trade-agreements-accords-commerciaux/topics -domaines/disp-diff/NAFTA-Interpr.aspx (accessed 29 April 2018)

Nouel, G. L., 'Arbitration Due to the Failed Privatisation Process of Belgrade Beer Industry (BIP)', *The Brief*, March 2013, 6–7

OAS, 'SICE the OAS Foreign Trade Information System', February 2018: (www .sice.oas.org/, accessed 28 February 2018)

OAS, 'Trade Policy Developments: Bolivia–Mexico', June 2010: www.sice.oas.org /tpd/BOL_MEX/BOL_MEX_e.asp#EntryintoForce (accessed 15 December 2018)

Obama, B., 'Presidential Proclamation – To Modify Duty-Free Treatment Under the Generalized System of Preferences and for Other Purposes', March 2012: www.whitehouse.gov/the-press-office/2012/03/26/modify-duty-free-treat ment-under-generalized-system-preferences-and-othe (accessed 13 March 2018)

OECD, *Convention on Combating Bribery of Foreign Public Officials in International Business Transactions* (OECD Publishing, 2011)

OECD, 'Draft Convention on the Protection of Foreign Property', *International Legal Materials*, 2 (1963), 241–67

OECD, 'Guidelines for MNEs', 2018: http://mneguidelines.oecd.org/about.htm (accessed 9 February 2018)

OECD, 'Implementation Procedures of the OECD Guidelines for Multinational Enterprises', *OECD Guidelines for Multinational Enterprises*, 2011 edn (OECD Publishing, 2011), pp. 65–89

OECD, *International Investment Law: Understanding Concepts and Tracking Innovations* (OECD, 2008)

OECD, *OECD Guidelines for Multinational Enterprises*, 2011 edn (OECD Publishing, 2011)

OECD, 'The Multilateral Agreement on Investment Draft Consolidated Text' (1998)

OECD, *Transparency and Third Party Participation in Investor–State Dispute Settlement Procedures* (2005)

OECD and WTO, *Aid for Trade at a Glance 2015* (OECD Publishing, 2015)

Office of the United States Trade Representative, 'U.S. Generalized System of Preferences (GSP) Guidebook', December 2012: www.ustr.gov/sites/default

/files/GSP%20Guidebook%20Dec%202012%20%20%20final%20version_0.pdf (accessed 13 March 2018)

O'Laughlin, P., 'ATPA's Impact on U.S. Economy, Drug Crop Eradication Still Negligible, Says USITC' (2014)

OPIC, 'Environmental and Social Policy Statement', January 2017: www.opic.gov /sites/default/files/files/final%20revised%20ESPS%2001132017(1).pdf (accessed 9 February 2018)

OPIC, 'Finance Eligibility Checklist', 2017: www.opic.gov/doing-business-us/appli cant-screener/finance-eligibility-checklist (accessed 16 January 2018)

Orrego Vicuña, F., *International Dispute Settlement in an Evolving Global Society: Constitutionalization, Accessibility, Privatization* (Cambridge University Press, 2004)

Ortiz, F., 'Spain Has few Ways to Pressure Argentina over YPF' (2012)

Oxford University Press, 'Investment Claims', February 2018: http://oxia.ouplaw .com/ (accessed 28 February 2018)

Paparinskis, M., 'Investment Arbitration and the Law of Countermeasures', *British Yearbook of International Law* (2008), 265–352

Paparinskis, M., 'Investment Treaty Arbitration and the (New) Law of State Responsibility', *European Journal of International Law*, 24 (2013), 617–47

Paparinskis, M., *The International Minimum Standard and Fair and Equitable Treatment* (Oxford University Press, 2013)

Paparinskis, M., 'The Limits of Depoliticisation in Contemporary Investor–State Arbitration', *Select Proceedings of the European Society of International Law*, 3 (2010), 271

Paparinskis, M. and J. Howley, 'Article 5. Submission by a Non-Disputing Party to the Treaty' in D. Euler, M. Gehring and M. Scherer (eds.), *Transparency in International Investment Arbitration* (Cambridge University Press, 2015), pp. 196–226

Park, W. W., 'Arbitration and the Fisc: NAFTA's "Tax Veto"', *Chicago Journal of International Law*, 2 (2001), 231–41

Parlett, K., 'Diplomatic Protection and Investment Arbitration' in R. Hofmann and C. J. Tams (eds.), *International Investment Law and General International Law: From Clinical Isolation to Systemic Integration?* (Nomos, 2011), pp. 211–29

Parlett, K., *The Individual in the International Legal System: Continuity and Change in International Law* (Cambridge University Press, 2011)

Parra, A. R., 'The Enforcement of ICSID Arbitral Awards', 24th Joint Colloquium on International Arbitration. Paris, November 2007 (2007)

Parra, A. R., *The History of ICSID* (Oxford University Press, 2012)

Paton, R. B., 'Corporate Social Responsibility: From Conflict Resolution to Conflict Anticipation', *Reflections*, 7 (2012)

Paulsson, J., 'Arbitration without Privity', *ICSID Review*, 10 (1995), 232–57

Paulsson, J., *Denial of Justice in International Law* (Cambridge University Press, 2005)

Paulsson, J. and G. Petrochilos, 'Neer-Ly Misled?', *ICSID Review – Foreign Investment Law Journal*, 22 (2007), 242–57

Paulus, A., 'Treaties of Friendship, Commerce, and Navigation', March 2011: www.mpepil.com/subscriber_article?script=yes&id=/epil/entries/law -9780199231690-e1482&recno=1&searchType=Quick&query=friendship (accessed 17 April 2018)

Pearce, C. C. and J. J. Coe Jr, 'Arbitration under NAFTA Chapter Eleven: Some Pragmatic Reflections upon the First Case Filed against Mexico', *Hastings International and Comparative Law Review*, 23 (1999), 311

Peels, R., E. Echeverria, J. Aissi and A. Schneider, 'Corporate Social Responsibility in International Trade and Investment Agreements', *ILO Research Paper, International Labour Office* 13 (2016)

Pellet, A., 'The Case Law of the ICJ in Investment Arbitration', *ICSID Review – Foreign Investment Law Journal*, 28 (2013), 223–40

Permanent Court of Arbitration (PCA), 'Arbitration between Aeroport Belbek LLC and Mr. Igor Valerievich Kolomoisky as Claimants and the Russian Federation', August 2016: https://pcacases.com/web/sendAttach/1865 (accessed 19 February 2018)

Perrone, N. M., 'The International Investment Regime and Local Populations: Are the Weakest Voices Unheard?', *Transnational Legal Theory*, 7 (2016), 383–405

Peters, P., 'Dispute Settlement Arrangements in Investment Treaties', Netherlands Yearbook of International Law, 22 (1991), 91–161

Peterson, L. E., 'After Settling some Awards, Argentina Takes more Fractious Path in Bond-Holders Case, with New Bid to Disqualify Arbitrators', December 2013: www.iareporter.com/articles/after-settling-some-awards-argentina -takes-more-fractious-path-in-bond-holders-case-with-new-bid-to-disqualify -arbitrators/ (accessed 29 September 2018)

Peterson, L. E., 'Argentina by the Numbers: Where Things Stand with Investment Treaty Claims Arising out of the Argentine Financial Crisis', February 2011: www .iareporter.com/articles/20110201_9 (accessed 29 September 2018)

Peterson, L. E., 'As Repsol Files Arbitration against Argentina, Row Erupts over Alleged "diplomatic protection" by Spain and the EU – Investment Arbitration Reporter (IAReporter)' (2012)

Peterson, L. E., 'How many States Are Not Paying Awards under Investment Treaties?', May 2010: www.iareporter.com/articles/20100507_3 (accessed 4 February 2018)

Peterson, L. E., 'Singapore Court Rejects Arbitrators' Extension of Chinese Investment Treaty to Macao', January 2015: www.iareporter.com/articles/ 20150121_1 (accessed 26 January 2018)

Peterson, L. E., 'South Africa Mining Arbitration Sees Another Amicus Curiae Intervention', February 2009: www.iareporter.com/articles/south-africa-mining-arbitration-sees-another-amicus-curiae-intervention/ (accessed 21 February 2018)

Peterson, L. E., 'UNCITRAL Meetings on ISDS Reform Get off to Bumpy Start, as Delegations Can't Come to Consensus on Who Should Chair Sensitive Process – Entailing a Rare Vote', September 2017: www.iareporter.com/articles/uncitral-meetings-on-isds-reform-gets-off-to-bumpy-start-as-delegations-cant-come-to-consensus-on-who-should-chair-sensitive-process-entailing-a-rare-vote/ (accessed 23 February 2018)

Pohl, J., K. Mashigo and A. Nohen, Dispute Settlement Provisions in International Investment Agreements (2012)

Polanco, R. and R. Torrent, Analysis of the Prospects for Updating the Trade Pillar of the European Union-Chile Association Agreement (European Parliament, 2016)

Polanco Lazo, R., 'Is There a Life for Latin American Countries after Denouncing the ICSID Convention?', Transnational Dispute Management, 11 (2014)

Polanco Lazo, R., 'The No of Tokyo Revisited: Or How Developed Countries Learned to Start Worrying and Love the Calvo Doctrine', ICSID Review, 30 (2015), 172–93

Polášek, P. and S. T. Tonova, 'Enforcement against States' in J. A. Huerta Goldman, A. Romanetti and F. X. Stirnimann (eds.), WTO Litigation, Investment Arbitration, and Commercial Arbitration (Wolters Kluwer Law & Business, Kluwer Law International, 2013), pp. 357–87

Posner, T., 'The Role of Non-Disputing States in Investment Dispute Settlement, 22nd Investment Treaty Forum (ITF), British Institute of International and Comparative Law (BIICL), 8 May 2014' (2014)

Posner, T. R. and M. C. Walter, 'The Abiding Role of State–State Engagement in the Resolution of Investor–State Disputes' in J. E. Kalicki, A. Joubin-Bret (eds.), Reshaping the Investor–State Dispute Settlement System (Brill, 2015), pp. 381–93

Potestà, M., 'Republic of Italy v. Republic of Cuba', American Journal of International Law, 106 (2012), 341–7

Potestà, M., 'State-to-State Dispute Settlement Pursuant to Bilateral Investment Treaties: Is There Potential?' in N. Boschiero, T. Scovazzi, C. Pitea and C. Ragni (eds.), International Courts and the Development of International Law (T. M. C. Asser Press, 2013), pp. 753–68

Potestà, M., 'Towards a Greater Role for State-to-State Arbitration in the Architecture of Investment Treaties?' in S. Lalani and R. Polanco Lazo (eds.), The Role of the State in Investor–State Arbitration (Brill/Martinus Nijhoff, 2014)

Potestà, M. and M. Sobat, 'Frivolous Claims in International Adjudication: A Study of ICSID Rule 41(5) and of Procedures of Other Courts and Tribunals to Dismiss Claims Summarily', Journal of International Dispute Settlement, 3 (2012), 131–62

Poulsen, L. N. S., 'Sacrificing Sovereignty by Chance: Investment Treaties, Developing Countries, and Bounded Rationality', London School of Economics and Political Science (LSE) (2011)

Poulsen, L. N. S., 'The Importance of BITs for Foreign Direct Investment and Political Risk Insurance: Revisiting the Evidence' in K. P. Sauvant (ed.), *Yearbook on International Investment Law & Policy 2009-2010* (Oxford University Press Inc, 2010), pp. 539-74

Ralston, J. H., *International Arbitration from Athens to Locarno* (Stanford University Press, 1929)

Ralston, J. H. and W. T. S. Doyle, *Venezuelan Arbitration of 1903* (US Government Printing Office, 1904)

Randelzhofer, A., 'Nationality' in E. Biglieri and G. Prati (eds.), *Encyclopedia of Public International Law* (Elsevier, 2014), pp. 416-24

Rayfuse, R. (ed.), 'Report of the Executive Directors on the Convention on the Settlement of Investment Disputes between States and Nationals of Other States (18 March 1965)', *ICSID Reports: Volume 1: Reports of Cases Decided Under the Convention on the Settlement of Investment Disputes between States and Nationals of Other States, 1965* (Cambridge University Press, 1993), pp. 23-33

Recanati, M., 'Diplomatic Intervention and State-to-State Arbitration as Alternative Means for the Protection of Foreign Investments and Host States' General Interests: The Italian Experience' in G. Sacerdoti, P. Acconci, A. D. Luca and M. Valenti (eds.), *General Interests of Host States in International Investment Law* (Cambridge University Press, 2014), pp. 422-44

Reed, L., 'Observations on the Relationship between Diplomatic and Judicial Means' in L. Boisson de Chazournes, M. G. Kohen and J. E. Viñuales (eds.), *Diplomatic and Judicial Means of Dispute Settlement* (Martinus Nijhoff Publishers, 2012), pp. 291-305

Reinisch, A., 'Will the EU's Proposal Concerning an Investment Court System for CETA and TTIP Lead to Enforceable Awards? - The Limits of Modifying the ICSID Convention and the Nature of Investment Arbitration', *Journal of International Economic Law*, 19 (2016), 761-86

Reisman, W. M., *Republic of Ecuador v. United States of America (PCA Case No. 2012-5). Expert Opinion with Respect to Jurisdiction, Prof. W. Michael Reisman*

Reuters, 'Argentina Unhurt in 2012 by U.S. Loan Hurdles-Source' (2011)

Reuters, 'U.S. Business Groups Urge Ecuador Trade Benefits Be Cut' (2012)

Roberts, A., 'Power and Persuasion in Investment Treaty Interpretation: The Dual Role of States', *American Journal of International Law*, 104 (2010), 179-225

Roberts, A., 'Recalibrating Interpretive Authority' (2014) *Columbia FDI Perspectives. Vale Columbia Center on Sustainable International Investment*

Roberts, A., 'State-to-State Investment Treaty Arbitration: A Hybrid Theory of Interdependent Rights and Shared Interpretive Authority', Harv. Int'l L.J, 55 (2014), 1

Rode, Z. R., 'The International Claims Commission of the United States: August 28, 1950–June 30, 1953', *American Journal of International Law*, 47 (1953), 615–37

Rosenberg, C. B., 'The Intersection of International Trade and International Arbitration: The Use of Trade Benefits to Secure Compliance with Arbitral Awards', Geo. J. Int'l L., 44 (2012), 503

Ross, A., 'Nicosia: Investment Arbitration – A View from Cyprus', *Global Arbitration Review*, 6 (2011)

Ruggie, J., 'Report of the Special Representative of the Secretary-General on the Issue of Human Rights and Transnational Corporations and Other Business Enterprises', *Neth. Q. Hum. Rts*, 29 (2011), 224

Sabahi, B., *Compensation and Restitution in Investor–State Arbitration: Principles and Practice* (Oxford University Press, 2011)

Salacuse, J. W., *The Law of Investment Treaties* (Oxford University Press, 2010)

Sauvant, K. P., *The Evolving International Investment Law and Policy Regime: Ways Forward. E15 Task Force on Investment Policy – Policy Options Paper. E15 Initiative* (International Centre for Trade and Sustainable Development (ICTSD) and World Economic Forum, 2016)

Schill, S. W., '"Shared Responsibility": Stopping the Irresponsibility Carousel for the Protection of Public Interests in International Investment Law' in A. Reinisch, M. E. Footer and C. Binder (eds.), *International Law and … Select Proceedings of the European Society of International Law* (Hart Publishing, 2016), pp. 160–9

Schneider, M. E., 'Investment Disputes – Moving Beyond Arbitration' in L. Boisson de Chazournes, M. G. Kohen and J. E. Viñuales (eds.), *Diplomatic and Judicial Means of Dispute Settlement* (Martinus Nijhoff Publishers, 2012), p. 119

Schneider, M. E., 'The Role of the State in Investor–State Arbitration: Introductory Remarks' in S. Lalani and R. Polanco Lazo (eds.), *The Role of the State in Investor–State Arbitration* (Brill /Martinus Nijhoff, 2014)

Schreuer, C., 'Calvo's Grandchildren: The Return of Local Remedies in Investment Arbitration', *Law and Practice of International Courts and Tribunals*, 4 (2005), 1

Schreuer, C., 'Investment Protection and International Relations' in A. Reinisch and U. Kriebaum (eds.), *The Law of International Relations: Liber Amicorum Hanspeter Neuhold* (Eleven International Publishing, 2007), pp. 345–58

Schreuer, C., *The ICSID Convention : A Commentary* (Cambridge University Press, 2001)

Schreuer, C. and M. Weiniger, 'A Doctrine of Precedent?' in P. Muchlinski, F. Ortino and C. Schreuer (eds.), *The Oxford Handbook of International Investment Law* (Oxford University Press, 2008), pp. 1188–206

Schwarzenberger, G., 'The Abs–Shawcross Draft Convention on Investments Abroad: A Critical Commentary', *Journal of Public Law*, 9 (1960), 147

Schwebel, S. M., 'In Defense of Bilateral Investment Treaties', *Arbitration International*, 31 (2015), 181–92

Scott, J. B., *Texts of the Peace Conferences at the Hague. 1899 and 1907, with English Translation and Appendix of Related Documents* (Ginn & Company, Boston and London, Published for the International School of Peace, 1908)

Shea, D. R., *The Calvo Clause: A Problem of Inter-American and International Law and Diplomacy* (University of Minnesota Press, 1955)

Shihata, I. F. I., 'Towards a Greater Depoliticization of Investment Disputes: The Roles of ICSID and MIGA', *ICSID Review*, 1 (1986), 1–25

Simons, P. and A. Macklin, *The Governance Gap: Extractive Industries, Human Rights, and the Home State Advantage* (Routledge, 2015)

Sinclair, S., 'Financial Services' in S. Sinclair, S. Trew and H. Mertins-Kirkwood (eds.), *Making Sense of the CETA* (Canadian Centre for Policy Alternatives, 2014), pp. 18–23

Skinner, M., C. A. Miles and S. Luttrell, 'Access and Advantage in Investor–State Arbitration: The Law and Practice of Treaty Shopping', *Journal of World Energy Law & Business*, 3 (2010), 260–85

Slater, M. D., 'The Energy Charter Treaty : A Brief Introduction to Its Scope and Initial Arbitral Awards' in Association for International Arbitration (ed.), *Alternative Dispute Resolution in the Energy Sector* (Maklu, 2009), pp. 15–54

Sornarajah, M., *Resistance and Change in the International Law on Foreign Investment* (Cambridge University Press, 2015)

Southern African Development Community (SADC), *SADC Model Bilateral Investment Treaty Template with Commentary* (2012)

Stuyt, A. M., *Survey of International Arbitrations: 1794–1989* (Martinus Nijhoff Publishers, 1990)

Sulzberger, C. L., 'Lack of Secrecy Makes Diplomacy Even More Difficult' (1975)

Summers, L. M., 'Arbitration and Latin America', *California Western International Law Journal*, 3 (1972), 1

Swiss Network for International Studies (SNIS), 'Diffusion of International Law: A Textual Analysis of International Investment Agreements', February 2018: https://snis.ch/project/diffusion-of-international-law/ (accessed 27 February 2018)

The Economist, 'Foreign Investment Disputes: Come and Get Me', February 2012: www.economist.com/node/21547836 (accessed 13 March 2018)

Tietje, C. and K. Kampermann, 'Taxation and Investment: Constitutional Law Limitations on Tax Legislation in Context' in S. W. Schill (ed.), *International Investment Law and Comparative Public Law* (Oxford University Press, 2010), pp. 569–97

Titi, C., 'The European Commission's Approach to the Transatlantic Trade and Investment Partnership (TTIP): Investment Standards and International Investment Court System – An Overview of the European Commission's

Draft TTIP text of 16 September 2015', *Transnational Dispute Management*, 12 (2015)

Titi, C., *The Right to Regulate in International Investment Law* (Beck/Hart, 2014)

Tomz, M., *Reputation and international cooperation: sovereign debt across three centuries* (Princeton University Press, 2007)

Torrent, R. and R. Polanco, *Analysis of the Upcoming Modernisation of the Trade Pillar of the European Union–Mexico Global Agreement* (European Parliament, 2016)

Trakman, Leon E., 'Investor–State Dispute Settlement under the Trans-Pacific Partnership Agreement' in Tania Voon (ed.), *Trade Liberalisation and International Co-operation: A Legal Analysis of the Trans-Pacific Partnership Agreement* (Edward Elgar Publishing, 2013), pp. 179–206

Transnational Dispute Management, 'Legal & Regulatory docs.', February 2018: www.transnational-dispute-management.com/ (accessed 29 December 2017)

Trevino, C. J., 'State-to-State Investment Treaty Arbitration and the Interplay with Investor–State Arbitration Under the Same Treaty', *Journal of International Dispute Settlement*, 5 (2014), 199–233

United Nations, 'Claims Commission Established under the Convention Concluded between the United States of America and Venezuela on 5 December 1885', *Reports of International Arbitral Awards*, 29 (2011), 223–98

United Nations, 'Commission for the Settlement of Claims under the Convention of 7 August 1892 concluded between the United States of America and the Republic of Chile', *Reports of International Arbitral Awards*, 29 (2011), 299–326

United Nations, 'French–Mexican Claims Commission (France, United Mexican States)' *Reports of International Arbitral Awards*, pp. 307–560

United Nations, 'Introducing Responsible Investment', January 2015: www.unpri .org/introducing-responsible-investment/ (accessed 27 February 2018)

United Nations, 'U.S.–Mexico General Claims Commission' *Reports of International Arbitral Awards* (United Nations, 2006), pp. 1–769

United Nations Commission on International Trade Law (UNCITRAL), 'Rules on Transparency in Treaty-Based Investor–State Arbitration. UN Doc. A/RES/68/ 462', April 2014: www.uncitral.org/uncitral/en/uncitral_texts/arbitration /2014Transparency.html (accessed 14 February 2018)

United Nations Commission on International Trade Law (UNCITRAL), 'Status UNCITRAL Rules on Transparency in Treaty-Based Investor–State Arbitration', February 2018: www.uncitral.org/uncitral/en/uncitral_texts/arbi tration/2014Transparency_Rules_status.html (accessed 20 February 2018)

United Nations Conference on Trade and Development (UNCTAD), *Dispute Settlement: State–State* (United Nations, 2003)

United Nations Conference on Trade and Development (UNCTAD), 'Improving Investment Dispute Settlement: UNCTAD's Policy Tools', *IIA Issues Note*, 4 (2017)

United Nations Conference on Trade and Development (UNCTAD), 'International Investment Agreements Navigator', February 2018: http://investmentpolicyhub .unctad.org/IIA/IiasByCountry#iiaInnerMenu (accessed 6 February 2018)

United Nations Conference on Trade and Development (UNCTAD), 'Interpretation of IIAs: What States Can Do', *IIA Issues Note* (2011)

United Nations Conference on Trade and Development (UNCTAD), 'Investment Dispute Settlement Navigator', September 2017: http://investmentpolicyhub .unctad.org/ISDS (accessed 15 September 2017)

United Nations Conference on Trade and Development (UNCTAD), 'Investment Dispute Settlement Navigator', February 2018: http://investmentpolicyhub .unctad.org/ISDS (accessed 26 February 2018)

United Nations Conference on Trade and Development (UNCTAD), *Investment Facilitation: A Review of Policy Practices. Follow-up to UNCTAD's Global Action Menu for Investment Facilitation* (2017)

United Nations Conference on Trade and Development (UNCTAD), *Investment Policy Framework for Sustainable Development* (2012)

United Nations Conference on Trade and Development (UNCTAD), *Investment Policy Framework for Sustainable Development (IPFSD)* (2015)

United Nations Conference on Trade and Development (UNCTAD), *Investor-State Disputes: Prevention and Alternatives to Arbitration* (United Nations Publications, 2010)

United Nations Conference on Trade and Development (UNCTAD), 'Reform of Investor-State Dispute Settlement: In Search of a Roadmap', *IIA Issues Note*, 2 (2013)

United Nations Conference on Trade and Development (UNCTAD) (ed.), *Reforming International Investment Governance* (United Nations, 2015)

United Nations Conference on Trade and Development (UNCTAD), *Scope and Definition: UNCTAD Series on Issues in International Investment Agreements II* (United Nations, 2011)

United Nations Conference on Trade and Development (UNCTAD), 'Special Update on Investor-State Dispute Settlement: Facts and Figures', *IIA Issues Note*, 3 (2017)

United Nations Conference on Trade and Development (UNCTAD), *World Investment Report 2016. Investor Nationality: Policy Challenges* (United Nations, 2016)

United Nations Environment Programme (UNEP), 'Corporate Social Responsibility and Regional Trade and Investment Agreements', 2011: http:// unep.ch/etb/publications/CSR%20publication/UNEP_Corporate%20Social% 20Responsibility.pdf (accessed 18 January 2018)

United Nations Human Rights Council, *Guiding Principles on Business and Human Rights: Implementing the United Nations 'Protect, Respect and*

Remedy', Framework, endorsed by the United Nations Human Rights Council on 16 June 2011 (2011)

United States, 'Statement on Open Hearings in NAFTA Chapter Eleven Arbitrations', http://www.ustr.gov/archive/assets/Trade_Agreements/Regional/NAFTA/asset_upload_file143_3602.pdf (accessed 23 February 2018)

United States Trade Representative (USTR), 'Generalized System of Preferences (GSP)', January 2015: https://ustr.gov/issue-areas/trade-development/prefer ence-programs/generalized-system-preference-gsp (accessed 6 February 2018)

United States Trade Representative (USTR), 'GSP in Use – Country Specific Information', February 2018: https://ustr.gov/issue-areas/trade-development /preference-programs/generalized-system-preferences-gsp/gsp-use-%E2%80% 93-coun (accessed 22 February 2018)

United States Trade Representative (USTR), 'Office of the United States Trade Representative. Generalized System of Preferences (GSP): Notice Regarding the Announcement of Petitions Accepted for the 2009 Annual GSP Country Practices Review, Acceptance of Pre-Hearing Comments and Requests to Testify for the 2009 Annual GSP Country Practices Review Hearing, and the Initiation of the 2010 Annual GSP Country Practices Review', www.gpo.gov /fdsys/pkg/FR-2010–08-11/pdf/2010–19745.pdf (accessed 13 March 2018)

US Commercial Service, 'Services for U.S. Companies', February 2018: www.trade .gov/cs/services.asp#commercialdiplomacy (accessed 24 February 2018)

US Department of State, 'Bilateral Investments, Other Bilateral Claims and Arbitrations', January 2015: www.state.gov/s/l/c7344.htm (accessed 24 February 2018)

US Department of State, 'CAFTA–DR Investor–State Arbitrations', February 2018: www.state.gov/s/l/c33165.htm (accessed 20 February 2018)

US Department of State, 'Investment Climate Statements', February 2018: www .state.gov/e/eb/rls/othr/ics/ (accessed 26 February 2018)

US Department of State, 'NAFTA Investor–State Arbitrations', February 2018: www.state.gov/s/l/c3439.htm (accessed 20 February 2018)

US Department of State, 'Understanding Concerning Certain U.S. Bilateral Investment Treaties, Signed by the U.S., the European Commission, and Acceding and Candidate Countries for Accession to the European Union', September 2003: www.state.gov/s/l/2003/44366.htm (accessed 16 January 2018)

'USCODE-2009-title22-chap32-subchapIII-partI-sec2370a.pdf'

Usoskin, S., 'Kyrgyz Republic's Mixed Fortunes in Investment Arbitration', May 2014: www.cisarbitration.com/2014/05/14/kyrgyz-republics-mixed-fortunes -in-investment-arbitration/ (accessed 9 February 2018)

Van Aaken, A., 'Control Mechanisms in International Investment Law' in Z. Douglas, J. Pauwelyn and J. E. Viñuales (eds.), The Foundations of International Investment Law: Bringing Theory into Practice (Oxford University Press, 2014), pp. 409–35

Van Aaken, A., 'Delegating Interpretative Authority in Investment Treaties: The Case of Joint Commissions', *Transnational Dispute Management*, 11 (2014)

Van Aaken, A., 'The Interaction of Remedies between National Judicial Systems and ICSID : An Optimization Problem' in N. J. Calamita, D. Earnest and M. Burgstaller (eds.), *The Future of ICSID and the Place of Investment Treaties in International Law* (British Institute of International and Comparative Law, 2013), pp. 291–324

van Harten, G., *Investment Treaty Arbitration and Public Law* (Oxford University Press, USA, 2008)

van Harten, G., 'TWAIL and the Dabhol Arbitration', *Comparative Research in Law & Political Economy. Research Report No 19/2011*

van Houtte, H. and B. McAsey, 'Abaclat and others v Argentine Republic ICSID, the BIT and Mass Claims', *ICSID Review*, 27 (2012), 231–6

Vermeer-Künzli, A., 'As If: The Legal Fiction in Diplomatic Protection', *European Journal of International Law*, 18 (2007), 37–68

Vermeer-Künzli, A. M. H., *The Protection of Individuals by Means of Diplomatic Protection: Diplomatic Protection as a Human Rights Instrument* (Department of Public International Law, Faculty of Law, Leiden University, 2007)

Viñuales, J. E. and D. Bentolila, 'The Use of Alternative (Non-Judicial) Means to Enforce Investment Awards against States' in L. Boisson de Chazournes, M. G. Kohen and J. E. Viñuales (eds.), *Diplomatic and Judicial Means of Dispute Settlement* (Martinus Nijhoff Publishers, 2012), pp. 248–77

Voon, T., 'Consolidating International Investment Law: The Mega-Regionals as a Pathway towards Multilateral Rules', *World Trade Review*, 17 (2018), 33–63

Waibel, M., 'Arbitrator Selection' in A. Kulick (ed.), *Reassertion of Control Over the Investment Treaty Regime* (2017), pp. 333–55

Waibel, M., A. Kaushal, K.-H. Chung and C. Balchin (eds.), *The Backlash against Investment Arbitration: Perceptions and Reality* (Wolters Kluwer Law & Business, 2010)

Wälde, T. and A. Kolo, 'Investor–State Disputes: The Interface between Treaty-Based International Investment Protection and Fiscal Sovereignty', *Intertax*, 35 (2007) 424–49

Wälde, T. W., '"Equality of Arms" in Investment Arbitration: Procedural Challenges' in K. Yannaca-Small (ed.), *Arbitration under International Investment Agreements: A Guide to the Key Issues* (Oxford University Press, 2010), pp. 161–88

Weeramantry, J. R., *Treaty Interpretation in Investment Arbitration* (Oxford University Press, 2012)

Weiler, T., 'NAFTA Investment Law in 2001: As the Legal Order Starts to Settle, the Bureaucrats Strike Back', *International Lawyer*, 36 (2002), 345–53

Weston, B. H., D. J. Bederman and R. B. Lillich, *International Claims: Their Settlement by Lump Sum Agreements, 1975–1995* (Martinus Nijhoff, 1999)

Whytock, C. A., *Domestic Courts and Global Governance: The Politics of Private International Law* (ProQuest, 2007)

Wong, J., 'The Subversion of State-to-State Investment Treaty Arbitration', *Colum. J. Transnat'l L.* 53 (2014), 6–48

Woolcock, S., *The EU Approach to International Investment Policy after the Lisbon Treaty* (Directorate-General for External Policies of the Union, 2010)

World Bank, 'News & Broadcast – Argentina: World Bank to Deepen Its Support to Social Programs', March 2012: http://www.worldbank.org/en/news/feature /2012/03/19/argentina-world-bank-deepen-support-social-programs (accessed 14 March 2018)

World Bank, *Report to the Development Committee and Guidelines on the Treatment of Foreign Direct Investment* (1992), vol. II

World Trade Organization (WTO), 'Dispute Settlement – Index of Disputes Issues', February 2018: www.wto.org/english/tratop_e/dispu_e/dispu_subjects_index_e .htm (accessed 26 February 2018)

Wu, C.-H., 'The Many Facets of States in International Investment Law' in S. Lalani and R. Polanco (eds.), *The Role of the State in Investor–State Arbitration* (Brill/ Martinus Nijhoff, 2014), pp. 405–29

Yackee, J. W., 'The First Investor–State Arbitration: The Suez Canal Company v Egypt (1864)', Journal of World Investment & Trade, 17 (2016), 401–62

Yen, T. H., *The Interpretation of Investment Treaties* (Martinus Nijhoff Publishers, 2014)

INDEX